Can't You Hear Them?

of related interest

Hearing Voices, Living Fully
Living with the Voices in My Head
Claire Bien
Foreword by Larry Davidson
ISBN 978 1 78592 718 8
eISBN 978 1 78450 322 2

Trauma is Really Strange
Steve Haines
Art by Sophie Standing
ISBN 978 1 84819 293 5
eISBN 978 0 85701 240 1

We're All Mad Here
The No-Nonsense Guide to
Living with Social Anxiety
Claire Eastham
Foreword by Natasha Devon MBE
ISBN 978 1 78592 082 0
eISBN 978 1 78450 343 7

‘An en… …oscience of voic… all their fascinating forms.’

– *Vaughan Bell, University Colleg… …don, UK*

‘A remarkable book about voice-hearing, which provides an accessible account of the science, but does not lose track of the meaning of the experience. It is compassionate, controversial and compelling!’

– *Chris Cook, Professor of Spirituality, Theology & Health at Durham University, UK*

‘On finishing this book my initial instinct was to re-read it in order to appreciate its insights for a second time. *Can’t You Hear Them?* is not only a work of impressive scholarship but a compelling, beautifully-written story of human experience and endeavour.’

– *Dr Eleanor Longden, Psychosis Research Unit, Greater Manchester Mental Health NHS Foundation Trust, UK*

‘With rigorous science, penetrating analyses, colourful and enjoyable prose, and an astonishing breadth of knowledge – Simon McCarthy-Jones has delivered a book that will undeniably be appreciated by many.’

– *Frank Larøi, University of Bergen, Norway and University of Liège, Belgium*

‘A brilliant and thoughtful travel into the complex experience of hearing voices. Superbly written, with intelligence, but also a delightful sense of humour, this book will become an indispensable addition to the bookshelves of clinicians, scientists and people who hear voices.’

– *Renaud Jardri, MD, PhD, Professor of Child and Adolescent Psychiatry, Lille, France*

Can't You Hear Them?

THE SCIENCE AND SIGNIFICANCE OF HEARING VOICES

Simon McCarthy-Jones

Jessica Kingsley *Publishers*
London and Philadelphia

Quotes in Chapter 1 from *The Day the Voices Stopped* by Ken Steele and Claire Berman, copyright © 2001. Reprinted by permission of Basic Books, a member of The Perseus Books Group.

Figure 25.1 is adapted and reproduced from Jardri, R. (2013) with kind permission of Oxford University Press.

Eric Morecambe quote on p.232 is reproduced with kind permission of the Eric Morecambe estate, managed by Billy Marsh Assoicates.

First published in 2017
by Jessica Kingsley Publishers
73 Collier Street
London N1 9BE, UK
and
400 Market Street, Suite 400
Philadelphia, PA 19106, USA

www.jkp.com

Library of Congress Cataloging in Publication Data
Title: Can't you hear them : the science and significance of hearing voices / Simon McCarthy-Jones.
Description: London ; Philadelphia : Jessica Kingsley Publishers, 2017. | Includes bibliographical references and index.
Identifiers: LCCN 2016048146 | ISBN 9781785922565 (alk. paper)
Subjects: LCSH: Auditory hallucinations.
Classification: LCC RC553.A84 M33 2017 | DDC 154.4--dc23 LC record available at https://lccn.loc.gov/2016048146

British Library Cataloguing in Publication Data
A CIP catalogue record for this book is available from the British Library

ISBN 978 1 78592 256 5
eISBN 978 1 78450 541 7

Printed and bound in Great Britain

ACKNOWLEDGEMENTS

I owe both an emotional and intellectual debt to my wife, Rose.

I've had the pleasure to work with, talk with or be helped by many people over the past decade, who I'd like to thank. These include Ben Alderson-Day, Paul Baker, Vaughan Bell, Richard Bentall, Jason Bridge, Peter Bullimore, Vaughan Carr, Anne Castles, Chris Cook, Christine Cooper-Rompato, David Copolov, Dirk Corstens, Aiden Corvin, Hywel Davies, Jacqui Dillon, Guy Dodgson, Rob Dudley, Sandra Escher, Charles Fernyhough, Judith Ford, Michael Gill, Melissa Green, Mark Hayward, Douglas Holmes, Renaud Jardri, Nev Jones, Kate, Cathy Kezelman, Rebecca Knowles, Debra Lampshire, Robyn Langdon, Frank Larøi, Eleanor Longden, Jane Macnaughton, Sara Maitland, Pete Moseley, Lena Oestreich, Tim Ollier, John Read, Phillip Resnick, Bruce and Faye Roberts, Marius Romme, Susan Rossell, Georgina Rowse, David Smailes, Iris Sommer, Kellie Stastny, Clara Strauss, John Sutton, Neil Thomas, Robin Timmers, Giles Tinsley, Filippo Varese, Amanda Waegeli, Flavie Waters, John Watkins, Tom Whitford, Sam Wilkinson and Angela Woods.

I am also exceedingly grateful to Pat Bracken, Christine Cooper-Rompato, Charles Fernyhough, Denise Harold, Renaud Jardri, Rose McCarthy-Jones, Joanna Moncrieff, Sam Wilkinson and, in particular, Vaughan Bell for reading and commenting on chapters of this book for me. This does not mean this book reflects their opinions, and any errors, of course, remain my responsibility.

Finally, to David Smail and Melissa Roberts, I'm sorry we never met in this world.

CONTENTS

Introduction

Voices are waiting to speak to you. They know your name. They could call it from the surrounds of sleep, on a bustling street, or from your car backseat. Samuel Johnson, Sigmund Freud, probably you, and definitely me, have all had at least this fleeting voice-hearing experience. A voice calls out our name. The experience is implausible, unreasonable and real. We heard. Many are called, but few are chosen for more. Voices only speak more than a few words to a select percentage of humanity. Such hearers are diverse, and their voices capricious. Voices deliver the mountaineer Joe Simpson down the Peruvian Andes and save his life. They depress the writer Virginia Woolf to a riverbed and end hers. They inspire the mathematician Francoise Chatelin, but discourage the musician Brian Wilson.[1] What causes people to hear voices? What does it mean to hear voices? Are they a symptom of a disorder, and if so, what can be done about them? Or are they meaningful messengers, and if so, what are they trying to tell us? If you've never had the experience and we could summon you an unseen muse through an electric crack of a neural whip, would you want it?

You may not, as voice-hearing is predominantly portrayed as an unambiguous harbinger of madness caused by a broken brain, an unbalanced mind, biology gone wild.[2] At the dawn of the twenty-first century, 76 per cent of UK psychiatrists believed voice-hearing involved biochemical disturbances and 62 per cent felt it resulted from brain damage.[3] This idea has burrowed deep into our culture, with J.K. Rowling telling us that even in the wizarding world hearing voices isn't a good sign.[4] It has been driven by an extreme biomedical account of voice-hearing, premised in pathology, promulgated by psychiatry and patented by pharmacology. This conceives of voice-hearing as synonymous with schizophrenia and explains both as caused by inner deviance: 'biochemical abnormalities, neuroendocrine abnormalities, structural brain abnormalities and genetic abnormalities'.[5] Here, events outside the person's cells are excommunicated as causes unless they too are biological: viruses, head injuries, a loss of oxygen at birth. A vague conception of stress is allowed as awakening a slumbering deformation, but we are told to expect that a psychiatrist 'may not even ask...about traumatic early life experiences'.[6] In the aforementioned survey of psychiatrists, only 22 per cent believed bad childhood experiences played a role in the development of voice-hearing. In this account, it is no one else's fault that you are hearing voices. Patriarchy, prejudice and poverty don't enter the frame as potential causes when voices are simply 'a symptom of brain disease just like blindness'.[7] As for cure, this account legislates psychiatry, and drugs called antipsychotics, to correct a purported chemical imbalance and to eliminate voices. The content of voices is irrelevant; if the only option is to medicate people, what difference does it make what the voices say? We are warned that people shouldn't be encouraged to talk to or about their voices; at best it will make them delusional, at worst, dangerous. We shiver.

This account is Ronald Reagan, it's Spandau Ballet, it sells futures on brick-size phones. It's Beverly Hills Cop, big hair, Bill Murray with a proton pack. It's the 1980s. Although this account's heyday was 30 years ago, it persists in popular consciousness, is still endorsed by some mental health professionals and is helpful to some people who hear voices. Its heart still beats because there is at least some oxygen of truth in its veins. There is a biological basis to voice-hearing. Antipsychotic drugs do help some people with their voices. Simply ignoring the voices is helpful for some hearers. Yet it also persists for darker reasons. It sells drugs, justifies professions and offers succour to right-wing ideologies that root the causes of people's problems inside them rather than outside in their social environment. An extreme biomedical model, almost entirely focused on factors inside the individual, may be an appropriate way to understand some people's voice-hearing experiences. Yet when the blanket of this account is thrown over all voice-hearers it is suffocating. Its hegemony silences other accounts. Indeed, the leitmotif of this account is silence. It is silent about the past; life events that may have birthed voices are overlooked or deemed dangerous to discuss. It is silent about the present; the first rule of voice-hearing is that you do not talk about voice-hearing. It seeks a silent future; recovery is the silence of the voices. As a result, many people who hear voices have found neither truth nor salvation in this framework. Instead, it has only brought them suffering, stigma and the rejection of what their lived experience tells them is the case.

The extreme biomedical model of the 1980s was, in part, a reaction to another extreme account associated with the 1960s. In this, voice-hearing was caused by bad parenting, traumatic life events and a sick society, leaving no space for genes, brains or chemical imbalances. Here, what the voices said was understandable in the context of the person's life and must be listened to. Voice-hearing was a breakthrough, not a breakdown. The hearer was a shaman, not a schizophrenic. The culture was sick, not the voice-hearer. There was no cure because there was no illness. Elements of this account are still with us for the same good and bad reasons: seeds of truth and ideological appeal.

But the sixties are over. Billy is bleeding; Captain America, dead. The eighties ended too, though this is less widely known. Today, we need to go beyond ideology to both honour people's experiences and acknowledge their biology. Yet, the continued endorsement of extreme positions, and the historical baggage they come with, makes this topic divisive. People want to be in a trench with a team, not sitting in no-man's land where the most likely outcome is a bullet in both ears. A central barrier to bringing these accounts together is, as the psychologist Vaughan Bell has observed, that 'people persist in seeing different levels of explanation as mutually exclusive'.[8] For example, if traumatic life events cause voice-hearing then this is taken by some as evidence that genes and chemical imbalances are not involved.

Evidence for Bell's argument is everywhere. Take this entirely accurate statement by a professor of the history of medicine: 'Psychiatry has always been torn between two visions of mental illness. One stresses the neurosciences, seeing the origin of psychic distress in the biology of the cerebral cortex, the other stresses the psychosocial side of patients' lives, attributing them to social problems or past personal stresses.'[9] The author follows this with the entirely inaccurate claim that these approaches are 'polar opposites, in that both cannot be true at the same time'. Today we know that both can be true. Just as a three-dimensional hologram is built from the interference pattern of multiple beams of light, we need the light generated by both biological and trauma-based research to create representations of voice-hearing that reflect reality. We now know how plastic the brain is. We can see trauma's fingernails scratched into it. We are beginning to understand how the world talks to our genome, as well as how our genome talks to the world.

In this book I will try to bring together biology-led and trauma-led perspectives. I have, for many years, been part of the Hearing Voices Movement (HVM). Led in large part by people who themselves hear voices, this movement has looked to reframe and reclaim the experience of voice-hearing and is strongly associated with trauma-based explanations. Yet, I also work in a university psychiatry department, where I undertake genetic and neuroimaging research into voice-hearing. I see my role as being to try and find a middle ground between these explanatory tribes, both of which have much to offer, and to look for a space where dialogue can take place. Let us be clear though, biology and trauma alone are not enough to understand voice-hearing. First, other ways are possible, such as spiritual explanations. I will not have the space to address this important framework here in any detail. This book is already long enough, so I must point you to other sources on this topic.[10] A second reason that we must go beyond biology and trauma is because causation has hidden hands. These are the causes of causes: poverty, unemployment, discrimination, income inequality and structural macro-economic factors. These cannot be allowed to sit over a causal horizon, unseen, untouched and unimpeached.

It is important to note that not all people who hear voices do so because of earlier traumatic life events. Nevertheless, I should warn you that it is impossible (although many have given it a good try) to meaningfully discuss voice-hearing without addressing the abuse and maltreatment that often do precede it. This may be, and indeed should be, distressing to read. Furthermore, if you are a survivor of such abuse yourself, what is recounted in the pages of this book is potentially triggering. The publishing industry (but not Jessica Kingsley Publishers, thankfully) has repeatedly told me that people don't want to read about such traumas and that, if I write about them, sales will suffer. It is quite possible, even probable, that they are right. Yet to turn away from these experiences is to betray survivors and collude with perpetrators.

To give you an early idea of the type of stories I am referring to, consider two famous people whose voice-hearing I have already mentioned: Virginia Woolf and Brian Wilson. You may be familiar with their work, but are less likely to be familiar with their childhoods. Both suffered abuse. Virginia Woolf was sexually abused by her two older half-brothers. The abuse by her half-brother Gerald began when she was 6 and he was 18. The abuse by her half-brother George began when she was 13 and he was 28.[11] The memory of this burned in Woolf until her suicide by drowning. Two months before her death, she wrote, 'I still shiver with shame at the memory of my half-brother exploring my private parts.'[12] Brian Wilson describes a childhood with a father who was 'volatile, unpredictable, violent'. This was a father who forced his son to defecate on the floor in front of him, demanding Brian's mother watch too. Brian describes how he felt 'beaten, abused, soiled'. He recounts, 'I've never forgotten this incident…the anger has never gone away… My dad yelled at or beat me so often that all he had to do was look at me and I'd flinch.'[13] It is understandable not to want to hear these stories, but we must as a potential prelude to understanding. They raise many questions. For example, was it just a coincidence that, before their voice-hearing, both Woolf and Wilson experienced threats and abuse that led to powerful feelings of shame?

It is also important to stress from the outset that some people live happily with the voices they hear, finding them benign or even helpful companions on life's journey. Some will never approach a realm where pathology is up for debate. Nevertheless, we will start this book by examining voice-hearing in people who have been distressed and impaired by their voices, resulting in a psychiatric diagnosis. We will do so because this is where the majority of the research has been done. Governments and other funders of research want problems to be solved, and in many people voice-hearing is problematic. For some it is a matter of life and death. Hearing voices in people diagnosed with schizophrenia, for example, is associated with an increased risk of suicide.[14] Some people you will meet in the pages of this book do not survive voice-hearing. A small minority of people who hear voices act on commands they hear to hurt or even kill others. A greater number act on demands of voices to burn, cut or kill themselves.[15] While the link between voice-hearing and violence should not be exaggerated, neither should it be ignored or denied.[16] For some people troubled by voices, medication will be the answer. Others will be able to move from having highly distressing voice-hearing experiences and an associated psychiatric diagnosis, to living happy, regular (and sometimes exceptional) lives while still hearing voices. We will explore what may enable people to transmute a hellish experience into a helpful one, and what the voice-hearer's stone could be that facilitates this. We will also examine what differentiates people who are troubled by their voices from people who are not. Understanding unproblematic voice-hearing will emerge as an important way to glimpse future methods of assisting people with problematic voice-hearing.

Let us now start our journey to try and understand this experience, not by beginning in the brain, in the blood or in the genes, but in the lives of people who hear voices. Such narratives are not the end of our journey. There will be things that people cannot tell us and that only magnets and centrifuges can reveal. But without the context of a person's life, our centrifuges may only spin lies and our magnets repel, not attract, truth.

CHAPTER 1

Desperately Seeking Silence

> The voices arrived without warning on an October night in 1962, when I was fourteen years old. Kill yourself… Set yourself afire, they said. I stirred, thinking I was having a nightmare, but I wasn't asleep; and the voices – low and insistent, taunting and ridiculing – continued to speak to me from the radio. Hang yourself, they told me. The world will be better off.[17]

This was Ken Steele's baptism of voice-hearing, described in his book *The Day the Voices Stopped*. His parents took him to their family doctor who gave him a diagnosis of schizophrenia. Ken had to visit the library to find out what this was. The answer involved words such as hallucinations, delusions, disorganized thoughts and emotional flatness, but it was two other words he read that stayed with him: 'incurable' and 'lifelong'. Today such a position would be seen as disempowering and demotivating, despite the grim results of a recent review that found only one in seven people diagnosed with schizophrenia was achieving a comprehensive recovery and that recovery rates had not improved over time.[18] Although, as we will see, the likelihood of finding ways to deal with distressing voice-hearing is increasing, with more ways being available to help people with their voices today than ever before, other problems are likely to remain for people with a schizophrenia diagnosis. It is not all about the voices, although this book, of course, is.

Ken told his grandmother what was happening to him. She was a Baptist and to her it was obvious who was behind the voices. If the devil's greatest trick was making the world think he didn't exist, he hadn't fooled granny. A devil-may-cause explanation predictably terrified Ken. The amount of suffering and disability voices cause is influenced by what the hearer believes about them and how much power they ascribe to them.[19] As such, believing your voice is a fallen angel who controls hell is naturally going to cause problems.

Ken's first experience of an antipsychotic drug was chlorpromazine (thorazine). It wasn't pleasant. As he recalls:

> …the dosage was so high, I couldn't stand or speak. It was like being a living potted plant… I lost track of everything. For a time, I even lost track of the voices. They were as sedated as I. And then they came back with a vengeance.

Six years after the voices started, Ken was gang raped while in a psychiatric hospital. In a small hospital in a nearby town, where he underwent surgery to repair the severing of his sphincter, the voices changed.

> 'You have to get even, Kenny,' they sang in chorus. 'You have to teach a lesson to those pigs who called you a ho. They fucked you. Now it's your turn. You have to fuck them back!… Kenny needs to hurt them bad.' Never before had the voices instructed me to harm somebody else. But there was something different about me now. The voices zeroed in on the rage I was feeling. 'We'll think up some great ideas for how you can get back at

> them, Kenny… Leave it to us. We'll find a way for you to exact vengeance.'

There was to be no justice. In fact, it was Ken who ended up handcuffed, chemically, thanks to the next antipsychotic he was given, haloperidol (haldol).

> The symptoms were similar to those in Parkinson's disease… Haldol made me feel like the Tin Man from the Wizard of Oz, without any oiling. I moved stiffly and with extreme slowness. My jaw was rigid, and I actually was afraid that I would swallow my own, swollen tongue… 'They're strangling you,' said my voices gleefully. 'Strangling you with your own tongue. That ought to put an end to this farce of a life.'

It was no coincidence that Ken experienced Parkinson's-like symptoms. When medicine first stumbled into the drugs that eventually came to be called antipsychotics (Chapters 34–37), these were thought to reduce hallucinations in people diagnosed with schizophrenia by causing the sort of brain damage associated with Parkinson's disease, resulting in its characteristic symptoms of slowed thinking and emotional suppression. A German psychiatrist even proposed that antipsychotics had been administered at an effective dose when a patient's handwriting reduced in size by 20 per cent.[20] Reduced handwriting size was a known symptom of Parkinson's, and at this size reduction, 'enough' Parkinson's was thought to have been caused to help. Unsurprisingly, the marketing of antipsychotics no longer takes this tack, although antipsychotics continue to cause brain tissue loss.[21]

Wait a minute, you might say, how did people come to think that causing brain damage to someone ostensibly already with a broken brain would be helpful? No one would suggest a punch in the face as a cure for a broken nose. This idea needs to be situated in the context of the 1950s when physical assault still masqueraded as a treatment for people diagnosed with schizophrenia. Indeed, interventions for schizophrenia have historically been a horror show. The aphorism ascribed, perhaps incorrectly, to Marx, that the only antidote to mental suffering is physical pain, appears to have been mistaken for a treatment plan for people diagnosed with schizophrenia. Such 'treatments' have included bleeding and purging (done by nearly everyone up to the 1800s), cocaine (Sigmund Freud), full-body ice-cold towel wraps (Michael Woodbury), self-administered electric shocks (Bucher and Fabricatore), inducing seizures (Ladislas von Meduna), inducing comas (Manfred Sakel), malaria (Wagner von Jauregg, winner of a Nobel Prize for this idea in 1927) and inserting ice picks through the eye socket to mash up the wiring of the frontal lobe of the brain (Antonio Moniz, also a Nobel Prize winning idea, this time in 1949). The period of history when this last approach was used has been referred to by a historian of psychiatry[22] as 'The Lobotomy Adventure', which is outrageously frivolous. No one would dream of using the phrase 'The Thalidomide Adventure' to describe that awful period in history, but the basic rules of human decency don't seem to apply to dealings with people diagnosed with schizophrenia. The end result of all this was that even if people who heard voices didn't have a broken brain before treatment, they damn well did afterwards.

Years passed for Ken. Alcohol, drugs, hospitals, electroconvulsive therapy, but always the voices. Aside from drugs, no help was given. Ken was told by a doctor to simply stop listening to the voices and to discipline himself. It is often said that hope is central to recovery, but the environmental activist Derrick Jensen has defined hope as longing for a future condition over which you have no agency.[23] Hope is the last refuge of the powerless. Ken had hope for recovery, but he also had a determination to make recovery happen himself. Eventually, he managed to obtain talking therapy.

His new therapist encouraged him to see another doctor. This doctor offered Ken a new drug called risperidone (risperdal) and told him that if he didn't like it then he could stop taking it. Ken was surprised; no other doctor had ever given him that choice before. He started taking it, albeit at a lower dose than prescribed. A number of other things also happened. He got his own one-bedroom apartment, just a few blocks from a friend of his. This was a bit frightening, but he could talk through his fears with his therapist. He had a cat, a canary and a housekeeper, who would come by three times a week to help with cooking and keep his spirits up. Three months later he was taking risperidone regularly. He started up a Mental Health Voter Empowerment Project, to get mentally ill people to register to vote. His therapy sessions started going better. Then, a revelation:

> On May 3, 1995, sitting on my living room sofa…I made a startling discovery. My voices had stopped. One minute the voices were babbling away; the next they were gone – replaced by a persistent, mantra-like 'om' from the living room air conditioner.

But this was not entirely welcomed by Ken, who had developed a not uncommon voice-hearing version of Stockholm syndrome:

> I wanted them to return! For thirty-two years, they had been my constant companions… Although they had criticized and insulted me, ordered me to abandon new relationships and quit safe harbors, and constantly commanded me to kill myself…voices had conferred a specialness to my existence. Without them, I felt very much alone.

Ken attributed his recovery, solely and squarely, to the antipsychotic, risperidone. He wrote a letter to his doctor, which simply said:

> Thank you for convincing me to try this medication. You didn't lie to me. The side effects are minimal. You've given me back my life.

Whether the silence of the voices was genuinely due to the effects of an antipsychotic, a placebo effect, the talking therapy, the therapeutic effects of his improved social situation or a combination of all these, we will never know. We will examine the evidence for the effectiveness of antipsychotics later in the book. For now, we will simply note that many other people report similar stories to Ken: the eradication of their voices after taking antipsychotic drugs, leading some patients to dub them 'miracle drugs'.[24] However, for some such people the side effects of antipsychotics are not minimal and the price of silence is too high. For example, Susan Mann was a successful, 23-year-old trainee lawyer when she experienced the full-blown onset of a range of unusual experiences, including hearing voices. For five years she avoided treatment, as she knew that a diagnosis of active schizophrenia would preclude her admission to the bar (being granted permission to practise law). Susan explains:

> Once I had been admitted to the bar, I tried to find a psychiatrist using every means I could and was eventually referred to a psychopharmacologist. The night I first took thioridazine [an antipsychotic], the voices, which had been screaming at me all day, fell silent and stayed that way all night.[25]

Despite this promising start, Susan soon began to experience tardive dyskinesia, a common effect of antipsychotic drugs,[26] characterized by involuntary movements of the tongue and mouth. As a lawyer, she could not function at work with this, so she stopped the drugs. The voices flooded back. This was not to be the last time a lawyer, an antipsychotic and tardive dyskinesia would cross paths.[27]

Such stories, and the way they are told, leave us with a range of impressions of voice-hearing, most of which are consistent with how the experience is widely thought of (or one could perhaps say, marketed): a symptom of schizophrenia that comes out of nowhere and is eradicable by antipsychotics that rebalance an unbalanced brain. But what stories aren't we hearing? Ken Steele's book was called *The Day the Voices Stopped*. It focused on the lead up to the cessation of the voices. But we need another book too, one that gives the contextualized back story. We need the prequel. We need *The Year the Voices Started*.

CHAPTER 2

Context, Not Cortex

Like Ken Steele, Melissa Roberts ('Mel') also first heard a voice when she was 14. 'Call me Ron,' it said.[28]

> I clearly remember sitting in the school toilets at lunchtime…and hearing a voice. It was a male voice and was clear as a bell. I must admit, I freaked! What was a man doing in the girls' toilets? The first word that came out of Ron's mouth was simply 'Hi'. Once I searched the toilets and realized that no man was actually there, I dismissed it. I thought that I was imagining things.

Ron told Mel that he was a spirit. Initially, he was unproblematic:

> Ron's presence became more frequent and I accepted him as a friend. I did think that I was a little old to be having imaginary friends but it was the only explanation that my mind could comprehend. I have never admitted this to anyone before but it was actually kind of nice to have my own secret friend. And at the self-conscious age of fourteen any friendship was a welcome one.

A year later, Mel started having noticeable mood swings. The next year she developed an eating disorder. When she was 18, one of her closest friends killed himself, and this seems to have been a trigger for Ron to change radically, just as Ken Steele's voices had become more negative when he was raped. Ron told Mel to hurt herself, to kill herself: 'Cut yourself. It will stop the pain... You'd be better off dead... Just give up, death is the only way... Kill yourself, it's all that's left.' He threatened her family to try and make Mel comply: 'Burn your wrist or there will be consequences to your family... Bash your head against the wall or someone you love will go to hell.' He demeaned her: 'Shut the fuck up! No one wants to hear what you have to say... You're a fucked-up slut, all anyone wants off you is sex.' He isolated her: 'You are all alone. You have nobody – nothing... We are all that's around, there's nobody else.' He told her others hated her: 'They hate you, you don't deserve to be loved... Nobody wants you alive... They want you dead.' He made her paranoid: 'Why is he looking at you like that? He's planning to hurt you... There are cameras everywhere... You are always being watched... There is a man following you, he is evil.' As Mel described him in her poem 'I know you're there':

> I know that you are there/ But I don't know who you are/ I know you want to harm me/ I know that you crave to scar.

Ron told Mel that he could control her: 'I can and will control you.' He told her there was no escape: 'I can see you all the time, you cannot hide from me.' He tried cutting her off from the love of her family: 'He's telling me that he will hurt Mum if she tries to stop me hurting myself, telling me that if Mum touches me he will kill her... I need to hug my Mum. It's killing me not to. I'm scared but I'm going to.' Mel described this pain in her poem 'You can NEVER touch me':

> I look at their heart-broken eyes/ As I urge them and force them away/ I want to reach out, to touch/ And hug and cry, 'please stay'.

Faced with this, Mel started self-harming:

> My 'cutting' began with a few scratches on the tops of my thighs. As I discovered the rush that one got from self-harming I began to increase both the severity and the frequency of this behaviour. I cherished the sight of blood. The messier the cut was the better.

Later she would note in a journal that 'I only get peace when I burn myself'. Eventually, Mel took an overdose of paracetamol and zoloft and was hospitalized.

The first place her psychiatrists looked for the cause of her voices was in her brain chemistry. Mel and her parents were told that antipsychotics should remove the voices in a couple of months. Over the next eight and a half years, she was given 12 different antipsychotics: chlorpromazine, clopixal, haloperidol, periciazine, trifluoperazine, flupentixol, fluphenazine, quetiapine, respiridone, olazapine, amisulpride, clozapine; nine different antidepressants: sertraline, fluoxetine, escitalopram, reboxetine, dosulepin, clomipramine, tranylcypromine, duloxetine, moclobemide; four different anti-convulsants: sodium valproate, clonazapan, lamotrigine, topiramate; two different anti-anxiolytics: diazepam, alprazolam; two different mood-stabilizers: lithium, carbamazepine; and an anti-Parkinson's medication, benzatropine. Although the medications came and went, Ron remained. When Mel wrote, in a twenty-first-century echo of Mallarmé,[29] that 'I've tried all the meds', she wasn't exaggerating. In her poem 'I'm here all alone' she conveys the feeling this resulted in:

> Too much of a risk/ I hear over again/ Nothing we can do/ Just increases the pain.

Along with the pills, the diagnoses also piled up: schizophrenia, schizoaffective disorder, borderline personality disorder, psychotic depression. One antipsychotic, clozapine, slightly dulled Mel's voices, but it also dulled her. It made her tired, not able to do anything, unable to think straight: 'Brain is not working. Mum asked me a simple maths problem, and I just couldn't get me head around it. I had no idea what she was talking about', and she gained massive amounts of weight. Ron used this against her, telling Mel she was fat and ugly.

When it was clear that drugs were not helping, a blunter trauma was applied to her brain in the form of 17 sessions of electroconvulsive therapy (ECT). Although there is no evidence that ECT helps people with their voices (though there is evidence that it causes memory loss and brain damage[30]), Mel's parents were assured by a doctor that four or five treatments of ECT would get rid of the voices. Given this assurance they in turn persuaded Mel to try this, but she hated the idea. As her father, Bruce, later recounted to me, 'It was the worst thing we ever did to her.' Mel describes the effects of ECT:

> Despite my initial nerves, I grew to love the feeling of being washed over with sleep as the anaesthesia kicked in… It was a quick and easy procedure, which began with that illustrious feeling and ten minutes later, I would wake up in the rather harsh surrounds of my hospital room. Unfortunately, the treatments were unsuccessful. One of the side effects of ECT is memory loss. I regrettably lost huge chunks of my past… When looking at the few photographs I have of my schoolies cruise [a holiday students take in Australia at the end of High School], I remember nothing. They are mere pictures of something that I thought I had never experienced.

Drugs failed, ECT failed, yet the search for the roots of the voices in Mel's brain continued undeterred. There was nothing in a CT scan: 'the ventricles, cisterns and sulci appeared normal', nor in an MRI scan: 'no structural abnormality identified to account for the patient's clinical symptoms'. Second opinions were sought: 'Overall it is difficult to see what more can be done to help this unfortunate young woman.' Mel's genes were unravelled to see if they were causing her to metabolize antipsychotics at an unusual rate – nothing was found that would account for why the drugs weren't helping.

Mel started to hear a new voice, a young girl, who also verbally abused her. She also started to see Ron, as well as hear him. By this point Mel was living at home with her parents, and one day she saw Ron in her bedroom. Mel was so terrified that she jumped out of an upper-floor window. Her terror at seeing Ron was so intense that she ran half a kilometre with a broken pelvis. She was eventually found, by her parents, sitting in a gutter, crying.

As Mel saw Ron more often, always watching her, she became afraid of doing things like having a shower. There was no escape. He was there in the day. He could appear in her sleep: 'had a dream, and "the voice" was in it'. He could be there when she woke: 'was sleeping and Ron was lying on me when I woke'. Lying down on the couch she felt like Ron was climbing on her. In her journals she reveals that 'Ron keeps telling me that he is the boss of me. I am his. I'm scared he will rape me.'

Mel's voices started in 1997, when she was 14 years old. The mental health system spent nine years looking in her brain for answers. It was looking in the wrong place. The mental health system spent nine years asking: 'What's wrong with you?' It was asking the wrong question. It should have looked in 1997 and should have asked: 'Mel, what happened to you?'[31] Mel experienced a sexual assault that year, perpetrated by strangers.

It was only in 2003, six years after the trauma, that Mel finally felt able to disclose this experience to a nurse and psychiatrist who engaged well with her. Having allowed Mel to feel comfortable in disclosing this, they then deemed her too unwell to delve any further. When trauma survivors disclose their experience and no supportive action is taken, rendering them silent and powerless, this can be deeply upsetting and harmful. It took seven more years for a doctor to suggest that Mel's voice-hearing might be a result of post-traumatic stress disorder. But by then it was too late. Mel's paranoia and fears that people were watching her and wanted to hurt her had intensified. She felt like Ron was taking over her body. She started to attack her parents, with knifes, perfume bottles, her bare hands around their throats. Mel wanted to die. She had wanted this for a long time. It appears that she was hanging onto life, in part, to help one of her friends, who was also suffering mental health difficulties. She asked Ron if she should stay around to help her friend. 'No,' said Ron, 'don't be stupid, you bitch.' Mel hung herself, in her bedroom, on a Thursday. She was 27.

Ron now only exists in a poem of Mel's, called 'Dear Ron':

When I was lonely you crept up to me,
You took my trust you threw it back.
When I was down you sheltered me,
You appeared to cut the slack.
You seduced me when I was all alone,
Plus showed me another place.
You protected me from imagined pain,
And shaded my burnt face.
You found your way inside my mind,
You claimed you protected me.
You scream of the forgotten race,
And try to make me see.
I deteriorate as days pass by,
My mind becomes more jumbled,
I will you away, I push for peace,
In the mirror, my face crumbled.
Everyday which ends with you,
Screaming in both my ears.
I feel a little less hopeful,
And often will turn to tears.
And then you cry for a little help,

To push me further down.
She pops right up, to assist you,
And adds to my deepest frown.
Now you all pull together,
To push me down all the more.
Once again I'm all alone,
And now I've hit the floor.

In contrast to Ron, Mel lives on in the hearts and lives of hundreds of people that she deeply touched during her short life. Six hundred people came to her funeral. She would regularly receive notes, letters and postcards from people with whom she had only had a few days' contact on a ward, but who nonetheless had been deeply touched by her care, warmth and compassion for others. It was a kindness she could never show to herself. Her friends were deeply loyal to her, reflecting Mel's concern for them even when she herself was in the depths of unimaginable suffering. She inspired her parents, Bruce and Faye, to set up the Hearing Voices Network New South Wales (HVN NSW), which has offered support to people hearing voices across New South Wales in Australia. Bruce and Faye also set up the Melissa Roberts Foundation, which aims to support HVN NSW, educate society about the meanings of hearing voices, create awareness and reduce stigma associated with hearing voices, promote recovery and advocate for change in the mental health system's approach to the treatment of people with distressing voices.

Mel's parents had initially put their faith in doctors. As they put it, 'you had to put your faith in someone, you have no choice'. Yet a primarily biological approach to Mel's voices was of little help to her. The only help Mel ever got from antipsychotics was a slight detachment with clozapine. In many ways this is not unexpected. As Shitij Kapur and colleagues explain, 'Antipsychotics do not eradicate symptoms, but create a state of detachment from them.'[32] They go on to describe that:

> it is widely known that for most patients antipsychotics provide only partial remission – and many aspects of psychosis as well as other aspects of the illness remain untouched. While some patients do actually achieve complete resolution of their delusions and hallucinations with antipsychotic treatment, for many patients a detachment from their symptoms is as good a resolution as antipsychotics can provide.

In line with this, people who hear voices commonly report that taking antipsychotics 'dampens the voices but doesn't stop them' and 'helps calm them [the voices] down, they're not so loud but [they] don't go away'.[33] Another group of people experience beneficial effects of antipsychotics, in which the voices remain, but the person simply doesn't care about them any more. For example, an early 1954 study by Elkes and Elkes found that chlorpromazine did not make voices disappear, but only made patients less bothered by them; they didn't shout and scream at their voices as much.[34] One patient stated that his voices 'did not worry him so much', and another who had been hearing a voice called 'Mr Knock', who put 'filthy thoughts into her mind', reported after chlorpromazine treatment that 'she did not bother any more with Mr Knock' as he 'did not annoy her so much'. Fifty years later, Mizrahi and colleagues, in a study of the effects of antipsychotic medication, found that before treatment patients thought that antipsychotics would both eradicate their voices and help them be more detached from them.[35] However, after six weeks the patients found that the drugs that helped them be more detached from their symptoms 'help deal, help stop thinking, and make the symptoms not bother', but were less effective in taking away the voices altogether.

Given this situation, we may wonder how a biomedical explanation of voice-hearing has come to so completely dominate our understanding of this experience, and to be the primary way that people like Mel's experiences are approached, with little offered in terms of alternatives. The answer is a surprising one and lies in history.

CHAPTER 3

Religion Weaponizes Medicine

Whether God is dead or simply resting, divine silence has its benefits. People claiming to hear God's voice are a religious official's nightmare. Often called mystics in the Judeo-Christian tradition, they have nearly always caused problems for the establishment. As has been observed:

> To the Church as an institution, the mystic is a maverick. He is a nonconformist and a troublemaker; he upsets efficiently functioning procedures; he rejects the authority of the institution whenever it conflicts with his private vision. The weight of numbers and of persons, traditions, convenience, decency, and respectability count for him as nothing in comparison with his inner conviction… [W]ith such individualists the Church has a simple alternative: It can either canonize them or expel them as heretics. It cannot ignore them.[36]

Historically, voice-hearing has played an important role in authorizing doctrines as coming from God. However, once these messages had been used to establish a theology, and create an earthly power structure, the divine voice-hearing tap needed turning off. God continuing to speak to laypeople would be destabilizing and could not be permitted. The situation is reminiscent of the Grand Inquisitor scene in *The Brothers Karamazov*. In this, Christ returns to Earth but is locked up by a cardinal because his message is deemed too challenging and would interfere with the work of the Church. Christianity disconnected the divine hotline using the doctrine of cessationism. This proclaimed that since the death of the last of the 12 apostles, God no longer spoke. The problem was that someone continued to speak. As a result, ways were needed to undermine people's claims that the voices they heard were God. Two tacks were taken. One was inconsistency of the voice with scripture; the other was a medical model of voice-hearing.

Judaism had already opted for the former tactic. It formally turned off the tap of infallible voice-hearing after the death of Malachi (around 420BC). He was the last person Judaism recognized as a prophet (an individual who encounters Yahweh, receives an infallible new revelation and delivers this message to the people of God).[37] Upon Malachi's death, the *Ruah Hakodesh* (similar to the Christian 'Holy Spirit') is said to have withdrawn from Israel. Yet voice-hearing continued. Greenspahn has argued that the claim that there were no more prophets after Malachi is not due to a lack of candidates, but resulted from the de-legitimization of people purporting to be prophets.[38] He reasons that:

> More than institutional self-interest may have motivated the rabbis to deny the legitimacy of contemporary prophets...[T]hese figures' eschatological mission posed a severe threat to the existing social order. To the extent that rabbinic authority was dependent on Roman support, the rabbis were unlikely to grant legitimation to so destabilizing an influence.

Voice-hearing couldn't be controlled, but voice-hearers could.

Post-Malachi, voice-hearing was understood in Judaism as a highly fallible experience called *bat kol*. This term literally means 'daughter of a voice', with the experience being thought of as a small remnant of God. Eliezer Ben-Yehuda defines it as 'a voice that is heard as though out of nowhere, so that it is impossible to know whence or from whom it comes'.[39] With the cessation of prophecy, *bat kol* was the sole means for God to communicate with humanity.[40] Despite seeming to allow new revelation, it doesn't. The voice can be wrong and overruled. Jewish texts give examples of rabbis disputing a point when a *bat kol* is heard seemingly offering support for one position. The argument is then made that the Law (Torah) has already been given, and that what the *bat kol* says cannot supersede this. If a *bat kol* contradicts scripture, it is wrong. Potentially explosive voice-hearing is theologically defused.

Some Christians took a similar tack after the divine hotline clicked back on in first-century Judea. Once Christian theology had been developed, God had to be gagged. One strand of Christian history is a two-thousand-year game of whack-a-mole. People pop up claiming to hear God's voice and are hammered back down if God said something politically inconvenient to the Church. As in Judaism, these Christian voice-hearers could be bludgeoned down by scripture, but another hammer of their God was available: medicine.

Those claiming to hear God's voice typically appeared at times of societal breakdown, when top-down control of the population was weakened. For example, in the early fourteenth century the papacy resided in Avignon, not Rome. Pope Gregory XI was persuaded by voice-hearing female visionaries such as Saint Birgitta and Saint Catherine to move the papacy back to Rome. Gregory's death led to the Great Schism when the newly appointed pope in Rome was challenged by a rival pope in Avignon. This crisis of authority led to what has been described as 'an unprecedented visionary activity, a phenomenon one could call mystical activism'.[41]

The use of voice-hearing to support political positions led people such as Jean Gerson (1363–1429), a prominent theologian, to try to undermine the authority of people claiming revelation from voice-hearing. He did this using a medical discourse, arguing that people should think of such voice-hearing 'as resulting from an injury done to the imagination and should worry about being ill in the same way that insane, manic, or depressive people are'.[42] He couldn't completely stop the draft of divine communications, as the Bible still technically wedged the door open, so he argued that people's personal characteristics should be considered when evaluating voices' messages. Only people who conducted themselves 'prudently and cautiously' were eligible for true visions and voices. In short, if you were a suspect character who heard a voice that challenged Church authority, it was not God speaking; you were simply ill.

Martin Luther (1483–1546) reversed this trend, returning to the strategy used by Judaism and backing away from medical interpretations. His thesis was that Christianity should be based in scripture, and that people could interpret this for themselves. Thanks to the newly developed printing press, this idea went viral. It radically undermined the Church's authority, allowing voice-hearing people to claim to be prophets. Luther insisted their messages be judged by their accordance with scripture.[43] To contrast this with Jean Gerson, imagine a theological version of the TV show *The Voice*. Martin Luther is sitting down with Father Levine and Sister Aguilera to judge whether a contestant is hearing God's voice, based only on what the voice said. In contrast, Jean Gerson in the fourth chair is spoiling the whole thing by constantly peeking over his chair and looking at the person, before deciding whether to press his button or not. Luther actively refused the medicalization of voice-hearing as a way to destabilize claims of divine revelation. He observed that people were 'taught by doctors…[to] say that one's complexion or melancholy is to blame, or the heavenly planets, or they invent some other natural cause'.[44] Instead, he argued that divine voices and visions were 'not melancholy dreams that have no bearing on reality'. He had called for *sola scriptura* in relation to voice-hearing. Half a millennium later we would take Solian™ as scripture.

Whereas Luther's tactic to control voice-hearers was relatively benign and pushed medicine away from voice-hearing, the Church of England weaponized medicine against religious voice-hearers. In seventeenth-century England there was anarchy in a decidedly un-united kingdom. The English Civil War (1642–51) convulsed the country until Charles II ascended to the throne, introduced tea to England, and everything naturally calmed down.[45] Until this happened there was a crisis of authority fermented by Luther's idea of a personal relationship with God.[46] English people started their own breakaway religious denominations based on voice-hearing experiences. Perhaps the best known of these today was George Fox, founder of the Quakers. The Church referred to these breakaway voice-hearers as enthusiasts, 'fanatical men, who either feign or presume to have God's breath and inspiration, and whether by diabolical, melancholic or voluntary illusions, deceive themselves and others that such inspiration should be assigned to divine revelation'.[47] The Church declared the voices and visions of these enthusiasts to be insane delusions based on false perceptions and diseased imaginings.[48] Such people were written off as 'melancholic' and as mentally sick. The Church had become the champion of medical interpretations of voice-hearing.

Medical accounts of voice-hearing started to enter into theological discourse in accounts such as that of George Trosse (1631–1713), a Presbyterian Minister.[49] Trosse at first thought he was hearing the voice of God, but came to conclude that it was the voice of the devil. He went on to argue that his voices, as well as those heard by competing religious groups such as the Quakers, were caused by a 'crack'd Brain, impos'd upon by a deceitful and lying Devil'. Three centuries later Trosse's 'crack'd Brain' was to become, in the title of Nancy Andreasen's popular book, *The Broken Brain*, but this transformation would take some work.

CHAPTER 4

Manufacturing Meaning

The idea that voice-hearing is due to a chemical imbalance in the brain and should be treated by other chemicals that correct that imbalance has been with us for over two thousand years. Only the chemicals have changed. In Greco-Roman humoral theory, an excess of black bile caused hallucinations by affecting imagination and reason.[50] This was to be treated with hellebore, thought to restore balance through its purging effects. Physicians could prescribe black or white hellebore depending on, and there is no delicate way to put this, which end of you they wanted the purging to take place from. Humoral theory did not replace religious understandings of voice-hearing. Christianity simply assimilated it. In the thirteenth century St Thomas Aquinas proposed that angels moved our humors to create divine voice-hearing experiences. In the fifteenth century Fathers Kramer and Sprenger explained witches' hallucinations using humoral theory in their infamous hammer of witches, the *Malleus Maleficarum*. After the impetus given to biomedical models of voice-hearing during the English Civil War, the next strong push came with the birth of psychiatry.

Medicine may have been the father of psychiatry but the Industrial Revolution was its mother. The factory age had led to the concentration of people into cities, giving rise to the asylum.[51] The presence of large numbers of patients in the same place enabled a new class of physicians to observe and treat them.

The psychiatrist was born, a term created by the German physician Johann Christian Reil in 1808, by joining 'psyche' (soul/mind) with '-iatry' (physician). Reil stressed that the mentally ill should not be treated by experts from other disciplines, such as philosophy, psychology or theology, but by this new type of doctor.[52] The obvious tack to take in order to gain acceptance of this viewpoint would have been to show that psychiatry was more effective than these other professions in treating mental illness. The problem was that psychiatry really couldn't do much to help people at this time. Even though humoral theory was redundant, hellebore was still being used as a treatment for insanity, including hallucinations. The revised basis for this was that if you had your insides coming out of you at either end then you would have more pressing concerns than attending to hallucinations.[53] Instead, two other tactics were employed to try and achieve psychiatric hegemony over insanity.

The first was to build a guild. The benefits of this can be seen in another late eighteenth-century organization which didn't take this approach. In 1796, a Quaker, William Tuke, introduced moral therapy. This was a regime of work, piety and moderation in a bright, clean and friendly, family-like atmosphere. Tuke's approach presented a challenge to psychiatry because he was a layman claiming authority to treat the mentally ill. Unlike the emerging discipline of psychiatry, he refused to build a guild. He didn't think a professional class was required. He refused jargon. He argued that previous abuses had resulted from 'the mystery with which many of those who have had the management of the insane have constantly endeavoured to envelop it'.[54] He was hence already teetering on the edge of the cliff of authority. This was not a safe place to be. A low-pressure system of biological explanation had been moving through society since the Renaissance. This then collided with the high-pressure system of the new machine age, which had led to the metaphor of mentally ill people as 'defective human mechanisms' that had to be repaired so they could go and function in the marketplace.[55] This produced a gale of biological explanation that blew Tuke to his death. In contrast, psychiatrists had the kite of medical training, which they were able to raise and they could then pull themselves up above the heads of all others.

The second tactic employed by psychiatry was therefore to stress the biological basis of insanity. Andrew Scull has argued that early psychiatrists were motivated to insist on purely physical causes of mental illness and to reject moral treatment, precisely in order to seize power from lay people and the clergy.[56] This may be true, but it can give the misleading impression that psychiatry focused on biological causation solely for its own self-interest. We should not forget that, from its inception through to today, psychiatry has focused on biological causes driven by the simple, honest and humane belief that this is the best level at which to understand the experience, that it is destigmatizing for patients, and that this can lead to desperately needed new treatments. We may question the validity of these beliefs, and highlight how money, power and prestige led to their uncritical propagation, but we must not forget the presence of essentially good motives. Indeed, not all early psychiatrists took a biological tack. Some, such as Philippe Pinel (1745–1826), argued that some mental disorders were not associated with physiological changes. Yes, as a result his colleagues deemed him soft on biology. And yes, one damned him for being 'too stingy with the blood of lunatics'.[57] And, yes, Pinel, perhaps somewhat overexcited by the French Revolution, created a form of psychological intervention which was less therapy and more 'terror-py':

> one of the major principles of the psychologic management of the insane is to break their will in a skillfully timed manner without causing wounds or imposing hard labor. Rather, a formidable show of terror should convince them that they are not free to pursue their impetuous willfulness and that their only choice is to submit.[58]

But alternatives to a strong biomedical account have existed in psychiatry since its inception.

By the mid-nineteenth century it was being stated that insanity was purely a disease of the brain and that doctors were now the responsible guardians of the 'lunatic' and should ever remain so.[59] Then, a single psychiatric diagnosis grabbed hold of voice-hearing and held it doggedly in its teeth for over a century. In 1896 Emil Kraepelin named hearing voices as a 'symptom peculiarly characteristic' of a new disease he had invented: dementia praecox, later schizophrenia. Kraepelin focused on biological causes, arguing that 'we must probably interpret [voices] as irritative phenomena in the temporal lobe [of the brain]'. He hired Alois Alzheimer (1864–1919) to find brain changes associated with dementia praecox, but none were found at the time.[60]

Conjecture was not enough for biological views of voice-hearing to dominate the explanatory landscape. It took a diverse range of events in the second half of the twentieth century for a biomedical model of voice-hearing to become the default explanation, with its high water mark in the 1980s. Perhaps the most important was the discovery of drugs – which we saw used with Ken and Mel – that came to be called antipsychotics (see Chapters 34–37). These could help some people with their voices, as well as with other experiences deemed symptomatic of schizophrenia. Researchers were able to find out how these drugs worked, uncovering a role for the neurotransmitter dopamine, which invigorated further research and development. Antipsychotics were hugely profitable for their manufacturers. Global sales of antipsychotics would peak at $22 billion in 2008.[61] Deliverance, dopamine and dollars reinvigorated the ancient chemical imbalance theory of voice-hearing.

Another part of the appeal of this strongly biomedical approach, particularly in the USA, was that it was a tool that psychiatry could use to strike back against the esoteric empire: psychoanalysis. This had risen to prominence in the first half of the twentieth century, but had descended into an incomprehensible obscurantism, a quagmire it had frankly never hovered far above. In many ways this was preferable to the occasions it did rise to the level of communicability. One such instance involved parents, typically mothers, being deemed responsible for causing their child to develop schizophrenia. This could be by being too caring and protective or not caring or protective enough. This led to the concept of the 'schizophrenogenic mother', prominent from the late 1940s until the 1970s, whose spread was helped by a wave of post-World War Two misogyny.[62] It ultimately led to a justified backlash. Parents and other family members formed powerful lobbying groups in the USA, such as the National Alliance for the Mentally Ill (NAMI, now the National Alliance on Mental Illness), which naturally rejected a role of parents in causing mental illness. Pharmaceutical manufacturers contributed nearly $23 million to NAMI between 2006 and 2008, representing nearly 75 per cent of all the donations it received.[63] NAMI's stance towards antipsychotics and the medical model of mental illness can be correctly inferred from this. Parents and psychiatry now partnered against psychoanalysis, both agreeing on a biomedical model of schizophrenia, giving it a potent mix of political, moral and scientific authority.

In this new political environment, psychiatry became afraid to suggest that parenting could have any impact on the development of schizophrenia, which further encouraged a decontextualized biomedical understanding of voice-hearing. For example, in 2004 a prominent psychiatrist wrote: 'Schizophrenia is not a disease that parents cause. Nor is it a disease that parents can prevent or arrest… Schizophrenia is a brain/mind disease.'[64] Anyone who puts evidence above politics will concede that the first and second of these statements are incorrect as blanket statements, and the third, whose context seems to imply brain diseases can't be caused by what is done to people, is just bizarre. Parents are quite capable of treating their children in a way that will cause them to develop experiences that will qualify them for a diagnosis of schizophrenia. Incest, for example, can result in voice-hearing, which may contribute to a diagnosis of schizophrenia.[65] Of course, it must be stressed that most people diagnosed with schizophrenia have not been sexually abused by their parents. If schizophrenia is not a disease that parents can prevent or arrest, then we may wonder why children at high genetic risk of developing schizophrenia who have good relationships with their parents are less likely to go on to be diagnosed with this condition.[66] The science hence suggests that parents can influence the probability that their child goes on to hear voices, although the size of this contribution, relative to all the other risk factors for voice-hearing, remains unclear. Yet the political environment makes this hard to discuss at all and may even obstruct facts coming to light. For example, one of my colleagues submitted empirical findings for peer-review on the relation between child abuse and psychosis only to receive the following comment from a reviewer: 'This data must never see the light of day. It is pure family blaming/what would NAMI say?'

Post-1970, it became hard to argue that people heard voices because bad things had happened to them, inside or outside the family. Proponents of such a view could be tarred with the brush of 'psychoanalytic environmentalism' and feathered with anti-psychiatry epithets. While there was much that was bad about psychoanalysis, not only was the baby thrown out with the bathwater, but the bathroom was demolished and a stringent denial maintained that there had ever been a bathroom in the first place.

One reason why environmental causes of voice-hearing could be so easily shouted down was because they were associated with silence. Many people did not feel comfortable disclosing what turned out to be relevant causes of their voice-hearing, such as child sexual abuse. In an anti-psychoanalytic climate, many mental health professionals did not want to ask about such experiences, discounted them as potential causes, or were simply not trained how to ask about or deal with them. This promoted silence and powerlessness in survivors.[67] For example, one voice-hearer who was sexually abused as a child has described how their therapist told them to swallow their medication, keep their mouth shut and 'keep the lid on the cesspool'.[68] This formed part of a wider and continuing problem of the consequences of traumas like sexual abuse being deemed indicative of the presence of a psychiatric disorder (e.g., schizophrenia, eating disorder, borderline personality disorder) without the trauma being recognized as causative of it.[69] Rape is not a problem with no name. It is a problem with many names in a psychiatric hall of mirrors, most of which never actually name it.[70]

The development of non-invasive brain imaging – the ability to see the structure and functioning of living people's brains – also spurred the medical model of voice-hearing. Magnetic resonance imaging (MRI) allowed researchers to see changes in the structure of the brains of people diagnosed with schizophrenia. Unfortunately, some (although not all) of these changes, rather embarrassingly, turned out to be due to the effects of antipsychotic drugs given to treat the condition.[71] Functional MRI (fMRI) drew back the curtain further, allowing researchers to see brain activity during voice-hearing in both real-time[72] and seductive technicolour. This was a stunning technological breakthrough, which has led to significant improvements in our understanding of voice-hearing. Yet the siren call of these images lured some researchers onto the rocks of biological reductionism. Only when research into the effects of traumatic life events on the brain nailed researchers firmly to the mast of reality could they consider the multiple potential meanings of these images.

Neuroimaging (see Chapters 23–26) revealed that when people heard voices, areas of the brain involved in speech perception increased their activity. Researchers spun this as a vindication of people's claims to be hearing voices, yet without a realization of what it revealed about how voice-hearers were actually being viewed. If you went to a doctor with a pain in your back, a subsequent MRI showing a slipped disc would be hailed as uncovering the cause of your pain, *not* as confirmation that you had pain, which wouldn't need proving. The historical legal prejudice against the testimony of 'lunatics' was shown to still be present as, despite people having said for millennia that they were hearing voices, it was only when a man in a white coat triumphantly wielded an image of a voice-hearing brain that this actually became truth. This prejudice is still with us today. One voice-hearer related a story to me of having visited their doctor in pain, only to be dismissed because they were deemed a delusional schizophrenic who was obviously unable to report anything accurately, even this most basic feeling. In schizophrenia, patients' truths are treated as hypotheses and professionals' hypotheses are treated as truths. So it goes. I make no claim that this is representative of all patients' experiences, but simply highlight it as a potential consequence of undermining people's first-person reports, an issue we will come back to in Chapter 45.

The results of brain imaging studies were combined with an either/or mentality of mental illness. Either you had a biological, genetic neurodevelopmental illness, which schizophrenia was deemed to be, or you had a non-biological, trauma-based illness, post-traumatic stress disorder. A lack of awareness of the plasticity of the brain and of the ability of trauma to cause biological changes falsely pushed people to see biology and trauma as mutually exclusive causes, forcing them to pick one. Given the climate, most opted for biology.

Economic factors may also have played a role in the prominence of a biological model. Warner has argued that during labour shortages a need to rehabilitate people leads to an optimistic model of mental illness, which places its causes in things that happen to people. When labour shortages then remit, the focus on mental illness becomes pessimistic and causes are placed in hereditary factors.[73] It is notable that in 1970s America, just before the broken brain boom (try saying that three times quickly) of the 1980s, a century of labour shortage ended.[74]

A more speculative proposal is that the 1980s became the zenith of the broken brain, biomedical model of voice-hearing in part because voices themselves became more malevolent, increasing the association between voice-hearing and psychopathology. One study that speaks to this hypothesis compared voice-hearing in patients admitted to a hospital in Texas in the 1930s with voice-hearing in patients admitted to the same hospital in the 1980s, to see howdy voices differed.[75] The commands of 1930s voices were mainly benign and religious ('live right', 'lean on the Lord'), whereas those of the 1980s were negative and destructive ('kill yourself', 'kill your mother'). The more negative commands of the later period could have reflected a more negative and hostile social environment. Unfortunately, we lack systematic data on how voices have changed over the decades in the West to be able to test this idea.

Despite this myriad of pressures towards a reductive biomedical mode of explanation, some people who found antipsychotics ineffective were able to find other ways to cope with their voices. Not content to be labelled 'treatment resistant', as if they themselves had failed rather than the drugs, some questioned whether biology was the most helpful level to understand their voices at, or at which to develop ways to help. When alternative forms of help weren't forthcoming, hearers moved to make recovery happen themselves. To understand this, let's look at the voice-hearing of two people who demonstrate an alternative approach in action.

CHAPTER 5

There's Still Steel in Sheffield

Ken Steele, who we met in Chapter 1, lived through an era when parents were often unfairly blamed for causing schizophrenia. He saw his parents worry that their behaviour may have caused his voice-hearing. 'How I wish my parents had known what I would learn decades later,' he lamented, 'that there's no one to blame for this illness.' Sometimes though, there are people to blame.

Walking through the east of Sheffield 40 years ago, 45,000 steel workers were dwarfed by mile after mile of belching behemoths, their ears pounded by the thundering of steel-hammers from factories jammed together in a Mordorian landscape of flaming forges and furnaces. You would think the surface of the sun itself was being made. Two decades later, 90 per cent of these jobs had vanished, with the fortunate remaining workers trudging through a post-industrial wasteland. Every month was cruel. By the turn of the millennium a third of Sheffield was unemployed and long-term illness was a quarter above the national average. It was to this city and in this context that I came to talk to Peter Bullimore to hear his story of voice-hearing.[76]

Peter started hearing voices when he was seven years old. It was two years earlier that the sexual and physical abuse by a female babysitter had started. Peter calls her a tormentor, as she not only abused his body but also his mind. As he puts it, his body healed, his mind didn't. Initially there was a single, benign voice. It would accompany him to the local putting green. He'd take a spare ball for it. As he got older, and the abuse continued, his body would sometimes react with arousal. He asked himself why he was enjoying something he didn't want. The voices multiplied and started telling him to hurt himself and others. At their urging he turned on a lawn-mower while his mother was cleaning it, only narrowly avoiding cutting her fingers off. When he was 13, the babysitter left, the abuse left, and so did the voices, for a while.

> The biggest mistake I made through that abuse was that I did not disclose. I never told anyone about it, it became suppressed, it became buried. But when I became a father at 18, and I saw the vulnerability of my child, that box started to open, the problems started to seep out.

Years passed, and Peter was now married with three children. He was under immense financial and emotional pressure, working 18 hours a day, seven days a week, to start a new business, and receiving criticism from his wife for his absence from the home. It made him feel as if the tormentor from his childhood was back. Visual hallucinations started to accompany the voices. Driving his van down a country lane at night, Peter glanced in the rear-view mirror and saw a Freddy Krueger-like being in the back of the van. Slamming the van to a halt, he started emptying the back of the van to find the creature. Cars started piling up behind him, honking their horns. 'Fuck off,' shouted Peter, 'I'm looking for Freddy Krueger.'

He ended up being involuntarily held in a psychiatric hospital, where he received a diagnosis of schizophrenia. Eventually, a social worker recommended he attend a group where people who heard voices could talk to each other about their experiences. Peter went. He found smart and presentable people who talked about experiences familiar to him. His family had told him not to talk about his experiences, but now he could take off his mask and talk about his voices. Despite this relief, while reflecting on his life Peter decided he was destined to kill himself. But before doing so, he thought he would go and tell Steve,[77] his psychiatrist.

> I went to see him and I said, 'Steve, I've worked it out.' So he said, 'Come on, what is it today?' Now, Steve's consulting room was very small, and when you've taken volumes of medication over years you forget words, and you get thought blocking, and I said to him, 'Steve, I was born to kill…', and for the life of me couldn't think of the word 'myself'. So I was continually saying to him, 'Steve, I was born to kill.' Well, you've never seen a chair go to that back wall as fast in all your life.

On being sectioned again, Peter's medication was increased to the point where his parents had to bring in tea towels to mop up the saliva that was pouring out of his mouth. Eventually he managed to lie his way out. Soon after, his mum was admitted to hospital with back pain. He went in to visit her and was bombarded with voices saying, 'Your mum's got cancer, she'll be dead in six months.' His mum was diagnosed with pancreatic cancer and died six months later. Peter can now put this down to coincidence but at the time it seriously screwed with his mind. The voices loved it though. 'You've killed your mother, you're a murderer, burn in hell,' they taunted. At her funeral, Peter was the only one who didn't cry. Antipsychotics had blunted his emotions. It was grist to the voices' mill: 'See, you're not crying, you're a murderer.'

Then came a turning point. Peter's dad had arranged to come and see him one day at 7pm, but by 8pm he wasn't there.

> The voices were saying, 'He's not coming, it's because you're a murderer, kill yourself.' I foolishly listened to them, went to my bed base, smashed open my razor,

> and slashed my wrists. Just as I'd done it, my dad walked in with a nurse, so you can imagine the commotion. And he asked me why I'd done it…and I said, 'Well it's your fault, you should have been here at seven, it's now turned eight.' He said, 'Pete, I'm in haulage, I got stuck in traffic, you know I always turn up.' Now my dad was a really big strong, powerful man and his next comments really shook me. He said, 'I've just lost your mum, I don't want to lose you,' and it was a look of utter despair in his face, and it made me realize 'stop being a selfish so-and-so cos you're hurting other people, not just yourself'. My mum and dad had done everything, so had Sarah [his occupational therapist[78]], so had Steve [his psychiatrist], there was only one person not trying and that was me. And the reason I wasn't trying was ten years prior a consultant psychiatrist had said, 'You will never, ever work again.' That's how powerful his words had been.

His occupational therapist, Sarah, told him that the local Hearing Voices Group had shut down and that Peter should start one up. As part of this process Peter invited the English Hearing Voices Network to Sheffield to hold an event.

> I was talking to the main speaker at the end. Now all this guy knew about me was that I was a voice-hearer, he knew nothing else. And I said to him, 'I like the way you work with voices, but you're talking about voices with identities; mine have no identity, they have no gender, they're demonic.' And he just looked me straight in the face and he said, 'Peter, address the demons of your past.' Now the demons of my past were my abuser, and as a grown man when I saw her I was still running away. So I decided somehow I had to address these demons, and I saw her one Saturday afternoon coming down the road. And my first instinct was to run, but I

> didn't, I kept walking. My heart was really pounding but I kept eye contact all the way. And as I got close to her, she wouldn't look me in the face, she looked to the floor. But just by getting her to look away I'd altered the power relationship. You have to remember in life no one can ever, ever give you any power, you have to take power. I had taken the power back from this woman.

Peter began to examine the meaning of his voices and realized that the reason that they were talking about emotional issues in his life relating to the abuse was because he had buried this away silently inside himself. He discovered that feelings of guilt surrounding the abuse were a key driver of the voices. He felt guilty because his body had reacted sexually, against his will, during parts of the abuse. To deal with this Peter now held a virtual court of law in his own head. He weighed up the evidence for and against his guilt and found himself innocent. He accepted that he was a child and did not choose to be abused.

For Peter, voices are emotions that have become overwhelming. Today he doesn't take antipsychotic medication, but still hears voices. The voices that continue to make unfounded allegations ('you killed your mother, you killed your son') would once have pushed him towards suicide, but he now treats them as helpful, albeit challenging, messengers reminding him to visit and honour the graves of those he has lost. And Peter thanks them for it. For him there is no silver bullet for the voices because it turns out they weren't werewolves in the first place. Peter has played a central role in the English Hearing Voices Network (Chapter 7), helped set up Hearing Voices Networks across the world and currently has health service funding in Sheffield for a project to help others decode their voices like he did. He has found his meaning. There is still steel in Sheffield.

CHAPTER 6

A Candle in the Dark

As a child the moon had nothing to hide. It was a lifetime of invisible gravitational clawing by the Earth that created a body with a dark side we never see.[79] The tidal forces on our planet owe as much to this unseen half of darkness as it they do to the moon's visible side of light. Kate became interested in the moon and astronomy as a child. This is not unusual. Many of us will have developed such an interest, perhaps fostered by a parent or a teacher, a movie or a museum. Kate became interested in astronomy because her mother locked her in a small, dark space at night, where the only light she could see was the moon.[80]

> I was just a child when I had my first voices speak to me, and being only four years old I didn't really understand what was going on. I didn't realize everyone else didn't have the same things going on in their heads. At the time I was suffering physical abuse, emotional abuse and neglect, and the voices came to me saying they were my friends and that they would help me, but they never did or could help me. I told my mother I was hearing voices and seeing things...and she just said it wasn't happening, it was just an imaginary friend. I thought mothers were supposed to protect and love their children, but mine just wanted to hurt me.

> She had many ways of punishing me, for whatever I had supposedly done, though existing seemed to be my worst crime. Locking me in the coal-bunker, with no food or water and sometimes with no clothes. If I created any fuss I was battered, so I learned to go in when I was told to. As the abuse expanded to include sexual abuse, by a family friend, she just ignored what was going on. I tried to tell her what he was trying to do with me but she wouldn't believe me and would punish me for lying.
>
> After my mother died, due to an incident when I was running away from her while she was trying to hit me, I was put into a children's home. Rather than this being the escape from a short lifetime full of abuse this opened up other avenues for the world to hurt me. From the age of 12 until I was 13 I was repeatedly molested, abused, raped by a member of staff and forced to perform sexual acts with the other children. I now call this man 'The Alien' as no human being could do such things to a child.

Kate then went to live with her grandmother for four years, until her grandmother also passed away.

> My voices took the place of the people who had hurt me over the years. The abuse I had suffered at their hands I now suffered in my mind, as I still do. I was first hospitalized after being raped, where I was diagnosed with post-stress paranoid schizophrenia. The initial reaction was to medicate me, in the belief that the medication would silence the voices. All the medication did for the 28 days that I was sectioned was weaken my resistance to the voices and make me sleepy. On release I was thrown back to the world with no support and a bottle full of pills that were supposed to cure me.

> To escape from the person who raped me I moved away. Three months later the police came looking for me, because The Alien had been arrested and was due in court with multiple charges relating to sexual abuse and rape occurring at the children's home I had been in. I was asked to give evidence, but the thought of being in court with The Alien was something I just couldn't face. The police were pretty good, not pressurizing me to give evidence, and when I was declared mentally unfit to give evidence they left me alone.
>
> The stress of these events and the horrors of my past that it dredged up caused me to decline. I was sectioned again and my children were taken into care. The voices worked on this, telling me that my children would go through what I had and it was all my fault. I figured out rather quickly that admitting to hearing the voices and seeing spaceships was not going to get me out. So to get my children back safe with me I lied through my teeth, telling the psychiatrists exactly what they wanted to hear about how their wonder drugs were working.

Most people encounter someone who is key to their recovery. For Peter (Chapter 5) this included his occupational therapist. For Kate it was a health visitor who pointed her towards the Hearing Voices Network:

> She was the first person who listened and tried to understand. Within the Hearing Voices Network I found for the first time in my life a group of people who actually understood what I was talking about and who believed me. Through shared experiences they helped me formulate my own coping strategies; gave me an understanding of what the voices could mean and tried to focus on the positives of hearing voices.

The voices had convinced me that everything that had happened to me was my fault. I deserved to be beaten, starved, half-drowned with my head down the toilet. The apparent affection and attention which had been shown while I was being sexually abused was something I had craved, never having had attention in a positive way. So the voices worked on the fact that I must have sought out the sexual side too and involuntary responses to the sexual situations just proved I was a whore, slag, or worse, and they kept reminding me of this every day. The Hearing Voices Network helped me realize that though I might carry the guilt, that guilt was misplaced. I was the victim rather than the one at fault and that the voices were just working on my deepest fears.

Left alone with them, without support, I relive the worst moments of my past again and again, night after night. Now with the support of the friends I have made at the Hearing Voices Network, I know I don't have to be alone with the voices; they have allowed me to reclaim my life. It is not a cure; there is no cure for hearing voices and it is not something that needs to be cured. It is what those voices say that we as voice-hearers have to try to interpret. It is when we are scared to discuss what is going on in our heads, when we live alone with them, that their more destructive potential can be unleashed.

Thankfully, there is a happy epilogue to Kate's story:

Once I was so medicated that I could barely stay awake through the day. Now five days a week I am out as a voluntary worker with the Hearing Voices Network. I facilitate groups in and out of hospitals, I train professionals and do workshops and visit universities

> trying to educate the next generation of professionals in a more empathic approach. So long ago it wouldn't have seemed possible for my life to have purpose, direction and meaning – now I work one to one with people in the state I once was in, showing them how to claim their lives back.

We have now seen the Hearing Voices Movement referred to in Mel's, Peter's and Kate's stories. What is this and where did it come from?

CHAPTER 7

The Psychiatric Reformation

Walls came down in 1989. This was the year that Kinzie and Boehnlein asked whether massive psychological trauma could lead to psychosis.[81] This was the year that Lorna Benjamin stressed the need to ask people hearing voices, 'How did it start?'[82] And this was the year when Marius Romme and Sandra Escher first published their work that was to lead to the Hearing Voices Movement.[83] The foundational event of this movement was a dialogue, a conversation between a psychiatrist, Marius Romme, and his patient, Patsy Hage. Before he met Patsy, Marius thought that what voices said were meaningless, and he regularly prescribed medication for them. Patsy argued with Marius about the reality of her voices, pointing out to him: 'You believe in a God we never see or hear, so why shouldn't you believe in the voices I really do hear?'[84] Marius recalls that 'Patsy was the first person in whom I accepted voices as reality'.[85] Patsy described how an alternative framework for understanding voices, which normalized the experience, helped her cope with and make sense of her voices. Marius's psychiatric certainties collapsed.

Marius, Patsy and the then science journalist Sandra Escher (now a PhD in psychology) reached out to other people who heard voices. This culminated in 20 voice-hearers speaking at a conference in Holland in the late 1980s, attended by

340 other people who also heard voices. Among other things, the conference revealed that hearing voices was not limited to people in the psychiatric system; many people in the general population also heard voices, finding them useful or beneficial and feeling no need to contact mental health services about this. People interpreted their voice-hearing using a variety of frameworks: psychodynamic, biomedical, parapsychological, mystical and technological. Romme and Escher concluded that treating voice-hearing as a symptom of an illness didn't always help people to cope with their voices. Instead, they recommended that people should try to understand the voice-hearer's frame of reference, support them to change their relationship with their voices and use the support of other people who heard voices (hearing voices groups) as a means of decreasing social isolation and stigma.[86] For many people who heard voices this approach provided an attractive alternative or adjunct to traditional psychiatric approaches, which were often experienced as simply trying to silence them and their voices. This approach became the Hearing Voices Movement (HVM). This holds an annual congress on voice-hearing where experts by experience (people with personal experience of hearing voices) share their stories of understanding, healing and recovery on an equal basis with experts by profession and training. These two groups are increasingly overlapping.

As the HVM grew it sought reform of what was seen as a dysfunctional psychiatric system. It sounded a call for a voice-hearing glasnost. People who heard voices demanded autonomy, the ability to define their experiences for themselves. They called for openness, a reconsideration of both the meaning and causes of voice-hearing and how effective psychiatry was in helping. They sought solidarity, the development of an international movement of people who heard voices. Calls for a psychiatric perestroika naturally followed: a restructuring of the provision of mental health services for people who heard voices. Organizing peer support became an important focus of the HVM, and hearing voices groups were welcomed by many voice-hearers as a safe space to explore and understand their voices and other experiences. Activists who heard voices, such as Peter and Kate who we met earlier, as well as people such as Jacqui Dillon,[87] Ron Coleman[88] and Eleanor Longden,[89] began providing training to mental health professionals and academics. The traditional power hierarchy was being turned upside down.

While the HVM includes people with a wide range of perspectives, there are six core values to which members generally subscribe.[90] The first is the normalizing idea that, as John Watkins puts it, voice-hearing is a common human experience.[91] Formal support for this proposition first appeared in 1894, when the first large-scale study of the prevalence of voice-hearing in the general population was undertaken.[92] This surveyed 17,000 people and found that around 3 per cent had heard voices. Similar surveys over a century later also found that a single digit percentage of people in the general population reported having heard voices while awake. Of course, who and how one asks influences the rate of voice-hearing that is reported. For example, in 1983 Posey and Losch asked US college students whether they had ever had experience of hearing a voice fully aloud 'as if someone had spoken' and found that a whopping 71 per cent said yes.[93] The most common single experience, reported by 39 per cent of students, was hearing one's name being called when no one was there. More expansive voice-hearing was also found, with 11 per cent of students having heard voices offering comfort or advice in situations similar to that of hearing a voice coming from the backseat of the car when driving. Voice-hearing emerged as being more common than people thought.

A second tenet of the HVM is that voices are not random or meaningless utterances, but understandable responses to things that have happened in one's life. It is argued that voices may be caused and fed by emotional life events that overwhelm and disempower the person, with the content and identity of voices frequently corresponding to broader issues in the person's life. Given this, there is naturally a focus within the HVM on the role of trauma in voice-hearing. However, a third key value of the HVM is that diverse explanations for voices are accepted and valued, including biomedical explanations, if they help. The HVM respects that people may draw on a range of explanations to make sense of their voices. Indeed, a fourth key value is that voice-hearers are encouraged to take ownership of their experiences and define them for themselves. Hearing voices groups often provide a safe space for this exploration. This links into the fifth key value of the HVM: peer support and collaboration as a fruitful means of helping people to make sense of and cope with their voices. Mutual support groups have a long association with the HVM, with an emphasis on group ownership rather than any specific predetermined structure.

The final core value of the HVM is that accepting and valuing voices is generally more helpful than attempting to suppress or eliminate them. Voices are accepted as a real experience, honouring the reality of the voice-hearer, and are recognized as something that the voice-hearer can – with support – understand and successfully deal with. However, consistent with the diversity of opinion valued by the HVM, if voice-hearers choose to take antipsychotic medications to manage or eradicate voices, this too is respected. Empowerment comes before ideology.

At its heart, the HVM looks to create a blank space where people can author their own meanings of their experiences. Its approach poses a significant challenge to conventional mental health services, some parts of which thought the HVM was trouble when it walked in. A 1994 review, published in the *British Medical Journal*, of Romme and Escher's first book on voice-hearing created early bad blood, proclaiming that a 'chill is sent down the reader's spine' and that the approach advocated was 'not just ill advised but potentially dangerous'.[94] Others have attached the antipsychiatry label to the HVM, but for the most part, through dialogue and engagement with mental health professionals,[95] the HVM has managed to shake it off. As Angela Woods has argued, the HVM has been able to create an entirely new identity for someone hearing voices that does not involve schizophrenia, namely that of being a 'voice-hearer'.[96] Before the HVM this style of being was simply not available. This idea has now been taken up by many people who now see voice-hearing as a part of their identity. As Taylor Swift might put it, players gonna play, hearers gonna hear. But it goes beyond this. Voice-hearing is viewed by many in the HVM as something potentially to be celebrated, paralleling Marcus Garvey's famous goal ('The world has made being black a crime… [I]nstead of making it a crime I hope to make it a virtue'). A major challenge this faces is that, on the surface at least, voices often have a distinct lack of virtue, as we will see next.

CHAPTER 8

Variety with Commonality

For a book ostensibly on voice-hearing, we haven't talked that much yet about voices themselves. To avoid this reaching the point of rudeness, we will now rectify this. Most voice-hearing research has been done with people diagnosed with schizophrenia, so let's ask what the typical voice-hearing experience is like there.[97] Of course, this assumes that there is a typical experience. This turns out to be only loosely true. Characterizing a typical voice-hearing experience involves more buts than the National Show of the American Goat Society.[98]

Most people who receive schizophrenia-related diagnoses will hear more than one voice (but around 20 per cent will hear only one voice). The voices will typically sound different from the person's own voice (but around a third will say the voices sound like their own voice). They are real, perceptual experiences, just like when someone talks to you normally (but a substantial minority of people will say they are more like ideas than external sensations, and some will report 'soundless' voices). They speak clearly (but many will also hear mumbling voices, and around 20 per cent will hear voices speaking gibberish). They will typically be heard as either coming from the outside world, like normal hearing, or from inside the head (but some will hear the voices coming from other parts of their body, such as the chest).

The voices will usually be either identifiable as people known to the person (but will be unknown people in a substantial minority of hearers) or beings like God or the Devil. The voices will typically be heard several times a day or most of the time (but the length of each instance can be highly variable, lasting from just seconds to continuing for over an hour). The voices will attempt to influence the voice-hearer's activity by issuing commands to perform specific actions and will judge them, typically negatively, through critical or abusive comments directed at him/her (but supportive voices will very often be reported too). Voices will tend to be very repetitive in what they say (but a minority will hear voices with novel content each time). Most will say the voices are not like memories (but nearly 40 per cent will say that the voices are in some way like 'replays' of memories of previous conversations they've had or overheard).[99] The person hearing them will have some control over their voices (but around 10 per cent will have no control at all), and the majority will be able to ask questions of the voices and get answers back (but around 20 per cent will not). Voice-hearers will generally be able to clearly recall the first time they heard the voice, and may report other forms of hallucinations as well, such as hearing music, clicks and bangs, seeing or smelling things, or feeling people touching them. The voices will become more frequent when the person is alone, and contextual factors (such as mood) will impact the frequency of their voices.

This variability in voice-hearing can pose real-life problems. For example, consider a defendant in a court case who claims that they were hearing voices at the time of their offence and wants to use this as justification for a plea of not guilty by reason of insanity (NGBRI). Of course, they would be doing this despite some studies suggesting that persons found NGBRI serve a longer time with loss of freedom than those who are found guilty of the crime, but anyway.[100] Now, imagine if there was some doubt as to whether they were really hearing voices, and so a professional was brought in to assess if the defendant was malingering (i.e., faking it for perceived gain). People have done this with voice-hearing in criminal cases,[101] sometimes to try and get a financial advantage,[102] and it has been claimed that voice-hearing is the most frequently faked symptom of psychosis by criminal defendants.[103] If the professional has in their mind a prototypical example of what voice-hearing is like and uses this as a yardstick to measure someone's alleged voice-hearing against, then given the variability in voice-hearing it would be easy for this to lead to an erroneous judgement.[104] If you're interested, you can consider the case of Senque Jefferson in a free-to-read paper.[105] Despite such variability in voice-hearing, certain aspects do echo through history.

Voices want you to do things. Over 80 per cent of people diagnosed with schizophrenia who hear voices receive commands from them. Some are petty prescriptions: 'get the milk'. More often they are darker directives: destroy yourself. Such voices can be found throughout history. In the 1600s a physician, the Reverend Richard Napier, recorded details of 2483 people he treated in general practice.[106] Twenty-eight patients reported that Satan appeared to them, either visibly or as a disembodied voice, urging them to commit suicide. In the 1800s, Esquirol described a patient who heard voices 'that accuse him…[that] are continually repeating in his ear that he has betrayed his trust – that he is dishonoured and that he can do nothing better than destroy himself'.[107] Voices can even intervene more directly to achieve this end:

> On one occasion, Mr. A experienced the voices 'taking over' and forcing his body to 'freeze' in the middle of a busy street. Meanwhile the voices cursed him and declared that the world was ending. Another time, the voices 'took control', causing his body to dive through a hospital window… Mr. A's experience was that the potentially lethal actions involved in these episodes

> derived entirely from the external agency of the voices, which had usurped his 'will'.[108]

Those who don't hear voices explicitly telling them to kill themselves are still likely to hear ones that chastise or abuse them. The majority of people diagnosed with schizophrenia who hear voices will hear a dominant voice that speaks in a tone which is angry or malicious, with content which is abusive, persecutory, derogatory, threatening or critical.[109] Again, such voices have a long history. In the 1500s Saint Teresa of Avila wrote of her voices that 'many of them are reproaches. He [God] sends them when I fall into imperfections. They are enough to destroy a soul.'[110] In the 1700s William Cowper described how 'Satan piled me closely with horrible visions and more horrible voices. My ears rang with the sound of torments.'[111] Such abuse is not random – voices know where to stick the knife. As one participant in a study of ours noted: 'The voices always played on what was your vulnerable point.'[112]

Voices ram these messages home through repetition, both of what they say and how they say it. Nearly 80 per cent of people diagnosed with schizophrenia who hear voices say that the general theme or content of what the voices say is always or mostly the same. Half say that their voices will often or sometimes use the same words or phrases repeatedly, like a stuck record.[113] This makes us think of the thoughts found in obsessive compulsive disorder (OCD). Are voices a perceptual form of OCD? We will pick this idea up again in Chapter 31.

Voices with negative content can nevertheless sometimes be felt to be benevolent, going all the way back to the story of Abraham and Isaac.[114] In a somewhat more recent example, Chadwick and Birchwood describe a patient who heard a voice telling her to kill her family and herself. She nevertheless believed the voice was a benevolent deity who was giving her the chance to see her dead daughter by going to heaven. Another patient believed his voices to be benevolent in spite of them telling him to kill his daughter.[115] The intention of a voice is very much in the ear of the beholder.

Other voices are genuinely nice. Around half of voice-hearing people diagnosed with schizophrenia will hear such positive voices. They can make them feel calmer, more confident and help with daily life.[116] They can also act as a buttress against negative voices. For example, one hearer describes how:

> One [voice] tells me to hurt myself… And I did in the past… It's very nasty…always criticizing…continually at you…'try and do yourself in', 'commit suicide'…they try and tell you how to do it…there's never anything good… Through time a girl appeared… She was more peaceful and more subdued…saying to me…'just don't pay attention to him'.[117]

Given these benefits, you can see why people can have mixed feelings about the medical elimination of their voices, as Ken Steele did in Chapter 1. Foes are lost, but so are friends. Positive voices often experience a natural attrition (to a greater extent than negative voices), either diminishing over time or becoming negative.[118] In some ways this latter experience can be more problematic than hearing voices which have always been negative. When a positive voice goes to the dark side it can take the influence it has gained with it. Angels become demons, leading to predictable distress and problems.[119] Positive voices can also be problematic in and of themselves, as they may encourage grandiose delusions, discourage help-seeking and impair people's functioning.[120] Furthermore, commands given by these voices are more likely to be followed. Positive voices are not without their problems.

Why are voices so often negative? What puts the ice in voices? We will later consider a role for traumatic life events (Chapter 20) and neurological factors (e.g., an involvement of right Broca's area, Chapter 30) but another possibility is that it is due to cultural factors. The preponderance of negative voices we have seen may be a peculiarity of the West, where most research studies are drawn from. Pakistanis diagnosed with schizophrenia and living in Pakistan are less likely to hear voices telling them to kill themselves or others than Pakistanis diagnosed with schizophrenia who live in Britain.[121] Whereas Americans typically hate their voices, a feeling that is apparently mutual, Indians and Ghanaians report predominantly positive experiences of voice-hearing.[122] Tanya Luhrmann and her colleagues, who found this, suggested that the Western sense of the self as private and bounded causes Americans to experience their voices as an assault and an intrusion into their private world, making the lack of control they have over their voices deeply distressing. We can see a parallel to this in the classic American film *Being John Malkovich*. Here, John Cusack's character finds a portal which leads him inside the head of John Malkovich. When Malkovich finds out what is happening his response is one that many of us would empathize with: 'That portal is mine and it must be sealed forever, for the love of God.' In contrast to Americans, Luhrmann and her colleagues argue that Indians and Ghanaians are more likely to interpret their voices simply as people rather than as signs of a violated mind. This means they can form relationships with them and are unsurprised that their voices cannot be controlled, as this is the nature of people. Hearing voices is cross-cultural, but how cross the voices are is cultural.

Going beyond cultural variation, hearing voices that issue commands appears a timeless and invariant experience. To test this proposition, we can ask if ears in ancient times also heard commanding voices. If we go back to some of the earliest written records, the cuneiform tablets of Ancient Mesopotamia and the papyri of Ancient Egypt, it is very hard to find reports of voice-hearing. This is despite both societies having a belief in spirits who could return to this world to harass the living, which would seem to encourage voice-hearing (if you're interested in more details on potential voice-hearing in Ancient

Mesopotamia, including Julian Jaynes' writings, you can read my *Silence of the Ancients* blog post).[123] Yet, oddly, many of the Hebrew prophets who intersected with these societies did report hearing voices, including notable numbers of commands. Ezekiel hears commands to eat a scroll and to cut his hair. Moses receives not ten observations, nor ten suggestions, nor even ten commandments, but ten Commandments. It is of course possible that these experiences, buried in time, are apocryphal.

We may have somewhat more confidence in reports from, to quote Poe, the glory that was Greece and the grandeur that was Rome. The most celebrated example of voice-hearing in Ancient Rome was that of Marcus Caedicius (391BCE) and involved a command. The historian Livy tells us that while Caedicius was standing on the famous Via Nova, 'he heard in the silence of the night a voice more powerful than any human voice bidding the magistrates be told that the Gauls were approaching'.[124] Cicero claims the voice said, 'The walls and gates must be repaired; unless this is done the city will be taken.' However, this story still has a strongly literary smell to it. Much more likely to be an early true report of a voice-hearing experience is that of Socrates in Ancient Greece. We are told that Socrates heard a voice that gave him instructions on what to do.[125] He was likely not alone. Dodds has argued that one of the most common types of hallucinations in Ancient Greece, experienced while awake, was hearing a divine voice which 'commands or forbids the performance of certain acts'.[126] Whether such ancient reports are true or not, they are nevertheless uncanny echoes of a key feature of contemporary experiences of voice-hearing. This leads us to suspect they were either real experiences, or inspired by real experiences others were having at the time.

Even if the typical voice-hearing experience is just that, hearing a voice, this is clearly the centre of an experience which ripples out into other forms. Approaching this disturbance of the pond of inner experience armed only with the term 'hearing voices' is like going into a sauna with only an eye patch. Only part of what needs to be covered will be so (though this may be a very English view of saunas). Language, as Eric Blair warned and Tony Blair showed, blinds as much as it reveals. The existence of the term 'hearing voices' encourages people to talk about or frame their experiences in a way that involves voices and hearing, yet, as we have noted, some people's 'voice-hearing' may neither involve a voice (being more thought-like) nor hearing (so called 'soundless voices'). More nuanced accounts of voice-hearing emerge when people are free to talk about their 'voices', rather than answering a checklist of questions. For example, Angela Woods and colleagues recently found that around a fifth of the people they asked about their voices (which included people with a range of diagnoses) said the term 'voice' was inadequate for their experience.[127] Instead they referred to 'intuitive knowing' or 'telepathic experience' and used terms such as 'alters', 'parts' or 'fellow system members'. Around 10 per cent reported voices with no auditory quality:

> I did not hear the voices aurally. They were much more intimate than that, and inescapable. It's hard to describe how I could 'hear' a voice that wasn't auditory; but the words the voices used and the emotions they contained (hatred and disgust) were completely clear, distinct, and unmistakable, maybe even more so than if I had heard them aurally.

The clinical focus on 'heard' voices can cause those with 'unheard' voices to feel that their experiences lack legitimacy. For example, Nev Jones and Mona Shattell describe the following powerful reaction when they told an audience about how voices can lack an auditory quality:

> A woman raised her hand, very hesitantly at first, and asked to confirm if what we were saying was indeed that 'voices without literal sound(s) were still legitimate

> symptoms'; yes, we responded, and then two other women in the room broke down in tears. 'I've always been afraid to say this to my doctor,' one explained, 'because the "voices" are terrible, but I don't actually "hear" them in a literal way, and I was worried that he wouldn't think they were real, would just say I was experiencing the same things everyone does.'

Another important caveat to the term 'voice-hearing' comes from the observation that very often a person is sensed, rather than just a voice. As Vaughan Bell has put it, 'voices are as much hallucinated social identities as they are hallucinated words or sounds'.[128] For example, as one participant in Woods and colleagues' aforementioned study noted:

> I hear distinct voices. Each voice has their own personality. They often try to tell me what to do or try to interject their own thoughts or feelings about a certain subject or matter[...] My voices range in age and maturity. Many of them have identified themselves and given themselves names.

As a result, it is not surprising that, as Laura Benjamin described, 'all the richness of social interaction can also be found in the internal world represented by the voice'.[129] Some people will report sensing the presence of the person whose voice they hear, even when the voice is not speaking. A person may stand behind the voice. Reflecting this, some voice-hearers have set up Facebook pages or Twitter accounts for their voices, where their voices can express what they think and feel. Many people's voices might pass an intra-psychic version of the Turing test. As we will see in Chapter 28, we may soon be able to find out if they actually can...

Although we started this book by inquiring into the experience of 'hearing voices' we may wonder if this is part of a wider class of experiences that we could call 'unshared communications'.

As Cynthia Wible has noted, many unusual experiences in schizophrenia 'revolve around the perception or feeling of an entity that is speaking, communicating, watching, following, observing, or spying'.[130] We could perhaps look beyond the form of these experiences (hallucinations, delusions) to an underlying unifying principle: unshared communications. The messages of these communications often appear to relate to physical or social threat, for reasons that are usually fairly self-evident given the life history of the person. Is there a core experience of threat or an unsafe world, which may manifest as a voice, an unspoken communication, or a persecutory delusion? And if so, why do different people experience this threat in different forms? As usual, we have more questions than answers.

To conclude this chapter, we may ask whether, even if voices are often not typical, certain features of voices are typically a sign of a specific mental disorder. Kurt Schneider (1887–1967) argued that two types of voices were specifically indicative of schizophrenia: voices talking to each other (conversing voices) and voices that keep up a running commentary on your behaviour and thoughts.[131] From 1980 to 2014, if you heard either of these two types of voices, and they caused you social and occupational dysfunction, then *this alone* was sufficient for you to get a diagnosis of schizophrenia. Don't let anyone tell you that someone would never have been diagnosed with schizophrenia simply because they were hearing voices.[132] In the latest version of psychiatry's dominant diagnostic manual (*DSM-5*), the idea that certain types of voices are indicative of schizophrenia has been quietly dropped. This change, on paper at least, in what certain types of voices are meant to signify resulted from the realization that a wide range of people hear such voices, not only people given schizophrenia diagnoses. This raises the question as to who else is hearing voices, and we will turn to this next.

CHAPTER 9

Doublespeak

Moving past schizophrenia can be difficult. Densely packed with history, professional and financial interests, and 100,000 research papers, it has developed a gravity all of its own. It can suck experiences into itself, which disappear over a schizophrenia event horizon, becoming unknown. We have come to call the darkness schizophrenia. Yet some things will not stay hidden.

Jane hears a voice. It first appeared at the age of ten when she was lying in bed at night, alone and terrified after another incestuous attack by her father. She felt so alone that it was unbearable and so she made up a 'friend' who began to comfort her. Her conversations with this friend grew more frequent and more complicated as time and the abuse went on. Jane is told she has paranoid schizophrenia.[133]

> **Client:** I started to hear voices, but they were not nice voices, they were horrible.
>
> **Interviewer:** Did you recognize them?
>
> **Client:** It was the man that abused me… I met this man that was a builder, in construction, you know? And he said that he wanted to give me a job, but they were all lies, he was trying to con me. He took me back to his house, he locked the door, and he had sex with me…
>
> **Interviewer:** When you went to hospital what did they say was wrong with you?

Client: Schizophrenia, paranoid schizophrenia.

Interviewer: What do you think personally?

Client: What do you mean?

Interviewer: Do you think it is what you've got?

Client: Oh yes, that's what I have got.[134]

Barbara is 18 and was raped a year ago. Her boyfriend kept saying that she was cheap and dirty for being raped and that no one else (apart from him) would ever want her. After their relationship ended, Barbara had a breakdown and heard voices telling her she was 'cheap and dirty'. Following a psychiatric assessment, she was diagnosed with a psychotic disorder and given antipsychotic medication. She was then referred to an early intervention in psychosis service, which found no delusions or bizarre behaviour and suggested that her experiences were consistent with post-traumatic stress disorder. The medication was stopped, and Barbara was offered psychological therapy instead.[135]

CHAPTER 10

Only God Knows

Mary is hearing voices and has just been hospitalized. In the last two weeks she has hurled knives at her family, choked friends, bit herself, thrown a puppy down a flight of stairs and had previously been found holding a knife to her head. Voices told her to do these things. In hospital she puts pictures of dogs and ducks on the door of her room and talks constantly about how they protect her. She has problems with attention, hyperactivity and impulsiveness. Her moods shift rapidly and she doesn't seem to enjoy things she used to. She can't sleep, and when she does, she has nightmares. Mary is five years old.

Mary has these experiences and acts this way because she was sexually abused, on a nightly basis, in her own bed, between the ages of three and four. She was raped and she was molested. A teenage uncle did this. The voice that tells her to do bad things is recognized by Mary as being his voice. Her belief that ducks and dogs are her protectors is not a delusion. It is a defenceless child's desperate attempt to feel safe. Dogs terrified her uncle. A stuffed cuddly duck was what she hugged while she was raped. The perpetrator is now locked up, but Mary still sleeps in the same bed where she was repeatedly raped. Mary's mum has found it hard to talk to her daughter about this. She too suffered sexual abuse. Abused, afraid and alone; this is not only Mary's story of voice-hearing, it is the story of many. Eight months after her discharge, with a diagnosis of post-traumatic stress disorder (PTSD) and a treatment plan, Mary is doing better. Her family are planning to move so she no longer has to sleep in that bed, and her mother is now able to talk to her about her abuse.[136]

Despite not being a named symptom of PTSD, hearing voices is often found in people with this diagnosis. People are diagnosed with PTSD after a trauma if they show a specific type of symptom; the big three are re-experiencing the trauma in some way, avoiding reminders of the trauma, and increased levels of anxiety and general emotional arousal. Of all common traumas, sexual assault is the most likely to result in PTSD. Kessler and colleagues found that 46 per cent of women and 65 per cent of men who rated rape as the only or most upsetting trauma they had suffered developed PTSD.[137] The awareness of sexual abuse in society has waxed but mainly waned (see Chapter 18 for potential reasons for this). Back in 1860s France, Auguste Tardieu reviewed 11,576 cases of people accused of rape or attempted rape and found that almost 80 per cent of victims were children, mostly girls between four and 12 years of age. Today, in the United States, 18 per cent of women and 1 per cent of men are raped in their lifetimes, with nearly half of this first happening before the age of 18.[138] Thirty-five per cent of women raped before 18 are raped again as adults. Being raped as a child increases your risk of hearing voices, and being raped again as an adult increases this risk further. It is unclear what percentage of people with PTSD resulting from rape will hear voices, but it can be estimated as in the range of 15 to 34 per cent.[139]

The leitmotif of both rape and voice-hearing is silence, so when the two co-occur the silence can be deafening. Survivors of rape are often made invisible and forced to be silent about their experiences for a variety of reasons, including the blaming, insensitive and ineffective reactions of others, and simply not being believed. Consider the experience of Marie. Her boyfriend had arranged for two strangers to take her home in their car:

> They drove to a wooded area where they held a gun to her infant son's head and raped her. When she got home, she told her mother who told her to keep the rape a secret: 'And I went home, and it was my fault. Shut up and don't you tell anybody what you did.' Marie also told two friends, but they blamed her and told her to try and forget that it happened: 'Forget it, it's over, it was your fault, leave it alone.' She then turned to her priest and told him about the assault in confession. But, he blamed her for the assault and told her that God was punishing her… 'I felt really, really, really bad. Feeling very bad. I couldn't talk, look at your face. I would, I would look down 'cause I'd think you'd look and I'd be filthy, dirty whore…feel less than a whore, dirtiest thing in God's earth.' Having exhausted all of the options she felt were available to her, Marie stopped disclosing.[140]

Here we see a number of themes that allow us to understand how a hearer with voices originating in childhood sexual abuse may find themselves imprisoned below five circles of silence.

The first circle is the silence during ongoing abuse that no one else knows about, cares about or believes. For example, Judith Herman reports a survivor's account of incest in a 'respectable' family:

> My mother lived at church and church functions. My father sang in the choir, and he molested me whilst my mother was at Sunday School… There was no drinking or smoking or anything the world could see. Only God knows.[141]

The second circle is post-abuse silence. One study found the average time it took women who had suffered child sexual abuse to tell anyone was 21 years.[142] This is often encouraged by the culture. As Catharine MacKinnon puts it:

> You cannot tell anyone. When you try to speak of these things, you are told it did not happen, you imagined it, you wanted it, you enjoyed it. Books say this. No books say what happened to you. Law says this. No law imagines what happened to you, the way it happened. You live your whole life surrounded by this cultural echo of nothing where your screams and your words should be.[143]

The third circle of silence consists of not talking about ensuing voice-hearing due to worrying about being stigmatized for it; being labelled a freak, dangerous, or even being made to feel 'like a different species'.[144] The fourth circle comes from the urging of the voices themselves. Invisible voices may wish to stay that way. Take the case of Joe. His voices told him not to tell his therapist about the sexual abuse he had suffered.[145] The final circle comes from silence being equated with cure. As Debra Lampshire, speaking of her personal experience within the mental health system, puts it:

> I learnt that success was silent, remaining silent, being invisible… To go unnoticed by the community that was the ultimate goal. No tell tale marks of your uniqueness… With almost surgical precision your differentness is removed, you became integrated, indistinguishable from others. This was the only route to freedom. Liberty lay in the resignation of your humanness.[146]

When we later come to consider how trauma might cause voice-hearing, we will have to consider the possibility that silence surrounding a trauma, and the lack of social support this is associated with, may encourage the development of voice-hearing.

Combat trauma is another well-studied cause of PTSD, where voice-hearing may be found. The concept of PTSD began in what was called 'post-Vietnam syndrome', and was driven by anti-war activists who wished to highlight the psychological injuries that US servicemen were returning with.[147] Young men had killed or witnessed the slaughter of millions[148] of Vietnamese men, women and children, and had also been present for the deaths and maiming of their own comrades. Repatriated to a societal backlash, they were often given no support. Many would end up hearing voices. Clinicians working with women who had been raped had long argued for the need for something like a PTSD diagnosis, but did not have sufficient influence or power to be heard.[149] Indeed, although war spurred the modern recognition that distressing mental experiences could have their roots in traumatic life events, Judith Herman argues that it was not until much later in the century that 'it was recognized that the most common post-traumatic disorders are those not of men in war but of women in civilian life'.[150] The numbers support this claim. For every man who returns from war with PTSD, three women at home have PTSD as a result of sexual assault. For every three men who come back from war with PTSD, one man at home has PTSD as a result of sexual assault.[151]

For an example of voice-hearing in the context of combat-related PTSD, consider David, who was 25 years old when he fought in the Lebanon War. He was a tank crew member and, some would say, a lucky one. When an artillery shell hit his tank he was picked up and thrown by the blast. David survived but other crew members were killed. In the days immediately afterwards he became restless and anxious. Worrying thoughts about the event kept coming into his mind. He didn't want to go outside. He could fly off the rails at the slightest provocation. His sleep was disturbed and he avoided weapons whenever he could. Several weeks later the voices started. His dead comrades were talking to him. They accused David of betraying them by remaining alive. They commanded him to join them by committing suicide. Fourteen years later, David is married with two children. Antipsychotics and psychotherapy have only given him a partial remission from these experiences. He has a diagnosis of chronic PTSD.[152]

Studies of voice-hearing in veterans with PTSD have found rates ranging from 20 to 65 per cent.[153] Although prevalence estimates vary, the voices themselves are remarkably consistent. The majority are related to the earlier combat situation, and co-occur with non-combat-related voices. Daniella David and colleagues found that the voices heard by traumatized veterans 'reflected combat themes and guilt', including hearing voices of dead comrades calling 'help' or 'medic' or 'people screaming in the back of my head'.[154] Such voices are not just auditory flashbacks. Although cries and groans are sometimes heard, veterans mostly hear voices they could never have actually heard, such as what an imagined non-English-speaking enemy soldier would say to them.[155]

Just like voices in the context of a diagnosis of schizophrenia, a common theme runs through the voices of veterans: kill yourself. They are often driven by feelings of guilt (including survivor guilt) and shame. For example, Mueser and Butler[156] give details of five veterans (of Korea/Vietnam) who had PTSD and heard voices. The first heard voices of people he believed he had killed in Korea, and of recently deceased relatives who cried to him, criticized him and encouraged him to kill himself. The second, a week after shooting a Korean soldier, started to hear the voice of this soldier urging him to kill himself. The third heard the voice of a friend who had been killed in combat, who sometimes just spoke to him, but at other times told him to kill himself. The fourth, hospitalized with guilt and depression over soldiers he had killed, heard voices of fellow soldiers telling him to kill himself and saying that it was time for him to join those he had killed. The final veteran was the only one not hearing voices to kill himself – instead he heard the voices of those he had killed, laughter, mortars and gunfire.

Although rape and combat are the traumas most commonly discussed in relation to voice-hearing, any trauma or emotionally overwhelming event can potentially lead to voice-hearing. Mary was a couple of blocks away from her adult son when she heard the gunshots that killed him. Now, once a week, she both sees and hears him. 'I don't know why they shot me, Mama,' he says. 'Come home [to heaven] with me.' James is in his mid-50s. After Hurricane Katrina he waited on his roof for three days to be rescued. As he waited, he heard others calling for help. After being rescued, he in turn rescued others. Yet there were many he could not save. Now he hears voices daily. They are unfamiliar voices calling out, trying to get his attention, trying to be saved.[157] Survivors of torture can also report voice-hearing:

> Once I was safe, I thought I was free of my torturers. I actually believed that I would never see them again, that I would never have to smell them or hear their voices. But what I soon realized was that they were within me; they literally had made their home inside my soul.[158]

Bullying is also linked to voice-hearing. Take the experience of 36-year-old Ruth.[159] She presented at hospital with depression, paranoia and hearing voices criticizing her. The voices happened when she had slept badly or when her mood was low. She believed her experiences were in part due to bullying at school, which no one (parents, teachers or friends) stopped from happening, even though she told them about it. She blamed herself for being bullied, believing it was a result of the sort of person she was and for her not wanting to be part of the bullies' peer group. She felt useless. In therapy, Ruth came to realize she was not to blame for the bullying, identified triggers for her voices (social situations, feeling she had made a mistake) and reframed the voices as self-critical, intrusive thoughts.

It is hard to estimate how many people with PTSD hear voices. A 2007 study found that 85 per cent of adolescents admitted to hospital with PTSD had auditory hallucinations,[160] yet some experienced PTSD clinicians report hardly ever encountering voice-hearing in patients. We have estimated that 20–65 per cent of veterans with PTSD will hear voices, with the equivalent estimate for survivors of sexual assault being 15–34 per cent. A reasonable overall estimate may be that one in four people with PTSD hear voices. Ample evidence suggests that voice-hearing should now be included as a characteristic symptom of PTSD.[161]

Now, think back to the earlier stories of voice-hearing by people who came to be diagnosed with schizophrenia. Traumas were in their back story too. Their voices said similar things to those heard by people with PTSD: hurt or kill yourself. Is voice-hearing in schizophrenia and PTSD the same thing? Arguments that the voices heard by people with PTSD are different from those heard by people diagnosed with schizophrenia hold water like a colander. One proposal is that people with PTSD recognize voices they hear as being their own thoughts (ego-syntonic 'pseudo-hallucinations' to use the jargon of the field), whereas voices heard by people diagnosed with schizophrenia are experienced as being someone else (ego-dystonic 'true hallucinations'). Yet both types of voices are found in both PTSD and schizophrenia.[162] A second argument draws on Schneider's argument that certain types of voices (running commentaries and voices conversing) are indicative of schizophrenia. However, there are no differences between rates of running commentaries or voices conversing between voice-hearing people with PTSD and voice-hearing people diagnosed with schizophrenia.[163] A third argument is that voices in PTSD typically take the form of auditory flashbacks (re-experiencing of auditions surrounding trauma), whereas voices in schizophrenia do not. Yet, voices in PTSD are distinct from auditory flashbacks where the person acts or feels as if the traumatic event is actually recurring.[164] In fact, when we directly compare voices heard by people diagnosed with schizophrenia and people with PTSD, they are remarkably similar.[165] I would wager that if you gave a clinician a description of a voice heard by someone with PTSD, but didn't tell them the patient's diagnosis, they would not be able to guess at rates better than chance as to whether the person had a diagnosis of PTSD or schizophrenia.[166]

An obvious conclusion is that whether you hear voices and have a diagnosis of PTSD or schizophrenia, traumatic life events may be at the root of your voice-hearing. Eugen Bleuler himself said of his much-misunderstood creation, schizophrenia, home of much of the world's voice-hearing, that we might be 'dealing with the effect of a particularly powerful psychological trauma on a very sensitive person rather than with a disease in the narrow sense of the word'.[167] But why stop here? Could trauma be associated with voice-hearing wherever it is found? To answer this let's turn to other psychiatric diagnoses with high rates of childhood trauma/abuse and see if the unseen speaks there too.

CHAPTER 11

Follow the Trauma

Kathy hears what she calls 'mean voices' in her head, as well as the sounds of children crying. She has flashbacks, is depressed, loses time and finds herself in strange places without knowing how she got there. Her therapist is able to talk to an alter personality of Kathy's, called Julie, who says that she helps Kathy during times of stress. Kathy cuts her arms with razors, burns herself with cigarettes and masturbates with sharp objects. Cutting helps her deal with the pain. Kathy's parents divorced when she was five years old, and a series of stepfathers physically and sexually abused her. As a teenager she lived on the streets, where she traded sex for food and shelter. Kathy has a diagnosis of dissociative identity disorder (DID).[168]

DID, the modern name for multiple personality disorder, is characterized by the presence of two or more distinct identities or personalities in a person. These have their own ways of thinking and viewing things. Some can grab the wheel to steer the person's behaviour. Those who can't can still make themselves known through speaking to the patient. Up to 90 per cent of people diagnosed with DID will hear voices, including voices commenting and voices arguing with each other. There is no clear evidence that the voices heard by people diagnosed with DID differ from those heard by people diagnosed with schizophrenia. While one study found that people with DID were more likely than people diagnosed with schizophrenia to hear voices that talk among themselves, and to hear voices that take the form of replays of things that have been previously said to the person,[169] another study of similar size concluded that the form and content of voices in DID and schizophrenia were 'remarkably similar'.[170] As we will see later, it may be that any differences that do exist between the voices of people diagnosed with schizophrenia and DID are due to the greater rates of childhood trauma in people with DID.

Let's meet someone with a different diagnosis. Moira was a 24-year-old student, admitted to hospital because she was threatening suicide. She had fluctuating moods and stormy relationships. Moira heard voices in her head telling her she was bad or advising her to kill herself. This did not occur on a daily basis, but only when she felt particularly distressed. Although she sometimes believed her voices while they were talking to her, once they stopped she knew that they were imaginary. She did not have any delusional beliefs. Moira received a diagnosis of borderline personality disorder (BPD, also referred to as 'emotionally unstable personality disorder').[171] Around one in three people diagnosed with BPD will hear voices.[172]

BPD is a victim of hallucination chauvinism. It is portrayed as being associated with hearing voices inside your head, which are dismissed as pseudo-hallucinations. This reflects a perception that only voices perceived as coming from the outside world are 'proper' hallucinations, and that these are associated with schizophrenia. This idea has deep historical roots. Augustine of Hippo (354–430) divided voices that people heard ('locutions') into three types. Corporeal locutions were those heard just like normal speech. Imaginative locutions were more interior, with clear words being heard but inside the mind. Finally, in spiritual/intellectual locutions a voice was heard but without any sound. This has been referred to as an 'inarticulate voice' which leaves more of an impression than definite words. It would be 'as if' a voice had told you to go jump in a river, for example. This classification system mattered at the time because Christianity assigned different importance to each type of voice. Corporeal (i.e., external) voices were most likely to be regarded with suspicion and dislike. Fifteen hundred years later and theological speculation had transmuted into psychiatric orthodoxy. Externally located voices were deemed to be associated with more severe psychiatric disorders. Unfortunately, there is no validity to this. The voices heard by people diagnosed with BPD are not notably different to those heard by people diagnosed with schizophrenia.[173] Furthermore, given the link between voice-hearing and trauma, it is unsurprising that a recent study found high rates of childhood trauma in BPD patients: 92 per cent reported emotional abuse, 87 per cent emotional neglect, 67 per cent sexual abuse, and 31 per cent physical abuse.[174] At this point, we may wonder if schizophrenia (in some but not all cases), PTSD, BPD and DID are simply subtly different reactions to trauma.

Take another psychiatric diagnosis associated with trauma: eating disorders.[175] These 'disorders' often represent attempts to deal with trauma. As Ellen Rome has described:

> Those of us who care for persons with eating disorders know that such disorders are often a solution to other problems, albeit a maladaptive one. My patients have ranged from a young lady repeatedly sodomized by a relative, and unable to put food in her mouth without gagging and vomiting, to a member of a wrestling team whose coach weighed-in the boys alone, naked, fondling (or worse) each teammate. My patient got himself off the team by starving himself to the point of hospitalization.[176]

As such, we might expect to find more voice-hearing in people with eating disorders than in the general population. This is an under-researched area, but voice-hearing, or something akin to it, can be found in people with eating disorders. This can be seen in something referred to as the 'anorexic voice'. Matthew Pugh[177] defines this as 'a critical-internal dialogue (i.e. a second or third commentary which is "heard"), orientated around shape, weight, eating and their implications for self-worth'. Take the following example:

> Mara Nottelman describes her daily struggle with an internal voice which forced her to vomit, even after ingesting a small amount of food… 'What a weak person you are! Did you just eat food? Crisps even. You have to vomit! Now!'… When Mara tried to argue with the voice it became even louder: 'Do you really want to keep that food inside your body? Impossible, you have to throw it up! Hurry up! The longer the food stays in your body the more calories will be absorbed.'… Eventually, Mara described obeying her critical voice and starting [sic] to vomit.[178]

Such voices appear to begin along with the eating disorder and may initially be perceived as a friend or protector. As the eating disorder gets worse, this voice can become negative and critical, and experienced as an enemy.[179] A preliminary study reported that 95 per cent of people with an eating disorder heard critical inner voices, with the remaining 5 per cent reporting very critical thoughts but not clearly 'hearing' an inner voice. This compared with rates of hearing critical inner voices in a comparison group of students of 30 per cent.[180] The lower someone's self-esteem, and the more they criticize themselves, the more severe this critical inner voice is. Thus, we have a voice-like experience, in a disorder associated with traumatic life events, which begins benignly, becomes hostile and critical, and which the person can feel compelled to act on. This is a lot like the other voice-hearing experiences we have encountered in this book. Nevertheless, it is not clear where this experience sits on the spectrum of routine inner speech and voice-hearing. Over half of the participants in the study described above had difficulties with the term critical inner *voice*, potentially due to the stigma associated with hearing voices, yet they could distinguish this 'voice' from more routine self-critical thoughts. Could there be a specific type of thinking, distinct from our normal thought, perhaps generated through thinking about how other people view us, which forms the basis for both the anorexic voice and the fully voice-like experience of voice-hearing?

At this point, for the purposes of balance, I should reiterate that not all people who hear voices have a history of trauma (and even if they do, it could still potentially be unrelated to any ensuing voice-hearing). This raises the question as to whether the voices heard by people with a history of trauma differ to those with no history of trauma. For example, we might predict that voices in the former group would be nastier.

This question was addressed in a study led by Martin Dorahy.[181] Dorahy examined the voices heard by people diagnosed with schizophrenia with low levels of childhood trauma, the voices heard by people diagnosed with schizophrenia with medium levels of childhood trauma, and the voices heard by people diagnosed with DID who had high levels of childhood trauma. A number of factors differentiated the groups. Children's voices were heard by 0 per cent of the low-trauma group, 13 per cent of the medium-trauma group and 97 per cent of the high-trauma group. Voices were replays of things previously said to the person in 22 per cent of the low-trauma group, 44 per cent of the medium-trauma group and 76 per cent of the high-trauma group. Voices talked among themselves in 12 per cent of the low-trauma group, 19 per cent of the medium-trauma group and 79 per cent of the high-trauma group. Commands were often heard by 44 per cent of the low-trauma group, 81 per cent of the medium-trauma group and 72 per cent of the high-trauma group. Voice-hearing started before the age of 18 years of age in 28 per cent of the low-trauma group, 38 per cent of the medium-trauma group and 90 per cent of the high-trauma group. This latter finding raises the question as to whether voice-hearing in people diagnosed with schizophrenia, which often starts at a later age (16–25 years old), is caused by a different (or additional) mechanism. This is a question we will come back to in Chapter 40. Let us now try and find more out about voice-hearing whose causes do not lie in childhood trauma.

CHAPTER 12

Certified Organic

In 1893, the neurologist Paul Julius Moebius, author of such works as *On the Physiological Weakmindedness of Women* (clearly absurd) and *On the Hopelessness of Psychology* (let's not rush to judgement on this one), wrote that the distinction between 'organic' mental disorders, where brain changes could be seen at post-mortem, and 'functional' mental disorders, where no such changes could be seen, was, simply put, 'useless'.[182] Forty years later the distinction was lethal. In the 1930s, Kurt Schneider argued that schizophrenia was an 'organic-constitutional…disorder'.[183] For him, psychosis was a disease and it was clear who was suffering from it and who was not. This became important in the context of the time. The Nazis asked psychiatrists which of their patients were *erbkrank* (congenitally mentally ill), a group which were then to be sterilized or murdered. People with a label of organic psychosis were deemed *erbkrank*. This led to a number of psychiatrists trying to save their patients from being killed by giving them diagnoses of functional disorders, such as neurosis, rather than schizophrenia.[184]

The historical echo of this organic-functional distinction can still be seen today in the differentiation between neurological disorders (e.g., Alzheimer's disease) and psychiatric disorders (e.g., schizophrenia). Given that the brain is clearly involved in both, why is there still such a differentiation? Historically, neurological disorders have been viewed as those involving problems with mood and thought, accompanied by physical symptoms, such as sensory (e.g., blindness) or movement (paralysis, shaking). In contrast, disorders of mood and thought, accompanied by no or only minor physical problems in the realm of movement or the sensory system, have been deemed psychiatric disorders.[185]

The hunch that neurological disorders and psychiatric disorders really are separate classes of disorder recently received some support from a neuroimaging study. This found that some regions of the brain tend to be altered only in people with neurological disorders. These include the basal ganglia, which are involved in the coordination of movements. Other regions tend to be altered only in people with psychiatric disorders. These include the medial prefrontal cortex, involved in self-reflection, thinking about social situations, and the sorts of spontaneous thoughts we have when our mind wanders. A final set of areas are altered in both psychiatric and neurological disorders, such as the hippocampus, involved in memory.[186] The human distinction between neurological and psychiatric disorders hence does appear to be reflecting two different types of problem in nature. This raises the question as to what voice-hearing is like in neurological disorders and whether it differs from that in psychiatric disorders. Given the lack of medial prefrontal cortex changes in neurological disorders, we might expect voices in this context to refer less to the person hearing them, and have content of less relevance to the person's ongoing thoughts and concerns.

Traumatic brain injury

A bang on the head can make you see stars, but can it make you hear voices? In some cases, it can. Both external blows and internal blowouts can lead to voice-hearing. Where on or in the head this occurs influences the probability of voice-hearing ensuing. A study of Finnish soldiers who received brain injuries in the Second World War found that 10 per cent went on to develop psychosis, particularly those with damage to their frontal or temporal lobes.

This is consistent with what we will find out about the neurology of voice-hearing in Chapters 24 and 25. What do these voices say? Braun and colleagues found that such voices did things such as telling the patient where to go (literally, not figuratively), and included 'haunting voices', that of a radio announcer, the patient's own voice, children crying or a murmuring crowd.[187] Braun and colleagues argued that these voices were different to those heard by people diagnosed with schizophrenia:

> the content of the hallucinated speech does not correspond to any apparent emotional or moral obsession of the patient (as seems to occur in psychosis), the speech is often a conversation among several people known to the patient or singing by a person heard previously by the patient, and the speech is often of a person of the opposite sex.

This fits with the prediction we made earlier, that such voices would be less reflective of people's ongoing concerns. Treatment of these voices with antipsychotics, antidepressants or benzodiazepines generally fails. The voices resulting from brain injuries may hence be underpinned by different mechanisms and require different types of treatment to those found in psychiatric disorders.

Epilepsy

An early account of hallucinations was proposed by Rene Descartes (1596–1650). Descartes employed the analogy of the bell-pull, used to communicate between rooms in large houses. Think of *Downton Abbey*. If Lady Mary was upstairs in her bedroom, unable to put her gloves on without assistance, she could pull a sash which had within it a wire that led down to a bell in the servants' quarters. It would ring and her maid, Anna, would hear it and perceive that Lady Mary was calling her. Now, imagine there was an animal fair at Downton, including orangutans brought in to amuse the Dowager Countess, and one of these orangutans escaped and got into the walls of the house. It then starts to pull on the wire that runs from Lady Mary's boudoir to the servants' quarters. Descartes argued to the effect that Anna would now 'hallucinate' a bell ringing in Lady Mary's room, in the sense that the bell would ring but it would have no source in the bedroom itself. This model thus proposed that any activation in the neural pathways between the ear and the emergence of a conscious perception of a voice could result in hearing voices that were not there. During seizures in temporal lobe epilepsy (TLE), this wire is likely to be pulled, and around 16 per cent of such people have seizure-related auditory hallucinations.[188] Even if voice-hearing in TLE were to be simply explainable as spontaneous, random tugs on the speech perception wiring in the temporal lobe, this model seems unlikely to be the cause of the voices in people with psychiatric diagnoses, such as schizophrenia, for a number of reasons.

First, the voices heard by people with TLE differ to those heard by people diagnosed with schizophrenia. One review concluded that hearing voices during a seizure almost never took the form of commanding or threatening voices talking in the third person.[189] Instead they seemed to be experiences from the patient's past. This is consistent with a range of other studies. A small study of six people found that only one epilepsy patient had voices which gave commands, and even then it was only 'sometimes', and only two patients had voices which talked about events in the world.[190] Another study[191] found that the voices TLE patients heard were usually limited to one voice, which was of their own gender, spoke in the second person, wasn't nasty, and was perceived to be coming from the opposite side to the hemisphere where their epilepsy originated (i.e., if it was left-hemisphere TLE then the voice would be heard coming from the patient's right-hand side), which is quite different from the voices heard by people diagnosed with schizophrenia.

Second, voices in epilepsy and schizophrenia appear to respond to different types of drugs. A recent paper reported that a woman with epilepsy who heard voices was not helped by antipsychotic medication, but that her voices were successfully eliminated by clonazepam, an anti-seizure medication used to treat epilepsy.[192] In contrast, there is no clear evidence for beneficial effects of this latter sort of drug in schizophrenia.[193] The claim that voices 'of neurological origin' differ to those 'of psychiatric origin'[194] hence appears to have some validity.

There is a temptation to portray epilepsy as a well-understood condition that can produce a specific type of voice-hearing through seizures in the temporal lobe, and to contrast this with schizophrenia as a distinct, less-well-understood condition that produces a different kind of voice-hearing experience through a different mechanism. Unfortunately, things are more complicated. First, there appears to be some relationship between schizophrenia and epilepsy. People diagnosed with schizophrenia are more likely to also have epilepsy than other people in the general population.[195] Second, while people with TLE can hear voices during seizures (referred to as ictal voice-hearing), they can also hear them in the days after a seizure (post-ictal voice-hearing) and during periods when there have been no seizures for a while (inter-ictal voice-hearing), where they may be more like the voices heard by people diagnosed with schizophrenia. We are left to conclude that while voice-hearing may result from spontaneous activity in the temporal lobe, this is unlikely to account for all the voice-hearing experienced by people with epilepsy, let alone people with other diagnoses such as schizophrenia.

As an aside, epilepsy has been used to try and explain many historical figures' experiences of hearing voices. Most of these attempts function as thinly veiled attempts to discredit religious accounts of voice-hearing. Medical materialism, William James called it.[196] One attempt which stands out is that offered by d'Orsi and Tinuper, who began by proposing, like many before them, that Joan of Arc's experiences were a result of epilepsy.[197]

Their innovation was to propose that Joan had a genetically inherited form of epilepsy and, because she sealed her letters with wax, to argue that it may be possible to find some of her hairs caught in one of these seals and hence to empirically test this hypothesis. Did her genes play a role in her road to Rouen? Perhaps, but it was not they that condemned her (Figure 12.1; see Colour plate 1).

Source: Paul Delaroche.

Figure 12.1: Joan of Arc being interrogated by The Cardinal of Winchester in her prison.

Alzheimer's disease (AD)

Mr H is 79 years old. Two years ago he was diagnosed with AD, and he started hearing voices a year later. He doesn't know who the voices are, but thinks that they might be those of colleagues who used to torment him before he retired. The voices create the same feelings that these colleagues used to.[198] Around 10 per cent of people with AD will experience auditory hallucinations, but twice as many will experience visual hallucinations. When voices are present they tend to comment on, or argue about, the person. Whereas there appears to be a clear line between voice-hearing in schizophrenia and voice-hearing in 'organic' disorders such as brain injury, this line seems to fade with AD.

There are multiple theories as to what causes AD. One is that it results from deficits in the neurotransmitter acetylcholine, which aids perception, learning, memory and thought. Indeed, a leading therapy is treatment with drugs called cholinesterase inhibitors, which help stop acetylcholine being broken down. There aren't many diseases for which the basis of treatment is a formally declared weapon of mass destruction, but AD is one; nerve gases, such as sarin, also work through cholinesterase inhibition, though obviously at much higher doses.[199] An involvement of acetylcholine in the visual hallucinations in AD makes sense, as acetylcholine is thought to play a key role in allowing the integration of visual stimuli with our knowledge of context, leading to an accurate visual experience of the world. If you were to ingest deadly nightshade (as the name suggests, this would be a bad idea) visual hallucinations would likely follow, due to this plant's ability to block the activity of acetylcholine in your brain. Similarly, visual hallucinations in people diagnosed with schizophrenia may also be successfully treated with cholinesterase inhibitors if antipsychotics have only successfully removed auditory hallucinations.[200] While what we have found about the causes of visual hallucinations in AD seems transferable to visual hallucinations in other diagnoses, we have not been blessed with a similar situation in relation to voice-hearing.

Parkinson's disease (PD)

Hallucinations occur in around a third of people with PD, but are typically complex visual ones, mostly of people, animals or objects.[201] As a result, most of the roughly 10 per cent of PD patients who hear voices will also have visual hallucinations.[202] Voice-hearing in the absence of visual hallucinations only occurs in 1 to 2 per cent of patients.[203] In one of the few studies to describe what these voices are like, Inzelberg and colleagues asked about the voices heard by ten of their 121 PD patients. Half heard voices that were incomprehensible, and 90 per cent heard voices which did not give commands and did not have threatening content. The voices were all heard externally, speaking in the first or second person, but not arguing. One patient identified the voice as that of her late husband, who would comment about her daily activities and sometimes give her instructions, which she would occasionally follow.[204] The lack of negative content in PD is typically taken as clearly distinguishing these voices from those heard in psychiatric populations.

An apparent paradox is that PD is caused by low levels of the neurotransmitter dopamine. Given that voice-hearing in schizophrenia is argued by many to be due to high levels of dopamine (see Chapters 34–37), one might wonder how someone with a condition involving low levels of dopamine could also be hearing voices. It is often argued that hallucinations in PD are a result of dopamine-increasing medications that patients take, such as levadopa (L-dopa). However, this can't be the entire story because, as Fénelon and colleagues note, a) there were reports of hallucinations in PD patients well before the introduction of L-dopa, and b) PD patients on greater doses of L-dopa do not appear to hallucinate more.[205] Whatever is causing hallucinations in PD, it does not appear to be simply due to increased dopamine levels.

Going forward

Voice-hearing in people diagnosed with psychiatric disorders appears to be a subtly different phenomenon to that occurring in people with epilepsy or brain injury. The dementias appear to be something of a middle ground, but remain under-studied. As a result, for the rest of this book we are going to focus on voice-hearing in people who are distressed by them and who have received psychiatric diagnoses, with one important exception. The voices heard by people with Parkinson's disease don't, on the whole, seem to be too troublesome. This raises the question as to whether someone experiencing benign voices, in the absence of any other problems, could be said to have a disorder at all, or whether this would be just a quirk of experience, an alternative way of being. If we could find significant amounts of voice-hearing in the general population this could force us to re-evaluate what we thought voice-hearing signified.

CHAPTER 13

Beyond Diagnosis

Mrs A is a 42-year-old divorcee, a mother of two, and a psychic healer who hears voices. The first began in childhood, and it has been joined by others over the years. She communicates with her voices, consulting them for the benefit of herself or her clients. Her voices also talk among themselves. Although her voices are not those of people she has heard in daily life, she is not afraid of them as they give her advice, comfort and care. She considers her voices as protective ghosts. In her childhood she was repeatedly physically and sexually abused, and she feels her voices helped her to get through this. It was only when, at the age of five, she was punished at school for repeating what her voices said aloud in class, that she realized that this wasn't an experience everyone had. She didn't discuss her voices with anyone else again for three decades. She has never been in contact with a psychiatric service, and based on a psychiatric assessment, doesn't meet criteria for any mental disorder.[206]

Mrs A is not alone. Many people hear voices unproblematically. If voices don't impair your ability to work or function in society then, by definition, you can't get a psychiatric diagnosis, in theory at least. Estimates of how many people in the general population hear voices vary almost as much as maths will allow. One review found rates that ranged from 1 per cent to 84 per cent.[207] Reasons for this variability include different questions being asked to different people. For example, asking people if they've had a specific example of voice-hearing seems to lead to higher rates, and students are more likely to indicate they've heard voices than the general population.

One situation where people will commonly hear voices outside the realm of psychiatric diagnoses is following the death of their partner. You may not know this, as less than a third of people who experience this will tell anyone else, often due to a fear of ridicule. Such voice-hearing ranges from simply hearing your partner call your name, through to being able to have a full-blown conversation with them. Bereavement hallucinations are found cross-culturally, but are treated as more normal in countries such as Japan than in places such as the UK.[208] If the communication of the dead is tongued with fire beyond the language of the living, as T.S. Eliot put it,[209] it is a short-burning flame, as the voices typically fade over time.[210] A study of people in their seventies found that 30 per cent heard the voice of their partner one month after bereavement, a proportion that fell to 19 per cent after three months and to 6 per cent after a year. Although some people in the West find these voices helpful, for others they may ultimately only increase feelings of isolation and loss.[211] Not everyone needs a love resurrection.

The death of anyone close to you can trigger bereavement hallucinations – it need not be a partner. Voice-hearing can occur in the wake of the death of your child. A 45-year-old woman who had lost her daughter to leukaemia heard, every day, most often while alone and during the night, the voice of her daughter. 'Mamma,' the voice would say, 'don't be afraid, I'll come back.' Another woman, who lost her daughter to a heroin overdose, heard her voice crying out, 'Mamma, Mamma!... It's so cold.' Sixteen years earlier, after the sudden death of her own mother, this woman had to be saved by passers-by when she tried to jump from a bridge to reach an apparition of her deceased mother.[212] Some people may be predisposed to hallucinate in such traumatic circumstances, and this is something we will explore later (Chapter 21).

Death does not become everyone. After the death of her mother, Julie started hearing her voice: 'She started calling me names like "slag" and "slut"…and "whore"…and telling me I wasn't fit to live…"take all your tablets".' Julie's relationship with her mother had been problematic, but she had never actually said such things to Julie. Julie was not able to dismiss what her mother said: 'It makes me question, is it true?…when you hear a thing often enough.' Sometimes what's dead should stay dead. But only sometimes. Aggie's boyfriend knew that he was terminally ill but hid this and broke off their relationship, in an attempt to spare her pain. After he had passed away, Aggie heard his voice saying sorry for pushing her away at the end. Aggie also partially blamed herself for his death and felt guilty about this. Hearing the voice helped her to forgive herself.[213]

Another place that voice-hearing occurs today, outside psychiatric contexts, is in religious contexts. In a study of 29 members of an evangelical Christian church, who reported having no previous treatment for mental illness, 59 per cent reported some form of voice-hearing experience, compared with a rate of 27 per cent in a non-religious control group.[214] Some religions actively encourage rummaging around in the contents of your consciousness for God's voice. For example, Tanya Luhrmann[215] has argued that contemporary American spirituality encourages people to:

> attend to the stream of their own consciousness like eager fishermen…to identify moments of discontinuity that are natural to the flow of our everyday awareness, and actually to interpret them as discontinuous. It encourages them to seek for evidence that they might be hearing a voice spoken by another awareness.

There is a great exchange in Shakespeare's *Henry IV, Part 1* in which Glendower boasts, 'I can call spirits from the vasty deep,' to which Hotspur replies, 'Why, so can I, or so can any man;

But will they come when you do call for them?'[216] It turns out that if you seek sufficiently, they may come.

Given the historical control religion has desired over voice-hearers (Chapter 3), it may seem odd that some religions should now encourage voice-hearing. Yet the content of contemporary religious voice-hearing is hardly iconoclastic. A recent study of people at an English Evangelical church who had experience of communicating with 'God' via voice-hearing found that such 'communications were generally concerned with present rather than future affairs, and were about practical, mundane matters rather than abstract, philosophical or doctrinal concerns'.[217] Similarly, a study of people at an English Pentecostal church concluded that 'God's voice often focuses on immediate issues. He seldom offers metaphysical insights. This seems like a way of regulating and evaluating daily activities and providing guidance to those whom He communicates with.'[218] For example, one participant in this study reported, 'I was looking in the mirror one day and God said to me "I don't want you to be afraid of growing your hair".' It's not exactly Exodus.

Unproblematic voice-hearing, or experiences with a family resemblance to this, can also be found in some creative writers. André Gide argued that:

> the poor novelist constructs his characters, he controls them and makes them speak. The true novelist listens to them and watches them function; he eavesdrops on them even before he knows them. It is only according to what he hears them say that he begins to understand who they are.[219]

As Gide suggests, the extent to which writers experience their characters as autonomous beings varies. At one end of this spectrum are writers whose characters are experienced as independent beings, whose presence is felt and whose voices are heard. For example, Marjorie Taylor and colleagues interviewed

50 adults who were fiction writers about the development of their characters and any experiences of childhood imaginary companions. All 50 'seemed to understand what we were asking about, and none of them looked at the interviewer in confusion when they were asked questions about whether they interacted with and heard the voices of people who were not real'. One writer described how 'It's like I am taking dictation. Their voices are quite alive to me; all I have to do is listen.' Another said of their characters: 'I live with all of them every day. Dealing with different events during the day, different ones kind of speak. They say, "Hmm, this is my opinion. Are you going to listen to me?"' The nature of inner voices in writers is still poorly understood, but the *Writer's Inner Voices* project, currently in progress at Durham University, may help to shed more light on this.[220]

Voices may also be able to help people who might not consider themselves 'writers' to create books. For example, recall Peter who we met in Chapter 5. Peter was able to write a book, entitled *A Village Called Pumpkin*, thanks to the help of his voices. He describes how:

> The process started when I was walking in the middle of the night and I heard this female voice which had no identity and it just kept saying 'a village called pumpkin'... The voice kept coming back at different times in the night and it would say 'it's a children's book' and then it gave me names of characters but I was thinking, 'I can't write a children's book.' Then it gave me a theme. The first chapter just flowed. Then I got stuck. I tried to write the next chapter without the voice and I couldn't do it. I was really stuck until the voice gave me the contents of another chapter... I always had to wait for inspiration from the voices. It could be a month or three or four months. I would sometimes try and write without being guided by my voices but there was just nothing there... It was an interesting

> process because the characters that the voice gave me would then start talking to me and they would ask me questions – what role am I playing? Do you need me in this bit?[221]

When the story was completed, the woman's voice, which had appeared in order to help him, disappeared. It is notable that the content the voice gave Peter was not without relation to his own life:

> About three years ago I was with someone from *Time* magazine and he looked at the draft and said, 'That's your life' – you know the themes – don't lose your childhood, stand up to bullies, atone for crimes, that kind of thing. It's just told in a different way.

When we try to add up all these different types of voice-hearing in the general population, it is hard to estimate how many people hear voices similar to those heard by people diagnosed with a psychiatric disorder (i.e., which say a reasonable amount, reasonably often) and yet are not troubled or impaired by them. No single study has asked about both the 'reasonable amount' and the 'reasonably often' criteria. This leaves us knowing how many people hear voices saying a reasonable amount, but not knowing how often they hear this, and knowing how often people hear voices saying things, but not knowing how much these voices say.

Louise Johns and colleagues found that 1.2 per cent of the general population reported having heard voices saying a reasonable amount ('quite a few words or sentences') in the space of the previous year.[222] Such experiences would likely range from the form of experience reported by Mrs A at the start of this chapter, through to the following example taken from another study of voice-hearing in the general population: 'I was sitting on a hillside letting my mind fully wander when I actually heard someone or something say "It's beautiful, isn't it?" It scared the hell out of me.'[223] After interviewing a subset of these people, Johns and colleagues found that 19 per cent did not meet the diagnostic criteria for any psychiatric disorder. This gives us a figure for non-clinical voice-hearing of around 0.2 per cent of the population (i.e., 1.2 per cent × 19 per cent). Another general population study, also by Johns and colleagues, found that, after excluding people with probable psychosis, 0.7 per cent of people reported the experience of having heard voices saying quite a few words or sentences in the space of the previous year.[224] Averaging the results of these two studies allows us to estimate that 0.45 per cent of the general population hear voices, saying a reasonable amount each year. In terms of the 'reasonably often' criteria, a recent study of the Norwegian population found that 0.3 per cent of people heard voices daily without seeking help, and 0.9 per cent heard voices at least several times a week. The number of people hearing voices reasonably often hence falls into the same ballpark as the number of people hearing voices saying a reasonable amount.

The fact that some people hear voices and are impaired, yet others hear voices and aren't, poses a problem for anyone who wants to define voice-hearing per se as being a symptom of brain disease. Imagine two people hearing exactly the same voice, which tells them to die. One of them, like Ken in Chapter 1, interprets it as being the devil and is understandably terrified by it. As a result, their life starts to fall apart and they enter psychiatric services, receiving a diagnosis of schizophrenia. The other person, a bit like Peter in Chapter 5, interprets this voice as representing a broken-off part of their own emotional life and as a warning that they need to make some changes in their life. They thank the voice for its help and for trying to protect them and get on with their life potentially helped by the voice. If voice-hearing is a brain disease, it appears to be unusual in that it is one that can simply vanish by someone thinking about it differently. This raises the question as to what influences whether hearing voices is going to cause you a problem or not.

The best study of this question identified a group of people from the general population who heard voices unproblematically, hence not meeting criteria for a psychiatric disorder, and compared them with a group of people diagnosed with schizophrenia who heard voices.[225] When all the differences inquired about were thrown into the mix together, there were four properties of the voices that uniquely predicted whether the hearer would have a schizophrenia diagnosis: *frequently* hearing voices with *negative emotional content* which they had *little control over*, with a *later onset*. On average the non-clinical voice-hearers started hearing voices when they were 12 years old and heard voices once every three days on average, which were seldom unpleasant and were controllable 60 per cent of the time. In contrast, on average people diagnosed with schizophrenia started hearing voices when they were 21 years old, and heard voices once an hour, which were mostly unpleasant and were controllable 20 per cent of the time. That frequency, negative content and controllability should be pinpointed makes intuitive sense. This type of voice would be, at best, hard to cope with, and at worse, hellish and would drive help-seeking. Negative emotional content (i.e., voices that were derogatory, abusive, insulting, threatening or critical) was a particularly prominent predictor of patient status. Simply knowing whether a person heard such voices allowed the researchers to predict with an 88 per cent probability whether the hearer was a patient or non-patient. The different age of onset of problematic and non-problematic voice-hearing makes us wonder whether they were caused by different events and processes. We will return to these non-clinical voice-hearing experiences later in the book.

Experiencing unproblematic voice-hearing doesn't mean that it will always be that way. Benign voices can become malevolent. The trigger for this change is often a trauma. For example, Escher and Romme describe Laura's experience of hearing friendly voices from the age of six, which suddenly became nasty when she was 12.[226] Laura was sexually abused by her boyfriend's friends when she was 12. Indeed, experiencing unproblematic voice-hearing increases your risk of developing problematic voice-hearing. If you look over the course of a year at adults in the general population who have a non-clinical psychotic experience for the first time, and compare them with people who have never had any such experiences, the new-onset people are 65 times more likely to have a clinical disorder two years later.[227] To put these numbers in perspective though, these studies also found that only 25 per cent of 11-year-olds with psychotic-like experiences go on to develop a clinical disorder.[228] Similarly, 84 per cent of adults who have a psychotic-like experience for the first time in a year will have no such experiences two years later, 8 per cent will still have such unproblematic experiences, and only 8 per cent will go on to develop a clinical disorder.[229]

As a result of such findings, Jim van Os and colleagues[230] have introduced what they called a psychosis proneness–persistence–impairment model. In this, psychotic-like experiences are viewed as being common, but mostly transitory. Only in a minority of cases do these become persistent, increasing the probability that they will start to impair the person and create a need for care. Factors which sabotage the normal evaporation of these experiences include traumatic life events, substance use, living in urban areas, and earlier developmental problems (such as walking/talking late).[231]

Just because voices are unproblematic, this doesn't mean their roots are not in problematic experiences. Rates of childhood sexual and emotional abuse have been found not to differ between non-clinical voice-hearers and voice-hearers with a psychiatric diagnosis, with both groups experiencing more abuse than the general population.[232] This is important as it suggests that trauma plays a role in generating voice-hearing per se, rather than just negative voice-hearing, as we might intuitively suspect. What influences why some people will hear supportive voices after a trauma, and others hear malevolent voices, is not at all well understood. However, there is preliminary evidence that traumas which continue to have an impact on the person, and that are hence unresolved, may be more likely to lead to negative and problematic voice-hearing experiences.[233] For example, Eleanor Longden describes how she came to learn from her own voice-hearing experience that 'each voice was closely related to aspects of myself and that each of them carried overwhelming emotions that I'd never had an opportunity to process and resolve – of shame, anger, loss, and low self-worth'.[234] Trauma may cause voice-hearing, with a continuing sense of threat making these voices more likely to be negative, problematic to deal with, and hence encourage entry into the psychiatric system. We will come back to the issue of the causal role of trauma in Chapter 19.

Unproblematic voice-hearing throws up a lot of questions, which are going to require more background before we can tackle them, and which we will hence return to in later chapters. Are the brain changes found in people with non-clinical voice-hearing the same as those in people diagnosed with schizophrenia who hear voices (Chapter 26)? Are the disturbances in neurotransmitters associated with voice-hearing in schizophrenia also found in unproblematic voice-hearing (Chapter 38)? Given that unproblematic voice-hearing tends to start earlier in life, does this follow a different developmental pathway to voice-hearing in people who come to be diagnosed with schizophrenia? Perhaps most importantly, how can one move, as Peter and Kate did, from being impaired by voice-hearing to having unproblematic voice-hearing? That we may be able to better help people with distressing voice-hearing experiences by better understanding unproblematic voice-hearing is becoming widely accepted. Indeed, the world's leading schizophrenia journal, *Schizophrenia Bulletin*, recently published a paper examining what can be learned from clairaudient psychics who may be able to help people with psychiatric diagnoses who are distressed by voice-hearing.[235] We will return to such questions in Chapter 44. Next we will try to sum up where we have got to, and to establish how many people in the West have frequent and extensive voice-hearing experiences, and who these people are.

CHAPTER 14

Two Point Five Per Cent

We have now seen voice-hearing in psychiatric and non-psychiatric populations, but just how common is it? Is it rampant, rare, or somewhere in between? The answer to this depends on who exactly we are talking about. At the moment we have focused on voice-hearing in cultures that have been termed WEIRD (western, educated, industrialized, rich and democratic).[236] Yet voice-hearing occurs all over the world: in Kenya and Uganda, Brazil and Java, in the mountain tribes in the heat of Borneo and the Inuit in the Arctic ice.[237] There are unlikely to be equal rates of voice-hearing across societies, as the culture or sub-culture you live in influences the probability you will hear voices. In the UK, relative to the white population, people of South Asian origin are half as likely to report hearing voices saying quite a few words each year, and people of Caribbean origin are twice as likely to report this experience.[238] In the USA, Hispanic veterans with PTSD are more likely to hear voices than other cultural groups.[239] Religion is also likely to affect the prevalence of voice-hearing. As we have seen, contemporary American spirituality actively encourages searching for God's voice. Any overall estimate of voice-hearing will hence not take into account the potential for significant cultural variation.

As the bulk of research on the prevalence of voice-hearing comes from WEIRD cultures, we are going to have to base our estimate on this unrepresentative group. Let's exclude neurological disorders (due to the different type of voice-hearing that appears to be occurring in these conditions) and dissociative identity disorder (due to its low prevalence), but include bipolar disorder (which we haven't previously discussed due to the similarity of voice-hearing in bipolar disorder and schizophrenia). We can now create estimates of both how many people hear voices saying quite a few words or sentences each year, and how many people will hear such voices in their lifetime. As you will see from the endnotes to this calculation, there is a great deal of uncertainty here. You can tweak this calculation yourself to see what you think a fair number is. With all these caveats in mind, my approximation is that 1.3 per cent of the adult population hears voices each year (Table 14.1), and 2.5 per cent of adults will hear voices in their lifetime (Table 14.2).

Table 14.1 How many people (and who) hear voices each year?[240]

Group	Annual prevalence	% of whom hear voices	% of all adults	% of all adult voice-hearing
Schizophrenia	0.34%	70%	0.24%	19%
Bipolar I disorder	0.4%	34%	0.14%	11%
Post-traumatic stress disorder	1.0%	25%	0.25%	19%
Borderline personality disorder	0.7%	29%	0.20%	16%
Non-clinical voice-hearers	0.45%	100%	0.45%	35%
Total			1.28%	100%

Table 14.2 How many people (and who) hear voices in their lifetime?[241]				
Group	**Lifetime prevalence**	**% of whom hear voices**	**% of all adults**	**% of all adult voice-hearing**
Schizophrenia	0.72%	70%	0.50%	20%
Bipolar I disorder	0.6%	34%	0.20%	8%
Post-traumatic stress disorder	2.0%	25%	0.50%	20%
Borderline personality disorder	1.4%	29%	0.41%	16%
Non-clinical voice-hearers	0.9%	100%	0.90%	36%
Total			2.51%	100%

It is hard to run too far with these numbers, given their approximate nature, but we may note that despite being the sacrosanct symptom of the sacred symbol of psychiatry,[242] the majority of people who hear voices in our society do not have a diagnosis of schizophrenia. Indeed, Table 14.1 suggests that for every person diagnosed with schizophrenia who hears voices there will be another person with PTSD who hears voices, another person diagnosed with borderline personality disorder who hears voices, and one, if not two, people who hear voices in the absence of any psychiatric disorder.

We may wonder if all these voices grow from a common seed. In reality, there is likely to be a packet of voice-hearing seeds. We have already seen enough to suggest that trauma is one seed, particularly child abuse. Other seeds may be hidden in the teeth of our DNA, and certain stretches of DNA may be particularly fertile soil for trauma seeds to grow into voices. We will now start our search for these seeds and soils – the causes of hearing voices.

CHAPTER 15

Where to Start with Causes

When we are conceived a genome is created whose string of nucleic acids has been crafted by both ancient unseen causes and our parents' recent shuffling. The emerging, still controversial, field of epigenetics is discovering that how our genome will function, how it will react to the challenges of life, has already been influenced by what happened to our parents before they met, and maybe even by what happened to our grandparents before they met. Our genome's functioning is then further shaped by what happens to us, first in the womb and then in the world, as it builds and operates a body and a brain. Our genes and brain will also influence the life events that the future throws at us by increasing our probability of ending up in certain situations, which will in turn alter the expression of our genes and hence our brain. The culture we live in, the political and economic system that we find ourselves thrown into, will also influence the life events we are exposed to, as well as how we interpret these events, which will again influence our genes and brain. Culture, life events, brains and genes are all interlinked in an ouroboric circle of causation that creates us; a baffled phenotype driven by a writhing genotype.

There is a temptation to dive straight into this circle of causes at the level of genes and the brain. The problem is that the water here is deep, and few return. An education in genetics and neurology can be like a recreational drug; an unpleasant world fades into the background and is forgotten. For example, in 1977 David Rosenthal and Olive Quinn published a study[243] that was remarkable for a number of reasons. It involved female quadruplets who all went on to hear voices and be diagnosed with schizophrenia. The authors estimated that this would only happen once in every 1.5 billion births, meaning this has happened less than a hundred times in all human history. What is even more remarkable is that this is not the most remarkable part of their study. A clear cause of the women's voice-hearing leaps off the pages of this study, yet the authors, dazzled by DNA, didn't see it. Instead they laid the cause of the quadruplets' experiences solely at the door of a 'schizophrenic genotype'. Given what we have discussed so far in this book, you can probably guess what happened to the quadruplets as children.

The four girls experienced a horrific childhood. Iris and Hester (not their real names) were found 'engaged in mutual masturbation' and, at the recommendation of a doctor, were circumcised and their hands tied to their beds for 30 nights. Another paper referred to this as the girls receiving 'less preferential treatment' from their parents.[244] They suffered genital mutilation. It is unclear why researchers dance around this. Another of the girls, Nora, was molested by her father, a threatening drunk. It seems unlikely he only sexually abused her, as all four girls suffered from bed-wetting and incontinence, potential signs of child sexual abuse.[245]

The quadruplets started hearing voices in their early twenties. Myra heard the voice of a man who had made sexual advances towards her when she was alone and frightened. Nora first heard voices after the brother of another hospitalized patient engaged in sex play with her. She also saw demons with fire around them. Hester's first hallucinations were visual, and also involved fire. Iris heard the voices of her co-workers and her father. A trigger for Nora's voices was lying down. Menstruation was a trigger for hallucinations in all the girls, as was getting ready for bed at night.

The authors do not comment on the utterly staggering, blindingly obvious reason why all this should be. Rosenthal and Quinn finish the paper by saying, 'If we listen intently to what these "voices" are telling us, we may achieve a better understanding of the mechanisms that underlie them.' The authors may have listened intently, but they didn't hear a damn thing. It is a notable irony that in studying experiences that others cannot perceive, researchers have failed to perceive what is staring them in the face. While it is possible that the girls' genes predisposed them to hear voices as a result of what happened to them, to focus only on their genes was a catastrophic oversight.

Lest you think this is a problem restricted to decades ago, let me give you another case from a few years ago. The background to this is that there exists a medical condition called 22q11.2 deletion syndrome, also referred to as velocardiofacial syndrome and DiGeorge syndrome. People with this syndrome are typically missing a large chunk of DNA (around three million base pairs) on their 22nd chromosome. Around half of sufferers have anomalies of the heart and face that are present from birth, most have learning difficulties, and perhaps a third will experience voice-hearing. A case of voice-hearing was reported in a Korean case study of a 25-year-old woman who was initially diagnosed with schizophrenia, but in whom a 22q11.2 deletion was later found by genetic testing.[246] The authors unambiguously portray the voice-hearing as being a result of the 22q11.2 deletion. Yet, there was another potential contributory factor to this young woman's voice-hearing, which the authors did not comment on in any detail. This appears to have been overlooked because the presence of a genetic change was deemed sufficient to account for the voice-hearing.

This was an unusual case from the start, as the patient showed no facial or heart anomalies. She also had other symptoms not consistent with 22q11.2 deletion, including frequent urinary tract infections. This last sentence, in conjunction with the previous chapters, may have given you a clue as to where this is going. Here is an excerpt from what the authors tell us:

> A 25-year-old female patient was admitted to the psychiatric ward due to auditory hallucinations. Eight months prior to the patient's admittance to the psychiatric ward, she experienced intermittent auditory hallucinations in the form of her ex-boyfriend's voice saying that he would kill her. During the month prior to her admittance to the psychiatric ward, the auditory hallucinations increased in severity and frequency, and the patient developed persecutory delusions. Additionally, the patient came to believe that she had been raped by her boyfriend. The patient also quit her job and withdrew from all social relationships.

This at least raises a concern that being raped may have contributed to the development of this woman's voices, potentially in conjunction with the documented genetic change. We cannot say from this limited information whether or not this is the case, but it reiterates the point that genetic explanations must not blind us to other additional potential contributory factors. Genes likely do matter, as we will examine in Chapter 40, but they will neither be the only nor final word.

While every seesaw we come to is slightly askew, in the voice-hearing world the hulking figure of biological causation sits so obdurately on one end of the seesaw that it propels trauma, maltreatment and abuse, sat on the other seat, high into the sky, almost out of sight. We will climb up onto this higher seat first, not because it is nearer the angels but because we find ourselves thrown into an unbalanced discussion in need of symbolic redress. So, let's start looking at life events as potential causes of voice-hearing. We won't start with events that meet formal definitions of trauma (e.g., actual or threatened death, serious injury or sexual violation), but with other worries people have, and consider how these may seed voice-hearing.

CHAPTER 16

Breast Pumps from Hell

> Has your breast pump ever sounded like it was trying to tell you something? No, I haven't lost it yet. But every time I pump, my 2004 Medela Pump In Style has a message for me. It's not a very nice one. But if you listen to the machine's rhythmic insistent lull, there it is, telling me to: 'Kill Bob, kill Bob, kill Bob.' OK, now you think I'm certifiably crazy. My husband did the first time I told him about it… But the next time I pumped, I made him listen. He listened closely: 'Kill Bob, kill Bob, kill Bob.' Indeed, he agreed. It did. I asked my pumping friends if they had ever heard anything. One told me her breast pump sounds like it's saying: 'What a ho, what a ho, what a ho.' Another said hers says: 'Go to bed, go to bed, go to bed.' Or are we all just crazy, sleep-deprived moms with big imaginations and, um, issues?[247]

These mums are not crazy. Tired, yes. Worried, yes. Mad, no. Hearing voices coming from the rumblings of breast pumps is both common and understandable, as documented in a great study by Christine Cooper-Rompato, whose interest in this area was sparked by her own experiences of a speaking pump. As Cooper-Rompato notes, whether to use a breast pump is an emotionally charged question. Many women may do it because they need to give their baby milk during times they can't breastfeed, such as when they are out at work. Others may do it to increase their milk supply or because their child has problems which make breastfeeding difficult or impossible. You may be able to start to imagine the emotions this could give rise to.

What do these pumps say to mothers? Many hear their child's first name called, but the most commonly reported utterances are to do with breastfeeding itself. Examples include 'nipple', 'gotta pump', 'feed the baby', 'give me more' and the creepily effusive 'you pump *good*'. Unsurprisingly, this can be troubling. As one mum put it, 'I think I've officially lost it. I can't pump any more without thinking that the damn thing is talking. "Fresh milk…fresh milk, fresh milk." I can't get it out of my head.' In relation to external employment, pumps damn mothers either way. Mothers working outside the house may be upset by the pump saying things such as 'get home'. Those not in outside employment may hear voices saying 'get a job, get a job'. Consistent with what we saw earlier about voices, commands are common: 'go shopping', 'read books', or even 'jerk off, jerk off, jerk off', as is abuse. 'I swear it was saying "retard, retard, retard",' reported one mum; 'cow-cow, cow-cow' said another, and one particularly succinct pump simply opined, 'mooooooooooo!' Some pump voices are straight from the pages of a Stephen King novel. One mum reported that her breast pump simply said 'be afraid'. Luckily, her husband was at hand to calm the situation: 'I made my husband listen, and he was hysterical. He said it was the beginning of the *worst* horror movie in history!' The voices may take a darker vein too. Some women have reported the pump saying 'kill you, kill you, kill you'. As Cooper-Rompato recalls from her own experience:

> After the birth of my second child, I remember being afraid that mine would speak to me in the middle of the night and convince me to do something awful. What if the pump urged me to hurt my baby?

The sort of thoughts that would generate such voices would not in any way be unusual. Nearly half of new mothers will have involuntary, intrusive thoughts about intentionally harming their baby.[248] It is a natural thing to happen, particularly if the mothers are receiving little social support or are very stressed, and the vast majority of mothers won't act on such thoughts. Indeed, what pumps say is often understandable in the context of the natural fears many mothers have surrounding having a new child, and feelings of guilt, shame or inadequacy that society may wrongly make them feel. As Cooper-Rompato summarizes, pump voices typically reflect anxieties about producing a healthy baby, milk production, and the mother's abilities to fulfil their baby's needs. Mothers typically recognize this. For example, one mother who heard her pump say 'fat pig, fat pig' explained it as: 'I think what we hear in each pump pretty much reflects what we are thinking at the time. I was dwelling on all the baby weight I still haven't lost.' Despite this, when mothers first hear these voices they may fear they are going mad. Hearing that other mothers have been through the same experience, or finding out that a partner or friend can hear the same words in the breast pump, often calms these fears.

The speaking pump phenomenon suggests that worries, concerns and feelings of shame can be seeds that, when fertilized by random noise and exhaustion, may grow into voice-hearing. Could this offer an explanation for some examples of clinically relevant voice-hearing? The hypervigilance theory of voice-hearing says yes.

CHAPTER 17

Hypervigilance Hallucinations

Meet Rick. He'd been involved in a violent confrontation with a local gang. Afterwards, he became very vigilant for any signs that reprisals were coming. He began to hear comments from people passing his house at night, suggesting that he would be assaulted. Rick was eventually hospitalized, medicated and discharged, but remained convinced that he was in danger and was reluctant to leave his house. His voice-hearing continued. Rick's psychologist worked with him to create an account of his experiences that could help him understand them. This account highlighted that it would be natural for Rick to become more conscious of threats after the violent incident. His position was likened to a soldier, for whom hypervigilance for threat has positive effects. In Rick's situation though, hypervigilance had more negative than positive effects, and his sense of threat was escalated by sleep deprivation, substance misuse and the voices. Rick found this story compelling and normalizing; it reduced the stigma he felt. Recognizing that the threatening comments he heard were a result of his scanning his environment for threat, rather than genuine indicators of a threat, enabled him to reassess the level of danger he was in. Soon Rick was able to leave the house again.[249]

Michael was admitted to hospital hearing voices calling him a 'nonce' (slang for paedophile) and mistakenly thinking other people thought he was a paedophile. A psychologist uncovered the following story. When Michael was 15, he masturbated to a variety of sexual fantasies, one of which was about his younger sister, who at the time was only eight. In his twenties, Michael became concerned that this meant he was a paedophile. He felt intense shame and became anxious about what would happen if other people knew about this. He feared someone else finding out and publicly labelling him a paedophile, as paedophiles were already being attacked in his neighbourhood. Michael became convinced that someone might know what he did, and he became hypervigilant for any signs of this. He started to actively scan the background noise from the street to see if anybody was calling him a 'nonce'. Sure enough, he came to hear a voice calling him this. Michael became even more anxious and hypervigilant, and this affected his sleep. He coped through drug use. As he had not disclosed his past to others, but he was nevertheless hearing a voice calling him a nonce, he started to believe that other people could read his mind. This made him even more hypervigilant and anxious. He coped with this by not going out and constantly listening to background noises to see if he could hear the word 'nonce'. This increased his sleep deprivation and anxiety, creating a vicious circle that led to his hospital admission.[250]

Based on Rick and Michael's experiences, their psychologists created the concept of a 'hypervigilance hallucination' (HVH).[251] This builds on the idea that our perceptual system is not designed to be as accurate as possible. Instead, it is designed to not miss threats, even if this means sometimes making mistakes. Nature hands out prizes for survival, not accuracy. HVH is proposed to result from an exaggeration of the normally adaptive perceptual bias that we evolved to allow us to detect threats. This bias reflects the fact that the benefits of being hypervigilant for threat normally outweigh the costs of the mistakes that this will lead to. For example, it is better to mistakenly think that you heard a bear behind you when there wasn't one, than to mistakenly think there wasn't a bear behind you when there was, and get eaten. To take another example, if smoke detectors only went off when they were absolutely positively sure there was a fire, you could already be dead by the time the alarm sounded. The price of this is false alarms. However, occasionally standing outside your building in your pyjamas is a price worth paying evolutionarily (unless you still wear Star Wars pyjamas, public knowledge of which could indeed diminish your reproductive fitness). However, if your bear-dar gets completely out of hand, and you constantly mistakenly think bears are there, this will cause a predictable set of problems.

In Guy Dodgson and colleagues' HVH model, a precipitating event makes someone worry about physical or social threats. This person then becomes hypervigilant for speech relating to this threat, reducing their threshold for detecting threats in the environment and increasing the chance of auditory 'false-positives' – that is, hearing a voice. But not just any voice. This model proposes this process will lead to hearing voices or sounds (such as laughter) which have threatening or derisive content relating to the person's concerns, and will be perceived as coming from the external environment. In some sense, the person 'expects' to hear the threatening content, and it is well known that both what you expect to perceive influences what you do perceive, and that things which are particularly salient to you are more likely to enter your conscious awareness. For example, a study by Warren and Warren played an audio-recording to participants in which they heard the word 'eel', then a pause, then another word.[252] If the second word played was 'wagon', the participant believed the first word they heard was 'wheel'. If the second word was 'shoe' they believed they had heard the word 'heel'. The second contextual word set up what people expected to hear, and influenced what they perceived. Add to this the fact that perception is motivated. Hunger makes you more likely to see images of food in ambiguous pictures.[253] In the verbal realm, not all words are created equal. Some are more salient than others and as a result are more likely to be promoted to your consciousness. Take the cocktail party effect. Imagine being at a party where you are bombarded by words and noise from everyone in the room. You aren't aware of this noise as you are focused on the conversation with the person you are having in front of you. However, if someone in another part of the room mentions your name, you will suddenly be aware of this, even though you were not listening out for it.

In terms of evidence for the HVH theory, a study I was involved in, led by my colleague Rob Dudley, found that inducing negative emotions in people (by playing them clips from the *Blair Witch Project*) causes them to be more likely to hear threatening words in white noise compared to a comparison condition which induced positive emotions (clips from the TV show *Friends*; and, yes, I know some people would find this more horrifying than the *Blair Witch Project*).[254] In another study bearing on the HVH hypothesis, we assessed four specific aspects of people's voice-hearing: 1) where people's attention was focused when they heard the voice; 2) the location of voice; 3) whether there was threatening content; and 4) whether it was heard in a noisy environment.[255] Using a technique called cluster analysis we found that the properties of hearing threatening voices, as well as hearing externally located voices, and having attention externally focused at the time of hearing the voices, tended to co-occur together, consistent with what the HVH model would predict. Evidence for HVH is tentative, but promising.

What can be done to help people with such voices? In another place or time, Rick and Michael could have received a diagnosis of schizophrenia, followed by long-term antipsychotic use and a conceptualization of their experiences as resulting from a brain disease. Yet HVHs are clearly understandable consequences of concerns in people's lives, reminiscent of the talking breast pump. Getting people with HVH to re-assess how realistic their perceived threats are should therefore be helpful. People who move from realms of extreme threat to low threat generally need to be helped through this transition. Take soldiers, for example. On returning from a war zone, in which you needed to be on your highest level of threat alert, a debrief is required to reinforce to you that the threat is now past, that you are no longer in danger, and that you can safely reduce your vigilance levels.[256] Improving safety for people with HVH, for example by arranging secure housing in a community, may also be needed. Recall Mary from Chapter 10 who was still sleeping in the bed she was raped in. Words alone are never going to make her feel safe. Once someone feels safe and can sleep, this can help reduce arousal levels. Anxiety may also be reduced by drugs such as benzodiazepines. Increasing the person's sense of (and actual) empowerment in their life may also help. A 2008 study found that people who were primed with situations which made them feel that events were out of control were more likely to perceive objects in ambiguous pictures.[257] It is possible the same may apply to perceiving words in ambiguous noise. The HVH framework is relatively new, and we are currently working to see if people identified as having such voice-hearing may be helped by tailored solutions.[258] Time will tell if our intuitions are borne out.

CHAPTER 18

What Have They Done to You, Poor Child?

Much of what we have heard in previous chapters screams out that suffering child abuse may cause people to hear voices, including, importantly, in the context of a schizophrenia diagnosis. This raises two key questions. The first is whether the scientific research supports this intuition. We will turn to this in the next chapter. The second, which we will concern ourselves with here, is why, given what we have already seen, isn't child abuse at least strongly mooted as a potential risk factor for voice-hearing? More to the point, why is this idea more muted than mooted?

That this idea has been at best neglected and at worst suppressed is suggested by John Read and colleagues who recently found that only 0.3 per cent of schizophrenia research has investigated the roles that child abuse and neglect may play in its development.[259] Claims that voice-hearing was related to child abuse could once upon a time be dismissed because everyone 'knew' voices were caused by schizophrenia, and schizophrenia was a genetically determined brain disease. Anyone diagnosed with schizophrenia who reported they were abused as a child could be discounted as delusional. Yet it turns out that people diagnosed with schizophrenia do not incorrectly allege sexual assault more than the general population does,[260] and that their reports of trauma tend to be consistent over periods of years and unaffected by how severe their psychotic symptoms are.[261] In fact, evidence suggests that people diagnosed with schizophrenia are likely to *under*-report child abuse.[262]

No one is saying that child abuse is the only cause of voice-hearing or schizophrenia, or that it should be the only thing we talk about, but when someone proposes that 'the *most important* etiological agent [cause of schizophrenia] may turn out to be a contagious cat',[263] and then proceeds to write a book on schizophrenia in which the words 'rape', 'incest', 'sexual abuse' and 'child abuse' do not feature in the index, then it is clear that something has gone horribly wrong. When someone feels that we have such a poor handle on the causes of schizophrenia that we need to start thinking, in apparent seriousness, if it may be caused by wearing high heels,[264] then we have gone beyond wrong into the fantastical territory of what Wolfgang Pauli called the 'not-even wrong'. I still hold out hope this latter theory is satire. As some papers on this topic emanate from a urology department, my suspicion that someone is taking the proverbial is strengthened.[265]

History offers reasons for why the relationship between child abuse and hearing voices has been neglected.[266] Before examining some of these, we should be clear that the term 'abuse' sanitizes what people have experienced. As the renowned pianist James Rhodes, himself a survivor of childhood sexual abuse, has put it:

> Abuse. What a word. Rape is better. Abuse is when you tell a traffic warden to fuck off… I was used, broken, toyed with and violated from the age of six. Over and over for years and years.[267]

Or, as another survivor of such abuse, Eleanor Longden, puts it:

> the impact of what those people did to me is beyond language. It was a blasphemy, a desecration beyond expression; and it left behind a tiny child whose mind broke and shattered into a million tiny pieces.[268]

Language must not be allowed to disguise or desensitize us to the horror that many people have suffered.

A key figure who obscured the relationship between child sexual abuse and hearing voices was a prominent Viennese cocaine user and novelist, with a sadomasochistic streak that involved dressing up as a scientist and then being very bad at it.[269] Sigmund Freud initially argued that hallucinations resulted from forgotten traumatic childhood experiences returning to consciousness. This returning material could be a memory of the trauma or simply the emotion associated with it. Freud believed the latter was particularly relevant to voice-hearing, arguing that 'repressed affect [emotion] seems to invariably return in hallucinations of voices'.[270] He pinpointed the sexual abuse of daughters by fathers as a key form of trauma. This formed the basis of his 'seduction theory'. Early in his career, Freud not only claimed that child sexual abuse was the caput Nili (source of the Nile) of hysteria, but went as far to propose that the motto of psychoanalysis should be: 'What have they done to you, poor child?'[271]

Freud later changed his mind, stating that 'surely such widespread perversions against children are not very probable'.[272] Jeffrey Masson portrays this as a cowardly rejection by Freud of what he knew to be true, resulting from pressure from colleagues and his clients' families.[273] In contrast, Allen Esterson has argued that Freud had good reasons to doubt many of the stories he was encountering.[274] Esterson proposes that many of Freud's patients' reports of abuse were driven by Freud getting the idea that child sexual abuse was the cause of their problems and effectively forcing this explanation onto them, leading them to recover memories of abuse. Esterson suggests that Freud was doubting reports of child abuse that were 'remembered' for the first time by patients when he questioned them using his specific techniques (such as applying pressure to the forehead), but not doubting memories that patients reported without his prompting. While the recovered memory literature remains contentious, and there is some evidence that adults can forget about having been sexually abused as children,[275] today it is generally held that memories of sexual abuse are not typically forgotten, but are actually remembered all too well.[276] Esterson concludes that it was the wider psychoanalytic community that later mistakenly encouraged psychoanalysts to treat all female patients' reports of childhood sexual abuse as fantasies.

Yet psychoanalysts who stressed the role of child sexual abuse in causing mental health problems received short shrift from Freud. In a 1932 speech, Sándor Ferenczi argued that sexual abuse caused mental health problems, describing how:

> ...sexual trauma, as the pathogenic factor cannot be valued highly enough. Even children of very respectable, sincerely puritanical families, fall victim to real violence or rape much more often than one had dared to suppose. Either it is the parents who try to find a substitute gratification in this pathological way for their frustration, or it is people thought to be trustworthy such as relatives (uncles, aunts, grandparents), governesses or servants, who misuse the ignorance and the innocence of the child. The immediate explanation – that these are only sexual phantasies of the child, a kind of hysterical lying – is unfortunately...invalid... The real rape of girls who have hardly grown out of the age of infants, similar sexual acts of mature women with boys, and also enforced homosexual acts, are more frequent occurrences than has hitherto been assumed.[277]

Ferenczi also detailed how abusers would often make children feel guilty for what had happened, and noted that children's disclosure to parents of what had happened would often not be believed, pointing out that both of these could play a role in the development of mental health problems.

Freud was present for Ferenczi's speech, and listened to it in shock. He lamented that Ferenczi had 'suffered a total regression to the etiological views that I believed in 35 years ago and renounced, that the general cause of the neuroses are severe sexual traumas in childhood'. He damned the speech as confused, stupid and dishonest. Worst of all, it would 'spoil the mood' of the conference. Freud may have been concerned about how Ferenczi got this information from patients, perhaps worrying it had come in the same suggestive way he had obtained such reports. Yet Ferenczi is clear that these were real traumas, corroborated by others. Other psychoanalysts dismissed Ferenczi's speech as a 'tissue of delusions', and his paper was blocked from being published in English until years later.[278]

Whatever version of the Freud story one wishes to believe, one has to concur with the conclusion of Webster that 'it is undeniably the case that Freud's repudiation of his seduction theory has repeatedly led to real instances of sexual abuse being overlooked or denied by psychoanalysts intent on treating memories as fantasies'.[279] In the case of incestuous sexual abuse, the situation became so bad that in the index of the psychoanalyst Otto Fenichel's 1945 book, *The Psychoanalytic Theory of Neurosis*, under 'incest' it simply says 'see Oedipus complex'.[280] Incest had become imaginary. Three decades later, in 1975, a respected psychiatric textbook estimated that only one in a million children experienced incest.[281]

Today it is recognized that, in girls, the rate of incestuous sexual abuse is nearly one in a hundred.[282] The earlier distortion caused, and continues to cause, real world damage. Take Helen's experience, for example. Helen describes seeking help from a psychologist for her voices and suicidal feelings, having suffered childhood physical and sexual abuse by her father. She reports how after a few sessions her psychologist 'described herself as a "Freudian therapist" and informed me that my experiences of abuse were "not real" but "the result of fantasy"'.[283]

The second figure to end up obscuring the relation between voice-hearing and trauma was R.D. Laing. He, quite rightly, argued that experiences associated with schizophrenia, such as hearing voices, were 'much more socially intelligible than has come to be supposed by most psychiatrists'. One of Laing's patients, Ruby, heard voices calling her 'slut', 'dirty' and 'prostitute'. In order to work out why, Laing undertook a series of interviews with Ruby and her family, and found that six months before hospital admission she had fallen pregnant.[284] Her family, on finding out she was pregnant, tried 'to pump hot soapy water into her uterus, [and] told her...what a fool she was, what a slut she was'. In interviews with the family, Laing was told 'with vehemence and intensity' that Ruby was 'a slut and no better than a prostitute'. Ruby had eventually miscarried at four months. Despite Laing's insights, due to his excesses of both argumentation and alcohol, his entire oeuvre came to be dismissed, obscuring the valid arguments he made for a relation between child abuse and voice-hearing. Laing is still spat in the faces of researchers today who empirically research relations between child abuse and voice-hearing. One of my colleagues, when presenting such findings at a conference, had to put up with the objection from the floor that 'you are just an un-reconstituted Laing-ian'.

A further contributor to the minimization of the role of child abuse in voice-hearing has been the *Diagnostic and Statistical Manual of Mental Disorders* (*DSM*), referred to as the bible of psychiatry. The analogy is apt. One is an international bestseller crammed full of voice-hearing and predominantly written by elderly, white patriarchs. The other is the central text of Christianity. The first edition of the *DSM*, published in 1952, included the term 'reaction' in the name of diagnoses (e.g., 'schizophrenic reaction', 'psychotic depressive reaction') to acknowledge the simple fact that people often have mental health problems because bad things happen to them. In later versions of the *DSM* the term 'reaction' was removed, ostensibly to 'be neutral with respect to theories of etiology'. However, as Howard Zinn puts it, you can't be neural on a moving train. Instead, the *DSM* encouraged a biological and decontextualized understanding of the causes of voices. The key exception to this was PTSD. The first problem here was that this became *the* trauma diagnosis. If you were given a diagnosis of schizophrenia, this could be taken to suggest that trauma wasn't a causal factor in your experiences. A further problem was, as we noted earlier, that voice-hearing was not, and is still not, listed as a symptom of PTSD, further shepherding voice-hearing into the open arms of schizophrenia.[285]

Researchers and the nature of the relation being researched may also have contributed to the overlooking of child abuse as a causal agent of voice-hearing. Some researchers may not have spent sufficient time listening to the life stories of people who hear voices. Their questions, as Dr King put it, 'suggest that they do not know the world in which they live'.[286] The same indictment was levelled by Carl Jung,[287] who saw a tendency for medical psychology to know 'far too little…of anything outside the medical department'. A lack of undergraduate medical teaching on the prevalence of child maltreatment and its potential causal role in mental health problems may contribute to this. There may also sometimes be a time lag between abuse starting and mental health problems, including voice-hearing, manifesting. For example, Teicher and colleagues found that depression and PTSD did not typically occur immediately after child sexual abuse started, but took almost a decade to emerge.[288] Such a lag would make causal relations harder to see. Thankfully, a renewal of interest in the relation between voice-hearing and childhood traumas, such as sexual abuse, has been driven by the women's movement, survivor activists, the Hearing Voices Movement, and researchers (among whom Professor John Read deserves special mention). Let's now see what this research has found.

CHAPTER 19

Can Child Abuse Cause Voice-Hearing?

As the twenty-first century dawned, a popular book on schizophrenia felt able to say that 'stress is no more than a very minor cause of schizophrenia, *if indeed it plays any role at all*'.[289] Even given the state of the research literature at the time, this was a breathtaking statement, sucking the air out of screaming lungs. We will now consider the evidence as to whether the association between child abuse and voice-hearing we have seen in previous chapters is a causal one. There are two possible ways to consider a causal role for child abuse in voice-hearing. First, child abuse could 'colour the content' of voices.[290] That is, child abuse may not cause the voices to occur, but when they do occur their content is shaped by the abuse. Alternatively (or additionally), child abuse could cause the voices to occur. We will examine if traumatic events can colour the content of voices in the next chapter, but here we will be concerned with whether child abuse can actually cause voice-hearing itself to occur.

One way to assess if the association between child abuse and voice-hearing is a causal one is to use criteria derived from a seminal 1964 US Surgeon General's report on whether smoking caused health problems.[291] To support a causal relation it would need to be the case that 1) a strong association exists between child abuse and voice-hearing; 2) there is a dose–response relationship

– that is, those who suffer more child abuse are more likely to go on to hear voices; 3) child abuse happens before voice-hearing starts; 4) child abuse stopping causes the odds of the person going on to hear voices to decrease relative to people in whom the abuse continues; 5) alternative explanations for the relation between child abuse and voice-hearing are unconvincing; and 6) there is a plausible mechanism for the relation.[292]

Voice-hearing is strongly associated with child abuse. A 2012 study of the general population by Bentall and colleagues found that experiencing multiple childhood traumas (two or more of the following: sexual abuse, physical abuse, bullying, being taken into care) was associated with voice-hearing to an extent comparable to the association of smoking with lung cancer.[293] This bears repeating: *experiencing multiple childhood traumas is associated with voice-hearing to an extent comparable to the association of smoking with lung cancer.* Child abuse is associated with voice-hearing in people with psychiatric diagnoses too. Honig and colleagues found that 65 per cent of people diagnosed with schizophrenia (and 80 per cent of people diagnosed with DID) had experienced a childhood trauma at the onset of their voice-hearing.[294] Another study, this time of 200 consecutively treated people at a mental health centre, found that child physical and sexual abuse were both individually associated with hearing voices, and that when someone suffered both these forms of events, rates of voice-hearing were even higher.[295] Only 2 per cent of patients with neither child sexual abuse (CSA) nor child physical abuse (CPA) heard voices commanding them to hurt themselves or others. If they had CPA only, this rate was 18 per cent, if they had CSA only, this rate was 15 per cent, and if they had both CPA and CSA then this rate was 29 per cent. Only 3 per cent of patients with neither CPA nor CSA had symptoms of psychosis that were related to the devil or evil. If they had CPA only, this rate was 12 per cent, if they had CSA only, this rate was 15 per cent, and if they had both CPA and CSA then this rate was 28 per cent. A further increase in rates of voice-hearing was found if CSA was incestuous (e.g., perpetrated by a father or brother). Consistent with this, another study found that *all* female (and nearly all male) incest survivors presenting to a psychiatric hospital experienced hallucinations.[296] Indeed, the type of child abuse most consistently linked to hearing voices is CSA. Being raped as a child increases an adult's odds of having heard voices in the past year sixfold (suffering childhood physical abuse increases the odds fourfold).[297] Yet the evolving evidence base in this area suggests that rather than specific types of abuse (e.g., child sexual abuse) causing specific experiences, such as voice-hearing, cumulative experiences of childhood adversities add up to increase the risk of a person hearing voices.[298] This brings us to the question of dose–response relations.

Not only is child abuse associated with voice-hearing, but there is also a dose–response relation. The greater amount of child abuse you experience (the 'dose'), the more likely you are to have the response of voice-hearing. Bentall and colleagues' study, discussed above, found that suffering more childhood traumas was associated with a greater risk of voice-hearing. Compared with people who had suffered none of the childhood traumas that this study enquired about, people who had experienced one childhood trauma had twice the odds of hearing voices, those suffering two childhood traumas had nine times the odds, and those with three childhood traumas had *18* times the odds.

In terms of temporal ordering, child abuse can precede people's first experience of voice-hearing. In a large Irish study, Kelleher and colleagues assembled a sample of adolescents who, when they were first interviewed, had never heard voices.[299] They found that those who had been physically assaulted or bullied in the last year were more likely to have heard voices when they were re-assessed three months and a year later. This effect has also been found for psychosis more generally. Janssen and colleagues asked 4000 people from the general population whether they had experienced child abuse, and then followed these people up two years later to see if any of them had experienced psychotic symptoms for the first time.[300] More people who had suffered child abuse went on to experience psychotic symptoms for the first time over this two-year period (1.4 per cent), than people without child abuse did (0.1 per cent). Even after factors such as a family history of psychosis had been controlled for, it was still found that people who experienced child abuse had nine times the odds of developing 'pathology-level' psychosis, compared with people who had not suffered child abuse. When child abuse stops, the probability of people hearing voices then goes down relative to people whose child abuse continues. Kelleher and colleagues' study found that those who had been bullied or physically assaulted, but were not bullied or physically assaulted again, were less likely to hear voices again than those in whom the abuse continued.

We can think of reasons why child abuse and voice-hearing occur together, which don't involve child abuse *causing* voice-hearing. I personally think that these arguments stretch credulity, but I nevertheless believe they are important to raise because we are looking for the truth. Querying a causal role for trauma could sound callous and uncaring. This is a hard position for someone to put themselves in, and I respect those who have the courage to do this. One such argument is that there could be a third variable that causes both voice-hearing and child abuse, meaning that voice-hearing and child abuse would tend to occur together but not actually cause each other. For example, Robin Murray and colleagues have noted that the possibility cannot be excluded that a child destined to develop schizophrenia in early adulthood (and to hear voices) may show early signs of this disorder in childhood, which increases the risk of them suffering child abuse.[301] As we will see in Chapter 41, research has found that the onset of schizophrenia is often preceded by subtle behavioural changes early in childhood.[302] As Murray and colleagues note, these changes are associated with greater risk for suffering emotional, physical and sexual abuse.

What Murray and colleagues are referring to is called an evocative gene–environment correlation. In this case it would involve a gene giving a child a genetic liability to develop psychotic symptoms in adolescence as a result of early childhood developmental problems that the gene causes. These developmental problems would in turn cause the child to evoke harmful experiences from their environment, which would give the illusion of these harmful experiences actually causing voice-hearing by both pre-dating it and being associated with it. The content of the trauma would also likely inform the content of the voice, further adding to the illusion that the trauma caused the existence of the voices, rather than merely shaping their content. If this were to be the case for some people (and it is a big 'if'), I would not use the word 'evoke', preferring to say that the gene's effects on neurodevelopment made the child more vulnerable to abuse, for example by increasing the probability they were physically ill as a child (a known risk factor for child sexual abuse[303]). In this way, blame for the abuse still lies firmly with the abuser.

Another non-causal explanation for the relation between child abuse and voice-hearing is that other negative events tend to occur to people who experience child abuse. A child who has been abused is likely to have had a childhood different in many ways from a child who has not been abused. It could be that it is these other events that cause the voice-hearing, not the child abuse. For example, in a (phenomenally controversial[304]) study, Rind and colleagues reported results suggesting that it was family conflict, not child (sexual) abuse, that was associated with mental health problems.[305]

Despite these counter-arguments, the best available evidence supports the idea that CSA *can* cause voice-hearing. For example, take another study which, although not examining voice-hearing specifically, pointed towards a causal role for child sexual abuse in mental illness.[306] Kendler and colleagues looked at female twins to see if CSA was associated with psychopathology. Over 1400 adult twins were assessed, and 30 per cent reported some form of CSA (8 per cent experienced forced sexual intercourse). The risk for psychopathology was greater in the twin with CSA than the twin without CSA, even though both had been reared in the same basic family environment, and both would have received the same genetic predisposition to psychopathology from their parents. If child abuse can cause voice-hearing, the next question is how exactly it does this.

CHAPTER 20

Voice-Hearing as Memories of Trauma

'It was clumsily done,' wrote Samuel Beckett in his book, *The Unnamable*. 'You could see the ventriloquist.'[307] In many cases of voice-hearing, it likewise does not take too much searching to find out where the voices have come from. An obvious way to explain how child abuse, as well as other traumas, can cause voice-hearing is through the idea that voices are based in memories of what was said during the trauma. There is certainly a strong overlap between what voices say and things that have previously happened to people. A recent study by Dirk Corstens and Eleanor Longden found that the content of 94 per cent of the voices heard by people diagnosed with schizophrenia could be related to earlier emotionally overwhelming events. Voices and adverse events often shared common emotions (e.g., both involving low self-worth, anger, shame and guilt) and common characters (e.g., both involving a family member, a past abuser).[308] This was consistent with previous research that had also shown that stressful events can form the themes of hallucinations.[309] For example, people at ultra-high genetic risk for psychosis who also have a history of sexual trauma have a nine-fold increase in their odds of having hallucinations with sexual content, compared with those with no history of sexual trauma.[310] More generally, it has been found that three-quarters of people diagnosed with psychosis who have also experienced child abuse have links between their abuse and the content of their hallucinations/delusions. In cases of child sexual abuse this can include hearing the voice of the rapist or a voice threatening rape.[311] What voices say clearly often relates to an uncontainable past.

A slight complication comes from the findings of a study by Amy Hardy and colleagues. This compared the voices heard by patients with and without a history of trauma. It found no differences between the two groups in levels of threats, humiliation or guilt in the voices.[312] This could be taken to suggest that either something other than prior traumas is causing the negative content of voices in both groups, or that trauma causes some people's negative voice content and another factor causes other people's negative voice content. However, these findings may have been influenced by Hardy and colleagues' focus on a limited range of traumas. When trauma is expanded to the more general concept of an emotionally overwhelming event, much more voice content can be linked to past events, as Corstens and Longden found.

Of course, we may worry that if we look hard enough we will always be able to find links between earlier life events and what voices say. We would perhaps feel happier that emotionally overwhelming events were the basis of voices' content if we could do an experiment to help someone cope better with a trauma thought to drive their voice, and to see if this also changed the content of the voice. For example, if someone heard a critical voice blaming them for being raped, then would helping them come to see that they were not to blame for this event cause the voice to ease off with its critique? Tentative evidence for this has come from a small case study of compassion-focused therapy (which will be discussed further in Chapter 42).

If what voices say is related to a memory of a trauma, then you might think that voices would turn out to be simply auditory flashbacks of the trauma. They would be a re-activated memory of what an abuser actually said, which has been burnt into the brain. There certainly are cases of voice-hearing which are like this.

For example, Anketell and colleagues found that 40 per cent of PTSD sufferers directly related their voices to past experiences of abuse or trauma.[313] For example, one patient who had been physically assaulted by two men subsequently heard the voices of two men saying, 'We'll kill you.'

Such voice-hearing appears to be the exception rather than the rule though. Many voices heard by PTSD sufferers have themes that only indirectly reflect the nature of the trauma. For example, Jessop and colleagues found that 46 per cent of PTSD sufferers reported a non-direct association between their voices and earlier traumatic experiences.[314] What the voice(s) said had themes that were understandable in the context of the trauma the person had suffered (e.g., 'you are hopeless', 'you deserve to die', in the case of childhood physical and sexual abuse) or related to derogatory things previously said to them, but were not verbatim replays of things actually said. The voices were like internalized shame relating to the trauma.

A similar pattern of relations has been found in people diagnosed with schizophrenia. Amy Hardy and colleagues found that the content of hallucinations (predominantly voice-hearing) in individuals with psychosis who had experienced trauma was directly related to these traumas in 13 per cent of cases, and indirectly (i.e., thematically) in 58 per cent of cases.[315] Voices tend to riff on the trauma, rather than repeat it. To adapt Mark Twain, voices don't typically repeat traumas, but they certainly rhyme with them.

These two ways in which voice-hearing can relate to earlier experiences – direct and indirect – are consistent with what we know about memory. Let's start with the voices that don't riff, but just repeat. These may originate from what Ralph Hoffman called a 'parasitic memory'.[316] This idea originally came from Charcot, who referred to traumatic memories as 'parasites of the mind'.[317] Hoffman suggested that parasitic memories could sneak into the mind and result in voice-hearing. He argued this would result in a voice having the form of 'a small number of rigidly repeated expressions', which he felt was consistent with his impression 'that voices are not very creative or expressive and frequently consist of a small number of rigidly repeated expressions'. This does indeed fit with how repetitive many voices are. But what would make a memory of an event parasitic?

One answer is that parasitic memories are those that cannot be integrated into our autobiographical memory base. They are the sheep that the sheep dog cannot get back into the pack. For example, Ehlers and Clark have argued that flashbacks in PTSD result from intrusions from memory, which in turn result from the original experience not being laid down into our autobiographical memory base.[318] Specifically, they propose that during trauma exposure our mental processing becomes data driven rather than conceptually driven. This means that there is more focus on processing the raw sensory impressions, and less focus on the meaning of the situation and on processing the event in a way that places it into context. Without the tent pegs of context holding them down, such sensory experiences are free to blow around in the wind of our heads. The more data-driven form of processing has been referred to as dissociative (meaning the stimulus is processed in an unintegrated manner) and has been proposed to result in what Chris Brewin has termed a situationally accessible memory. This is a memory that is difficult to recall voluntarily, but easily involuntarily triggered into consciousness when something associated with the original trauma is encountered.[319] A sight, a smell or a sound can trigger a memory, or even a reliving, of the trauma. Situationally accessible memories are good candidates for Hoffman's parasitic memories.

While the term 'parasitic memory' has the ring of pathology about it, we could nevertheless understand voices that recapitulate parts of the trauma as being an attempt of the mind to protect the person. For example, Anke Ehlers and colleagues have put forward ideas that would allow us to understand some voice-hearing as resulting from a person having identified a warning signal of what happened to them.[320] They note that many of the intrusive thoughts and memories experienced by people with PTSD represent things experienced shortly before the part of the trauma with the largest emotional impact. As such, they could be understood as things that warned of what was coming. To illustrate this, they give an example of a childhood sexual abuse survivor who kept hearing the voice of the perpetrator saying, 'Get me the sugar cube.' This is what he had said shortly before the assault. Why, you may ask, would such warning signals be auditory? Why not visual or in some other modality? Ehlers and colleagues note that warning signals do indeed occur in other modalities and give examples. A woman, who had been raped in her home, kept seeing the rapist standing inside her bedroom door, which was as she had seen him when she woke up before the rape. Another rape victim who was attacked from behind kept feeling hands being put over her eyes. Ehlers and colleagues argue that voice-hearing is particularly likely to follow trauma if something heard preceded what was about to happen more clearly than something seen or felt. For example, they suggest that if there was no visual signal of the danger, such as if someone was attacked in the dark or from behind, then voice-hearing is more likely to emerge. This idea remains to be tested.

Despite such theories being able to account for one-to-one correspondences between what was said during the trauma and what voices say, the question remains as to why voices are not typically simple re-experiences of trauma, but are typically only thematically related to them. One explanation, based on models of memory, comes from Chris Brewin and colleagues.[321] They start from the concept of situationally accessible memories (SAMs). These are memories that you can't intentionally recall, but which situations can trigger, which they propose form the raw material of voices. They argue that SAMs (and hence voices) can be 'automatically altered or added to whenever some or all of the information they contain happens to be paired with changes in concurrent bodily states or contents of consciousness'. If a SAM was created by trauma, then absolution of responsibility for the trauma or further self-shaming information should change the SAM and hence the voice, making it nicer or nastier respectively. They suggest that this may occur through an associative process. For example, a SAM of the trauma occurs and is followed by the thought 'I should kill myself'. This new thought then becomes a SAM in itself, and forms the basis of voice-hearing. The malleability of the original SAM at the hands of current events, thoughts and goals would therefore explain why voices are related to the original trauma but not identical to it.

This all starts to sound quite technical, but the ideas at the heart of this are straightforward. As Charles Fernyhough explains:

> The truth is that autobiographical memories are not possessions that you either have or do not have. They are mental constructions, created in the present moment, according to the demands of the present… We remember the past through the lens of the present: what we believe now, what we want now.[322]

Fernyhough explains how the PTSD literature shows that we 'appear to construct flashbacks about what we feared might have happened rather than what actually did'. This helps explain why people are hearing voices thematically or symbolically related to their trauma. They may be having a form of re-experiencing, but with the content strongly shaped by their current fears and concerns (e.g., of what the abuser thinks about them, or would do to them if they were there). This reiterates what we noted in earlier chapters, namely that problematic, distressing voice-hearing may derive from not feeling safe in the world.

We are still left with the question as to why people experience a voice rather than an intrusive memory. One possibility is that this is because the atoms of the trauma memory have a strong sensory component, which give memories derived from them a sensory quality. Alternatively, it could be that the unexpectedness (i.e., the intrusiveness and automaticity) of this mental visitor leads our best guess to be that it is a voice, leading it to be experienced as such. A further reason why a person's best guess would be that an escapee from memory is actually a voice is because trauma has affected what is called their source-monitoring ability.

Source monitoring is a catch-all term covering our ability to determine the source of an event or a thought. This includes what is called reality monitoring, which is our ability to decide whether a given event was something that actually happened to us, or whether it was something we internally produced ourselves (i.e., that we imagined). The classic example here is Paul McCartney and his song *Yesterday*, but as McCartney ranks number six on my list of favourite Beatles (behind Lennon, Harrison, Starr, VW and scarab), I'm going to use another example – Hunter S. Thompson. He and his attorney (after having sampled grass, mescaline, acid, cocaine, uppers, downers, screamers, laughers, poppers, tequila and rum) picked up a young hitchhiker. Driving along at a hundred and ten, Thompson lets us into his stream of consciousness:

> How long before one of us starts raving and jabbering at this boy? What will he think then? This same lonely desert was the last known home of the Manson family. Will he make that grim connection when my attorney starts screaming about bats and huge manta rays coming down on the car? If so – well, we'll just have to cut his head off and bury him somewhere. Because it goes without saying that we can't turn him loose. He'll report us at once to some kind of outback nazi law enforcement agency, and they'll run us down like dogs.
>
> 'Jesus!' Thompson then thought, 'Did I say that? Or just think it? Was I talking?'[323]

Reality-monitoring abilities can be tested experimentally by getting you to read some words aloud, getting an experimenter to read some other words aloud, and later seeing how good you are at recalling whether a given word was read aloud by you or the experimenter. Alternatively, you could be asked to read some words aloud, imagine some other words being read aloud, and then later try to remember which words you spoke aloud and which you only imagined reading aloud. On average, people who hear voices have worse reality-monitoring skills than people who do not hear voices.[324] Similarly, people who suffer traumatic life events, such as child sexual abuse, have worse reality-monitoring skills than those who have not been traumatized.[325] It is therefore possible that child abuse alters the brain's ability to distinguish between internally generated thought and externally originating perceptions, resulting in voice-hearing (see also Chapters 24 and 39).

Despite the evidence that child abuse can cause both the onset and content of voice-hearing, Robin Murray and colleagues have correctly noted that even if we accept that child abuse is sometimes a cause of voice-hearing, it is neither necessary for someone to hear voices (plenty of people hear voices who have not experienced child abuse) nor sufficient (not everyone who experiences child abuse goes on to hear voices). This raises the question that we will address next: why do only some people hear voices after trauma, and what circumstances may push a person down this route?

CHAPTER 21

What Encourages Voice-Hearing After Trauma?

Life is a five-chambered gun; four are loaded. Eighty per cent of us will experience a traumatic event in our lifetime.[326] What the trauma is will be influenced by a range of factors, including our sex. Women are more likely than men to be raped, both as children and adults. Men are more likely to experience combat trauma, a car crash, or to witness injury or death.[327] What specific problems such traumas will lead to is also influenced by a range of factors. Unfortunately, we have little idea of what these are. Suffering a trauma increases the risk for a wide range of problems and psychiatric diagnoses, but may also lead to none of these. For example, suffering childhood trauma increases the risk of you hearing voices, but also increases your risk of being diagnosed with non-voice hearing versions of PTSD, depression, anxiety disorders, oppositional or conduct disorders, eating disorders, substance abuse and personality disorders.[328] General mechanisms have been set out for why childhood trauma leads to vulnerability to such problems. These include emotional dysregulation – a loss of control of how emotions are felt, experienced and expressed. This is found to some degree across all the post-traumatic problems listed above. Yet it is not at all clear why, for example, one person goes down the path of developing an eating disorder after a trauma while another develops PTSD.

At this time, we are essentially left to speculate as to the reasons why someone goes on to develop specifically voice-hearing after a trauma. Answers to this can take four broad routes (you may be able to think of more). First, culture may play a role in the form post-traumatic reactions will take, by providing a range of socially sanctioned reaction patterns and a mould into which the trauma can be poured.[329] Second, aspects of the trauma itself, such as its chronicity and the identity of the perpetrator, may also influence the form of the reaction to it. We have already seen evidence that incestual child sexual abuse is more likely to lead to voice-hearing than non-incestual child sexual abuse. Third, individual differences in our 'mysterious mixture',[330] our pre-existing biology and psychology, may push us down a certain pathway after a trauma. Finally, the meaning someone makes of a trauma, or has made for them by a perpetrator, family or friends, may influence the path they take.

One possibility I would like to focus on here is that certain emotions following trauma increase the probability of voice-hearing developing. As we have already seen, themes of shame and guilt pervade many people's voices. A recent study found that 60 per cent of the voices heard by people diagnosed with schizophrenia embodied feelings of shame and guilt.[331] Another study found that 35 per cent of people's voices had a specific theme of shaming. Based on what we saw in the previous chapter, it seems likely that voices with content involving shame and blame are driven by events involving shame and blame (even if the shame and blame are completely undeserved). To reiterate this point, a study that reported on the content of the voices heard by four people who had been raped found that three of these people heard voices blaming them for the rape they had suffered.[332] I would like to argue that shame, in particular, is hallucinogenic.

In order to assess if shame could contribute to the development of voice-hearing we currently have to rely on hints from the PTSD research literature. Levels of shame following trauma influence how severe PTSD symptoms are. For example, Andrews and colleagues examined what factors led victims of violent crime (actual or attempted physical or sexual assault, or bag snatch) to develop PTSD symptoms.[333] A month after the crime, shame (feeling they should have done more to stop the attack, thinking that they looked bad to others during it, or carrying bodily signs of the crime) and anger with others predicted people's levels of PTSD symptoms. Six months after the trauma, only shame surrounding their experience of crime remained a predictor of symptoms. In addition to shame, guilt and self-blame may also encourage PTSD to develop.[334] For example, Canton-Cortes and colleagues found that female students who had experienced child sexual abuse and who blamed themselves had more severe PTSD symptoms than those who did not blame themselves.[335] Given the links between PTSD, re-experiencing symptoms and voice-hearing, this offers some proxy support for the idea that shame and self-blame after a trauma could encourage voice-hearing. In order to consider if there is a plausible mechanism through which shame could cause voice-hearing, we need to understand what shame is.

The threats we encounter from others today are more likely to take the form of social threats to our reputation and social standing, than physical threats to our body. Such social threats imperil our basic human need to belong and to be valued. They threaten what Paul Gilbert has called our social attention holding power – our ability to elicit positive attention and social rewards in the form of approval, praise, acceptance, respect, admiration and desire.[336] This makes such threats a fundamental part of our consciousness and a driver of our behaviour. As George Orwell once put it, 'my whole life…was one long struggle not to be laughed at'.[337] Experiences of being disgraced, devalued, demoted, dishonoured, degraded, discredited, humiliated, ridiculed, shunned, ostracized or scorned, as Paul Gilbert notes, are signalled to us through the emotion of shame, the feeling there is something flawed, bad or worthless about us.[338] The emotion of shame is a social threat detection system warning us that other people are viewing us negatively and may punish us.[339] This belief may come to be internalized, leading us to believe that we are contemptible, wretched and worthless failures. In such internal shame, we become both the judge and the judged.[340]

The hypervigilance hallucinations framework (Chapter 17) offers one way to understand how shame and its effects on altered perceptions of the social environment could lead to voice-hearing. Simply put, shame leads people to become hypervigilant for signs that their social status (and potentially their physical safety) is threatened. We can conceive of the case of Michael in Chapter 17 as having shame at its heart. Sources of shame such as social threat and social defeat, when examined in rats, have been found to lead to increases in dopamine levels in the same pathways targeted by antipsychotic medication (see Chapters 34–37),[341] offering a way to link shame to the biology of voice-hearing.

Once you have this framework in mind, you can see numerous historical examples of voice-hearing that are consistent with this. Take a case of voice-hearing during the First World War. The patient was a 31-year-old private, admitted to hospital hearing voices.[342] The voices were of his brother, elder sister and brother-in-law, telling him what to do and what not to do. It emerged that five years earlier he had slept with a prostitute. At first he was not disturbed by this, but later he thought he could 'detect a strangeness in the behaviour of his family, as if they knew of his misdeed'. It was only then that he began to hear voices, such as those of his brothers and sisters, coming from the wall. Recall from Chapter 8 that the French psychiatrist Esquirol had a patient who heard voices 'that accuse him…[that] are continually repeating in his ear that he has betrayed his trust – that he is dishonoured, and that he can do nothing better than destroy himself'.[343] The patient in question had been the head of a large German city whose inhabitants attacked the French army, resulting in disorder in the city. The gentleman felt so ashamed of this that he cut his throat with a razor, surviving, but only for voices to start. If you want another example, go back to the case of Ruby in Chapter 18. These examples span the centuries.

Other ways in which shame could contribute to voice-hearing have also been suggested. Shame could increase the likelihood of someone trying to suppress thoughts and emotions related to the trauma, causing them to, ironically, rebound with greater vigour unexpectedly into consciousness.[344] Indeed, voice-hearers diagnosed with schizophrenia who try to suppress their emotions more tend to hear more frequent and louder voices.[345] One reason for undertaking emotional suppression is that social support is not available to help you deal with your emotions. This suggests that a lack of social support could also encourage voice-hearing. Although no research speaks directly to this, a lack of social support has been found to predict whether PTSD will develop after a trauma.[346] In a related manner, shame could also lead to social isolation, which has also been proposed to be at the root of some voice-hearing. Hoffman argued that due to the social nature of the brain, our temporal lobes will spontaneously generate speech if none is forthcoming for an extended period. This is called the social deafferentation (lack of social input to the brain) theory[347] of hallucinations. It is already accepted that some visual hallucinations can be explained by a similar mechanism. For example, a lack of input to the visual cortex in people with Charles Bonnet syndrome can lead to bizarre hallucinations of small figures bounding around in costumes and hats, or of grotesque and distorted disembodied gargoyle-like faces.[348] These are referred to as release hallucinations, with the theory being that the normal perceptual processes that would inhibit the sensory cortices and keep them occupied are absent. This causes these areas to act in an unconstrained manner producing spontaneous perceptions.[349] There are therefore converging reasons to believe shame and its sequelae may encourage the development of voice-hearing.

Revictimization (or chronic abuse) may also make voice-hearing more likely. *Two of every three people who are sexually victimized will later be revictimized.*[350] It has been found that 15 per cent of psychiatric patients who have suffered child sexual abuse will hear voices commanding them to do things, whereas 29 per cent of psychiatric patients who have suffered child sexual abuse, and were then sexually revictimized as adults, will hear such voices.[351] Despite this, another study found no evidence that adult trauma helps translate childhood trauma into psychosis. In this study, childhood traumas appeared sufficient for this on their own, and did not depend on revictimization.[352]

In addition to looking at the trauma and its sequelae, we may also consider how factors preceding the trauma may influence the probability that someone goes on to hear voices. One possibility is that a child's attachment style may influence the probability that traumas experienced later in life lead to voice-hearing. Attachment is the emotional bond that children form with their main caregivers (e.g., mum and/or dad). Attachment can vary in the degree to which it makes the child feel safe and secure, and in how it shapes their view of themselves and others, which John Bowlby referred to as an internal working model.[353] If the primary caregiver is felt to be responsive, accessible and trustworthy, a secure attachment develops, but if they are seen as unpredictable or rejecting, then attachment is deemed to be insecure. Insecure attachment has been proposed to come in three types: anxious (positive view of self, negative view of others), avoidant (negative view of self, positive view of others) and fearful (negative view of both self and other).[354] While no clear evidence shows that the probability of someone developing hallucinations after a trauma is influenced by their attachment style, preliminary evidence suggests that childhood neglect increases the risk of hallucinations in people with avoidant and anxious attachment styles.[355] Our understanding of the mediating steps between trauma and voice-hearing is still in its infancy.

Even if factors such as levels of post-trauma shame, retraumatization or attachment influence the probability that people go on to hear voices after a trauma, we are still left with the nagging problem of specificity. Why do some people respond to trauma with hearing voices specifically? One possibility is that it depends on your biology. Biological factors, such as people's neural make-up at the time of trauma, or their genome, could help explain why trauma is specifically transduced into voice-hearing. Before jumping into this, it should be stressed that it doesn't appear that someone *has* to have some form of biological predisposition in order for stress or trauma to cause them to hear voices. Events such as child abuse may be able to cause voice-hearing whatever genes you have. For example, Arseneault and colleagues failed to find that people at high genetic risk of psychosis who had suffered child abuse were any more likely to report psychotic symptoms as adults than people at low genetic risk of psychosis who had suffered child abuse.[356] Given this, John Read and colleagues have concluded that 'bad things happening, often enough, early enough or sufficiently severely, can drive us mad with or without a genetic predisposition'.[357] Nevertheless, we will now investigate the possibility that biological factors can influence the probability that someone hears voices after a trauma. To do this we are going to need to understand our brain and our genes. This will also allow us to answer many other questions about voice-hearing, such how the brain is able to produce voice-hearing at all.

Colour Plate 1: Joan of Arc being interrogated by
The Cardinal of Winchester in her prison

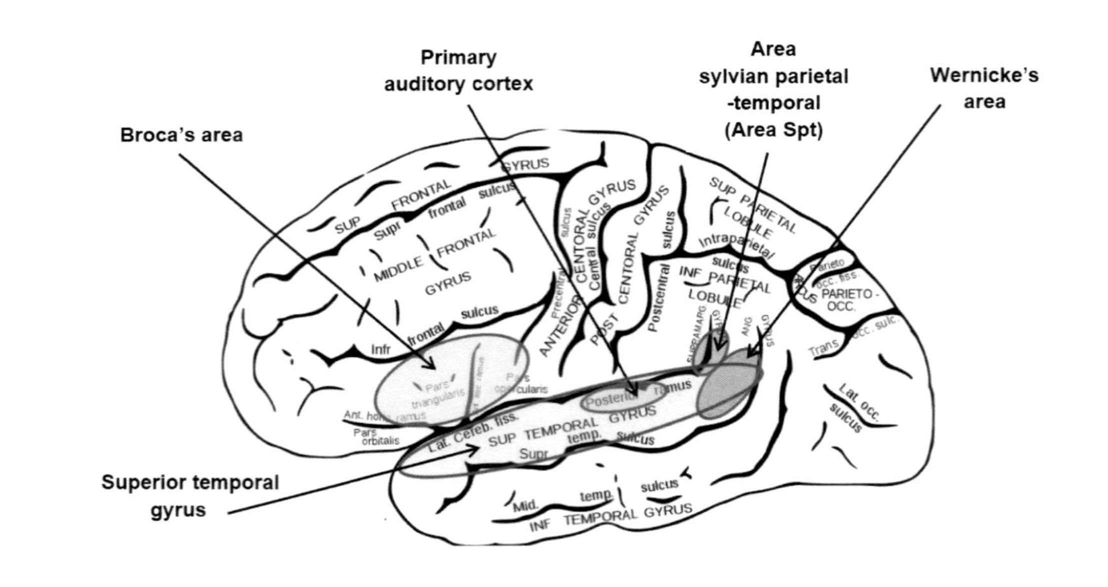

Colour Plate 2: Cortical areas of the brain involved in speech production and perception

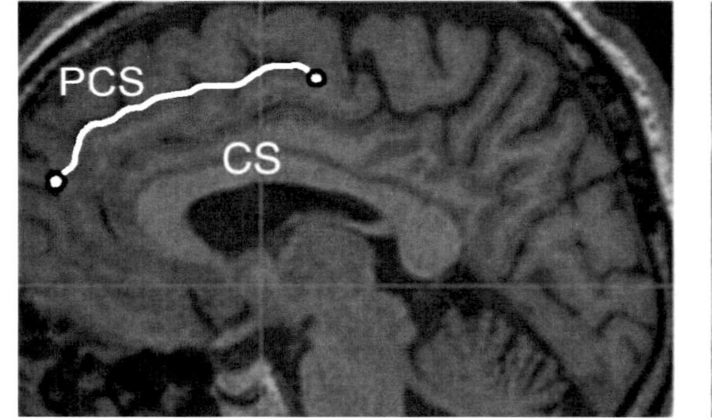

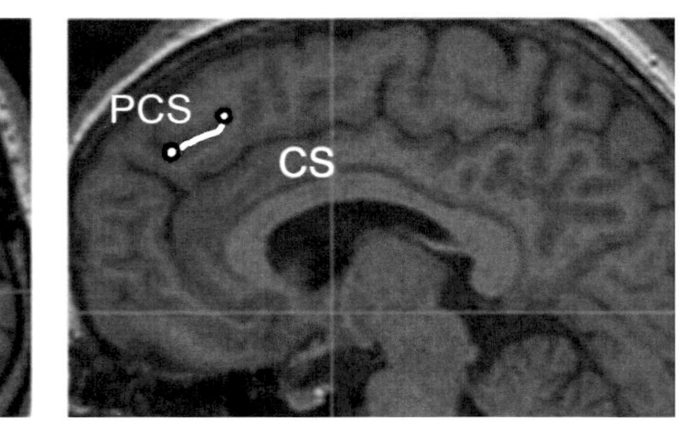

Colour Plate 3: Inter-person variation in paracingulate sulcus (PCS) length

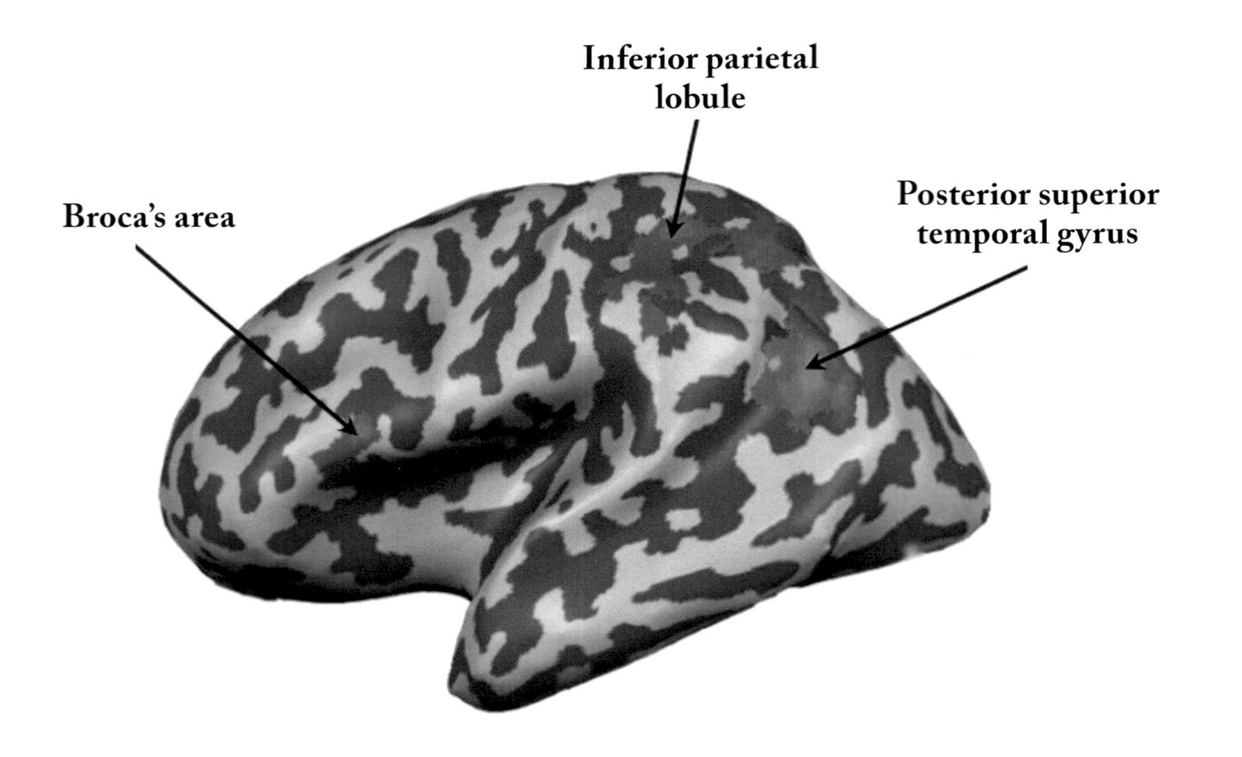

Colour Plate 4: Left hemisphere cortical activity associated with hearing voices

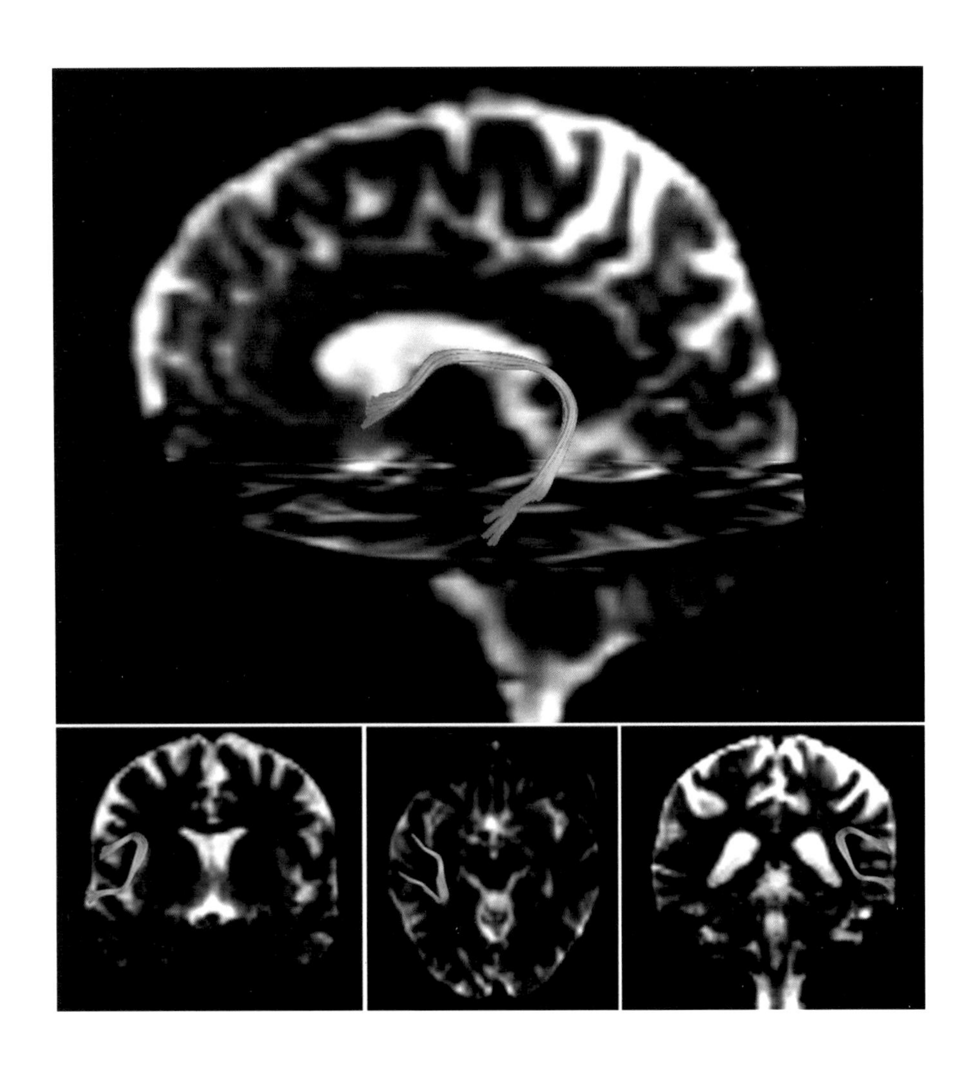

Colour Plate 5: The left hemisphere arcuate fasciculus

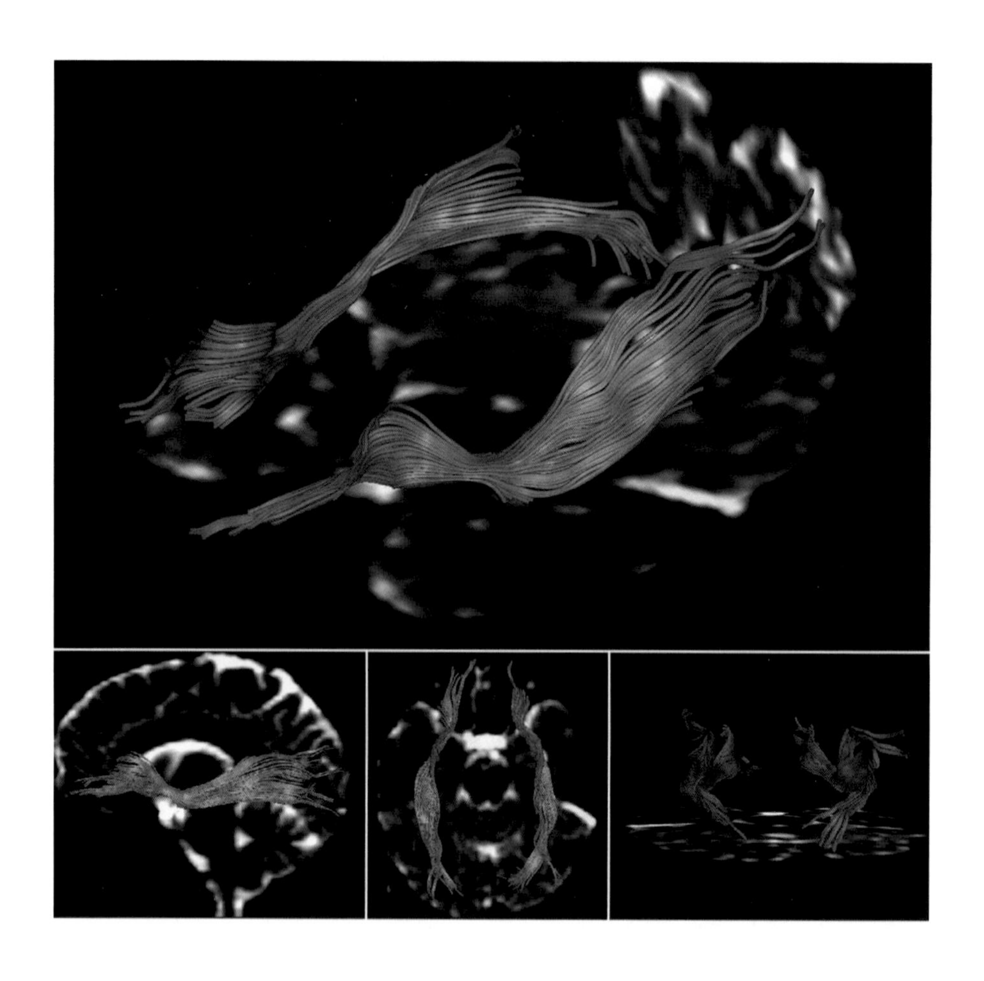

Colour Plate 6: The left and right inferior occipito-frontal fasciculi (IOFF), extracted using diffusion tensor tractography

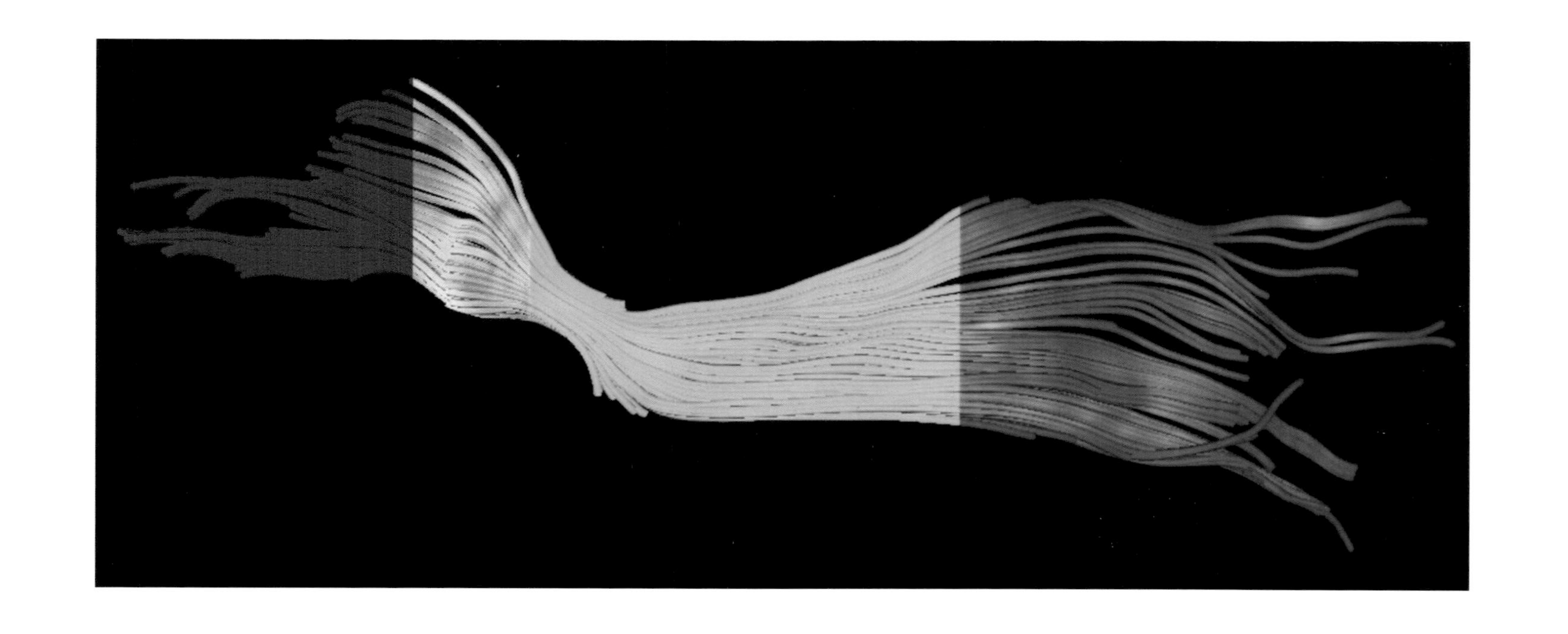

Colour Plate 7: The four sub-regions of the inferior occipito-frontal fasciculus: frontal (red), fronto-temporal (yellow), temporal (green) and occipital (blue)

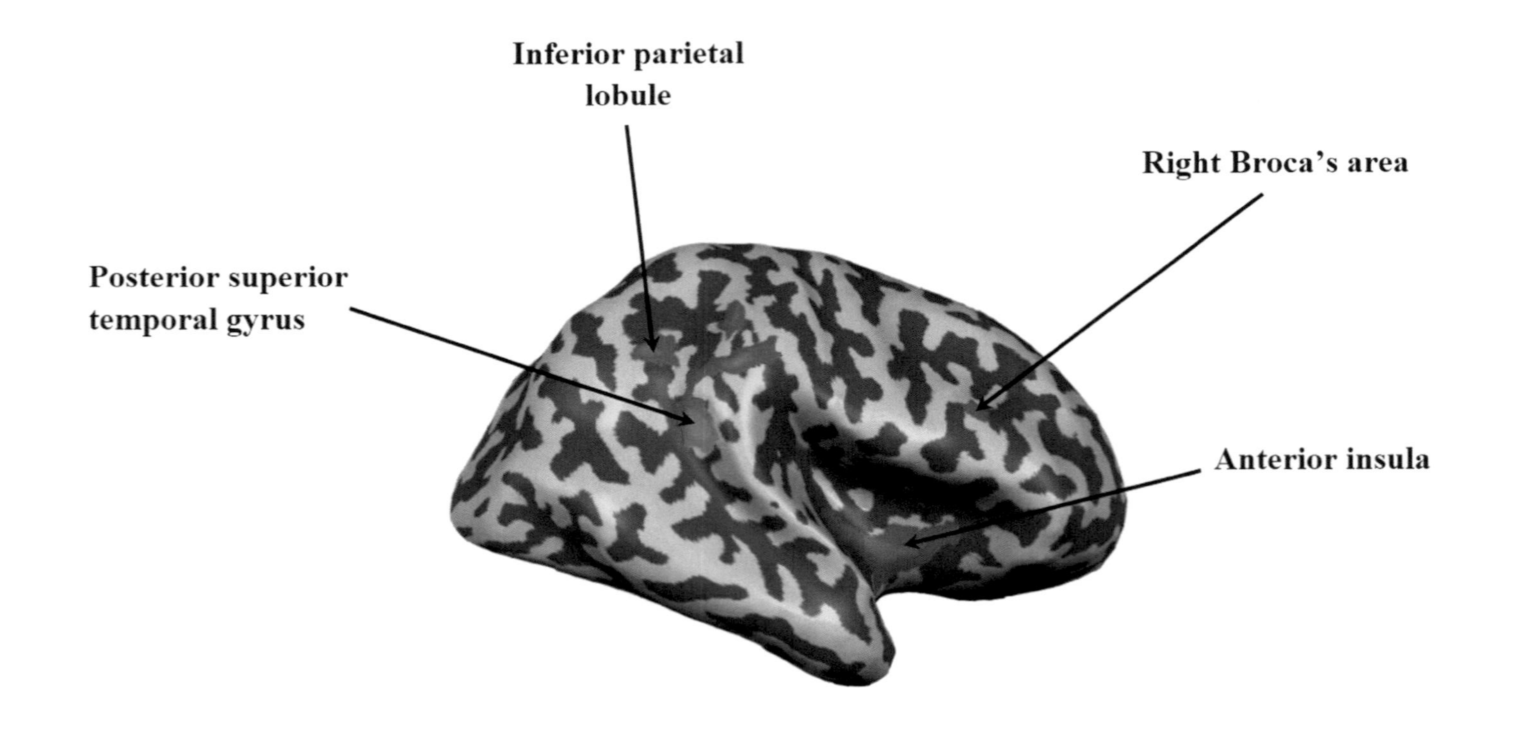

Colour Plate 8: Right hemisphere cortical activity associated with hearing voices

CHAPTER 22

The Galaxy in Your Head

The United States of America consumes 20 per cent of the world's energy but makes up only 5 per cent of the world's population. The brain is one of the few things that can make this look restrained. It consumes 20 per cent of our body's energy but makes up a mere 2 per cent of our body weight.[358] Similarly, just as events in the USA often defy understanding, what is happening in the brain also remains largely inexplicable. To move towards some kind of understanding, let's start by considering what the brain looks like to the naked eye.

The brain is a triumph of engineering but not aesthetics. The most complex and sophisticated object in the universe looks like a ball of pasta sheets that a cat spat up. The bark of our brain, the cortex, is folded such that it has deep, diving ravines (sulci) and rising ridges and plains (gyri). The cortex in each hemisphere is typically visualized as being split into four parts: the frontal lobe (involved in reasoning, decision making and the planning and execution of movements), temporal lobe (hearing, memory), occipital lobe (vision) and parietal lobe (touch, spatial awareness). The brain can be seen in Figure 22.1 (see Colour plate 2), which provides a map of the key language areas. Key structures to note for our purposes are the superior temporal gyrus (STG), which sits at the top of the temporal lobe, and the inferior frontal gyrus (Broca's area), which sits towards the bottom of the frontal lobe.

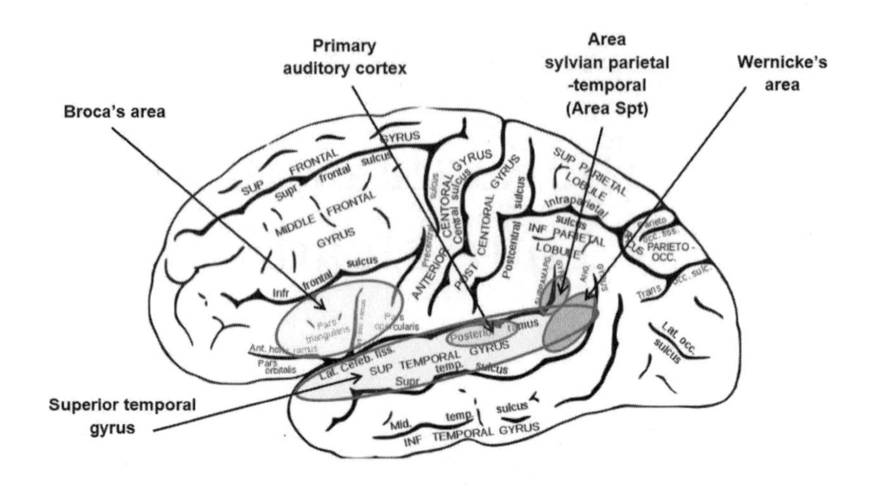

Source: Gray, H. (1918) *Anatomy of the Human Body*. Accessed at https://commons.wikimedia.org/wiki/File:Gray726.svg. Public Domain. Annotations by the author.

Figure 22.1: Cortical areas of the brain involved in speech production and perception

Below the cortex lurk a range of evolutionarily older structures, including the thalamus (which relays information received by your sense organs to the rest of the brain), the basal ganglia (involved in control of voluntary movements) and the limbic system (e.g., the hippocampus and amygdala, involved in memory, emotion and reward/motivation). All these parts of the brain have a greyish colour and are therefore referred to as grey matter. Cut a slice through a brain and you will see that much of the internal part of the brain is made up of a white-coloured material, which is, unsurprisingly, called white matter. What are these two different coloured types of matter, and what do they do?

The cells that make up the brain come in two basic types: neurons and glial cells. Let's take neurons first. We have a lot of neurons in our brain, between 80 and 100 billion. That's a big number, greater even than the number of *Police Academy* films (at the time of writing), and roughly equal to the number of stars in the Milky Way. We're each walking around with a galaxy in our head. Neurons come in many types, but a typical one consists of three parts. At one end is an antenna, which receives signals from other neurons. This large, branching structure is called a dendrite. Signals come in the form of chemicals called neurotransmitters, such as dopamine and serotonin. This signal is then transmitted to the centre of this branching structure, where the main body of the cell is. This contains the cell's nucleus and its DNA stash. Grey matter looks grey because it is where the cell bodies of neurons cluster. If the brain was a city, grey matter would be the homes and factories. Extending out from the cell body is a long, thin strip called the axon that leads away from the reception end of the neuron down to its transmission end. Electrical signals travel along the axon, and to make this process quick and efficient, the axon is surrounded by a white-coloured, fatty insulating substance called myelin. Long-range myelinated axons are what make up the white matter we see in the brain. They are the brain's wiring or, to continue the city analogy, the brain's highways.

This brings us to glial cells. These are the neuron's personal assistants; their job is to help the neurons do theirs. They come in multiple types. One type is called oligodendrocytes. These are responsible for producing myelin. Altered oligodendrocyte function appears to be the main cause of neural disconnectivity and other white matter changes in schizophrenia.[359] The decay of oligodendrocytes can have neurotoxic effects by activating another type of glial cell called microglial cells. These are the guardians of the neural galaxy, resident immune cells which make up between 5 and 20 per cent of all cells in the brain. They are a bit like Steven Seagal in *Under Siege*. They have a resting state in which they do a useful everyday job, but at a given signal they turn into highly effective killers. ('You're not a cook.' 'Yeah, well, I also cook.') At rest, they manage the activity and development of synapses.

When they detect microbes that have invaded the brain, or dying neurons, they head over to them and either release an arsenal of cell-killing weapons, or eat them in a process called phagocytosis or 'cell eating'. The Seagal parallel ends there, unless I have missed one of his more disturbing films. Both oligodendrocytes and microglia therefore serve vital functions, but both can also lead to neural damage.

When electrical signals reach the end of the axon there are a series of branches called axonal terminals. These produce, store and release neurotransmitters that are used to broadcast signals to be picked up by the dendrites of other neurons. Communication between neurons occurs at synapses, where the axonal terminals of one neuron meet the dendrites of another neuron. We have approximately one quadrillion synapses in our brains, making each of us better connected than even Kevin Bacon. The axonal terminals of the neuron sending the signal are called the pre-synaptic site, and these store neurotransmitters in pods called synaptic vesicles. When a neuron fires, these neurotransmitters are released into the synaptic cleft, the gap between the axonal terminal of the first neuron and the dendrites of the second neuron. They then dock in receptor sites on the dendrite, called postsynaptic sites, sending information into the second neuron. There are over 100 varieties of neurotransmitter. Some cause neurons to become more excitable, some less excitable, and others can do either, depending on the context. Once they have docked and passed on their signal, neurotransmitters are recalled by the pre-synaptic neuron that released them, and gobbled back up in a neural version of Hungry Hungry Hippos, formally called reuptake. All this is a dynamic process in which the number of neurotransmitter vesicles, receptors at the pre-synaptic site and receptors at the post-synaptic site can increase or decrease.

If someone is having unusual experiences we hence have a range of usual neural suspects that we can round up for questioning, which could hand us the keys to voice-hearing. Of course, just because a part of the brain looks or acts differently, this neither means that it must be pejoratively labelled an abnormality, nor that the state or experience it results in is necessarily an undesirable disease state. That is a decision for you to make, not for the brain to dictate. Now we know what to look for, we need to know where to look. Given that hearing voices often involves hearing speech, we need to know how and where speech is perceived and produced in the brain.

When someone talks to us, sound waves hit our ears and are converted into an electrical signal which is relayed, via the thalamus, to an area of cortex in your left hemisphere called the *primary auditory cortex* (also referred to, anatomically, as Heschl's gyrus). This sits in the upper middle part of the superior temporal gyrus (STG). The primary auditory cortex performs a preliminary analysis of the basic properties of the sound, such as its frequency and intensity. This information is then sent to the surrounding cortex, which is called the secondary (or association) auditory cortex. This includes the superior temporal sulcus (STS), a groove in the cortex between the superior and middle temporal gyri. The STS works out what basic word sounds (phonemes) the signal represents (e.g., 'ba', 'ma', 'ca'). This information is then sent into the middle temporal gyrus (MTG), which works out what these word sounds mean.

What about producing speech? The start of this works like the previous process, but in reverse. You have to find the words to communicate your meaning, and recall the sounds of these words. This involves the MTG and STS. Your brain then has to work out how to get your mouth to produce this sound. To do this, information from the MTG/STS about what sound is required is sent to an area at the border of the temporal and parietal lobes called area spt (sylvian parietal temporal region). This sits at the boundaries of the parietal and temporal lobes. Area spt calculates what motor command is needed to produce the required sound and sends this information to a region of the left hemisphere frontal lobe called Broca's area. This then starts the job of articulating the word. Broca's area allows us to both speak out loud and speak silently to ourselves in our heads (inner speech).

If you've heard of Broca's area, you've probably also heard of Wernicke's area. Anatomically, Wernicke's area is poorly defined, but broadly speaking it covers the posterior (back) end of the STG (which we will henceforth refer to as pSTG), sneaking into the junction of the temporal lobe with the parietal lobe, hence covering the STS and the area spt. If you have a lesion to Wernicke's area you will be able to hear speech, but you won't understand it. The experience would be like a person who only speaks English listening to someone speaking Chinese; they would be able to hear what was said, but they couldn't understand what it meant. Lesions to this area will still allow you to speak fluently, but what you say tends to be meaningless, for example 'the big and big for my and over again'.[360] Wernicke's area is therefore involved in both perceiving and producing meaning in speech.

Since Paul Broca and Karl Wernicke identified these areas of the brain (in 1861 and 1874 respectively) that came to be named after them, their work has been used to create two distinct classes of theories about voice-hearing. The first focuses on Broca's area and proposes that voice-hearing is a disorder of speech production. The basic idea is that your brain produces speech from Broca's area but you don't recognize it as being your own, due to source-monitoring errors. The second proposes that voice-hearing is a disorder of speech perception, and focuses on abnormal function of Wernicke's area. As we will see, this debate continues today.

Now we have some idea of how speech is processed in the brain, we can look at what areas of the brain appear to be involved in voice-hearing with some frame of reference. The first question we might ask is simply whether the brains of people who do and do not hear voices look different.

CHAPTER 23

Grey Matter Changes in the Voice-Hearing Brain

In 1965 Dylan went electric. Fifteen years later neuroscience, not to be outdone, went magnetic. The development of magnetic resonance imaging (MRI) allowed the structure of living people's brains to be looked at in a safe, non-invasive manner. Well, a fairly safe manner; an MRI scanner did once shoot someone, but in its defence it was in an excited state.[361] Whereas Dylan faced an immediate backlash, neuroscience's relation with MRI had an extended honeymoon period. This recently ended, after an embarrassing encounter with a dead salmon[362] and an up-swell of scepticism leading to an inconvenient truth being mooted: namely that MRI 'does not allow us to make firm inferences about the primary biology of mental disorders'.[363] Although the ground is therefore currently moving under our feet somewhat, there is a picture emerging of voice-hearing being associated with changes to grey matter structures involved in speech perception and source monitoring.

Individual studies have found a range of grey matter changes to be associated with voice-hearing. However, meta-analyses, which aggregate the results of all previous studies and are normally seen as the polished pyramidion of evidence, have found few changes to emerge reliably. Within people diagnosed with schizophrenia who hear voices, meta-analyses have found more severe voice-hearing to be associated with a smaller superior temporal gyrus (STG) volume.[364] Yet these meta-analyses have not provided evidence that the STG differs in size between people with schizophrenia who do and do not hear voices, although there have been few individual studies of this question. Individual studies performed since these meta-analyses have continued to suggest that smaller STG volumes are associated with more severe voice-hearing,[365] and have also further advanced our knowledge. First, they have clarified what is driving this volume change. The volume of any part of your cortex is determined by how thick it is and the size of its surface area. It is reduced cortical thickness of the STG that appears to be associated with more severe voice-hearing.[366] This is interesting as there is a notable genetic effect on the thickness of the STG,[367] suggesting this could form a basis of a genetic predisposition to voice-hearing. Second, these studies have continued to indicate that STG volumes are not different between people diagnosed with schizophrenia who do and do not hear voices, suggesting that other neural changes are required, in addition to STG reductions, for voice-hearing to emerge.[368]

Structural changes to parts of the brain involved in reality monitoring may be one candidate for this. A part of the brain called insula plays a role in reality monitoring, helping us decide whether we imagined something or actually perceived it.[369] To find this structure you need to put your hands down into the sulcus between the frontal and temporal lobes, pull them apart, and peer in. Meta-analysis has found that having a smaller insula in the left hemisphere is also associated with more severe voice-hearing.[370]

Structural differences in another part of the brain, the paracingulate sulcus (PCS), have also been linked to both altered reality-monitoring abilities and hallucinations. You might think that all our brains have pretty much the same basic pieces.

The PCS is a bit different though. If Lego were to make a human brain, it would have to make a tricky decision about what to do about the PCS, because some of us have big ones, some of us have small ones, and some of us don't have one at all. Figure 23.1 (see Colour plate 3) shows the PCS in two different people; as you can see, one is notably longer than the other. The PCS is formed during the third trimester of pregnancy, when the cortical pasta sheets of the brain are being folded into shape. Variations in this structure may hence be influenced by genetic and/or pre-natal events. People in the general population with shorter PCS tend to be worse at reality-monitoring tasks.[371] Does this mean that people with a shorter PCS will also be more likely to hallucinate? It appears so. My colleagues and I recently found that the size of the PCS in people diagnosed with schizophrenia was related to the probability they had experienced hallucinations.[372] Having a 1cm-shorter PCS was associated with a 20 per cent increase in the odds that the person had experienced hallucinations. The BBC referred to the PCS as a 'brain wrinkle', leading to Star Trek's Mr Sulu to suggest that hallucinations could be treated by Botox.[373] That wasn't a sentence I ever expected to be writing when we were designing our study.

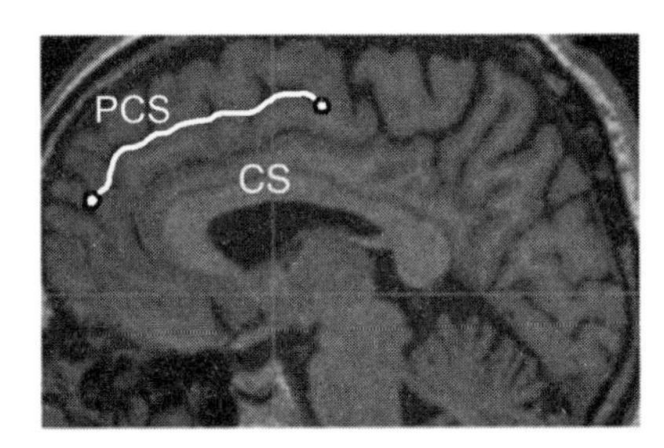

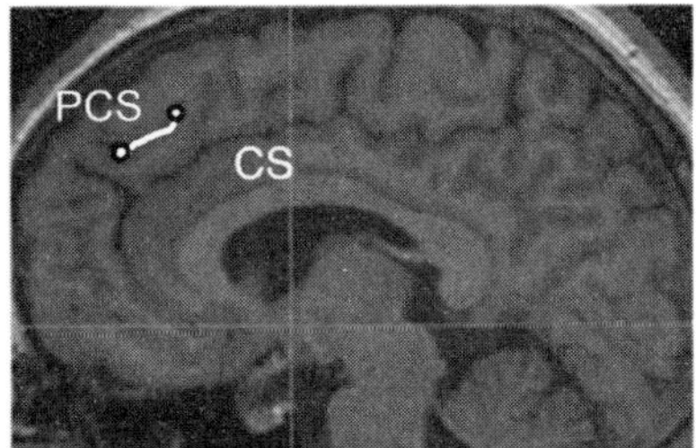

Note: PCS = paracingulate sulcus, CS = cingulate sulcus. The left-hand image shows an individual with a long PCS, whereas the individual in the right-hand image has a much shorter PCS.

Reprinted from Garrison, J. *et al.* (2015) 'Paracingulate sulcus morphology predicts hallucinations in schizophrenia.' *Nature Communications,* 17(6), 8956, licensed under a Creative Commons Attribution 4.0 International Licence.

Figure 23.1: Inter-person variation in paracingulate sulcus (PCS) length

Thus, there is some evidence that structural changes to parts of the brain involved in auditory perception and reality monitoring are associated with voice-hearing. However, structural differences do not necessarily translate into differences in function. The next question is whether or not there is any evidence that the STG functions differently in people who hear voices, and if such altered function can cause voice-hearing.

CHAPTER 24

Where Wilder's Things Roam

Before Celine and before Justin, the title of greatest living Canadian was held by a neuroscientist, Penfield Wilder. He had always been a bit of a whack-it-and-see type of chap. Back in his Oxford days, he reflected on how a fellow rugby player swore when he bumped into him. 'Next time,' he wrote in his diary, 'I'll bump him hard and see what is joggled out of him.'[374] A number of decades later Penfield and his colleague Phanor Perot were performing brain surgery on people with epilepsy. After removing parts of patients' scalps to expose the cortex below, Penfield was able to resurrect his youthful poking prowess and use a probe to electrically stimulate specific areas of the brain. As the patients were still awake,[375] they could report on the subjective experiences that this stimulation caused. After studying over 500 patients, Penfield and Perot found that it was only when one specific region of the cortex was stimulated that (some) patients reported having auditory hallucinations – the left STG.[376] When the primary auditory cortex (Heschl's gyrus) was stimulated, only clicks, bangs and whizzes were heard by patients, but when the electrode was slid into the secondary auditory cortex (Wernicke's area), voices emerged. Based on what we discussed about the brain's speech production/perception system in Chapter 22, this is what we would expect. These findings gave succour to Wernicke-inspired speech perception theories of voice-hearing.

Is it possible to explain voice-hearing as simply resulting from a naturally occurring form of Penfield's poking; that is, spontaneous neural activity in the left pSTG? This idea has its proponents. Michael Hunter and colleagues propose that spontaneous fluctuations in the STG may seed voice-hearing.[377] An fMRI study by this group found that when (non-voice hearing) individuals sat in silence there were periodic sharp increases in the electrical activity of the left pSTG, including the primary auditory cortex. Although such experiences did not result in voice-hearing, Hunter and colleagues argued that a greater magnitude of such fluctuations could be the acorns from which voice-hearing grows. They suggest that these spontaneous fluctuations could lead to people's expectations of hearing words being fulfilled, as the brain interprets these fluctuations as words it was expecting to hear.[378] This is called the expectation–perception model of voice-hearing. It echoes parts of the hypervigilance hallucination theory we saw earlier, and foreshadows the predictive coding framework we will examine later in Chapter 38.

If the left pSTG is involved in voice-hearing, then we might expect that tweaking its activity in people who hear voices should alter their experience of voice-hearing in some way. We can do this using transcranial magnetic stimulation (TMS). TMS involves what looks like a double-headed ping-pong bat being placed over a specific region of your scalp. When the bat is turned on, a rapidly changing magnetic field is created which penetrates just far enough into your brain to induce electric currents in your cortex. It is painless. The results are often incorrectly referred to as a virtual lesion. What actually happens is that TMS makes neurons fire, meaning that they can't do the jobs they would normally do for us. A juggling monkey can't scratch his ass. The longer-term effects of TMS are a reduction in the excitement of the cortical region targeted, as well as alterations in the strength of the connectivity between the targeted region and other areas of the brain it is connected to.

Targeting the left pSTG with TMS can reduce this area's excitability, providing a way to test the hypothesis that an overactive left pSTG contributes to voice-hearing. TMS for voice-hearing is normally applied slightly more posteriorly in the brain than where the left pSTG is, over an area covering the confluence of the left pSTG and the left parietal lobe (the temporoparietal junction or TPJ; see Chapter 32). Nevertheless, a few studies have targeted the left pSTG with TMS in voice-hearers. Good studies have employed a sham TMS condition too, to ensure that any effects found are not simply due to placebo effects. Sham TMS involves tilting the coil slightly away from the head, so people still hear the clicks and bangs of the procedure, and experience contractions of their scalp muscles, but don't get the proper targeted effect of TMS. The largest and most recent study to target the pSTG found that people diagnosed with schizophrenia who were given five daily sessions of 16 minutes of TMS over the left pSTG came to hear their voices less often than patients who were only given sham TMS.[379] Although the frequency of voices decreased, the number of different voices that were heard, the extent to which they caught the hearers' attention and altered their ongoing thought and behaviour, their loudness, reality and length of utterance, and the amount of distress caused, did not change. Furthermore, other studies have failed to find any beneficial effect on voices of TMS over the left pSTG. Such an approach is clearly not a voice panacea.

Another problem for an account in which spontaneous left pSTG activation is viewed as causing voice-hearing is that the voices summoned by artificially stimulating this region differ to those heard naturalistically by people diagnosed with schizophrenia. Penfield and Perot's stimulation led to patients hearing things such as 'my mother and father talking' and 'something like a crowd'. Anthony David has argued that these experiences are strikingly unlike the voices heard by people diagnosed with psychotic disorders.[380] Indeed, the voices Penfield and Perot summoned were more like remembrances of things heard in the past by the patient. As they noted, 'the patient usually recognizes it [the induced voices] spontaneously as coming from his past'. Similarly, voices occurring during naturalistic epileptic seizures in the temporal lobe also often have the flavour of verbal memories (Chapter 12). Although, as we have seen, some people diagnosed with psychosis report such voices, the majority of their voices seem more focused on, and interested in, ongoing events in people's lives, rather than being memory traces. This suggests that it may not be spontaneous epileptic-like activation in the pSTG that results in the voice-hearing of people who do not have epilepsy.

To sum up, there is evidence that activation of the left pSTG can cause voice-hearing, but whether it is the sort of voice-hearing that we have been talking about is unclear. There is also some evidence that toning down the excitability of the left pSTG can help diminish some people's voice-hearing. What we need to know next is whether the activity of this area of the brain actually increases when people naturalistically hear voices and, if so, given that spontaneous epileptic-like activity in this region seems not to be its source, where else in the brain this activity has come from. To do this we need to catch voices in the act.

CHAPTER 25

What is the Brain Doing When Someone is Hearing Voices?

Voices can run deep into the recesses of a person's mind, but they can't hide. In fMRI 'symptom-capture' studies of voice-hearing, a voice-hearer lies down in the scanner and either presses a button to indicate when they are hearing voices, or is scanned and afterwards reports whether they heard a voice or not. The researcher calculates the brain activity when the person was hearing voices, and then subtracts from this the brain activity when they were not hearing voices. This leaves them with a change in brain activity that is uniquely associated with the experience of hearing voices.

A 2011 meta-analysis of symptom-capture studies in people diagnosed with schizophrenia, led by Renaud Jardri, found three areas/networks of the brain to be activated when voices were being heard.[381] The first was the left hemisphere language network of the brain (we will come back to the rest in later chapters, as this first one will take us a while to run with). You can see this network in Figure 25.1 (see Colour plate 4).[382] This shows the areas of the brain that increased their activation in the left hemisphere of the brain when patients heard voices in the scanner. First, you can see that the left STG increases its activity when people hear voices. In particular, its posterior part, corresponding to Wernicke's area, is activated, extending into the MTG below it, suggesting the involvement of the superior temporal sulcus, which is consistent with the perception of speech. Left Broca's area is also seen activating, as is a region of the inferior parietal lobe near to where it joins the temporal lobe, a region not too dissimilar to area spt. These areas light up both when people diagnosed with schizophrenia hear voices and when non-clinical voice-hearers hear voices.[383] This is what you would expect given that the two groups are having similar experiences. Voice-hearing therefore involves activation across the left hemisphere speech production and perception network.

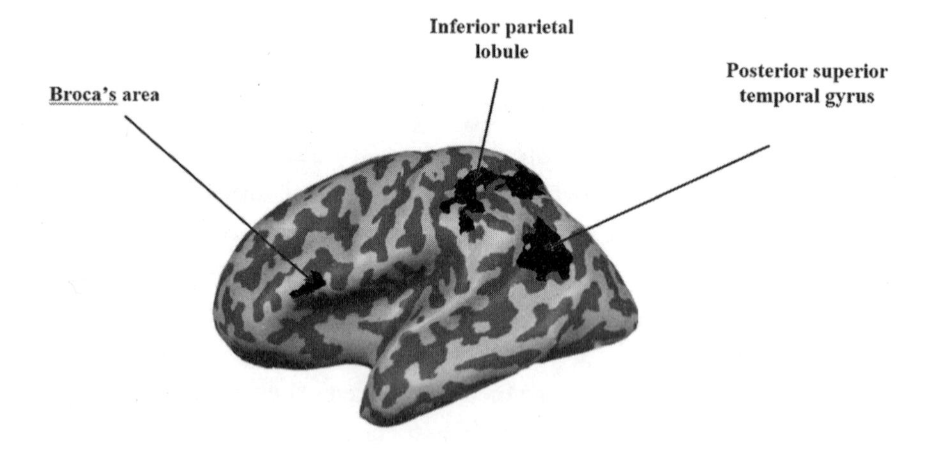

Data represents results of an fMRI analysis of voice-hearing in 20 adolescents with brief psychosis disorder.

Adapted from Jardri, R. *et al.* (2013) 'The neurodynamic organization of modality-dependent hallucinations.' *Cerebral Cortex,* 23(5), 1108–17, with permission.

Figure 25.1: Left hemisphere cortical activity associated with hearing voices

You may object that it is hard to separate cause from effect here. Were these areas activated before the person heard voices, and hence caused the voices, or were they activated after the voices, and hence were an effect of the voices? Although there are few studies of this question, there is evidence that activity in the left pSTG and Broca's area occurs *before* the person experiences the voices, increasing our confidence that they are causes, not effects, of voice-hearing.[384]

We can also learn something from the cortical dogs who don't bark when people hear voices. First, the left primary auditory cortex wasn't found to be activating during voice-hearing in this meta-analysis. Jardri and colleagues later found that although the cortex of the left pSTG of patients who heard voices was thinner than healthy non-voice-hearers, it was not thinner in the specific part of the STG that includes the primary auditory cortex. On the basis of this, they suggested that when individual studies have occasionally found primary auditory cortex activation during voice-hearing,[385] this has been due to the back propagation of activity from the pSTG. This allows that primary auditory cortex activation may influence factors such as how vivid voices are, but that its activation may not be necessary for the experience of voice-hearing. Variation in primary cortex activation during voice-hearing may explain the sensorial continuum voice-hearing lies on, running from hearing clear voices through to more thought-like experiences and soundless voices. It may also impact the perceived reality of the voices that are heard. During voice-hearing, the perceived reality of voices is related to the strength of connectivity between the left Broca's area and left primary auditory cortex.[386] The back propagation model suggests that within the wider class of auditory hallucinations, voice-hearing may be the primary form of experience. Non-verbal auditory hallucinations could be seen as mere overspill of left pSTG activation into the primary auditory cortex, resulting in more perceptually vivid voices along with a click–bang–whizz commotion.

It is notable that areas in the left hemisphere that light up during voice-hearing are similar to those that activate when people talk to themselves silently in their heads (inner speech). Yet inner speech is also associated with activation of the supplemental motor area (SMA), a strip of cortex approximately in the middle of the top of your head. We don't see the SMA increasing its activation when people hallucinate voices. This is the second cortical dog that isn't barking during voice-hearing. So, what is a lack of SMA activation, or damage to this area, associated with? SMA damage is found in alien limb syndrome, where your arm makes movements, such as reaching out and grabbing things, but you don't feel as if you caused it to do it.[387] We can start to imagine how an inner speech version of Dr Strangelove's arm could result in voice-hearing.[388] Inner speech without SMA activation could give you the experience of hearing speech but without the feeling you caused it. It would be understandable if the brain then labelled this as being the experience of hearing someone else's voice.

Alternatively, it may not be a lack of SMA activation during inner speech that leads to voice-hearing, but rather a different *timing* of activation. David Linden and colleagues used fMRI to compare the activity in the brain of people when they were hearing voices to the activity in the brains of the same people when they were simply imagining other people talking to them.[389] When imagining other people speaking, voice-hearers' brains first activated in the SMA and then, after a short delay, activity began in Broca's area and Wernicke's area. When the same people were hearing voices, the SMA, Broca's area and Wernicke's area all activated at roughly the same time. Linden and colleagues suggested that normally we gain the experience of producing speech through a planning stage involving the SMA, but that if this doesn't happen, then voice-hearing can result.

Ever since the first symptom-capture study peeped into the brain of someone hearing voices, and found left Broca's area to be activated during the experience, this has been used as prima facie evidence of an involvement of inner speech.[390] A spoke was recently thrown in the wheel of this interpretation by a study that found left Broca's area was only activated during *planned* inner speech (i.e., when you plan to say something to yourself in your head, such as something an experimenter has told you to do), and not when you spontaneously undertake inner speech. In this study, Russell Hurlburt and colleagues examined brain activity both during inner speech that people were told to do and during inner speech that people undertook spontaneously.[391] Planned inner speech led to activation in line with previous studies: left Broca's area increased its activation and there was no change in the activity of primary auditory cortex. However, when participants spontaneously undertook inner speech, left Broca's area didn't increase its activation, but the primary auditory cortex (Heschl's gyrus) did. Spontaneous inner speech seems to be more like what Hurlburt and colleagues have termed 'inner hearing', than 'inner speech', and inner hearing seems much closer to voice-hearing than inner speech is. The implications of this intriguing study for models of voice-hearing are yet to be worked out. We will come back to inner speech models of voice-hearing in Chapter 26.

Another way to think about the separable contributions of the left hemisphere language network to voice-hearing was recently provided by Kühn and Gallinat. They considered how Broca's area and the left STG might cause voices, and suggested they were both involved in subtly different ways. Changes to the pSTG may confer vulnerability to voice-hearing, with activation of Broca's area creating the experience itself. In essence, the STG digs a hole, and Broca pushes you in. Kühn and Gallinat examined the neural differences between someone when they were and were not hearing voices (state differences in voice-hearing), and also the neural differences between voice-hearers and non-voice-hearers during tasks such as imagining words being spoken (trait differences in voice-hearing).[392] In a meta-analytic review they found evidence that trait differences in voice-hearing involved the left STG (including primary auditory cortex), whereas state differences involved Broca's area bilaterally (i.e., in both the left and right hemispheres). They concluded that the momentary experience of hearing voices was associated with activation in brain areas related to speech production (i.e., Broca's area), coinciding with a more permanent alteration in activity of the temporal lobe.

In summary, when people experience voice-hearing there are increases in activation across a network of grey matter structures that form the left hemisphere language network, and yet an absence of increased activation in a region known to be associated with the feeling of having caused something. Let's next look at the white matter tracts that act as the wiring within this left hemisphere language network, to see if this may contribute to the development of the voice-hearing experience.

CHAPTER 26

White Matter Changes in the Voice-Hearing Brain

The total length of the wiring in one human brain is over 100,000km, which means, should you be sufficiently dextrous and motivated, you could use your brain to lasso two earth-size planets.[393] To put it another way, the total length of the white matter in the heads of the seven billion of us on this planet is over 100 light years. Our brain has a literally astronomical amount of wiring. This is one of many reasons why you should never let a cat play with your brain.

Some white matter diseases are associated with voice-hearing, others are not. Both give clues as to what white matter changes may contribute to voice-hearing. Metachromatic leukodystrophy is a rare white matter disease most commonly caused by a mutation in the arylsulfatase A gene.[394] This mainly results in damage to the myelin in the frontal and temporal lobes of the brain. Up to half of people with metachromatic leukodystrophy with adolescent or early adult onset will experience voice-hearing.[395] This is a *dys*myelination disease; it involves problems with the normal formation of myelin. Other white matter diseases are *de*myelination diseases. In these, white matter develops normally, but becomes damaged later in life. Multiple sclerosis (MS) is probably the best known example of a demyelination disease, with its average age of onset being around 30 years of age. Although MS patients can report voice-hearing, it is much rarer than in people with dysmyelination diseases. This suggests we should look for the causes of (at least some) voice-hearing in early adulthood changes to myelin in the fronto-temporal regions of the brain.

We can examine the structural integrity of white matter wiring in the living brain with a neuroimaging technique called diffusion tensor imaging (DTI). This examines the direction of movement of water in the brain. Imagine you have a series of long wires all parallel to each other running down a slope. If you poured water both over and through these wires, then the water would pretty much all flow in the same direction, parallel to the wires. In the jargon of DTI, such water flow would be said to have high fractional anisotropy (FA) and would suggest high structural integrity of the wires. If, however, a cat got hold of the wires, made a right tangle of them and punctured them with its claws, then when you poured water over and through them again, the water would go sideways here, back again there, in a zigzagging path, as well as spurting out through the holes. Such water flow would be deemed to have low FA, suggesting both structural problems with the wires and that you should have got a dog.

DTI has primarily been used in studies of voice-hearing to examine the fronto-temporal white matter tracts in the left hemisphere that link Broca's and Wernicke's areas. Imagine you are sitting in Wernicke's area and you want to head up to Broca's area. You can take the high road or you can take the low road. The high road is called the dorsal language pathway. To remember what dorsal means, think of a dorsal fin poking out the top of a dolphin – it means 'upper'. The dorsal language pathway connects Broca's area to the pSTG (part of Wernicke's area), via the parietal lobe, through a white matter tract called the arcuate fasciculus (r-q-ate fass-ick-u-luss; it's a neuroscience shibboleth). Figure 26.1 shows this tract from one of our studies (see Colour plate 5).

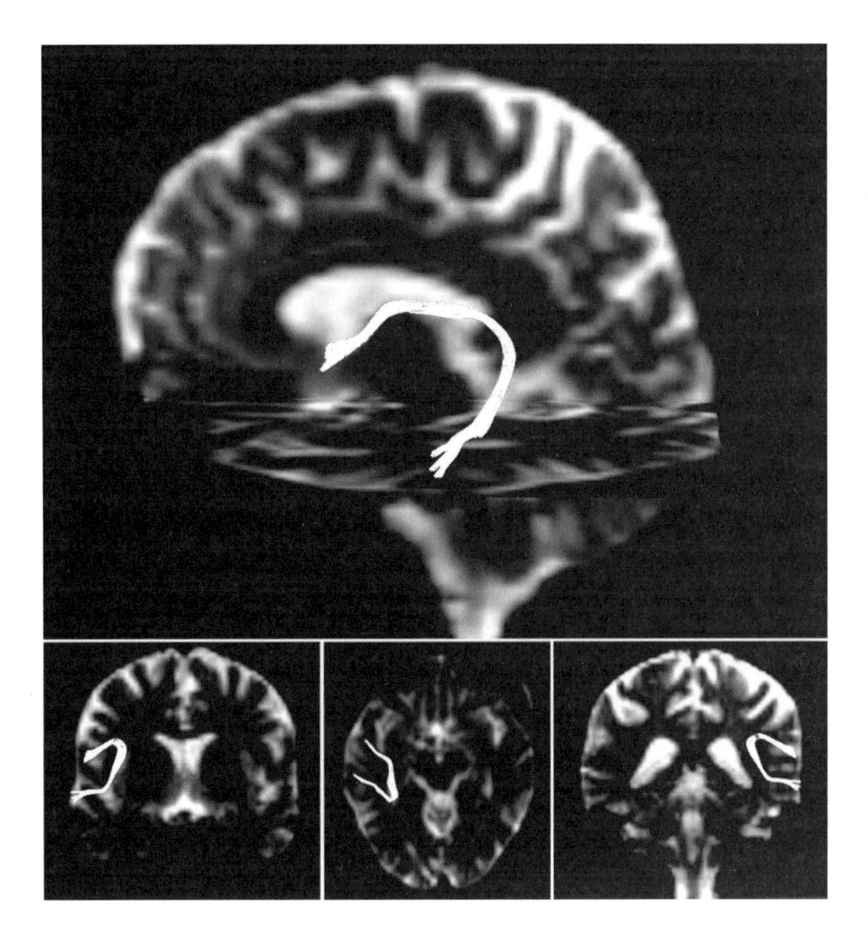

Note: Top = side view (front of brain on left side). Bottom left = view from behind head. Bottom middle = view from above head looking down. Bottom right = view from in front of head.

Unpublished image created by Lena Oestreich from data published in McCarthy-Jones, S. *et al.* (2015) 'Reduced integrity of the left arcuate fasciculus is specifically associated with auditory verbal hallucinations in schizophrenia.' *Schizophrenia Research,* 162(1–3), 1–6.

Figure 26.1: The left hemisphere arcuate fasciculus

We saw earlier that the only area of the cortex that, when stimulated, created voice-hearing was the STG. When we delve into the wiring of the brain, it emerges that Penfieldian poking of the arcuate fasciculus in the left hemisphere can also cause voice-hearing. In a 2016 study, researchers electrically stimulated the frontal part of the left arcuate in three people with epilepsy, who were awake, to see what they would experience.[396] As the stimulation began, the first participant started hearing a voice speaking. Although the participant was not Italian, she described the voice as speaking English with an Italian accent, like something out of *The Godfather.* As the intensity of the electrical stimulation was increased, she stopped hearing the voice and instead felt an urge to say the same phrase the voice had been saying. The second participant reported that 'I feel like I am talking to myself in my head even though I was not… It is like hearing myself, but not saying anything… It is kind of like I am hearing something I am saying, but I am not really.' When the third participant was stimulated she said, 'That was really weird. I just said "ah ha", and I did not say it.' As the power of the stimulation increased, she described the experience as: 'It is like I'm talking out loud but there is nothing coming out…it is weird…my mouth isn't opening, is it? I feel like I'm yelling.' Another time she exclaimed, 'I just said lights… I had no control over it. I said "lights" without intending to, it just came out.' Such findings encourage us to look further at a potential involvement of the left arcuate fasciculus in voice-hearing.

A 2014 meta-analysis found that people diagnosed with schizophrenia who heard voices had lower average FA (suggesting reduced structural integrity) in their left arcuate fasciculus, compared with healthy people.[397] A problem in interpreting this finding as indicating that this change is due to voice-hearing is that many things will differ between these two groups of people that might account for the difference found, not just voice-hearing. The two main differences are likely to be antipsychotic drug usage, delusions and substance abuse. The three main differences are likely to be antipsychotic drug usage, delusions, substance abuse and depression. The four main... You get the idea. There are many differences between people with and without schizophrenia diagnoses, in addition to voice-hearing, that could be *la razón de la materia blanca cambia este análisis encontrado* (no one expects the Spanish exposition).

To try and assess if reduced left arcuate fasciculus integrity is specifically associated with voice-hearing, my colleagues and I undertook a more detailed study.[398] We compared two groups of people diagnosed with schizophrenia who were highly similar in most ways (e.g., age, gender, depression, delusions, duration of illness, antipsychotic usage, substance abuse and IQ), except that one group had experienced voice-hearing and the other had not. We found reduced FA of the left arcuate (we're on first name terms with this tract by now) in the voice-hearing group. We also found a suggestion that the nature of this change involved damage to the myelin of the arcuate. DTI can generate other measures in addition to FA, including radial and axial diffusivity. These measures are thought to tell us something specific about the biological nature of the change to the white matter we are investigating. If you demyelinate axons in mice, but don't damage the underlying axon, radial diffusivity goes up, but axial diffusivity remains the same. Conversely, if you damage the axons of mice, but leave the myelin sheath around it unscathed, radial diffusivity is unchanged, but axial diffusivity drops.[399] If you damage neither the axons nor the myelin of mice then neither axial nor radial diffusivity is changed, and you can enjoy Disney films with a clear conscience. In our study, the voice-hearing group had higher radial (but no different axial) diffusivity compared with all other groups. This suggested voice-hearing could be associated with reduced myelination of the axons in the left arcuate, although post-mortem study would be needed to confirm this.

Lest you should think that such talk necessarily points to a genetically determined neurodevelopmental problem, it is quite possible that what we are seeing is the result of childhood adversity. A 2009 study reported that healthy young adults who had suffered verbal abuse as children had lower structural integrity in their left arcuate than those who had not suffered such abuse.[400] More recently, a 2015 study found that the more adverse childhood experiences people diagnosed with schizophrenia had experienced, the lower was the structural integrity in a raft of white matter tracts in their brain, including a tract called the superior longitudinal fasciculus, of which the arcuate is a part.[401] Alterations to the left arcuate therefore offer us what we were searching for in Chapter 19, a plausible biological mechanism through which child abuse may cause voice-hearing.

Before we get carried away by this story, we need to consider some objections. First, studies do not find that every patient who hears voices has reduced FA in their left arcuate; there is simply a lower average FA between the voice-hearing and non-voice-hearing groups. This means that reduced arcuate integrity is likely to be neither sufficient nor necessary for voice-hearing to occur. Second, most DTI studies have examined voice-hearing in people diagnosed with schizophrenia, a group which has a lot of other things going on, and it is hard to be absolutely sure that any changes you find relate to voices specifically. Our fears here can be assuaged somewhat, as FA reductions in the left arcuate have also been found in people diagnosed with schizophrenia who have never taken antipsychotics.[402]

One further way to dodge such potential confounds is to use DTI to explore what is happening in the white matter of non-clinical voice-hearers (Chapter 13). A study which did this compared the integrity of the arcuate between: 1) people diagnosed with schizophrenia who heard voices; 2) people with no psychiatric diagnosis who nevertheless heard voices (non-clinical voice-hearers); and 3) people with no psychiatric diagnosis who did not hear voices ('healthy controls').[403] It found that while people diagnosed with schizophrenia who heard voices had reduced FA in the left arcuate compared with healthy controls, there was no difference between the voice-hearing people diagnosed with schizophrenia and the non-clinical voice-hearers. However, this study also used another measure called magnetization transfer ratio (MTR). This measure was increased in the arcuate of both people diagnosed with schizophrenia who heard voices and non-clinical voice-hearers, compared with healthy controls. Although the authors were unsure how to interpret the biological meaning of this finding, they were clear that increased MTR values indicated some form of reduction in structural integrity of the arcuate, be it to the axon or the myelin, and that this was specifically associated with hearing voices. Thus, the best evidence continues to point to some role for changes in the left arcuate in voice-hearing.

Let's now turn to the low road from Wernicke's area to Broca's area: the ventral language pathway, a road less travelled by voice-hearing researchers. The most notable ventral language pathway is part of a much longer tract called the inferior occipital frontal fasciculus (IOFF), which spans the length of the brain, starting in the bottom of the frontal cortex and running all the way back to the occipital cortex at the rear of the brain. You can see what this looks like in Figure 26.2 (see Colour plate 6), taken from one of our studies.

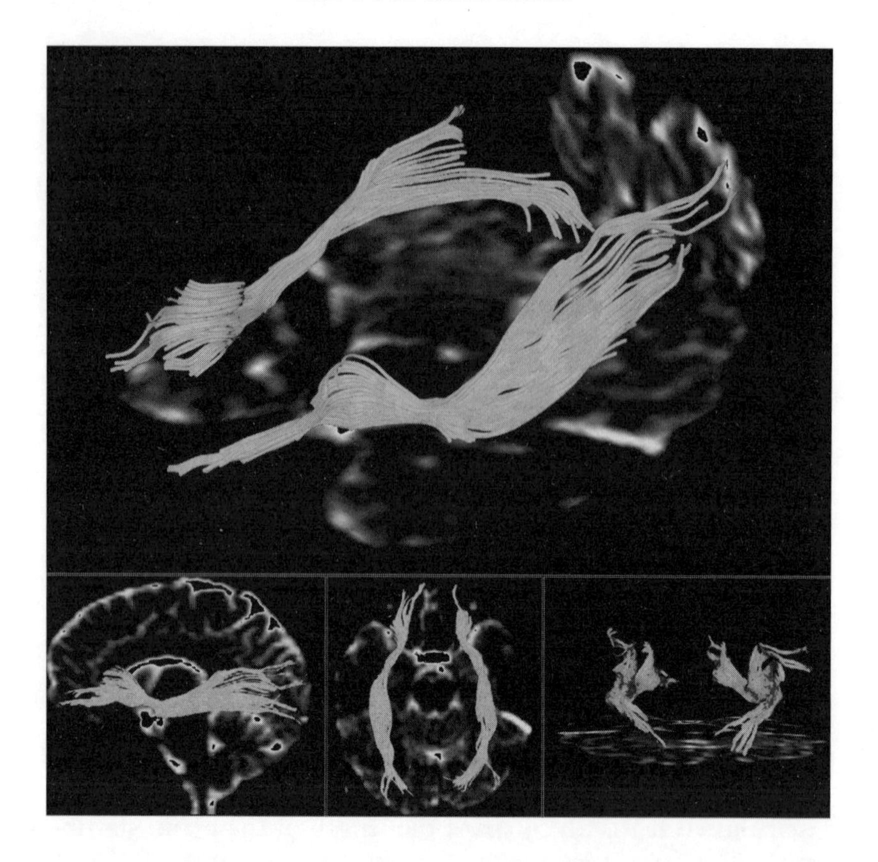

Sources: Oestreich, L.K.L. and McCarthy-Jones, S. (2016) 'Decreased integrity of the fronto-temporal fibers of the left inferior occipito-frontal fasciculus associated with auditory verbal hallucinations in schizophrenia.' *Brain Imaging and Behavior*, 10(2), 445–54; Whitford, T.J. (2015) Australian Schizophrenia Research Bank, © Springer Science+Business Media, New York. Reproduced with permission of Springer.

Figure 26.2: The left and right inferior occipito-frontal fasciculi (IOFF), extracted using diffusion tensor tractography

A study of the left hemisphere IOFF by Branislava Ćurčić-Blake and colleagues found reduced structural integrity in the frontal part of this tract to be associated with hearing voices in people diagnosed with schizophrenia.[404] My colleagues and I also recently looked at this tract, splitting the left hemisphere IOFF up into four parts. As shown in Figure 26.3 (see Colour plate 7), we divided it up into a frontal section (red), a fronto-temporal section (yellow), a temporal section (green) and an occipital section (blue). We found that the only part of the left IOFF where reduced integrity was associated with voice-hearing was the fronto-temporal section – that is, the key part of the connection between Broca and Wernicke's areas.[405] Again, such changes could be due to a number of reasons, although it is notable that the more adverse childhood experience people diagnosed with schizophrenia have suffered, the lower the structural integrity of their IOFF tends to be.[406]

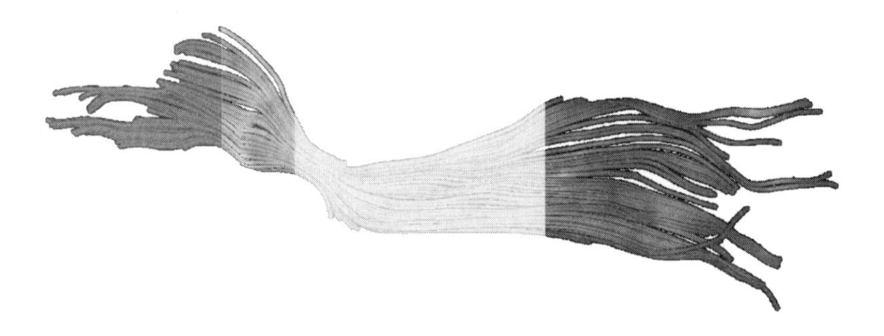

Sources: Oestreich, L.K.L. and McCarthy-Jones, S. (2016) 'Decreased integrity of the fronto-temporal fibers of the left inferior occipito-frontal fasciculus associated with auditory verbal hallucinations in schizophrenia.' *Brain Imaging and Behavior,* 10(2), 445–54; Whitford, T.J. (2015) Australian Schizophrenia Research Bank, © Springer Science+Business Media, New York. Reproduced with permission of Springer.

Figure 26.3: The four sub-regions of the inferior occipito-frontal fasciculus – from left to right: frontal, fronto-temporal, temporal and occipital

Other methodologies have also provided evidence that altered fronto-temporal connectivity is associated with voice-hearing. Transcranial direct current stimulation (tDCS) involves passing a weak electrical current through your brain. This isn't like electroconvulsive therapy. There are no seizures and the most you feel is a weak tingling. I've had tDCS done on me, and all I felt was a slight warmth and itching (keep your STD jokes to yourself, please). The procedure involves two electrodes being placed on your head: an anode (cortical activity under this electrode will increase) and a cathode (activity of the cortex under this will decrease). tDCS doesn't only alter activity in the cortex below the electrode sites of the brain, it changes the connectivity between the two parts of the cortex targeted. The first tDCS study trying to help people who hear voices placed the cathode over part of the left temporal lobe (specifically the left temporoparietal junction: TPJ) and the anode over part of the left prefrontal cortex, and applied tDCS for 20 minutes twice a day for five days. It also used sham tDCS with other patients, as a control group.[407] At the end of treatment, patients who had received the real tDCS experienced a 31 per cent reduction in the severity of their voices (a combined measure of frequency, loudness and salience), which compared with only an 8 per cent reduction in the group who had received a sham treatment. Was this improvement in voice-hearing due to fronto-temporal connectivity changes resulting from the tDCS though?

This question was addressed by a 2015 study that used the same approach.[408] It first replicated the finding that tDCS applied over the left TPJ and left prefrontal cortex reduced the severity of voice-hearing. It also measured how tDCS altered the connectivity between different parts of the brain and how this related to the improvements in patients' voices. The study found that tDCS altered the connectivity of the left TPJ with a range of areas across the prefrontal cortex; however, it was only the decrease in connectivity between the left TPJ and the left anterior insula following tDCS that correlated with the extent to which voices improved. The authors argued that the role of the insula in reality monitoring was the reason why altered connectivity between the left TPJ and insula improved people's voices.

To sum up, there is reasonable evidence that altered connectivity between frontal and temporal regions of the brain may contribute to voice-hearing. The next question is why such changes could lead to voice-hearing. Damage to the IOFF can cause verbal preservation (the repetition of words).[409] This is notable given how repetitive voices tend to be. IOFF changes may be responsible for this specific property of voices. In contrast, changes to the left arcuate may be responsible, at least at a neural level, for the emergence of the voices themselves. But how?

CHAPTER 27

Who May I Say is Calling?

There are many good reasons why soldiers don't advance on enemy lines at night carrying boom boxes belting out their favourite tunes. These include difficulties in finding universally liked tunes, no one wanting to advance behind twerking comrades, and the not universally lamented post-1990 decline of the boom box itself. Most importantly, the benefits of a boom-box-based advance, such as drawing your commanding officer's attention to your bravery, are likely to be more than outweighed by you not being able to hear the enemy sneaking up on you. If you are a cricket though, you have a built-in boom box. Imagine what it must be like to be the creature from which this ear-ringing racket emanates.[410] Deafening yourself to all other noises around you, such as the advancing sounds of hungry badgers, *I'm a Celebrity... Get Me Out of Here!* contestants and angry Pharaohs (or whatever enemies crickets have), doesn't seem like a great survival strategy. But evolution has come up with a cunning plan.

The part of the cricket's brain that creates the wing movements from which its chirping emanates simultaneously sends a signal to the cricket's auditory perception areas. This is exactly timed to dampen down the responsiveness of the cricket's auditory cortex to the noise it is exposed to as a result of its chirps, but to still allow it to hear the sounds of other things around it. This dampening signal is called a corollary discharge. We make use of these too. One of their functions is to help our brain figure out whether auditory verbal information it encounters is coming from the voice of someone else out there in the world, or whether it was internally generated and resulted from us talking to ourselves in our head. When we speak, motor regions in our frontal cortex use a corollary discharge signal to give our auditory processing regions in the temporal lobe (e.g., the pSTG) a heads-up that the sound it is about to process comes from us, dampening down their activity. This system also functions when we talk to ourselves silently in our heads, in what is termed inner speech.

Inner speech is one of those experiences whose ubiquity can only be appreciated when it is no longer there. For example, after a left hemisphere stroke caused her to lose her inner speech for a number of weeks, Jill Bolte Taylor described 'the dramatic silence that had taken residency inside my head'.[411] Now, consider what would happen if you produced inner speech, speaking silently to yourself in your head, but the corollary discharge signal from your frontal lobes didn't get to your pSTG. Your brain wouldn't be told that the speech it was processing was its own production, and instead it would be treated as an external signal – a spoken voice. One theory proposes that this is what happens when people hear voices. It doesn't claim that the corollary discharge signal fails to reach the pSTG though, but rather that it gets delayed along the way, meaning it doesn't get to the pSTG in time.[412]

This argument hasn't yet been fully tested in relation to voice-hearing, but it has been found that when people diagnosed with schizophrenia press a button to create a self-produced sound, their STG shows a greater response to this sound (i.e., it is less effectively dampened) than when healthy people do the same task.[413] Now, let's say that this problem occurs because the corollary discharge signal in people diagnosed with schizophrenia is delayed for 50ms. What would happen if such a person pressed the button to produce the sound and the experimenter introduced a 50ms delay before a sound was actually produced? In theory this means the sound from the button would be 50ms late reaching their temporal lobe, but the patient's corollary discharge would also be 50ms late, meaning they would actually both arrive at the same time, just as in healthy people. When this elegant experiment was done, the introduction of a 50ms delay meant that the temporal lobe of people diagnosed with schizophrenia behaved in the same way as when healthy people did the task without the delay – that is, a dampening of the response to the sound was seen.

The question then becomes, what could cause a 50ms delay to occur in the brains of people diagnosed with schizophrenia? You will recall that the purpose of myelin surrounding axons is to make signalling in the brain occur rapidly. If the myelin surrounding the tract linking frontal motor regions to the pSTG was damaged, then signals would travel slower along this pathway. As these signals appear likely to pass down the left arcuate, this ties nicely into our finding from the last chapter that voice-hearing may be associated with reduced myelination of the left arcuate. However, if this theory were true, you would expect that all inner speech in people who heard voices would be experienced as a heard voice. This isn't the case. A study by my colleagues and I found that people who hear voices have inner speech pretty much just like everyone else.[414]

Another challenge to the corollary discharge account comes from a study by Ćurčić-Blake and colleagues that used fMRI to get an idea of how well signals were able to pass between Broca and Wernicke's areas. A technique called dynamic causal modelling allowed them to see whether any change in connectivity along this pathway in voice-hearers was due to alterations in signals going from left Broca's area to left Wernicke's area, or vice versa. Whereas the corollary discharge model assumes that alterations to structural connectivity affect the ability of left Broca's area to send signals to dampen activity in left Wernicke's area, Ćurčić-Blake and colleagues found changes in the *opposite* direction. They suggested that the weaker connectivity from Wernicke's area to Broca's area in patients who heard voices may allow frontal regions to be less constrained by the input they receive from Wernicke's area, and freer to liberally interpret this input as being whatever it expected it to be. We will come back to this idea when we discuss predictive coding in Chapter 38.

We have been moving towards the idea that altered connectivity between Broca and Wernicke's areas may cause a change in the way we experience our own inner speech, leading to voice-hearing. However, if we really want to see if inner speech is involved in voice-hearing, we need to leave neuroimaging behind us temporarily to consult other sources of evidence.

CHAPTER 28

Take into the Air My Quiet Breath[415]

For hundreds of years, people have suggested that voice-hearing results from talking to yourself in your head, but not recognizing that this is what is happening. In the 1500s the Spanish mystic St John of the Cross railed against people who claimed to hear God as, in his view, they were actually just 'saying these things to themselves'.[416] In the 1800s, the French psychologist Eggers argued voices were simply inner speech asserting itself with greater insistence than normal. One way to test these ideas is to take advantage of the fact that when we undertake inner speech, whether through silently reading, imagining others speaking, or mentally going back over the witty retorts we should have just made, a small but detectable amount of activity occurs in our speech musculature. This can be measured by placing electrodes on the throat and lips, in a process called electromyography (EMG).

Evidence for EMG activity accompanying voice-hearing is mixed, and has tended to come from older studies. However, a 2013 EMG study, the first of its kind for over two decades, studied 11 French people diagnosed with schizophrenia who heard voices that said the usual complimentary things, such as 'Tu es stupide' (although at least the voice had the manners to use the familiar form of address).[417] Activity in patients' lips, but not their arm muscles, accompanied voice-hearing, suggesting it was specifically lip movements and not a general muscular tension that accompanied voices.

If speech musculature is active during voice-hearing then you might wonder if attaching a sensitive microphone to the throat of someone while they are hearing voices could make this most private of experiences public, allowing the voice to speak directly out of the person. Louis Gould tried this in 1949 with a woman whose voices had begun soon after her husband's death. The woman's subvocal speech was about twice as quick as her ordinary voice, had a male quality to it, and had content which closely matched her voices. For example, when the amplified subvocal speech was heard to say, 'I don't think this is fair, do you?… On the level…something else,' the woman reported her voice as saying, 'I don't think this is fair. Isn't she on the level with you or something else?'

This finding was successfully replicated three decades later by Green and Preston.[418] Their study examined a 51-year-old man diagnosed with schizophrenia, referred to as R.W. (let's call him Rigsby), who heard a female voice that claimed her name was 'Miss Jones'. When Rigsby heard this voice, simultaneously and unbeknownst to him he made quiet, unintelligible whisperings. When a throat microphone was attached to his larynx a voice could be heard saying, 'You shouldn't speak to him' and 'It's me. We're on tape.' Miss Jones claimed Rigsby was her boyfriend, but also claimed to have another boyfriend (ooh Miss Jones!). When Rigsby addressed Miss Jones aloud saying 'Where's your other boyfriend?' the amplified whisper said, 'He's here with you,' and Rigsby reported that his voice had just said, 'He's here with me.' More generally, the whispers tended to refer to Rigsby as 'he', commented on his actions, gave him instructions, used vulgar phrases that Rigsby did not typically employ, and interrupted him while he was saying something else.

So it appears that at least in a subset of cases, no one knows what percentage, people are producing the speech that forms the basis of their voices. Technological advances, such as a subvocal speech recognition system recently developed by NASA,[419] may facilitate future tests of this theory. NASA's interest in this area stemmed from wanting to allow astronauts to be able to control machinery, such as the Mars Rover, using only their inner speech: 'turn left', 'stop', 'stay on target'. Their technology has now advanced to the point that sensors attached to your throat can allow your inner speech to appear in front of you on a computer screen as you think it. Could people's voices soon be read off a screen? The more one thinks about this, the more intriguing the implications of an ability for voices to speak to the world become. Could a voice, which could now reach out into the world to communicate its presence, be said to be a person in any sense? We speculated in Chapter 8 that some voices would likely pass the Turing test. This new technology would now allow us to test this idea.

Returning to immediate reality, other tests of the inner speech hypothesis are also possible. If your voices are based in your own inner speech, then impairing your ability to perform inner speech should temporarily stop the voices. Bick and Kinsbourne[420] tested this by asking people who heard voices to open their mouths wide for a minute, a task thought to disrupt the ability to perform inner speech. Try it for yourself (in private, please). The majority of participants found their voices spoke less often while they were doing this. Performing a control task, such as fist clenching, didn't affect the voices' frequency. A later study failed to replicate this, but did find that people's voices spoke less when they were humming.[421] As humming activates both Broca's area and the STG, it is unclear if this has its effects by blocking inner speech production or by commandeering speech perception regions of the brain. Another tactic is to stop messing around with tasks thought to impair the ability of people to produce inner speech and simply use neurostimulation to directly knock out left Broca's area temporarily. This has been done using transcranial magnetic stimulation over left Broca's area. It was not found to reduce people's voices in the days after stimulation, although (frustratingly) it was not reported whether people were less likely to hear voices during the stimulation itself.[422]

Even if we accept that self-produced inner speech is involved in some voice-hearing, this idea still faces the challenge of how we get from speaking in our own first person voice in our head to the voice of another person talking to us. When we look more closely at what inner speech is, we start to see that we may be asking the wrong question.

CHAPTER 29

Meet You in Malkovich

Our heads are clown cars. 'You' are in there, but so are a lot of other people, and at any second they may all start pouring out. Such a claim sits uncomfortably with the intuition that our skull is a car with us as the lone driver inside, chatting away to ourselves. If we view inner speech in this way, then the inner speech theory of voice-hearing faces the problem of trying to explain how we get from our own voice in our head to hearing the voice of someone else. It would appear that we would need to invoke some form of mysterious transformation. This problem starts to melt away when we look more closely at what inner speech is like and consider the clown car nature of consciousness.

It makes sense that we can talk to imaginary versions of people from our social world 'offline' in our head. This 'social-assessment' function of inner speech[423] allows us to fine tune our future interactions with people by simulating what they might say or do in a given situation.[424] It seems plausible that such inner speech, based on taking the voice and perspective of other people on ourselves, could form the basis of voice-hearing. Experiences of shame appear particularly likely to be able to summon these others in our head into action. All this fits with the self-produced speech of others coming out of voice-hearers we saw in the last chapter. That inner speech often takes this 'dialogic' form involving us and an 'other' appears to be a result of the way it develops.

Charles Fernyhough has argued that children develop inner speech from external speech in stages.[425] First, they engage in out loud, social speech. A child and parent might talk together when trying to solve a jigsaw puzzle together ('Where do you think that piece goes?'; 'I don't know, but it must go with the rest of the blue pieces'; 'Well, according to the picture they're all up on the left', etc.). The next stage is private speech, where children conduct these same dialogues out loud, by themselves. This speech is not aimed at communicating with others, but is just to help them think. Private speech eventually dies out in children, but it does not vanish entirely. It simply goes underground and becomes inner speech. As speech starts in the form of a dialogue we should expect that our inner speech will inherit this form. Indeed, Socrates defined thought as 'the talk which the soul has with itself… [The soul] when it thinks, is merely conversing with itself, asking itself questions and answering.'[426] We can see this in the writings of Richard Feynman, who says, 'I argue with myself. I have two voices that work back and forth.' He gives the example of saying to himself: "The integral will be larger than this sum of the terms, so that would make the pressure higher, you see?" "No, you're crazy." "No, I'm not! No, I'm not!" I say.'[427] Going beyond specific people, little is known about what sort of archetypal people we talk to in our inner world, and what they say back. One study suggested a typology which involved five main types of interlocutor: Faithful Friend, Ambivalent Parent, Proud Rival, Helpless Child and Calm Optimist.[428] If you think these sound more like a range of badly marketed scented candles than a reliable and rigorous classification of inner speech, I would have some sympathy with you. But it is a start, and there is little that is reliably known about this area yet.

Another commonality between inner speech and voice-hearing is that both often involve the regulation of behaviour. Lev Vygotsky argued that developing inner speech helps children to control their actions. Although we cannot (yet) directly observe the inner speech of others, the private speech of children is observable. Studies of this have found children often use such silent speech to tell themselves what to do, taking the roles of questioner, adviser and director in controlling their activity. As Vygotsky put it, children come to be able to control their behaviour from the outside.[429] If we have a track of silent self-instruction developmentally seared into our brain, should we be surprised that when voices come they run on these rails?

Despite these commonalities, we are still left with the feeling that voices are still different from inner speech in important ways other than the obvious. Although inner speech helps us cajole ourselves into doing things, the urgings of voices seem to have a more compelling feel. Could voice-hearing be a distinct or, and God forgive me for using this phrase, pimped-up version of inner speech that we evolved in order to give ourselves compelling instructions in extreme situations, as it was found to have greater imperative weight? For example, Oliver Sacks describes dragging himself home along a mountain path after dislocating his knee in a fall.[430] He stopped due to exhaustion and thought to himself in his normal inner speech 'why not a little rest – a nap maybe'. This was then answered by what he describes as a strong, clear and commanding voice that said, 'You can't rest here – you can't rest anywhere. You've got to go on.' This is similar to Joe Simpson's experience, briefly mentioned in the Introduction, in which he was crawling down a mountain with broken limbs.[431] He too heard a voice that was 'clean and sharp and commanding', which told him to 'go on, keep going'.

If we want to follow the hunch that voice-hearing is like inner speech but still somehow something very different, we can pursue it in another way. Normal inner speech is produced by Broca's area in the left hemisphere. But left Broca's area has a doppelganger in the right hemisphere. And, as with all good doppelgangers, it turns out to be suitably nasty.

CHAPTER 30

Right is Might

It turns out Mulder was right. We are not alone. But the being of which we speak does not live in Zeta Reticuli. It lives much, much closer to home. It is chained up in the right inferior frontal gyrus of our brains: right Broca's area. And it is not happy. This slightly exuberant claim is going to take a bit of unpacking.

So far, we've only looked at one set of regions of the brain that alter activity during voice-hearing: the *left* hemisphere language network. And it has taken a while. Let's now look at the second set of areas that Renaud Jardri and colleagues' meta-analysis found to increase activation when people heard voices. These are in the *right* hemisphere of the brain (see Figure 30.1, Colour Plate 8), and include the right hemisphere twin of Broca's area and the right anterior insula hidden in the sulcus below it. Right Broca's area was first argued to be involved in voice-hearing after a 2008 study led by Iris Sommer[432] found this area increasing its activation when people heard voices. So, what does right Broca's area do?

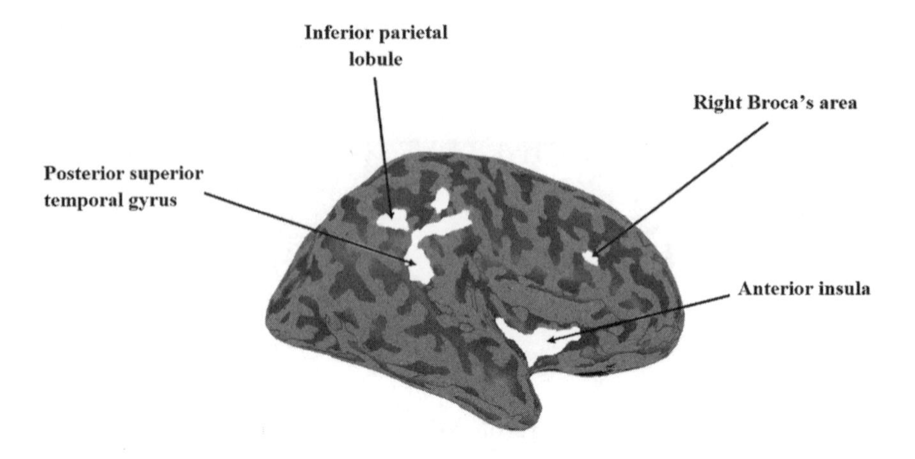

Data represents results of an fMRI analysis of voice-hearing in 20 adolescents with brief psychosis disorder.

Adapted from Jardri, R. *et al.* (2013) 'The neurodynamic organization of modality-dependent hallucinations.' *Cerebral Cortex*, 23(5), 1108–17, with permission.

Figure 30.1: Right hemisphere cortical activity associated with hearing voices

Although, as we have seen, left Broca produces words themselves, right Broca is involved in aspects of speech such as rhythm and musicality. In normal circumstances the Broca twins work together. In great oratory, both take full flight.[433] The distinct contributions of right and left Broca to language can be seen most starkly if someone uses transcranial magnetic stimulation (TMS) to temporarily knock out your left Broca's area. You would now not be able to say the words 'The hills are alive with the sound of music', but, sadly for all concerned, you could still sing them. Similarly, TMS applied over left Broca prevents you performing inner speech, whereas you can still chat away merrily to yourself in your head while TMS is applied over right Broca's area.[434]

It isn't that right Broca can't speak, but rather that left Broca normally keeps it under lock and key. Left Broca actively inhibits

its cranky right hemisphere twin. If left Broca is out of action, right Broca is finally freed from its oppressor and, like a student on Summer Break, goes wild. For example, studies of speech in people who have suffered left hemisphere strokes that have incapacitated left Broca have found that right Broca can speak. Such people frequently say repetitive, simple things that often consist of terms of abuse and swear words.[435] Although they can't speak when you ask them to, cursing flows fluently. John Cleese might have been the first to say 'fuck' at a televised funeral but, thanks to right Broca, Iris Sommer's team were the first to say 'motherfucker' in a leading neurology journal.[436] Why does right Broca produce such vitriol? One possibility is that it is because this area normally plays a role in the inhibitory control of behaviour,[437] including inappropriate behaviour, but we really don't know.

Similarly, other studies show that if you knock out the left hemisphere and allow the right hemisphere to communicate then a very different personality ascends. Take the patient referred to as P.S. who had his corpus callosum (the white matter bundle which is the main route of communication between the two hemispheres) severed for medical reasons.[438] When he was asked what job he would like to do, he replied, using speech generated by left Broca, that he wanted to be a draughtsman (someone who does technical drawings and plans). What did his party hemisphere want to do? P.S.'s right Broca wasn't able to speak, so in order to find out the experimenters had to develop a cunning plan to allow the right hemisphere to communicate. They smuggled information into the right hemisphere by presenting information to P.S.'s left visual field and left hand, which meant the information went directly into the right hemisphere, leaving the left hemisphere unaware of what was going on (because the severed corpus callosum couldn't transfer this information from the right to the left hemisphere). As the right hemisphere controls the left hand, the experimenters were able to get P.S.'s right hemisphere to communicate by using his left hand to pick out scrabble tiles to spell words. P.S.'s right hemisphere was then able to let the researchers know what it wanted to be: a racing driver.

Given such findings, Iris Sommer and colleagues have interpreted voice-hearing as instances of right Broca's area speaking, generating the repetitive, short, abusive phrases typical of many people's voice-hearing. The reason such output is experienced as the voice of another person is argued to be because it is harder for the brain to correctly determine the self-other source of speech when speech input comes from both hemispheres, and not just the left. This theory solves a key problem that the left hemisphere inner speech theory has no good answer for, the selectivity problem: why is some but not all inner speech of people who hear voices experienced as a voice?[439] The right Broca's area model offers a simple answer to this: normal inner speech is experienced because left Broca's area is working fine (explaining why voice-hearers have normal inner speech), and it is only the occasional spewings of right Broca's area that are experienced as a voice.

This account still has problems. First, if people heard only one voice, and it was angry and abusive, then this would fit with what we know right Broca can do, yet people typically hear more than one voice. Second, right Broca is involved in many processes, not simply language. For example, right Broca and the right TPJ are involved in the detection of events in the world, particularly salient or unexpected ones.[440] Given this, we could interpret right Broca's activity during voice-hearing as a consequence of the unexpected experience of hearing a voice, or as involved in hypervigilance processes which originate the voices. Despite these problems, the right Broca account offers a glimpse of a theory of voice-hearing that can explain the content of people's voices in purely neural terms and doesn't need to draw on, for example, traumatic life experiences to account for why voices are so negative. The value of this occurs when you meet people whose voices say the most awful things about them, yet they insist that they don't feel this way about themselves. Unless we want to go down the road of proposing a quasi-Freudian unconscious self-hatred, which I don't, something like a right Broca account feels necessary.

If some people's voices were to have a right Broca origin, others a basis in inner speech that takes the perspective of another on oneself, and yet others a basis in memory, this starts to seem horribly unparsimonious. This may just be the way things are. However, let's unsheathe Occam's razor to try and cut this down to one unifying account. It could be that voice-hearing arises from self-monitoring errors occurring when we push this ability to its limit by taking another's perspective on ourselves using our inner speech, and that creating the words of such another requires us to draw on our memories of them, with right Broca's activation either preventing such thoughts from being inhibited or making them salient. This is a little contorted, but perhaps points to a way forward. Although we have discussed how memory may be related to voice-hearing, at the moment we are acting a little on supposition. However, we have one set of areas, which Jardri and colleagues' meta-analysis found to be activated during voice-hearing, left to discuss.

CHAPTER 31

Speak, Memory

It's a warm summer evening in Ancient Greece, as the esteemed Dr Sheldon Cooper would say, and Aristotle is trying to figure out why people hallucinate. Imagine, he says, if frogs were placed at the bottom of a barrel with salt on their heads to weigh them down. As the salt dissolved, the frog would rise. Hallucinations, Aristotle reasoned, are unchecked frogs rising from the depths of our soul.[441] Later writers used similar analogies. In the nineteenth century, Baillarger argued that hallucinations resulted from a failure to control one's memory/fantasies, drawing a parallel with a school child who, let loose to run at recess, brings back unrequested ideas, images and memories.[442] By the twenty-first century, Aristotle's frogs were popping up in vivid colour in neuroimaging studies of people hearing voices.

The third and final regions that Jardri and colleagues' meta-analysis found to change their activation during voice-hearing were the left hippocampus and parahippocampal region. Both of these are involved in memory, with the latter, as Jardri and colleagues note, known to 'presensitize' regions, such as the STG, to link a given input with a memory. Changes in parahippocampal activation levels (a deactivation) precede voice-hearing, making it likely to be a cause rather than a consequence of the experience.[443] We could see this deactivation of the parahippocampal region as indicating a failure to tell the STG that the input it is about to receive is in fact a memory.

If we want to know if memory is involved in voice-hearing, we can do more than just see if neural areas associated with memory alter their level of activation during voice-hearing. We can simply ask people if their voices are like memories. Recall from Chapter 8 that nearly four in ten people diagnosed with schizophrenia who hear voices say that their voices are in some way like 'replays' of memories of previous conversations they've had or overheard. If we are happy that memories are involved in some voice-hearing, then we can move from the frogs onto the salt.

A series of studies have probed whether there are memory changes in people who hear voices, and whether they have poorer control over memories. These studies form part of Flavie Waters and colleagues' proposal that voice-hearing results from the unintentional activation of memories, due to hearers having an inability to keep them down.[444] Waters and colleagues argue that the first step in voice-hearing is a failure in 'intentional inhibition' – the ability to keep information out of consciousness. To test this theory they gave a task to people diagnosed with schizophrenia in which they had to complete the last word of a sentence, but not with the obvious word.[445] Thus, the participant may be given the sentence, 'The cat sat on the…' If the participant said the word 'mat', this would count as a failure of intentional inhibition. Waters and colleagues found that the more severe were the voices heard by people diagnosed with schizophrenia, the worse they performed on this task. Of course, you could argue that if you have more severe voices, then you are more likely to get distracted by them and make mistakes on this task. This would mean that reduced intentional inhibition was a consequence and not a cause of voice-hearing, but let's run with the idea it is a causal factor, for the moment.

If you only had reduced intentional inhibition, then you would simply experience thoughts coming into your head that you would recognize as your own but could not stop. This should lead to OCD-like experiences, rather than voice-hearing. Therefore, Waters and colleagues proposed that a second problem was necessary for voices to emerge, a context memory deficit. Context memory allows us to bind different contextual evidence together to help us locate a memory in its original context, and to hence be able to identify it as a memory. Recall from Chapter 20 that this is the sort of thing you would have problems with if you had dealt with a trauma in a dissociated manner. Waters and colleagues found that people diagnosed with schizophrenia who heard voices had worse memory for context than people diagnosed with schizophrenia who did not hear voices.[446] When they then looked at both intentional inhibition and context memory deficits, they found that 90 per cent of people diagnosed with schizophrenia who heard voices had deficits in both of these abilities compared with only 33 per cent of their counterparts who did not hear voices.[447]

The relationship between voice-hearing and cognitive changes associated with OCD is particularly intriguing. Diagnoses of schizophrenia and OCD often co-occur,[448] and the idea that voice-hearing shares something in common with obsessions goes back to at least 1895 and the French psychiatrist Jules Seglas. He coined the term *hallucination obsédante* (obsessional hallucinations) to refer to a hallucination accompanied by the characteristics of an obsession. There are clear parallels between thoughts in OCD and what voices are like. Obsessional thoughts in OCD are by definition repetitive and often centred on a common theme, just as voices often are. Thoughts in OCD have a compelling nature. You don't have to go home to check whether you left the gas on, but you feel a strong urge to, and when you do your anxiety lifts. This parallels the commanding nature of many voices: you do not have to respond to the voice telling you to hurt yourself but it can be very hard not to, and temporary relief may be gained by compliance.[449] It is possible that people sometimes act on the urgings of voices not simply because of specific beliefs they hold about the voice, such as that it is an all-powerful demon who will punish them and their family for non-compliance, but because there is something inherently, viscerally compelling about the voice. Parallels between voice-hearing and OCD may also be echoed at the neural level. We already noted in Chapter 26 that voice-hearing is associated with changes to the inferior occipital frontal fasciculus, a tract which when damaged can lead to someone saying the same thing over and over with minor variation. Changes to this tract are also found in patients with OCD.[450]

The inter-relations between voice-hearing and OCD become even clearer when we see voices emerging from what were initially only obsessions:

> Since the age of 18 Emma has heard voices which curse her and repeat phrases such as 'yes, correct'. Her first psychiatric problem occurred when she was 12 [we are not told what happened to her, if anything, at this age] when she became preoccupied with aggressive and sexual thoughts and fears of saying the wrong thing [something clearly happened to her when she was 12]. As a result she started a range of compulsive checking, counting and repetitive behaviours for up to 2–3 hours a day. At 19 she developed 'obsessive auditory hallucinations' as well as delusions.[451]

Given these parallels, could drugs with anti-obsessional effects, as used to treat OCD, help people who hear repetitive voices? There are hints that they could. Massoud Stephane and colleagues reported two cases of psychiatric patients who heard voices with repetitive and fixed content (e.g., 'Do it, hang yourself in the bathroom'), which did not respond to treatment with antipsychotic medication, but did decrease and stop after treatment with fluvoxamine, a drug known to have anti-obsessional effects.[452] This could offer an alternative pharmacological route to alleviate some people's voices. It would also be cheap: fluvoxamine is out of patent, although this actually raises problems. As Fuller Torrey and Davies have noted, because antipsychotics are such major sources of revenue for pharmaceutical companies, 'it is unrealistic to expect the companies to promote less expensive alternatives…[T]here is little or no financial incentive for pharmaceutical companies to promote repurposed drugs, there are no three-page, glossy ads or drug representatives to purchase pizza for the clinician's office staff.'[453] To the many reasons we have seen for lack of progress in helping people with their voices, we can now add the absurdity of a lack of free pizza.

So far we have discussed inner speech, memory and obsessional thoughts. Words, words, words. Something is missing. We highlighted Vaughan Bell's observation in Chapter 8 that voices are often more than just words. They can involve hallucinated social identities. We need to explain why this may be the case. We need to account for the speaker, not just the spoken. As Felicity Deamer and Sam Wilkinson put it, we need to find the 'speaker behind the voice'.[454] Our discussions of trauma have highlighted why a specific person might be felt to be the source of the voice, but another way we can think about this is to consider how the brain can give us the feeling that someone is lurking nearby.

CHAPTER 32

TPJ

Biblical events occur where the temporal and parietal lobes collide. The temporoparietal junction (TPJ) is the hyped location of the neural 'God spot', an area whose stimulation is claimed to lead to transcendent experiences. Going beyond the headlines, stimulation of the left TPJ is more likely to result in feelings of a 'shadowy presence', a creepy feeling that an unseen person is close by, than a one-on-one with the Godhead.[455] The more mundane functions of the TPJ are to help create our experience of voices and gestures, including threatening or emotionally negative gestures. It is a key area involved in the detection of social threats.[456] Activation of the TPJ hence underpins experiences of threatening, social communications involving both language and the felt presence of another. This seems a reasonable approximation of what many people who hear voices experience (at least, those distressed by them). If aberrant TPJ activity could cause voice-hearing, could tweaking the TPJ with neurostimulation undo voice-hearing?

Before answering this, let's pause to consider what we may have just done here. We have reached into the brain for a cause of voice-hearing, and tacitly implied that the TPJ activation may be its fountainhead. In fact, we may merely be offering a recapitulation at the neural level of what we have previously said at the psychological level: people being hypervigilant for threat causes voice-hearing. The psychological-level explanation appears much more informative compared to referencing a decontextualized neural process. The neural-level explanation may obscure, rather than improve, our understanding of voice-hearing. Indeed, targeting the TPJ with neurostimulation as a therapeutic intervention could be seen as seeking an artificial and illusory short cut to perceived security for someone who lives in an unsafe world, which is doomed to failure. Of course, it could also be that something has happened to the TPJ that is unrelated to anything out there in the world, but at the moment we don't know which account is correct. Either way, having now provided a suitable caveat, let's see if neurostimulation of the TPJ can do anything for voice-hearers, in the short term.

Transcranial magnetic stimulation (TMS) pulses sent into the left TPJ have beneficial effects for some people distressed by voices.[457] Yet not everyone is helped. Why? It appears that different people may have different neural underpinnings associated with their voices, and TMS only helps voice-hearers with a specific neurology. People with voices that respond to such TMS over the left TPJ have been found to differ from people whose voices do not respond by having a more excited left STG before treatment.[458] Another study found that people who continuously heard voices were more likely to respond to such TMS if they had worse connectivity between right Broca's area and Wernicke's area, and that those with more intermittent voices were more likely to respond to TMS if they had lower levels of activation in Broca's area (in both hemispheres) when they heard voices.[459] This starts to suggest that our hacking at multiple accounts of voice-hearing with Occam's razor in the last chapter may have been unnecessary. Maybe there are multiple routes to voice-hearing, parsimony be damned.

When TMS over the left TPJ does help voice-hearers, how does it do this? One possibility is that it reduces activity in the TPJ itself. Another is that it makes cortical regions that the TPJ is connected to, such as the left primary auditory cortex, less excitable. Kindler and colleagues found that resting levels of blood flow in Broca's area, the cingulate cortex and primary auditory cortex all decreased after TMS over the left TPJ, but that voices only become less severe when resting primary auditory cortex activity decreased.[460] But why should making such regions less excitable reduce voice-hearing?

One theory, mentioned in passing earlier, is based on the idea that one factor that helps us differentiate between thoughts and perceptions is the level of left pSTG activity, with this being greater during perception than thought. If the difference between your resting pSTG activation and the activation of your pSTG during the external perception of speech is shallower than usual (i.e., there is less of a difference between the two), then ongoing verbal thought is more likely to be confused with external perception. This should lead to worse reality-monitoring abilities. Imagine two twins who are identical except for the fact that one is 5ft tall and other is 6ft tall. You have a clear way of telling them apart. But if the taller twin had a freak Rick Moranis style accident, and ended up being 5ft 1, then you would be much more likely to confuse the twins. You may fear where I am going with this, and you'd be right to; yes, this is the *Honey, I increased the resting activation of the left posterior superior temporal gyrus* theory of voice-hearing. Catchy.

This theory predicts that dampening down the resting activity of this region should reduce voice-hearing. We have already seen mixed evidence that TMS applied over the left pSTG, which dampens down its activity, has some ability to reduce voice-hearing (Chapter 24). Another prediction on the flip-side of this theory is that if the resting activity of the left pSTG could be increased in people who don't hear voices, then it should make them more likely to confuse their own thoughts for externally heard voices, leading to hallucinations. Evidence for this was found in a neat study led by Peter Moseley.[461] This used transcranial direct current stimulation (tDCS) to temporarily increase the activation in the left pSTG of students while they tried to decide if a word was being played to them in the midst of some white noise or not. Sure enough, cranking up the pSTG made the students more likely to hear a word spoken in the white noise when none was present. This mimicked the performance on this task of voice-hearing people diagnosed with schizophrenia, in the absence of any tDCS, who are more likely to hear words that aren't there than other people. Whether tDCS could be used to cause frequent and extended voice-hearing on command, either as a way to help provide evidence for the underlying causes of voice-hearing, or to provide an on-demand muse for those who wanted one, remains to be seen.

Another prediction of the *Honey, I* theory gets into mechanisms. If we use TMS to reduce the resting activity of the left pSTG of people who hear voices, then this should improve their reality-monitoring skills. The extent to which these improve should directly relate to how much their voice-hearing improves. This hasn't been looked at directly in relation to the pSTG, but if TMS is applied over the left TPJ of people diagnosed with schizophrenia then their reality-monitoring skills improve, and the more they do the less severe their voices become.[462] One reason for applying TMS over the left TPJ, rather than over the left pSTG directly, is that this may have a double-whammy effect. It may make the pSTG less excitable and reduce feelings of sensed presences and perceived threats. This in turn may make the person less expectant of hearing a voice (see Chapter 38). Another possibility is that the left TPJ can reach parts of the brain that other parts of the temporal lobe cannot. Targeting the left TPJ with TMS may lead to improved connectivity between this and frontal lobe structures involved in reality monitoring, whereas targeting the STG with TMS may not result in such changes. No brain region is an island, and the TPJ is no exception. Indeed, recent research has found that the brain is made up of spatially distinct areas that work together in networks to create certain states of mind. An important network that the TPJ is involved in is one that whirrs into action when, to an external observer, we may appear to be doing nothing at all. It is this we turn to next.

CHAPTER 33

Vigorously Resting

Sitting quietly in a chair we can travel to the ancient past or an imagined future, traverse our own planet or Tatooine, converse with the dead or Scooby Doo, and still return in time for tea. We spend nearly as much of our time in our heads as we do in the world, with 30–50 per cent of our waking day spent engaged in thoughts unrelated to ongoing activities.[463] We decouple our attention from the demands of a busy, noisy world and enter a world of our own thoughts and imaginings. This is referred to as stimulus-independent thought or mind wandering.

During mind wandering, a specific network of regions across our brain, termed the default mode network (DMN), whirrs into action. As soon as the world beckons us back, activity in the DMN decreases and activity in another network, the central executive network (CEN), increases as it takes over the unenviable task of dealing with the world. The switch, which moves our spotlight of attention between the outer and the inner and flicks our brain between the DMN and CEN, is located in a third brain network called the salience network. By signalling that an event is salient, the activity of this network makes the event 'pop-out' at us, appearing in our consciousness and wrenching us out of our DMN reverie and into CEN alertness as the world comes knocking.

Renaud Jardri and colleagues have found that people diagnosed with schizophrenia who experience hallucinations have a more unstable DMN.[464] They suggest that this may contribute to the development of voice-hearing by causing 'aberrant transitions between resting and conscious sensory states'. There is little other evidence that speaks to this hypothesis yet, but Jardri and colleagues note that when you look at what psilocybin (magic mushrooms) does to the brain to cause hallucinations, it turns out that their main effect is not on sensory areas, such as the STG, but on the functioning of the DMN.

What could cause the DMN to be unstable? One possibility is that it is due to problems with the switch that turns it on and off – the salience network. This network needs to be structurally intact in order to efficiently regulate the level of activation of the DMN.[465] It turns out that core parts of the brain involved in the salience network are the insula and anterior cingulate cortex. In Chapter 23 we saw that a smaller left insula was associated with more severe voice-hearing, and that a smaller left paracingulate sulcus, a structure whose size is related to the size of the anterior cingulate cortex, was also reduced in patients with hallucinations. In addition, in Chapter 31 we noted right insula activation during voice-hearing. It turns out that the right insula has a particularly critical role in switching between the DMN and CEN.[466] It is hence plausible that some of the brain changes we have found to be associated with hearing voices have the effect of altering the function of the salience network, which in turn creates instabilities in the DMN, leading to internally generated thoughts becoming experienced as externally generated perceptions.

Another effect of damage to the salience network which could also contribute to the development of voice-hearing is to change levels of a particular neurotransmitter: dopamine.[467] This is a good point to segue into an examination of how and why dopamine may be involved in creating voice-hearing. This story starts with dopamine-blocking drugs,[468] more commonly referred to as antipsychotics.

CHAPTER 34

A Tranquillizer by Any Other Name?

In 1950 a Frenchman synthesized indifference. A Gallic shrug in a pill. It could have simply been called 'meh!', but the chemists christened it chlorpromazine. The genesis of this drug was a decade earlier when the first antihistamines were synthesized. These drugs caused drowsiness and sedation. When French scientists added a soupçon of chlorine, chlorpromazine was created. One of the first people to administer this drug to patients was Henri Laborit. Those he gave it to became disinterested in what was happening around them, and on this basis he suggested that it might be useful to psychiatric patients. Other French doctors started using chlorpromazine as an unusual type of painkiller; it didn't make patients feel less pain, it just made them not care about it.

By 1952, Delay and Deniker were describing the effects of chlorpromazine on psychiatric patients as being 'apparent indifference', 'emotional and affective neutrality' and 'decrease in both initiative and preoccupation'.[469] In 1954 the first randomized, placebo-controlled trial of chlorpromazine for schizophrenia took place,[470] and its findings echoed Delay and Deniker. The authors of the trial noted that 'in no case was the content of the psychosis changed. The schizophrenic [sic]...patients continued to be subject to delusions and hallucinations, though they appeared to be less disturbed by them.' Other studies found that indifference to hallucinations was a way station to their elimination. A 1955 study described how, at first, there would be 'psychic indifference', where hallucinations would persist yet not have the same emotional impact, and later they would fade away.[471] Twenty-first-century studies have found similar progressions. A 2011 study examined how voices treated with antipsychotic medication changed over time.[472] Of the 40 per cent of patients who stated that antipsychotic medication reduced their hallucinations, reductions in loudness and disruption occurred after four weeks, but reductions in frequency and changes in the beliefs regarding the origin of the voice were only found after ten weeks. There hence appeared to be a two-stage effect of antipsychotics on voices.

In the early 1950s, chlorpromazine was charitably viewed as a sedative that could be helpful by causing hearers to become indifferent about their voices. In this sense it was equivalent to aspirin: it masked a problem without remedying its underlying cause. The psychiatrist Henri Ey explicitly referred to chlorpromazine as 'psychiatric aspirin'.[473] Another conception was also available. Deniker argued that chlorpromazine was a drug that caused brain damage, akin to that found in Parkinson's disease, but that this actually had beneficial effects for people diagnosed with schizophrenia (as we discussed in Chapter 1). The idea of curing a brain disease by causing brain damage may seem odd to us, but this was a time when many therapies were thought to help people diagnosed with schizophrenia by causing brain damage. For example, in a 1941 paper entitled 'Brain damaging therapeutics', Walter Freeman, a man with the decency not to disguise his aims but the indecency to pursue them, wrote: 'The greater the damage, the more likely the remission of psychotic symptoms… Maybe it will be shown that a mentally ill patient can think more clearly and more constructively with less brain in actual operation.'[474] This was simply not true. Patients could go home from hospital, but they would live out their lives as pale shadows of themselves. As Benny Hill once put it, just because nobody complains doesn't mean all parachutes are perfect.

By the 1960s, particularly in the USA, chlorpromazine and its cousins were being referred to as major tranquillizers. In 1964 a major randomized controlled trial found evidence that this family of drugs decreased voice-hearing in people diagnosed with schizophrenia, relative to a placebo.[475] As a result, the authors suggested that the term tranquillizer be dropped and the new term 'anti-schizophrenic' be introduced, which eventually morphed into our modern term 'antipsychotic'. Despite this, our popular culture has retained an awareness of the tranquillizing effects of these drugs, with this even being referenced in the 1984 movie *Ghostbusters*.[476]

Psychiatry needed these drugs. It had stood naked on the battlefield for 150 years, save for a white coat, and this was now so covered in bone, brain and blood that it could be mistaken for any old coat.[477] Some of these stains would never come out.[478] With the advent of antipsychotics, psychiatry was now close to having the authority to pronounce on schizophrenia and voice-hearing, and becoming a respectable member of the medical community. To achieve this though, it wasn't sufficient to have found psychiatric aspirin, which was viewed as barking up the wrong tree. Since the introduction of antibiotics in the 1940s, as Joanna Moncrieff has noted, medicine had been associated with drug treatments that addressed underlying causes, not ones which simply masked problems.[479] Psychiatry therefore simply adopted the mantra that antipsychotics corrected an underlying problem. Comparisons between antipsychotics and masking agents such as aspirin stopped, and explicit or implicit analogies began with drugs that cured disease, such as antibiotics. By 1998 Edward Shorter was opining that 'chlorpromazine initiated a revolution in psychiatry, comparable to the introduction of penicillin in general medicine'.[480] In a moment we will turn to an examination of how these drugs work, but first we need to more clearly establish the extent to which they do.

CHAPTER 35

Antipsychotics: Heart-Warming and Heart-Breaking

Simple questions rarely have simple answers. A case in point is: do antipsychotics help people who hear distressing voices? One of most recent reviews of the effectiveness of treatments for hallucinations presented data from a trial that looked at the effects of five different antipsychotics in 362 people having their first episode of schizophrenia.[481] The average patient in this trial started with marked-to-severe hallucinations, but after a year of antipsychotic use they only had absent-to-minimal levels of hallucinations. The percentage of patients with more than mild hallucinations decreased from 100 per cent to only 8 per cent. Wow, you might say, antipsychotics seem to almost completely eliminate hallucinations in over 90 per cent of people, that's great! However, there was no placebo, or other form of control group, in this trial so we don't know how many people's hallucinations could have improved simply due to natural remission, other aspects of being taken into care, or placebo effects.

Placebo effects are likely to be important. A recent six-week randomized controlled trial (RCT) examined the effects of placebos and antipsychotics (olanzapine) in 420 people diagnosed with schizophrenia, whose onset was typically over a decade ago.[482] Analyses focused specifically on positive symptoms – a combined measure of hallucinations, delusions and confused thought. Patients fell into four distinct categories of response type. Ten per cent were classed as 'dramatic responders', and had on average a 74 per cent decrease in positive symptoms. All these patients turned out to be in the group taking antipsychotics. To put it another way, 17 per cent of all patients taking antipsychotics had a dramatic response. In contrast, people classed as 'responders' and 'partial responders', who made up 70 per cent of patients, were not statistically more likely to have come from the antipsychotic group than the placebo group. Around 80 per cent of the patients in this trial had previously been on antipsychotics, which they were taken off to participate in this trial of a new antipsychotic. Given this, it is even more remarkable that more patients in the placebo group didn't show huge exacerbations of positive symptoms following being withdrawn from their other antipsychotics, and even more remarkable that over half of the placebo group had their positive symptoms *improve* once taken off their antipsychotics (being classified as responders or partial responders). The study hence simultaneously supported and questioned the use of antipsychotics for voice-hearing.

The existence of a group of rapid responders to antipsychotics was also found in a 2014 study that examined the response to antipsychotics of people diagnosed with first-episode schizophrenia.[483] This study had the limitation of not using a placebo group, but was at least looking at people who had never been on antipsychotics before. It found that 10 per cent of participants could be classified as rapid responders. Only one factor predicted whether a patient would have a rapid, compared with a gradual, response. This was whether the person had a job when they started taking antipsychotics. It could be objected that this was just a proxy measure of how severe people's symptoms were, and that those with less severe symptoms were those who responded best, but this was not the case. Symptom severity did not differ between gradual and rapid responders. There are hence hints that predictors of rapid treatment response may include social factors as well as biological ones.

Placebo effects highlight the need to examine RCTs that have compared the effects of antipsychotics on voice-hearing with that of a placebo. Today, it is rare to see such a design as it would typically be deemed unethical to withhold antipsychotics from first-episode patients. It would also normally be viewed as unethical to suddenly take people on stable doses of antipsychotics off them, due to the high probability of relapse. This means we mainly have to resort to older studies, taken from the land before consensus, to find placebo-controlled studies. Data published in the 1960s, stemming from six-week RCTs of the effectiveness of antipsychotics and placebo for newly admitted people diagnosed with schizophrenia, despite some statistical concerns, provide evidence of greater voice-hearing improvement in people taking antipsychotics than in people given placebos.[484] However, from what we saw earlier in this chapter, it may be wondered to what extent this effect was driven by a relatively small number of dramatic improvers in the antipsychotic group.

Going beyond individual trials, what can systematic reviews of this area tell us? A 2007 review of RCTs reporting on the efficacy of the antipsychotic chlorpromazine compared with a placebo came to the following conclusion: 'Even though chlorpromazine has been used as an antipsychotic drug for decades, there are still a surprisingly small number of well-conducted randomized, placebo-controlled trials measuring its efficacy.'[485] This is indeed surprising. The authors continue: 'In spite of 45 years of research on this benchmark anti-psychotic treatment, very little can be said from trials regarding its direct effect on mental state in general or specific symptoms of schizophrenia.' What can be said is that 'for every six people treated with this compound, five may have been given the drug with no important clinical responses beyond a placebo effect'. This begs the question as to why this drug with such a powerful side-effect profile is so widely used. The authors tell us that '[t]he use of chlorpromazine for millions of people is based on clinical experience rather than the poorly reported trials that involve, in total, only a few thousand participants'. So, anecdote is the basis for the effectively mandatory use of antipsychotics? Perhaps we could write this off as simply being the case for chlorpromazine, one of the older, 'typical' antipsychotics. We must have better evidence for the effectiveness of the newer, 'atypical' antipsychotics, mustn't we? You know, those 'newer medications' which, in the film *A Beautiful Mind*, John Nash credits for his recovery.

Individual trials look promising. McEvoy and colleagues found that 64 per cent of patients treated with olanzapine, 58 per cent of patients treated with quetiapine, and 65 per cent of patients treated with risperidone had their hallucinations improved to the point where they only experienced infrequent hallucinations.[486] Again though, there was no placebo group. Furthermore, 62 per cent of patients stopped using their medications during the year-long trial, and this could have in part been because their hallucinations were not responding to the drugs. Indeed, a major reason for patients dropping out of trials is that the antipsychotics aren't working. For example, in one large trial by Kahn and colleagues,[487] 22 per cent of patients dropped out of the trial (representing 53 per cent of all drop-outs), because their psychiatrist deemed that the antipsychotics had insufficient efficacy. Another reason for drop-out is the side effects of these drugs. In reality, John Nash stopped using his medications as he felt they fogged his intellect. The line in the movie about the newer medications causing his recovery was 'a fabrication, and a conscious one'.[488] Anecdotes aside, consider the health effects of one of the newer antipsychotics, olanzapine (global sales in 2008 = $5.4 billion). In Kahn and colleagues' trial, patients gained an average of 14kg, one in five developed hypertriglyceridaemia (high blood fat levels), one in four developed hyperglycaemia (high blood sugar), one in three developed hypercholesterolaemia (high cholesterol), and a quarter of the women participants developed sexual dysfunction. Given this, it is unsurprising that people diagnosed with schizophrenia have a staggeringly reduced life expectancy of 10–25 years compared with the general population.[489] Although 40 per cent of this difference is attributable to a greater rate of 'unnatural' causes, such as suicide, the other 60 per cent is due to 'natural' causes, such as cardiovascular disease.[490] It seems odd to term as 'natural' a cause of death that likely, in large part,[491] results from drugs people were given. For many patients, the effects of antipsychotics are literally heart-breaking.

Going beyond the results of individual trials, a recent systematic review of RCTs of the effectiveness of the atypical antipsychotic risperidone versus placebo began by noting a clear beneficial effect of risperidone on psychiatric symptoms.[492] Then the waters became murkier. Of the seven RCTs examined, there was one outlier, an equivocal trial which was sponsored by a research charity. As the authors note, the other studies 'were sponsored by an interested pharmaceutical industry… We found very few data reported on mental state for the comparison of risperidone versus placebo and what we do have is difficult to trust.' They then describe how the majority of trials were funded by the manufacturer of the drug itself, that many of the studies' authors had affiliations with the drug industry, and that industry-funded studies tended to favour the drug treatments more than non-industry-funded studies did. They conclude: 'Risperidone may well help people with schizophrenia, but the data in this review are unconvincing. People with schizophrenia or their advocates may want to lobby regulatory authorities to insist on better studies being available before wide release of a compound with the subsequent beguiling advertising.'

On balance it seems that antipsychotics will help some people, but we cannot clearly say how many, or know in advance who will be helped. If we assume that antipsychotic trials have a 60 per cent drop-out rate, and that most of these drop-outs are due to the drugs not working or having intolerable side effects, and that of those remaining maybe 75 per cent will experience remission of their hallucinations, then we are looking at antipsychotics being effective treatments for less than half of all people's voices. This is in the ballpark of what clinicians report. One study examined reports by 872 physicians of symptom changes in 3845 patients with hallucinations (of all forms, not just voices), and found 51 per cent of hallucinations were reported as generally well controlled by antipsychotics.[493] However, they were rated as providing little or no control of hallucination in 11 per cent of patients, and only some control in 38 per cent of patients. Yet not only is what 'control' means unclear, but the studies we have reviewed above suggest that a significant amount of such effectiveness may be due to placebo effects. Once we discount for placebo, it could be that antipsychotics are effective treatments for less than half of people's voices. One can take a glass half-full or glass half-empty perspective on this. Many drugs deemed successes nevertheless fail to help everyone who takes them.

Thus, while evidence suggests that antipsychotics can help with voice-hearing, this effect may be limited to a small subgroup of people, a lot of the evidence in this area is potentially hard to trust, and the widespread use of these compounds may be based on clinical experience rather than hard evidence from RCTs. This raises the question as to why psychiatrists' clinical experience is acceptable as an evidence base when claims voice-hearers make on the basis of their lived experience, such as that their voices were caused by trauma or that a psychological therapy was helpful for them, are written off as unreliable 'anecdata'. It also suggests that people being prescribed antipsychotics may want to look at the pen that writes their prescription and the paperweight that stills their records. Mike Shooter, then President of the UK's Royal College of Psychiatrists, put the problem this way:

> I cannot be the only person to be sickened by the sight of parties of psychiatrists standing at the airport desk with so many perks about them that they might as well

> have the name of the company tattooed across their foreheads. It simply will not do.[494]

Indeed, a recent review of the relation between doctors' exposure to information from pharmaceutical companies and the quality, quantity and cost of their prescribing (for prescription medications in general, not antipsychotics specifically) concluded by recommending that 'practitioners follow the precautionary principle and thus avoid exposure to information from pharmaceutical companies'.[495]

Going forward, there is a need to develop ways to accurately predict whose voices will and will not be helped by antipsychotics in order to avoid people, who are being given these drugs primarily for their voices, unnecessarily taking these potent drugs. Although predictors of the response of specifically voices to antipsychotics haven't yet been examined, studies have looked at what factors predict whether psychosis per se (hallucinations, delusions and thought disorder) will respond to antipsychotics. These have been found to include neurology, genetics, trauma, and length of untreated psychosis. Patients with either lower white matter integrity across a range of tracts (potentially including the arcuate fasciculus[496]) or greater levels of childhood trauma (particularly child sexual abuse[497]) have been found to be less likely to respond to antipsychotics. This may again set us off wondering if there are subtypes of the voice-hearing experience that are reached by different routes, and hence best exited by different routes. Longer durations of untreated psychosis are also associated with worse treatment response,[498] as is variation in a gene involved in creating dopamine receptors.[499] This latter finding highlights that one way both to better help people with distressing voices and to understand the underlying mechanics of the experience is to understand the role of dopamine in the experience. It is hence to dopamine, or 4-(2-aminoethyl)benzene-1,2-diol as we should perhaps formally address this member of schizophrenia royalty, that we turn to next.

CHAPTER 36

Enter Synapse

For the past four decades certain things have remained synonymous with each other: Spielberg and film, Greer and feminism, Selleck and moustaches. To this list can be added schizophrenia and dopamine. There have been three iterations of the dopamine theory of schizophrenia. Version 1.0 became widely adopted by the late 1970s. It was based on research showing that the more an antipsychotic bound to dopamine receptors in the brain, the better it worked. Here, voice-hearing was understood as resulting from too many post-synaptic dopamine receptors, causing too much dopamine signalling.[500] This was superseded by dopamine theory v2.0, released in 1991 to a mixed reception. This argued that too little dopamine in frontal areas of the cortex caused too much dopamine in a deeper part of the brain called the striatum, which was the cause of voice-hearing. Seven thousand research papers later, Howes and Kapur upgraded us to the current version of dopamine theory (v3.0) in 2009.[501] This argued that voice-hearing was caused by too much dopamine being stored and released at pre-synaptic release sites in the striatum.

The striatum is a region of the brain below the cortex that receives input from the cortex and the hippocampus, and then sends signals back to the cortex via the thalamus. Activation of the striatum occurs when we encounter new things, or things associated with reward or danger; in short, when we encounter something salient. It has two parts: the putamen and caudate nucleus. The putamen is involved in helping us to spontaneously produce speech. A recent (but as yet unreplicated) study found the putamen to be smaller in voice-hearers,[502] and another found greater connectivity in voice-hearers in a neural circuit involving the putamen and two staples of voice-hearing, left Broca and the left STG.[503] For these reasons, if altered neurotransmission in the striatum were to play some role in voice-hearing, it would not be entirely surprising.

Evidence for the dopamine theory v3.0 has come from a careful analysis of dopamine transmission in people diagnosed with schizophrenia. Dopamine transmission is influenced by four things: how much you make (capacity for pre-synaptic dopamine synthesis), how much you release (degree of dopamine release in response to stimuli), how much you have floating about (concentration of extracellular dopamine in the synaptic cleft), and how much is currently in action (density/availability of post-synaptic dopaminergic receptors). Position emission tomography (PET) can be used to inject people with various dopaminergic radiotracers to tell us about each of these aspects. Let's look at these in turn, drawing on very helpful papers by Oliver Howes and colleagues.[504]

People diagnosed with schizophrenia make more dopamine in their striatum. Elevated pre-synaptic striatal dopamine synthesis capacity in people diagnosed with schizophrenia has been found by nearly every study that has looked at this. This includes studies of chronic patients, first-episode patients, and those in the prodromal period (i.e., before the use of antipsychotics). It is, as Howes and Kapur put it, 'the single most widely replicated brain dopaminergic abnormality in schizophrenia'.[505] A number of studies have also found increased dopamine release in people diagnosed with schizophrenia, with greater levels of release being associated with a greater likelihood that the person has positive symptoms (i.e., hallucinations and delusions).[506] Not only is there more dopamine released, but there appears to be a greater baseline level of it floating around in the synapse.[507] There is less convincing evidence that dopamine receptor density (or to be more specific, density of a specific type of dopamine receptor called the dopamine D2 receptor) is altered in people diagnosed with schizophrenia. The overall picture that emerges is of schizophrenia, and hence potentially voice-hearing, being associated with making more dopamine, releasing more dopamine, and having more dopamine floating around in the synaptic cleft.

This throws up a quandary. Antipsychotics block *post*-synaptic dopamine D2 receptors, but v3.0 of the dopamine theory suggests the primary problem is *pre*-synaptic dopamine release. This suggests that antipsychotics don't address the primary problem, but rather only the downstream effects of this problem. Indeed, by blocking post-synaptic dopamine D2 sites, antipsychotics may actually cause the brain to try to compensate for this by producing even more dopamine. This can explain why people who suddenly stop their antipsychotic medications often find their symptoms get worse (worse even than they were in the first place); their unblocked post-synaptic dopamine receptors now face a tidal wave of dopamine. As Howes and Kapur note, this suggests the need for new drugs that focus on altering pre-synaptic striatal dopamine function.

If dopamine function is altered in people diagnosed with schizophrenia (even before they start using antipsychotic drugs), how did this happen? One possibility is that this has a genetic basis. We will look at how variations in a gene involved in creating the dopamine D2 receptor (the DRD2 gene) may be associated with schizophrenia in Chapter 40. Another possibility is that life events cause these changes. We already saw in Chapter 21 that life events linked to shame, such as social threat and social defeat, can increase dopamine levels in the striatum, at least in animal models. Stress in general also has the potential to do this, as it has a neurotoxic effect on the hippocampus. Lesions to animals' hippocampi have been found to cause increases in spontaneous firing of dopamine neurons in their striatum.[508]

But why exactly would greater levels of striatal dopamine signalling cause you to hear voices? An early proposal was that this was because dopamine is involved in signalling salience to us, and therefore excess levels could make thoughts and memories stand out more, coming to be experienced as voices.[509] This argument has now been more tightly specified, drawing on research showing that dopamine indicates to us how certain we can be about whether we've actually seen or heard something. Increased levels of dopamine have been proposed to lead to source-monitoring errors by increasing people's uncertainty as to whether events were thoughts/memories or something happening out there in the world.[510] We will come back to this in the context of predictive coding models in Chapter 38.

Another line of evidence for an involvement of dopamine in voice-hearing would be if experimentally increasing someone's dopamine levels caused them to hear voices. Giving dopamine-increasing drugs to animals is one way to get at this. We already know that giving mescaline to mice reduces emotional defecation[511] (don't ask), giving phencyclidine to fish makes them swim in circles[512] and giving meth to monkeys makes them fiddle with their asses.[513] If these animals had gone on to work in Hollywood, things could have been very different. On the upside, the Mickey Mouse Clubhouse would have been a lot cleaner, and Nemo would never have got lost. On the downside, Willy would never have been freed, and what was already the scariest part of the Wizard of Oz would have become simply horrific. But we have digressed. Returning to the matter in hand, increasing dopamine levels in monkeys using amphetamines has been found to lead to behaviours that suggested they were hallucinating.[514] Yet in humans, drugs that increase dopamine (e.g., cocaine, apomorphine) only rarely cause voice-hearing. A study that gave a low dose of dopamine-increasing drugs (bromocriptine/lisuride) to 600 patients with pituitary tumours found that less than 1 per cent went on to hear voices.[515] Neither do dopamine-increasing drugs worsen voice-hearing in people who already hear voices.[516]

For example, giving people diagnosed with schizophrenia a drug called L-dopa, which increases dopamine, doesn't exacerbate hallucinations or delusions.[517] One possible reason why dopamine-increasing drugs don't cause or worsen voice-hearing is because dopamine never caused it in the first place. We will turn to this idea in the next chapter, but first let's look at a potential role for another neurotransmitter, glutamate.

In some people diagnosed with schizophrenia who do not respond to antipsychotics, striatal dopamine levels are normal, but levels of another neurotransmitter are altered: glutamate.[518] Glutamate is the most common excitatory neurotransmitter in the brain, and the most widespread in prefrontal and temporal regions of the brain. If you take drugs such as ketamine or phencyclidine (PCP) you will be likely to hallucinate. These drugs have their effects by blocking a glutamate receptor in the brain called the N-methyl-D-aspartate (NMDA) receptor.[519] Autoimmune-related damage to a particular part (the NR1 subunit) of the NMDA receptor has been proposed to be the cause of around 2 per cent of cases of schizophrenia. In what is called antibody-driven NMDA receptor encephalitis (inflammation of the brain), the person has antibodies in their system which damage their NMDA receptors, and can cause psychosis. Treatment for this disorder is recommended to include steroids, plasmapheresis (cleaning of the blood) and intravenous immunoglobulins (which help regulate an overactive immune system),[520] not antipsychotics. As an aside, even though NMDA-blocking drugs such as ketamine can cause voice-hearing,[521] generally their effects are not limited to just this form of hallucination. Indeed, as someone insightfully noted at a discussion after a recent talk of mine, there are no drugs that will cause you to hear voices without also experiencing other forms of hallucinations. As over half of people diagnosed with schizophrenia who hear voices do not have any other forms of hallucinations[522] (e.g., visions or hallucinated smells), this means there is no known drug that can mimic the experiences of people who hear voices, which, when you think about it, is profoundly odd.

A 2015 study by Kenneth Hugdahl and colleagues found that people diagnosed with schizophrenia had, on average, lower glutamate levels than healthy controls in both temporal and frontal lobe areas.[523] Yet, within the patients they found that glutamate levels were higher in those with hallucinations than in those without hallucinations. Another study found that increases in glutamate in the anterior cingulate cortex, an area we have previously seen to be involved in reality monitoring, were linked to hallucinations.[524] This is an evolving area of research, which ties nicely into the regions of the brain we have seen to be linked to voice-hearing. Whether we can move from glutamate theories of voice-hearing to glutamate therapies for voice-hearing remains to be seen. This is not the only doubt we face. A larger uncertainty of Heisenbergian proportions has recently begun to rumble.

CHAPTER 37

The Truths They Are A'changing

If I had to pick my favourite joke by Tim Vine, it would be this: 'So I got a job at Burger King, and Andrew Lloyd Webber walked in. He said, give me two Whoppers. I said, you're good looking and your musicals are great.'[525] Anyway, according to Lloyd Webber, time changes everything. In the world of voice-hearing research, it is a paper snappily entitled 'Dopaminergic function in the psychosis spectrum: an [18F]-DOPA imaging study in healthy individuals with auditory hallucinations' that threatens to change everything, although it is unlikely to ever be adapted for Broadway. In this study, led by Oliver(!) Howes, people who heard voices, yet did not have any psychiatric diagnosis (non-clinical voice-hearers), had pre-synaptic dopamine function measured in their striatum.[526] This was then compared with that of healthy people who didn't hear voices. The potential confounds of schizophrenia studies (e.g., medication use) were therefore removed. It was found that the voice-hearers did not differ in striatal pre-synaptic dopamine function to the healthy people who didn't hear voices. On the face of it, this suggests that a striatal dopamine imbalance is not associated with voice-hearing.

To prove Thomas Kühn[527] right, let's try to explain this away. First, this was only a small study, with just 16 voice-hearers. Perhaps it didn't have enough juice (or statistical power, as it is more formally referred to) to detect dopamine differences between healthy people who did and did not hear voices. The authors' retort to this was that their study was big enough to reliably detect differences in dopamine synthesis capacity of the size found between people diagnosed with schizophrenia and healthy controls. But, you may say, these people didn't have schizophrenia diagnoses, so maybe you would expect a smaller difference, which this study couldn't detect. The authors had an answer to this too: their study had sufficient numbers of participants to detect differences in dopamine synthesis capacity of the size found between people with a sub-clinical form of schizophrenia (schizotypal personality disorder) and healthy controls, so it would still be expected that if these people with sub-clinical voice-hearing had an altered dopamine synthesis capacity their study would have detected it. Next objection: these non-clinical voice-hearers were having different voice-hearing experiences to people diagnosed with schizophrenia. This is true in some senses – by definition the non-clinical voice-hearers' voices didn't cause them distress and dysfunction. However, factors such as the number of voices heard and their loudness were similar to those seen in people diagnosed with schizophrenia.

Let's try another tack. What if only *problematic* voice-hearing is associated with increased striatal dopamine levels? This would allow us to accept Howes and colleagues' finding, without abandoning the link between dopamine and voice-hearing in schizophrenia. The question then becomes: why would increased striatal dopamine only be associated with problematic voice-hearing? We could try and explain this following Palaniyappan and Liddle's suggestion that we need to consider the implications of the existence of two types of salience for hallucinations: proximal and motivational.[528] Proximal salience is the 'what's that?!' moment, the creation of a momentary state of awareness of a stimulus. Motivational salience is the 'do something!' moment, which signals whether this stimulus is something we need to act on. Both types of salience involve dopamine, but in different regions of the brain: the insula and anterior cingulate cortex for proximal salience, and the striatum for motivational salience. If motivational salience only played a role in clinically relevant voice-hearing, then we would expect to find altered striatal dopamine in patient populations but not in non-clinical voice-hearers. But why would motivational salience only be associated with problematic but not non-problematic voice-hearing? One possibility is that increased motivational salience could be responsible for the perception that voices are powerful entities with commands that have to be followed. This could get you into trouble, and lead to a clinical diagnosis, but not be found in non-clinical populations. However, hints that acting compulsively is associated with problematic voice-hearing are limited.[529] This theory leads to the testable prediction that, in contrast to the striatum, dopamine levels should be elevated in cortical regions of the salience network (the insula and anterior cingulate cortex) in both clinical and non-clinical voice-hearers.

On the one hand, it could be that at least a subset of people who hear voices do so because of altered striatal dopamine function. On the other hand, it could be that altered striatal dopamine is genuinely not associated with voice-hearing in anyone. At this stage, we just don't know. If the latter possibility were to be true, then we would need to explain why dopamine-reducing drugs (antipsychotics) help people with their voices. The answer here may be akin to the reason why painkillers work: masking (Chapter 35). Antipsychotics predominantly act by reducing the salience of voices and making people indifferent to them, but just because dopamine blockage reduces the salience of voices, this does not imply that it was an excess of dopamine that caused the voices. Every week we hear hype about paradigm shifts, but Howes and colleagues' study may actually provide one. Dopamine may have been the phantom of the voice-hearing opera.

Given this, it is notable that revisionist accounts are already appearing that claim psychiatry never endorsed a chemical imbalance theory of schizophrenia (and by extension, voice-hearing). Ronald Pies, a professor of psychiatry, writes: 'In truth, the "chemical imbalance" notion was always a kind of urban legend – never a theory seriously propounded by well-informed psychiatrists.'[530] There are two ways to take this statement. One is that it is clearly disingenuous, like a blushing ten-year-old denying ever having believed in Father Christmas. A second is that it is true, which then raises the question as to why voice-hearing patients have been told (and continue to be told) by their psychiatrists that they have a chemical imbalance. Answers to this question essentially boil down to people being told white lies for, what is perceived by others to be, their own good. Such white lies are argued to have three benefits.

The first is helping people not to feel blame for their illness. Pies suggests that 'some doctors believe that they will help the patient feel less blameworthy by telling them, "You have a chemical imbalance causing your problems."'[531] Unfortunately, it turns out that biomedical accounts may have the effect of *increasing* stigma against people diagnosed with mental disorders.[532]

A second perceived good is that it makes patients more likely to take their medication. To take an example from another field, a pharmacologist has argued that patients will feel more comfortable taking antidepressants 'if there was this biological reason for being depressed, some deficiency that the drug was correcting'.[533] Similarly, a psychiatrist describes how he tells depressed patients that they have a chemical imbalance that drugs can correct:

> ...not because I really believe it... I think I say that because patients want to know something, and they want to know that we as physicians have some basic understanding of what we're doing when we're prescribing medications. And they certainly don't want to hear that a psychiatrist essentially has no idea how these medications work.[534]

This is not a modern quandary. Over 300 years ago the physician Samuel de Sorbière reported being in two minds about whether to be truthful with patients or whether to make them unconditionally confident in him to serve the purposes of cure.[535] Plato had long since opted for the lie.[536] It is unclear how all this sits with the modern Hippocratic Oath,[537] which explicitly states that physicians 'will not be ashamed to say "I know not"'. Probably rather uncomfortably.

This ties into a final, and related, perceived good, namely that promulgating the chemical imbalance theory enhances the authority of the psychiatrist, which is of benefit not simply because it encourages patients to take prescribed medications but because it is potentially curative in its own right. Psychiatry has often seen authority as being part of its therapeutic method, in part through encouraging placebo effects. It has been argued that psychiatrists themselves are (or have the potential to be) walking, talking placebos, healing by 'the confidence they display…their prestige…and by their socially sanctioned authority'.[538]

To be clear, the issue here is not that psychiatrists prescribe antipsychotic drugs to help with voice-hearing. As we have seen, for some people this is indeed helpful. The issue is why some psychiatrists still tell their patients that antipsychotic drugs correct a chemical imbalance if 'well-informed psychiatrists' never 'seriously propounded' this idea. Mike Shooter[539] notes that patients 'are entitled to ask their doctor why he or she is so keen on something whose mechanism is so little understood', yet they cannot do this if thcy arc not aware that these mechanisms are poorly understood. The three perceived goods of promulgating a chemical imbalance story actually turn out to have the potential to result in increased stigma for patients, increased prestige for psychiatrists, and treatment that is not based on informed consent and which is hence coercive. You could conclude that this white lie is actually a whopper.

CHAPTER 38

The Untamed Prediction

After every joke I got a tremendous round of applause. Then I found out there was a waiter trying to get some HP Sauce out of a bottle.

Eric Morecambe

Eight minutes ago hydrogen atoms were fused together in the heart of a star. This propelled photons 150 million kilometres across the solar system, where they bounced off a mix of protein and dead cells, and into me. This was just part of a wider maelstrom of electromagnetic bombardment I faced, while simultaneously being pounded by compressed air from all directions. This sounds mysterious, dramatic and overwhelming. It wasn't. I saw a dog. It barked. Our ability to figure out what is going on 'out there' when faced by such a full spectrum onslaught is remarkable.

One way to draw together some of the findings from previous chapters is through a new approach to understanding perception. Traditionally, the brain has been viewed as passively drinking in signals from the external world and translating these into perceptual experiences; what you see is what you get. An alternative approach to perception is offered by the predictive processing framework. This conceives the brain's job as being to predict what is going on 'out there'. The best prediction your brain comes up with, not the actual data that comes into your sensory organs, is what you consciously perceive. In the predictive processing framework, what you see is what you predict.[540]

How does the brain decide on its best guess as to what is going on? First, it cheats. It doesn't start from a standing position (well, technically it often does, but you know what I mean) but instead uses prior knowledge. It peeps at the past to predict the present. Before the brain encounters a stimulus it has some idea as to how likely certain things are to happen. This is called the 'prior probability' of an event. Before I leave home in the morning, the prior probability of there being a dinosaur in my office is a good deal lower than the prior probability of there being a coffee maker in there (Wednesdays excepted).

Once I get to my office, if I hear a roaring sound coming from inside I can come up with a range of hypotheses as to what the cause of this sound might be. The sound, taken in isolation, might be an equally good fit with the hypothesis that there is a dinosaur in my office and the hypothesis that I left the (very old and creaky) coffee machine on last night. Although when taken in isolation both hypotheses have the same likelihood of being true, when combined with the prior information I have (dinosaur in office unlikely, coffee machine likely), the coffee machine option becomes more probable overall. In technical terms, its 'posterior probability' is higher. This prediction wins and is what I perceive. Standing outside my office door I hear the sound of my coffee machine.

For the sake of argument, we assumed that the sound referred to earlier, when taken in isolation, was an equally good fit with the dinosaur and coffee pot hypotheses. In reality it would not be, unless it was either a very odd dinosaur or a substantially broken coffee machine. To assess each of these hypotheses, the brain calculates the difference between what it has predicted and what the actual stimulus it receives is – that is, how wrong it is. This is called prediction error. The brain's job is to pick the hypothesis that minimizes prediction error. In this case, the coffee pot hypothesis would be closer to the actual sound coming from inside the door, and would minimize prediction error. A huge benefit of this approach is that because we have already made a prediction, our higher cortical areas no longer need to deal with all the information received from the senses, but only with the small fraction of this information that deals with how far out the prediction is – that is, the prediction error. This is a very efficient way of dealing with the world.

The use of predictions means our higher prefrontal cortical regions can act in a 'top-down' manner to actually generate activation in lower sensory cortical regions. As Andy Clark describes, as part of learning to perceive we develop the ability to self-generate perception-like states from the top down, by driving the lower cortical regions into the predicted patterns of activation. For example, a system which can learn to perceive a cat is also a system which can use higher cortical regions to create much of the neural activity that would ensue in the visual presence of an actual cat. This is what imagination is. This becomes a routine thing for the brain to do. As Richard Dawkins has noted, 'To simulate a ghost or an angel or a Virgin Mary would be child's play to software of this sophistication.'[541]

In addition to the roles of prior expectations and prediction error in perception, a third variable that gets thrown into the mix is the judgement as to how accurate and reliable the prediction error calculation is. We only want to use prediction error to revise our predictions if we are happy the prediction error is correct. We hence need to make a second-order judgement and predict how accurate we think the prediction error is going to be. This is called precision. For example, I don't believe aliens have landed on Earth. If someone tells me aliens have been here (akin to generating a prediction error), then I have something that contradicts my belief, which I may need to revise to minimize error. First though, I am going to have to make a judgement as to how reliable the source is, and the amount of noise received with the signal, in order to decide whether I should place any weight on the prediction error, or discount it. If David Icke tells me about the aliens, I might think this is unreliable and discount this. If Stephen Hawking tells me, I might think this is more reliable, give weight to this error signal, and revise my belief about aliens to be that they have landed, minimizing error. Another way to look at this is to consider the amount of noise accompanying the signal. If I am in a noisy pub and someone is talking to me, I will place less weight on prediction error (in technical terms I 'turn down the gain' on it), and give more weight to my prior expectation than if I was in a quiet room. In the pub it may objectively sound like my friend said 'I know the bear', but I know the signal is corrupted by all the background crowd noise, so I will turn down the gain on the prediction error, giving greater weight to my prior expectation of what he may be saying. As a result, 'another beer' will be deemed the best prediction, and will be what I actually hear.

The activity registered by the sensory regions of your cortex will be consistent with what your prediction is, not the actual thing 'out there'. If your best prediction is that an object seen out the corner of your eye is a face then, even if it is actually a tree, the regions of your brain involved in processing faces (known as the fusiform face area) will fire in response to this non-face stimulus.[542] Your perceptual areas can be activated not by the stimulus itself, but by top-down processes.

The way that our brains implement precision is by influencing the extent to which prediction errors are able to propagate through our neural system to force revisions to predictions. The more precision I attribute to a prediction error, the more it is allowed to propagate through levels of processing and to revise my prediction. In the case of a noisy or unreliable signal, prediction error ignorance is bliss.

So how is all this of relevance to hallucinated voices? The first thing to note is that, in some sense, all perception has its basis in hallucination. As Metzinger elegantly puts it, the brain 'constantly hallucinates at the world...vigorously dreaming at the world and thereby generating the content of…experience'. Hallucinations only remain referred to as hallucinations if they are untamed by prediction error. To understand voice-hearing more clearly in a predictive coding framework, we can start from the first (and only) equation in this book,[543] which summarizes what we have discussed:

$$\hat{c} = c_0 + k(s-\hat{s})$$

Here $\hat{c}$ is your prediction (i.e., what you actually perceive/experience), c_0 is your prior expectation, k is the Kalman gain (a measure of precision, i.e. the confidence you have in the accuracy of the sensory input you are receiving, relative to your confidence in your prior expectation), and $(s-\hat{s})$ is the prediction error, i.e. the difference between the sensory input your prior expectation would predict ($\hat{s}$) and the actual sensory data (s). These three elements that influence our perception could each contribute to voice-hearing.

First, consider your prior expectation. Renaud Jardri and Sophie Denève suggest that if your prior expectation is mistaken for incoming sensory data, it would wrongly be treated as a perception, leading to a hallucination. Auditory perception results from a negotiation between what we expect to hear (top-down information) and actual sensory input (bottom-up information), which minimizes prediction error. Normally, information about our expectations only travels from the top to the bottom of the network, but if there are failures in the inhibitory loops that let this information only go in one direction, expectations could also come back up the network. This would lead to these signals being treated by the brain as if they were sensory information coming in. As inhibition in the brain is driven by the neurotransmitter GABA (gamma-aminobutyric acid), whose activity is modulated by dopamine, this can be linked back to the neurochemical findings of the previous chapters.

Another way your prior expectation could be treated as a perception is if the top layers of your neural network don't get the prediction error message, meaning inaccurate predictions are not updated. This brings us to the role of *k*, your confidence in the reliability of sensory input. Karl Friston has argued that if someone thinks the level of noise or level of uncertainty in the signal is lower than it actually is (i.e., they underestimate *k*), this leads to too little weight being given to the prediction error and, conversely, too much weight being given to your prior expectations.[544] By discounting the prediction error's message that your prediction is wrong, you will hear what you expect to hear, not what is actually there. A study showing that voice-hearers are more likely to hear a voice in ambiguous white noise after they have been induced to expect to hear it[545] demonstrates this effect in action; prior expectations are given too much weight.

Alternatively, prediction errors may be given an appropriate weighting, but the prediction error information may not be able to ascend up the network to correct the prior expectation. Again, in Jardri and Denève's model, damage to the brain could cause this. Higher cortical regions would then not be able to be informed that their prediction that someone is speaking to you is wrong. Some evidence was found for this in a 2014 fMRI study by Horga and colleagues, which found that, in an auditory learning task, people diagnosed with schizophrenia who heard voices had weaker prediction error signals in their right hemisphere superior temporal sulcus (STS) and middle temporal gyrus (MTG).[546] Patients with weaker prediction error signals also had greater levels of resting activation in these regions during silence. If speech was predicted by a prior expectation, driving activation of the auditory cortex, but none was actually perceived, then prediction error signals would normally dampen down the activity of the auditory cortex by forcing the prior expectation to be revised. However, a failure of prediction error to propagate up the network would not allow this in voice-hearers, leading to the prior expectation being retained as the best explanation and consequently over-activation of the auditory cortex being seen. This fits with the work of Ćurčić-Blake and colleagues in Chapter 27, which found problems in information flow from Wernicke's area to Broca's area, as this could be interpreted as meaning that prediction error could not flow back up to the prefrontal cortex to correct expectations.

This framework also allows us to reframe some of the questions we have been asking. For example, we have discussed models where the brain produces inner speech and something goes wrong, such as a reality-monitoring problem. This leads to the inner speech being wrongly labelled as someone else's speech and transformed into a perceptual experience of another's voice. In contrast, Sam Wilkinson has argued that within a predictive coding framework it is not the case that we 'do' inner speech, which can then be experienced as inner speech or a perception.[547] Instead, the brain either predicts that there is inner speech occurring or it predicts that an external perception of speech is occurring. Wilkinson makes a profoundly important point when he states that '[t]here is no experience of inner speech first, which is somehow then transformed [into a voice]'.

The question then becomes, is the basis of voice-hearing a prediction that the person themselves will speak, or a prediction that the person will hear speech? This brings us back to the age-old debate between speech-production and speech-perception models of voice-hearing, although it frames the question in a different way. The prediction we will hear speech would drive activation of the auditory cortex, leading to the perception of a voice (or a voice-like experience). If there was a problem with prediction error signals this prediction would not be updated and speech would be perceived. Yet this wouldn't explain why the speech musculature is activated during (some) people's voice-hearing. Speech musculature involvement would seem to necessitate not that the person predicts that speech will be heard, but rather that the person predicts that speech will be produced, and then the brain minimizes prediction error by actually creating speech (albeit not to the stage where full vocalization occurs). Another possibility that Wilkinson has raised is that inner speech production involves the prediction that speech will be produced, but the gain on prediction error is turned right down (i.e., it is deemed to have low precision), meaning that action (i.e., actual speech production) need not occur to try and minimize it, nor need the prediction be revised based on a lack of speech being produced. How inner speech can be understood within a predictive processing framework is still being worked out, effectively placing a bar on applying it to voice-hearing at the moment.

Whatever the details, the therapeutic implication of this for someone who wishes to be rid of their voices is that their brain (not necessarily the person themselves though) needs to be persuaded that what it is experiencing is not best predicted as being a voice, but rather as being inner speech or a memory. This means addressing all the cues the brain is getting as to what the experience is. For example, in hypervigilance hallucinations, one cue that what is being experienced is a voice from the external world is the bodily feelings that are accompanying the stimulus, for example muscle tension from fear or anxiety.[548] Simply relaxing the person, either through breathing exercises, relaxation, medication or getting more sleep, may start to remove cues that this stimulus is a voice.

In summary, the predictive processing framework suggests that the *content* of voice-hearing may be driven by prior expectations, and the *occurrence* of voices may be caused by altered estimates of precision or changes to the network itself. Prior expectations can be seen to be driven by life events, which would explain why so many voices are thematically related to earlier traumas or ongoing concerns, and are affected by the socio-economic and cultural milieu one is raised in. What could be altering the structure/function of the network itself though? To understand this we need to consider a person's development. Indeed, any predictive processing model of voice-hearing needs to be developmental.

CHAPTER 39

Neurodevelopmental Theories

Among neurons, our impending death must be a source of much frustration. These are the longest living cells in our body. When we die they could happily live on for many more years, if transplanted into someone else. People, from a neuron's eye view, have no stamina. Nevertheless, neurons undergo lots of changes as we age, learn and grow, particularly in terms of the number and strength of connections between them. A neurodevelopmental model of voice-hearing asks what brain changes happen, when and why, to cause this experience. Such models echo neurodevelopmental models of schizophrenia, which are told as two-hit stories. A first hit causes subtle neural changes in childhood, and then the full-blown emergence of schizophrenia is triggered by a second hit in early adulthood.

Sometimes you can see something subtly different in children who will later go on to be diagnosed with schizophrenia. Walker and colleagues (cf. Chapter 19) examined home videos of young siblings, only one of whom went on to later be diagnosed with schizophrenia. The sibling who would go on to be diagnosed with schizophrenia had worse dexterity, gait and other movement problems. Other studies have found that children who go on to develop schizophrenia reach developmental milestones, such as walking and talking, later. This also appears to be the case for voice-hearing. Seven-year-old children who hear voices are more likely to have shown some developmental delay in motor and social skills in their first year of life, compared with non-voice-hearing children.[549] At the level of the brain, the STG may be developing in a different way. Children with a high genetic risk of receiving a diagnosis of schizophrenia have reduced STG volumes. This fits with the work of Kühn and Gallinat, mentioned in Chapter 25, which suggested that altered STG volumes could be an underlying risk factor for voice-hearing.

So, what could be a first hit that causes these early changes? This is typically proposed to be the result of genes, pregnancy complications or maternal illness during pregnancy. Preeclampsia and extreme premature birth double the risk of children eventually being diagnosed with schizophrenia,[550] as do pregnancy complications (e.g., bleeding, diabetes), abnormal foetal growth and development (e.g., low birthweight, reduced head circumference), and complications of delivery that involve hypoxia (a loss of oxygen to the foetus).[551] At least some of the genes found to be associated with schizophrenia by the Schizophrenia Working Group of the Psychiatric Genomics Consortium (Chapter 40), such as GRM3 (which affects glutamate), have also been found to have their levels of expression altered by hypoxia.[552] Genes and pregnancy complications could work together to increase risk for schizophrenia and, by extension, voice-hearing. Being exposed to infections while in the womb, whether they be viral (e.g., herpes), bacterial (e.g., chlamydia) or parasitical (toxoplasma gondii), is also linked to an increase in the odds of someone later receiving a diagnosis of schizophrenia.[553] For example, having antibodies to toxoplasma gondii in your blood when you are few days old doubles your odds of later being diagnosed with schizophrenia.[554] In terms of voice-hearing specifically, mothers of voice-hearing children (compared with mothers of non-voice-hearing children) have twice the odds of having had an infection during pregnancy.[555] However, the evidence for a causal role of such infections in voice-hearing is too scant to form firm conclusions yet.

What could happen in early adulthood to cause experiences associated with a diagnosis of schizophrenia to emerge from these subtle early developmental changes? What forms the second hit? There are two schools of thought on this. The first argues that it is the turbulent emotional crucible of this time. The second argues for a role of a prominent change that naturally occurs in the brain at this time. We'll focus on the second here as a) we have already discussed in detail the role of life events in voice-hearing, and b) we have all been teenagers. Cortical development during the teenage years involves a substantial reduction in the number of synapses in the brain.[556] As the brain does not become littered with dead neurons, this suggests that neurons aren't being killed off, but rather that there is a reduction in the connections between them. This is referred to as synaptic pruning.

Excessive synaptic pruning could lead people to hear voices. This may sound speculative, but we already know it can cause computers to hear voices. Hoffman and McGlashan created a computer model of the brain to simulate speech perception,[557] and then damaged it in a variety of ways to see what would cause the system to produce verbal outputs when there was no verbal input to it – that is, a computer version of a hallucination. Simply removing nodes in the network (equivalent to killing neurons) did not produce hallucinations. What did cause the computer to hallucinate was a severe reduction in the number of connections between nodes in the network. The computer performed best at speech perception when the number of 'synapses' it had was reduced by 29 per cent. This is comparable to the number of synapses the average person loses during adolescence. A further reduction of 20 per cent of 'synapses' led to the onset of hallucinations in the computer. This mirrored the 20 per cent reduction in the volumes of frontal axon and dendrite branches found in people diagnosed with schizophrenia compared with healthy controls. Despite this finding, a recent review concluded that altered synaptic pruning is an attractive hypothesis for a cause of schizophrenia, but we remain 'rather remote from its proof'.[558]

Life events are easy to weave into a neurodevelopmental account because they have neural consequences. This has been done in John Read and colleagues' traumagenic neurodevelopmental model of psychosis.[559] This argues that the brain changes found in people diagnosed with schizophrenia compared with healthy adults are similar to those found between people who have and have not suffered childhood trauma. It then proposes that the changes to the brains of people diagnosed with schizophrenia are in fact due to their experiences of childhood trauma, rather than any distinct schizophrenia disease process. In this view, there are no 'schizophrenic brains', only traumatized brains.

There are some commonalities between what child abuse does to the brain, and the changes found in the brains of people who hear voices. Changes in superior temporal gyrus (STG) size are associated with suffering childhood traumas such as neglect, physical abuse, sexual abuse, emotional maltreatment[560] and verbal abuse.[561] Child abuse is associated with changes to white matter tracts associated with voice-hearing.[562] Early life stress alters the connectivity of the STG to other regions of the brain[563] and the functioning of the default mode network,[564] and may be associated with reduced activity of the supplemental motor area[565] – all related to the neural changes associated with voice-hearing. Enduring stress early in life is also associated with increased dopamine release in the striatum in response to stressful events decades later,[566] although as we have seen, there is some ambiguity as to whether such changes are associated with voice-hearing. Commonalities cannot blind us to differences though. The grey matter change most reliably associated with stress exposure is a reduction in the size of the hippocampus, and although this is reliably associated with schizophrenia, it is not associated with voice-hearing specifically. The best-evidenced white matter change associated with childhood adversity is a reduction in the integrity of the corpus callosum,[567] yet such a change has not been reliably found to be associated with voice-hearing.[568] Given that not all child abuse leads to voice-hearing, and not all voice-hearing results from child abuse, we would not expect a perfect overlap between their neurology. Furthermore, as we have seen (Chapter 19), there are better ways to test for a relation between child abuse and voice-hearing than comparing their associated neural changes.

Traumatic life events do not need to be seen as a one-hit story. For some people, voice-hearing may occur straight after a trauma, while for others voices may only start after a second hit, which could also take the form of a traumatic life event. As Judith Herman has noted, survivors of child abuse may successfully manage adult life until defensive structures break down due to stressful things happening, such as the breakdown of a marriage, the birth of a child, or the death of a parent. This has been described as the 'sleeper effect' of trauma.[569] Of course, talk of single or dual hits is likely to often be a gross oversimplification. Traumas may instead be, as Debra Lampshire[570] has put it, 'a kaleidoscope of bumps and bruises and harsh words which blend and melt into each other'. The one- vs two-hit approach is a useful yet limited heuristic.

Continuing with this simplification gives us a situation where a first hit could be caused by pre-birth biology (genetics/infection/pregnancy complications) or by traumatic life events, and a second hit could be caused by synaptic pruning or traumatic life events, giving us four different two-hit routes to voice-hearing:

1. First hit = pre-birth biology; Second hit = synaptic pruning.
2. First hit = pre-birth biology; Second hit = trauma.
3. First hit = trauma; Second hit = synaptic pruning.
4. First hit = trauma; Second hit = retraumatization.

It could be hypothesized that routes involving synaptic pruning would be associated with voice-hearing starting in early adulthood (typically associated with a schizophrenia diagnosis), whereas earlier/later onset could be associated with non-synaptic pruning, trauma-based routes. This would fit in with the finding discussed in Chapter 11 that childhood trauma is associated with voice-hearing that begins before the age of 18. It could also be hypothesized that those whose route to voice-hearing involved trauma would have distinct cognitive and neurobiological profiles compared with those whose routes did not. As suffering childhood trauma leads to greater levels of inflammation in adult life,[571] it could hence be predicted that people who hear voices due to developmental pathways involving trauma (routes 2–4 above) should have greater levels of inflammation than those who develop voice-hearing through non-trauma pathways (route 1 above). It is already known that people diagnosed with schizophrenia who have experienced childhood trauma have greater levels of inflammation than equivalent people who have not experienced such trauma.[572]

It is hence possible to create plausible trauma-related and non-trauma-related neurodevelopmental accounts of voice-hearing. We have flagged genes as playing a potential role in both these routes. This brings us back to the question we broached in Chapter 21: could someone's genome, and the specific kind of brain it has built, influence whether or not a trauma will lead to voice-hearing in that person? We can now try and explore this in more depth, but to do this we are going to need to know something about genes.

CHAPTER 40

Are there Genes for Hallucinations?

Charles Darwin's family produced ideas that, it is safe to say, met with varying degrees of success. His grandfather, Erasmus, proposed the idea that roundabouts could cure mental illness by unclogging the congested brains of patients who rode them, but also had an idea for a rocket engine. Thankfully, he never combined the two. Charles' cousin, Francis Galton, published a letter in the world's premier scientific journal on how to best cut a cake, devised a beauty map of women across Britain that ran from attractive to Aberdeen, but also helped develop the concept of heritability.[573]

A commonly cited statistic is that schizophrenia is 80 per cent hereditable. This does not mean that the child of someone diagnosed with schizophrenia has an 80 per cent chance of developing schizophrenia. In fact, only 7 per cent of people diagnosed with schizophrenia have a first-degree relative with any form of psychotic disorder.[574] Nor does it mean that 80 per cent of schizophrenia is caused by genes, and 20 per cent is caused by life events. A trait can be 100 per cent hereditable but still caused by an environmental event. As Richard Bentall notes, if everyone smoked 20 cigarettes a day, then the heritability of lung cancer (if smoking was its only cause) would be 100 per cent, because the only variability in whether people got lung cancer would be due to their genes.[575] Heritability is the extent to which variability between people in something (e.g., height, presence of schizophrenia, etc.) is influenced by genetic variations between them, but it does not tell us the whole story about causation. As Danielle Dick argues, it is likely to be much more informative to try to understand the pathways of risk than to ask whether genes or the environment were the critical factor.[576]

Early studies found that 30–40 per cent of the variability in hallucination-proneness between people in the general population could be explained by genetics.[577] However, a recent study of over 9000 twins found that only 15–32 per cent of the difference in hallucination-proneness between twins (lower range, males; upper range, females) was due to genetics.[578] The majority of the difference in hallucination-proneness between twins was due to the different environmental events they experienced. Studies of hallucinations in people diagnosed with schizophrenia have found that genetic factors account for 43 per cent of the difference between patients. These figures are in the ballpark of the upper range of findings from PTSD research which have found genes account for 13–30 per cent of the difference in levels of re-experiencing symptoms between veterans.[579] This relatively low heritability for hallucinations is consistent with the important role we have seen that traumatic life events often play in the development of voice-hearing. Whatever the extent of genetic involvement, it is clear that there is something that people can inherit in their genes that increases their risk of hearing voices. The first way to explore this is to see if the structure of our genome, specifically the sequence of nucleotides in it, alters our probability of hearing voices. As always, we need a bit of background first.

If you were to take the DNA in the 46 chromosomes most people have, iron its double helix structure flat, and lay it all end to end, you would have something looking like a very, very long ladder, with lots and lots of rungs. A stairway to human, if you will. Each leg of the ladder would be a six-billion-letter word written using only four letters (nucleotides), A (adenine),

C (cytosine), G (guanine) and T (thymine). Each rung on the ladder would be a hydrogen bond, either joining a 'C' on one leg with a 'G' on the other, or joining an 'A' with a 'T' (base pairs). If these rungs were 6cm apart from each other, you would have a ladder that a mouse could climb up to reach the moon. As the rungs are actually only about three nanometres apart, mice will have to pin their hopes on Elon Musk instead.

This is our sequential genome. If you zoomed in on part of one leg of the ladder it might read something like ATGCCGGAGGCCCCGCCTCTG. DNA code looks like hieroglyphics, but is actually much simpler. Egyptian hieroglyphics have three different alphabets and no punctuation. In contrast, the four letters of DNA are only ever used to write three-letter words (codons), resulting in a mere 64 words being in the DNA dictionary. Samuel Johnson should have been a geneticist. Some codons are instructions for making amino acids, the building blocks of proteins, while others act as punctuation (start/stop instructions). Our genome doesn't make great bedtime reading, although it is still preferable to *Atlas Shrugged*.

In some parts of the genome, codons are put together into sentences that act as instructions for making a protein. Broadly speaking, this is what a gene is. A gene has three parts. First, there are exons (short for '*ex*pressed regi*on*'), which are instructions for making amino acids (constituent parts of proteins). These only make up just over 1 per cent of our DNA. So what does the rest of the genome do? Well, imagine that you had a set of instructions for how to make concrete and another set for how to make windows. If all you did was churn out windows and concrete, you would be rather unlikely to end up with a cathedral, unless Picasso had designed it. You need to know when, where and how much of each to produce. This is where the rest of the genome comes in. Exons are separated by introns. These don't contain information for what protein to make, but can be involved in regulating the amount of protein created. Upstream of the exons and the introns in the DNA sequence are regions called regulators. Regulators include promoter and enhancer/silencer regions. Promoter regions are found just before the part of the gene containing the exons and introns, and are where proteins called transcription factors bind to control the rate at which the gene takes the first step (called transcription) towards producing a protein.

Enhancer/silencer regions serve similar functions, but may be located either much further away from the exons/introns or found within the introns themselves. It is now thought that many genetic variations associated with disease are not to be found in exons, but instead lie in introns and regulators. This is because exonic changes would directly impact the protein that is built, potentially wrecking it and causing life-threatening problems for the person. In contrast, changes to the amount of a protein that is made may have a noticeable, but non-catastrophic, effect.

There are a large number of steps involved in a gene expressing itself and in creating a protein from a DNA sequence. Changes at any of these steps could contribute towards voice-hearing. Let's focus on some key steps. First, changes to the DNA sequence in a gene may impact the type of protein that results (if the changes occur in exonic regions), or the amount of protein that is created (e.g., if the changes are in promoter regions). This could involve a change in a single base pair at a specific part of a gene (termed a single nucleotide polymorphism – more on this shortly), or stretches of DNA that would normally be present once in a gene region being either missing altogether (deletions) or present multiple times (duplications), termed copy number variations.

Second, to get the information out of the DNA, a copy of its protein-building instructions must be created and transported out of the cell nucleus to the protein-building machinery in the cell. To do this, an enzyme called RNA polymerase reads off the gene, creating a molecule called pre-messenger RNA (pre-mRNA) from which the intron regions are cut out through a process called splicing, and creates a messenger RNA (mRNA) molecule informed only by the content of the exons. This process is called transcription. One factor affecting transcription is if other molecules bind to the DNA, effectively closing the DNA book so that RNA polymerase cannot read it. An example of this is methylation, where methyl molecules bind to the DNA and block the transcription process.

Third, mRNA heads out of the cell nucleus where it is used to assemble a protein in the cytoplasm of the cell. Post-transcriptional regulation of gene expression refers to factors that influence the ability of mRNA, once produced, to actually go on to make a protein. One such factor is microRNA. These are small molecules, typically only 22 nucleotides long, which nevertheless have a significant effect on post-transcriptional expression by breaking down mRNA and thereby decreasing a gene's ability to make proteins. In effect, microRNAs shoot the messenger. Now that we understand some mechanisms, let's consider how changes to the structural genome itself (i.e., the As, Cs, Gs and Ts) and microRNAs may contribute to voice-hearing, before we come to look at a potential role for methylation in Chapter 41.

Single nucleotide polymorphisms, more simply referred to as SNPs (pronounced 'snips'; our second shibboleth), are a common type of genetic variation. If more than 1 per cent of people have different nucleotides at an exact given point on the genome, this genetic variation is referred to as a SNP. These occur about once every 300 nucleotides, meaning there are roughly ten million SNPs in the human genome. Each SNP is given an alpha-numerical name which starts with 'rs' (which stands for reference SNP) and is followed by a number. For example, take the SNP rs4680. About 20 million letters into chromosome 22 nestles the COMT gene. This gene codes for the catechol-O-methyl transferase protein, an enzyme that helps breaks down dopamine in the prefrontal cortex. When we wander 158 codons into the COMT gene, we find that some people have a GTG sequence.[580] This leads to the amino acid valine being produced. For other people the first G is an A instead, creating the codon ATG, which leads to the production of a different amino acid, methionine. People whose 158th codon creates methionine, on either one of their copies of chromosome 22, have a much less active COMT enzyme. This means dopamine isn't broken down as quickly in their prefrontal cortex, resulting in higher levels of prefrontal dopamine, which changes the way they perceive the world, including making stressful events feel more stressful.[581]

In this example, G and A are referred to as alleles. As genes come in pairs (you get one on the chromosome which came from your mum, and one on the chromosome from your dad), each SNP involves a pair of alleles. The combination of alleles you have is referred to as your genotype. For example, if a SNP involves a C→T polymorphism, the alleles are C and T, and you could have a CC, CT or TT genotype. Most SNPs are relatively benign. Others aren't. For example, take the SNP rs1447295, which is to be found on chromosome 8. If a man has an A allele (i.e., either an AA or AC genotype) then his odds of developing prostate cancer are increased.[582]

Where in our genome should we start looking for SNPs that might be associated with voice-hearing? One place may be in genes that influence dopamine and glutamate transmission. Dystrobrevin binding protein 1 (DTNBP1) is a gene implicated in schizophrenia susceptibility, and influences both dopamine (D2) and glutamate neurotransmission. DTNBP1 has reduced levels of expression in both the STG and hippocampus in people diagnosed with schizophrenia, making it a particularly plausible candidate as a voice-hearing SNP. Indeed, a SNP in this gene (rs4236167) has been found to be associated with voice-hearing in people diagnosed with schizophrenia.[583] As this SNP is located in an intron of this gene, if it was causally involved in voice-hearing it would likely be through affecting the transcription of DTNBP1. Another gene linked to schizophrenia and which affects dopamine release is the cholecystokinin (CCK) gene. A number of studies have found evidence that CCK SNPs may be related to voice-hearing specifically.[584]

Another place to look is in the gene that enables us to talk. At about the same time as we started to walk on two legs (around 400,000 years ago) there occurred a change in the Forkhead Box Protein (FOXP2) gene. This allowed humans to vocalize a new range of sounds. The role of the FOXP2 gene in language was discovered when the genes of a family with a specific language disorder were analysed and a rare mutation was found in the 553rd codon in this gene (causing the codon to produce histidine rather than arginine; hence termed an R553H mutation).[585] Given what the previous chapters have shown us about the neural areas involved in voice-hearing, the neural effects of this rare R553H mutation are particularly interesting. This mutation is associated with grey matter alterations to left Broca's area, the STG bilaterally, and putamen[586] – the components of a neural circuit we saw proposed to be associated with voice-hearing in Chapter 36. The R553H mutation is also associated with reduced Broca's area activation during both overt and covert word production.[587] The proposal that common FOXP2 SNPs may have similar, although less drastic, effects to those of the rare R553H mutation can hence lead to the hypothesis that common FOXP2 SNPs may alter the likelihood of you hearing voices.

This hypothesis has received mixed support. Tolosa and colleagues examined 27 FOXP2 SNPs in 293 people diagnosed with schizophrenia, and then compared the 77 patients who heard voices to the remainder who did not.[588] They found a trend towards an association between some SNPs (rs2396753, rs2253478 and rs1456031) and voice-hearing. However, when my colleagues and I looked at these same three FOXP2 SNPs in 211 people diagnosed with schizophrenia-spectrum disorders with a lifetime history of voices and 122 without, we failed to replicate these findings.[589] There was an interesting kicker to our study though, which we will return to in Chapter 42.

Another place in the genome where SNPs may contribute to voice-hearing is in microRNA genes (miRNA) which, as we have seen, impact the ability of other genes to express themselves. Little work has been done on miRNAs in relation to hallucinations, but a SNP (rs3746444) in the miRNA gene miR-499 has been found to be associated with hallucinations in people diagnosed with schizophrenia.[590] It is thought that this gene plays a role in the immune response. In terms of miRNA genes that could plausibly be linked to voice-hearing, miR-219 has been linked to schizophrenia[591] and found to regulate the maturation of oligodendrocytes, hence potentially altering myelination.[592] More generally, it is notable that a 'striking deviation' has been found in miRNA expression in the STG of people diagnosed with schizophrenia.[593] This means people diagnosed with schizophrenia have a marked difference in the post-transcription gene regulation environment in a key region involved in voice-hearing. Such miRNA has been proposed to influence the expression of a range of genes linked to schizophrenia, including those affecting dopamine and glutamate transmission, offering a post-transcriptional mechanism that could account for some of the changes found in people hearing voices. miRNA changes offer a promising way forward for voice-hearing research.

Returning to studies of candidate SNPs for voice-hearing, a key problem is that these have all been small by genetic standards. Much larger studies have examined what SNPs are associated with schizophrenia. Although 70 per cent of people with this diagnosis hear voices, SNPs associated with schizophrenia still only hint at being associated with voice-hearing specifically. Most recently, a large international collaborative study looked at 9.5 million SNPs in over 30,000 people diagnosed with schizophrenia and over 100,000 healthy controls.[594] This found changes in 108 distinct regions of the genome to be associated with schizophrenia, including in genes associated with the dopamine D2 receptor (DRD2), glutamate neurotransmission (e.g., GRM3), white matter integrity (ZNF804A), and immune function. It is possible that some of these changes may pertain to voice-hearing specifically, although this remains to be seen. In the interim, it should be noted that the genetic variations that were found by this study accounted for only around 3 per cent of the variability between people as to whether they had schizophrenia or not; genetic contributions of SNPs to schizophrenia and voice-hearing are likely to be multiple and small. My personal view is that genes involved in regulating oligodendrocytes and the myelin they spin appear particularly likely to be involved in voice-hearing, as people diagnosed with schizophrenia have the largest differences in the expression of these genes in neural regions linked to voice-hearing (the cingulate cortex, superior temporal gyrus and hippocampus).[595] Consistent with this, a study of around 2500 people diagnosed with schizophrenia hinted that hallucinations might be associated with SNPs in genes involved in a demyelinating disorder (CTDP1).[596]

Going beyond SNPs, deletions of significant chunks of DNA have also been linked to hearing voices. We have already mentioned 22q11.2 deletion syndrome in Chapter 15. Around a quarter of people with this syndrome will go on to be diagnosed with schizophrenia,[597] and it is estimated that 1 per cent of all people diagnosed with schizophrenia will have 22q11.2 deletion syndrome.[598] Voice-hearing in this syndrome may start at the typical age of schizophrenia onset (16–25 years) or much earlier, and can be of the same form and content as that we have seen to be associated with schizophrenia. For example, a study of 30 pre-adolescents (aged 9–12 years) with 22q11.2 deletion syndrome found that five (17 per cent) heard voices.[599] These included hearing a child yelling, strangers talking and voices giving orders. All were experienced as disturbing and unpleasant.

Studying 22q11.2 deletion syndrome gives us hints at genes that might be involved in voice-hearing, and the mechanisms through which they have their effect. Of the multiple genes that would normally be in this deleted stretch of (one copy of) chromosome 22, perhaps the most obvious candidate whose deletion could contribute to psychosis is the COMT gene. We have already discussed its role in influencing cortical dopamine levels. At the level of neurology, it is notable that adults with 22q11.2 deletion syndrome show changes to fronto-temporal white matter pathways,[600] and altered anterior cingulate and auditory cortex activity.[601] We have already seen that such changes are associated with voice-hearing. Mouse models of 22q11.2 deletions have also been examined. One such study suggests that the deletion of the DGCR8 gene on one copy of chromosome 22 may cause increases in dopamine (D2) receptors in the thalamus (a relay station which ferries information from your sensory organs to your cortex for processing), which disrupts its connectivity with the auditory cortex, a problem which can be rectified by antipsychotics.[602]

Despite all these theories of how 22q11.2 deletion syndrome can lead to voice-hearing, a fundamental question that remains unanswered is why this only happens to less than a third of people with this deletion. What else needs to happen? Could traumatic life events also be necessary, perhaps along the lines of the example we saw in Chapter 15? Similarly, the underwhelming evidence for an involvement of SNPs in hallucinations may be because it may not be sufficient to simply have certain SNPs in order for your voice-hearing risk to increase significantly – trauma may also be needed. We are talking here of what is termed a gene–environment interaction, to which we now turn in more detail.

CHAPTER 41

When the World Speaks, the Genome Listens

Two men with different aldehyde dehydrogenase genotypes walk into a bar. This isn't the start of a bad joke (or a good one), but is likely the start of a bad hangover for one of the men. The specific variant of the aldehyde dehydrogenase (ALDH2) gene you possess influences your sensitivity to alcohol. Two people with different versions of this gene could drink the same amount and yet one would have a worse hangover than the other.[603] This is an example of a gene–environment interaction – the extent to which an environmental event (drinking) results in something (a hangover) is influenced by your genes (ALDH2). The idea that common genetic variations may influence the probability of you receiving a psychiatric diagnosis after a stressful life event was ushered into public consciousness by Caspi and colleagues.[604] They reported that variation in a gene involved in serotonin neurotransmission influenced the probability that people reported depression and suicidality after a stressful life event. Back in Chapter 21 we asked what factors may influence whether someone hears voices after a trauma. A possibility we can now address is that your sequential genome is one such factor.

Possessing certain genes may build your brain in such a way that when you encounter a trauma you are more likely to react in a certain way. For example, Pitman and colleagues studied sets of twins, only one of whom went to fight in Vietnam.[605] They began by examining something that was clearly going to be a consequence of combat trauma: heart rate response to a sudden loud sound. They found what you would expect. A combat veteran twin with PTSD had a greater heart rate response when exposed to such sounds than their non-combat-exposed co-twin. This suggested that increased heart rate response after sudden loud noises was an acquired sign of PTSD. It was then examined whether a similar pattern of findings was present for neurological changes often thought to be a consequence of PTSD, such as a smaller hippocampus. They found that decreased hippocampal volumes were present in the twin who had been to Vietnam and come back with PTSD, *and* their twin who had stayed at home. In contrast, in twin sets where one had been to Vietnam and not come back with PTSD and one had stayed at home, neither had decreased hippocampal volumes. PTSD seemed to emerge from having genes which set people up to have lower hippocampal volumes, plus the experience of trauma. Could the same be the case for voice-hearing? Could trauma be particularly likely to lead to voice-hearing if your genes have set you up with a smaller left superior temporal gyrus, a shorter left paracingulate sulcus or decreased myelination in your left fronto-temporal white matter?

There is only preliminary evidence that SNPs may influence the probability of trauma resulting in voice-hearing. A study of gene–environment interactions in relation to voice-hearing was undertaken by me and my colleagues in Sydney, as mentioned in Chapter 40. We looked at a specific set of SNPs in the FOXP2 gene and four types of parental child abuse (sexual, physical, emotional and neglect). People diagnosed with schizophrenia who had suffered parental emotional abuse (verbal abuse/humiliation) and had the CC genotype of the FOXP2 SNP rs1456031 were more likely to hear voices than patients who had suffered similar such abuse but had an AA genotype. Another study reported that a SNP in the brain-derived neurotrophic factor (BDNF) gene,[606] which creates a protein that helps new neurons to grow and existing neurons to survive, altered the probability that survivors of child abuse experienced psychotic-like experiences as adults. The SNP in question (rs6265) involved a change to the 196th letter of the BDNF gene, resulting in the 66th codon in this gene being either valine (Val) or methionine (Met), and is hence referred to as the Val66Met BDNF polymorphism. People who suffered child abuse (emotional, physical or sexual abuse) and had at least one Met codon had greater levels of psychotic-like experiences than people who suffered child abuse and had no Met codons. This was interpreted as being due to Met carriers being more vulnerable to the neurotoxic effects of stress and its knock-on effects on dopamine transmission. It is hence plausible that future research will find specific SNPs that influence the probability of someone specifically developing voice-hearing after child abuse.

No replication has yet been attempted of the above studies and, historically, only around a third of such studies are able to be replicated by other researchers.[607] Furthermore, we should recall the findings of a study by Arseneault and colleagues from Chapter 21. They found that the rates of psychotic experiences people reported following childhood trauma were not significantly different in people at low, high and very high genetic risk of developing psychosis. Based on the current state of evidence alone, which consists of unreplicated findings and suggestive theories, we must conclude that the evidence that child abuse can cause people to hear voices is far stronger than the evidence that the probability of this occurring is influenced by variations in people's sequential genome.

Although we have focused on the negative aspects of gene–environment interactions, genetic differential susceptibility theory (GDST) suggests a potential upside. Whereas the implication above has been that there are 'risk' genes for voice-hearing, GDST proposes that 'risk' genes may actually be 'susceptibility' genes. Susceptibility genes are responsive to both the effects of positive and negative environments. Such a gene would increase the probability of a negative outcome in the presence of adversity but increase the probability of a positive outcome when the person is in a supportive environment. GDST is nature rolling the dice. There is some evidence that possessing the same genotype that increases the risk you will develop behavioural problems if you encounter adverse child experiences also makes you more likely to benefit from supportive psychotherapy environments.[608] Similarly, although children who possess a Val-Val version of the catechol-O-methyltransferase Val158Met (COMT) polymorphism are more likely than their Met-carrying counterparts to show increased aggression after problematic life events, they have lower levels of aggression than their Met counterparts in the absence of such problematic life events.[609] As such, we could speculate that the same genotype that encourages a person to hear voices should they suffer a childhood trauma could have beneficial effects for that person should they not experience such a trauma.[610]

We have considered how the sequential genome we inherit might be involved in voice-hearing, but DNA carries two levels of information. The second layer sits on and around your DNA and controls the volume of your genes – that is, their ability to produce proteins. This is the epigenome, and it is shaped by the world. If your genes are in the music studio, knocking out tunes, then the world is at the mixing desk, fading up and down your genes' song, and the knob it turns to do this is the epigenome. Identical twins have the same sequential genome, but the different life experiences they have mean that they will have different genes turned on or off, or up or down; they have different epigenomes. Some life events will have epigenetic effects that cause your genes to be temporarily turned on or off, whereas other events will cause permanent changes to your genes' expression. Some genes will only be open to epigenetic modification during specific times of your life (critical periods), whereas others will always be amenable to altering their expression. The early social environment appears to be a particularly important period when life events can shape the activity of genes in this way.

Your epigenome doesn't just bear the marks of the living. Generations of cold, dead hands can still be seen imprinted on it. Your epigenome is shaped by what happened in your parents' and grandparents' lifetimes. It was originally a tenet of genetics that what happened to you in your lifetime had no effect on the genome of any subsequent offspring you had. Your DNA is fixed, and the half of your child's DNA that you will contribute only differs to yours due to random mutations and recombination. There was no known mechanism through which you could actually update or change your DNA to give something to your children. The reassuring implication of this was that whatever you did to yourself before you had children (e.g., heroin, self-flagellation, weight lifting, accountancy), or had done to you (e.g., abuse), your children would still receive a clean genetic slate.

There is now an emerging, although still controversial, evidence base that this is not the case. For example, Dias and Ressler gave male mice electric shocks every time they (the mice, not the experimenters) smelt acetophenone, a chemical used in perfumes that smells of cherries and almonds.[611] The mice naturally came to shudder at the smell of this. The odd thing was that when these mice later had children, they too feared the smell even though there was no reason for them to do so; they had never received shocks in relation to the smell. Not only that, but the children of these children also feared the smell. How was this possible? It emerged that the mice who were shocked, as well as their descendants, had altered olfactory neurocircuitry which enabled this effect to occur. This suggested that what had happened to the shocked mice somehow led to changes in the DNA in their sperm and was passed on to their children. This is not the only finding of this kind. Other studies have found that the normally raised children of rats whose parents had been repeatedly and unpredictably ripped away from their mothers still showed more signs of rat depression, such as simply giving up on tasks, than the normally raised children of rats whose parents had normal rat childhoods.[612] What exactly is happening here at the level of DNA?

The world can speak to your genes through a range of processes, with a particularly important one being methylation. This doesn't involve changes to your sequential genome, but rather the attachment of methyl groups to it. The best known mechanism involves methylation of parts of the promoter region of a gene, with the effect of silencing or down-regulating the expression of the gene.[613] If a mother mouse is undernourished while pregnant with a boy mouse then, when the child is born, the DNA in its sperm is methylated in a different way. It was recently found that the male children of mother mice who had been undernourished while pregnant had DNA with sperm that was less methylated in 111 regions, relative to sperm from male mice whose mothers had been normally fed while they were pregnant.[614] When this sperm was used to make another baby mouse this altered methylation was passed on. This effect did not pass on to the third generation though. Methylation seems to visit the lives of parents onto only the first and second generations (contra Numbers 14.18). The existence of this mechanism makes a lot of sense, as it allows children to be prepared to deal with the type of world they are likely to face.

While intergenerational inheritance of methylation patterns is controversial, it is less controversial that life events alter the methylation of your genome and hence the expression of your genes. When you come out of the womb (as well as potentially while you are still in the womb), the world you are exposed to impacts you through methylation. The amount that a mother rat licks her pup alters the methylation of promoter regions of genes involved in the stress response, causing pups who are licked more to have a less extreme physiological stress response, an effect that persists into adulthood.[615] Similarly, we now know that child abuse is associated with epigenetic changes involving altered methylation of the genome that are present deep into adulthood.[616]

Epigenetics has not yet been directly examined in relation to voice-hearing, although the methylation of the genome of people diagnosed with schizophrenia is beginning to be studied. A recent study looked at the methylation of over 7000 sites in the genome of people diagnosed with schizophrenia and found an association between methylation at a number of these sites and the levels of reality distortion experiences (i.e., delusions and hallucinations).[617] Increased levels of reality distortion were associated with less methylation near some genes (e.g., LAX1, TXK, PRF1, CD7) and greater methylation near other genes (CD244, MPG). What many of these genes have in common is that they are involved in the body's inflammatory response (e.g., its response to infection).

Gene–environment interactions and epigenetics have the potential to improve our understanding of the causes of voice-hearing by bridging the 1960s and 1980s to create a model that integrates genetics with life events. However, at present we lack hard evidence that genes can moderate the relation between trauma and voice-hearing or that epigenetics mediates this relation. This will be for future studies to test. If this is found to be the case, then this has the potential to have important consequences for how we think about ways to help. Changes in methylation can be reversed by both pharmacological *and* psychological means. Words and pills may sometimes end up working through the same mechanisms. This is a good point to turn to the question of how people distressed by their voices can be assisted.

CHAPTER 42

Turning to Recovery

Different people want different ways to be assisted with overwhelming, distressing voice-hearing experiences. We recently found that people hearing voices had one of two basic stances towards recovery.[618] The first was 'turning away'. Here, people generally noticed a turning point when they were prescribed medication that helped. As one participant put it, 'I can function better, and I can think better, and I've been able to pass my courses.' Medication eliminated voices in some people and allowed others to change their response to their voices. For example, instead of being overwhelmed by the voices, they were able to listen to them for a few minutes and then distract themselves. People with a turning-away approach tended to accept a medical model of the experience, viewed their voices as being symptoms of an illness and had a strong sense of wanting to put the experience behind them and get on with their lives. This echoes what has been termed a 'sealing over' recovery style, characterized by cordoning off psychotic experiences from the rest of one's life,[619] and what Frank has referred to as a quest memoir narrative: acceptance of illness with trials, told stoically, and with no special insight gained.[620]

For people who want to pursue this course, a range of other biological interventions could become available in future. Pharmacologically, we have already mentioned the possibility that drugs with anti-obsessional effects could be useful for people with repetitive voices. We have seen intimations that inflammation may contribute to the development of voice-hearing, potentially due to earlier trauma, and there is some evidence that anti-inflammatory drugs (e.g., aspirin[621]) may be helpful for hallucinations in people diagnosed with schizophrenia. Oestrogens also have an anti-inflammatory effect and there is some evidence that these can improve hallucinations in women diagnosed with schizophrenia.[622] In addition, oestrogens aid the growth and repair of neurons, including re-myelination, offering an alternative explanation for any beneficial effect they have. Other agents with neuroprotective effects, such as omega-3 fatty acids, have also been found to have some beneficial effects, such as reducing the probability that someone at high genetic risk of psychosis will actually go on to develop psychosis.[623] Given the potential for myelin damage to fronto-temporal white matter pathways to be involved in voice-hearing, drugs currently being developed to aid in re-myelination, such as anti-LINGO-1, may prove of help to some people with distressing voices.[624]

Another new biological intervention may arise from considering how we can create a therapy from the significant body of neuroimaging data we now have on what areas of the brain are lighting up when people hear voices. One way is to simply try and get people to change the activity in these regions of their own brain, themselves. In his book *Do Androids Dream of Electric Sheep?*, Philip K. Dick described a machine that could change your own neural activity and corresponding mental state. He called this a 'Penfield mood organ' (inspired by the work of Penfield and Perot – see Chapter 24). Dialling a number into this machine would induce a specific emotional state in you:

> From the bedroom Iran's voice came. 'I can't stand TV before breakfast.'
>
> 'Dial 888,' Rick said as the set warmed. 'The desire to watch TV, no matter what's on it.'

> 'I don't feel like dialing anything at all now,' Iran said.
>
> 'Then dial 3,' he said.
>
> 'I can't dial a setting that stimulates my cerebral cortex into wanting to dial!...'
>
> 'I'll dial for both of us,' Rick said, and led her back into the bedroom. There, at her console, he dialed 594: pleased acknowledgment of husband's superior wisdom in all matters.

It turns out we may be able to jettison machines and alter our neural activity in clearly defined parts of the brain at will. Neurofeedback is a way in which you can learn to control your brain using techniques learnt from receiving real-time feedback from your brain activity. One version of this uses fMRI to show people the real-time activity in a specific region of their brain. In user-friendly set ups, the participant is shown a screen with an object such as a submarine on it. The submarine represents the level of activity in a specific region of the brain, say the left pSTG. The participant is then asked to try and use mental strategies to increase the level of activity in this area, and if this activity does actually change then the submarine rises to give them feedback. People can then use these mental techniques, learnt in the scanner, to alter their brain activity when they are back in the real world.

This sounds like science fiction, but is not. Neurofeedback allowing people to influence the activity in their anterior cingulate cortex has been found to help with chronic pain.[625] Neurofeedback could similarly be employed by people hearing voices,[626] with an obvious area to target being the left pSTG. Gaining control over this region could allow people to downregulate its activity of the left pSTG during voice-hearing, potentially reducing the severity of the voices. This would also have the advantage of allowing people to quieten down the voices they dislike, as they spoke, while still allowing valued voices to speak. Trials are currently underway.

What about people who want to have a different type of recovery journey, who aren't helped by drugs or who have understandings of their voices that don't sit well with biological interventions and who want to go beyond this? This might be someone like Lucy, a hearer who described how her doctors 'just wanted to put me on medication instead of dealing with why I was hearing the voices'.[627] Our recovery styles study found another group of people with voices whose recovery stories involved a 'turning towards' approach. These people were characterized by a tendency to turn to face problems, to actively engage with voices, to be curious about what voice-hearing meant, to test their beliefs about voices, and to change their relationships with voices. Some hearers may actively choose such an approach, while others may only turn to this if medication has failed. Indeed, in turning towards narratives, the importance of medication in recovery was either not emphasized, noted as ineffective or had costs outweighing its benefits.

The people who took this approach described how they had been transformed through experiencing voice-hearing and its associated challenges. They, like Peter in Chapter 5, had come to understand voices as communicating something valuable, albeit in a distressing manner. They described a transformation in their identity as a result of becoming unwell and hearing voices, including becoming less angry and more empathic toward others, more communicative about their emotions, and having a stronger sense of self. One stated, 'In a way it's been good that I got sick because I'm a lot less angry… It gives me heaps of empathy for other people too.' People with this recovery style would challenge their voices or test their beliefs about them. This wasn't easy; as one person put it:

> Challenging the voices…they might say the whole world will end and your mother will die or people will

> come round and kill you. But I actually learnt if I said no, no one would come round and kill me.

Another technique was to interpret challenging comments as a metaphorical expression of voices' concerns, which were deserving of attention (like Peter did in Chapter 5). For example, one participant responded to threatening comments by framing her debate with her voices as a series of poetry:

> It was a way to be able just to listen to them in an artistic way. So rather than take it at face value…it sort of was speaking in a more metaphorical sense. They weren't necessarily out to get me, it was more like they were concerned about something and I wanted to make sense of what was going on at the time.

Such a change in perspective has been nicely described elsewhere by Debra Lampshire,[628] who writes about how she came to view her voices as 'actually trying to help me, yet they just had very poor communication skills, and it was my responsibility to interpret what they were saying into something that was helpful and useful for me'.

Our study also found that listening to what voices were saying and responding in a moderate and reasonable manner was characteristic of recovery. As voices were understood as being part of the person, learning more about voices and engaging with them also meant learning more about oneself. This resonated with the Māori concept of voices as a 'difficult gift' which is nonetheless an ordinary part of daily life.[629] Coming to hold a normalized account of what it means to hear voices was pivotal in turning towards recovery narratives, opening up the possibility of a normal, non-pathologized identity:

> It really opened up my mind to this as an experience that was normal in the world… Whereas before that

> I thought it was my shame. My shame, my fault, my illness. You know, it was all about me and me broken.

People's different recovery journeys should be respected and supported, going beyond simply talking about choice and actually offering it. Mental health services need to work out ways to achieve what a given person wants as their outcome, rather than provide a one-size-fits-all service. Providers must start from 'what do you want to do?' rather than 'this is what I do'.[630] Talking is central to this. Indeed, talking can be a therapy in itself.

CHAPTER 43

The Long Talk to Freedom

What do you do if someone complains that a demon is speaking to them from inside their stomach? This was a problem faced by a nineteenth-century physician, Anton Müller. His answer was to apply a blistering agent to the patient's stomach. As a blister rose, he cut it open, bent down and pulled a small statue out of it. This, he told the patient, was the source of the voice. He then cast it to the floor where it shattered into a thousand pieces.[631] Bizarrely, the voice the patient heard did indeed vanish, although this wasn't the end of the story. The patient became convinced that another demon had entered the wound, except this one didn't speak.[632] The type of technique used by Müller was called the 'pious fraud'. Psychological techniques have long been used to work with people's belief systems to try and rid them of voices.

Today's psychological therapies neither use the pious fraud nor aim to rid people of voices. Instead they work to help people transition to hearing voices unproblematically. Psychological therapies (and the Hearing Voices Movement) have been much more open than pharmacological interventions to the idea that recovery can be achieved even if the person is still hearing voices, and have developed an array of approaches to try to help people. These include cognitive behavioural therapy (CBT), acceptance and commitment therapy (ACT), avatar therapy, compassion-focused therapy (CFT), competitive memory training (CMT), hallucination-focused integrative therapy (HIT), relating therapy, and the Maastricht interview approach of the HVM.

In terms of funding, evidence base and availability, CBT leads the pack. This approach is based on the cognitive model of voice-hearing, which proposes that the distress voices cause is a product of what the hearer believes about their voices, rather than due to their presence per se. As noted earlier, believing the voice you hear has great power, and that you have no means to control it, is associated with greater levels of distress. What people believe about their voices is in turn influenced by the mental maps (schema) they have about their social world. For example, schema about power and subordination (e.g., 'I am weak' – 'other people are strong') influence how much power people think their voices have.[633] Such schema typically develop in early childhood and reflect early childhood experiences. Suffering child abuse, for example, may lead you to position others as powerful and yourself as powerless. Early life experiences hence influence what you believe about the world, which shapes what you believe about your voices, which in turn influences the amount of distress and disability you experience as a result of the voices. To address this, CBT is built around working out the links between what someone thinks about their voices and what they feel/do in response. Beliefs that lead to distress and disability are then examined with the hearer, to see if alternatives may be possible. This sounds somewhat abstract, so let's take an example.[634]

Raymond, aged 40, was hearing threatening voices saying things such as 'You've wasted your life, you screwed it all!' and 'You should be punished and dead, you will pay!' He also had paranoid delusions and high levels of anxiety. As a result, he lived an isolated life, alone in his house in which he had installed surveillance cameras and where he barricaded his bedroom at night. During his initial assessment with a psychologist, Raymond identified some of the triggers of his voices. He would hear voices while he was bored at home, when he was silent or had nothing to occupy his mind with, and when night drew in. Raymond then set goals for his psychological therapy: he wanted better ways to cope with his voices, delusional beliefs and anxiety, so as to become autonomous at nights again.

The first technique used to achieve these goals was for Raymond to understand links between his own thoughts and his voices. He realized his voice-hearing was frequently preceded by recurrent negative internal dialogues he had when bored, and that what the voices said represented his own worries. To address this, Raymond began changing his inner dialogue, saying things to himself such as: 'I do not need to be punished for anything, as I have never hurt anyone. I have already improved my life, quit drinking and drugs, and deserve to be happier.' Second, Raymond was encouraged to challenge negative appraisals of the voices, by considering if what he believed about the voices was true. Guided discovery, which involves the therapist gently pointing out inconsistencies in a client's beliefs, in the manner of the TV detective Columbo, was used to help Raymond see that there was no evidence to support his persecutory beliefs about voices, and to help him realize that he had remained safe and had not been attacked or even threatened by anyone for years. Third, he was encouraged to examine his safety behaviours, to see that they stopped disconfirmatory evidence being obtained, and to use behavioural training to change this. Raymond had the assumption that '[i]f I do not remain isolated and vigilant, activate the security system and barricade the bedroom, then I'll be assaulted'. He learnt that by barricading himself in his room he was never able to see if this assumption was actually true. The assumption was slowly challenged by first getting Raymond to remove the doorstop, then to unlock the bedroom door, then to substitute watching security cameras in the evening with watching movies, and eventually to remove the barricade. He was also encouraged to get involved in social situations, such as taking walks, shopping and visiting family.

Whereas before therapy Raymond felt that his voices were 'scary and they freak me out', at the end of therapy he felt that '[t]hey're still there but I don't attend to them as much now'. Whereas he used to think his voices meant that 'I'm being chased and will be punished', he now felt that '[t]hese are probably my own thoughts'. As a result, he said that 'I'm not as anxious as before. I can relax more often now', whereas before he'd feel 'I cannot cope. I'm losing control.' As a result, his abilities to cope with voices and persecutory beliefs increased and his anxiety reduced. This allowed Raymond to be able to follow his goal to go back into education.

One problem in assessing the evidence base for CBT for psychosis (and hence for voice-hearing) is the potential for bias. It is well publicized by psychologists that psychiatric drug trials sponsored by a pharmaceutical company in which at least one of the authors has a declared financial conflict of interest are nearly five times more likely to report a positive result than an independently funded trial.[635] However, for some reason, studies of the effectiveness of CBT for psychosis being led by clinicians whose livelihood is in part dependent on them providing CBT for psychosis are not seen as introducing equivalent bias. The meta-analyses we currently have somewhat disagree on the effectiveness of CBT for psychosis, in part because of methodological differences between them. Overall, though, the emerging picture is that CBT has a moderate benefit for people who hear voices.[636]

This moderate overall effect appears likely to represent a situation in which some people with voices are helped by CBT, and others not so much. One factor which influences whether someone is helped or not is how well they get on with their therapist. Goldsmith and colleagues have shown that the therapeutic alliance between therapist and client affects how effective CBT is for people with psychosis.[637] In situations where there is a good therapeutic alliance, more therapy sessions lead to a better outcome, but in situations where the therapeutic alliance is bad, more sessions lead to worse outcomes. Could it be that the therapeutic alliance is the only important aspect of therapy, with it mattering *who* you see but not what specific model or technique they use? This idea is called the Dodo bird conjecture. It seems unlikely to be true. For example, a trial of CBT for PTSD found this technique to be more effective than a more generic 'supportive therapy' intervention. Both the therapeutic alliance and the specific psychological techniques employed appear to contribute to the effectiveness of CBT for psychosis.[638] The same seems likely to be true for voice-hearing.

Particular aspects of voices are more likely to be helped by CBT than others. The power people perceive their voices to have seems amenable to re-evaluation, with an ensuing reduction in the probability that people will follow any harmful dictates of their voices or believe that their voices can hurt others.[639] To illustrate this more clearly, one of my voice-hearing colleagues describes that a turning point for her was when she asked her voices, who claimed to be all powerful, to do the washing up. Obviously, the voices could not do this, which was bad news for the state of the kitchen, but good news for her as she realized that the voices could perhaps not do all that they claimed, such as hurting her family.

Instead of focusing on the person's beliefs about their voices, a slightly different approach has been taken by relating therapy, developed by Mark Hayward.[640] This differs from CBT by viewing voices not as sensory or thought-like stimuli that people hold *beliefs about*, but as social, people-like, entities with whom the voice-hearer has a *relationship*. For example, Julie had heard voices since the age of 18. There was a dominant male voice, which was abusive, commanding and continuous. Julie responded to the voice by pleading and often responding to its commands by self-harming. She constantly felt as if she wanted to die. Therapy focused on trying to change Julie's relationship with this voice. It was proposed that Julie's sense of powerlessness and submissiveness to the voice may have been reinforcing its dominant attempts at control. Using role play it was explored how the voice responded when she was pleading (it became more powerful), angry (it goaded her more) and assertive (the voice was taken aback). As a result, Julie started to feel more in control of her voices, even though the tone of the voices remained critical.[641]

How to make nasty voices nicer is a big problem for psychological therapies because, as we have seen, negative content is a key determinant of the amount of distress that voice-hearing causes. It is hence concerning that there is no evidence that CBT can change the negative content of voices. In contrast, hallucination-focused integrative treatment (HIT), which integrates CBT techniques, family therapy, rehabilitative efforts, mobile assertive crisis intervention and antipsychotic medication in routine treatment, has been found to reduce both the distress *and* negative content of voices in chronic patients, compared with treatment as usual.[642] The effectiveness of this approach suggests that addressing the wider milieu of the person may be necessary to change the nastiness of voices.

Another potential way to reduce the negative content of voices is offered by compassion-focused therapy (CFT). This builds on the idea that people with high levels of shame find it hard to be self-supporting or self-reassuring, in part because they have never learnt to be this way, due to a history of being shamed and criticized. By helping people to develop self-compassion and self-soothing, perceived threats can be reduced. You can see a short video on CFT as applied to voices on YouTube.[643] Research has found that the greater capacity someone hearing voices has to self-reassure themselves, the less shameful content their voices have, suggesting that CFT has the potential to reduce such negative emotions.[644] Although CFT is only starting to be empirically trialled as a way to help people with their voices, preliminary evidence suggests it can reduce negative content. In a small pilot study of three people, CFT 'had a major effect on voice-hearers' hostile voices, changing them into more reassuring, less persecutory and less malevolent voices'. [645] The histories of the participants in this study were notable, given our previous discussion of shame. One 'had a sexual secret that he was ashamed of, that led him to worry about others discovering this secret and then punishing and rejecting him'. Another heard a voice telling him he was a paedophile. These stories echo those discussed in the context of hypervigilance hallucinations in Chapter 17.

The ideas of CFT fit with the benefits of self-forgiveness in situations where an abuser has made a victim wrongly believe that they were responsible for what happened. This can be a hard belief to shift. Simply saying 'it's not your fault', as Robin Williams does to Matt Damon in the film *Good Will Hunting*, may not be sufficient to convince people of their innocence if they have lived with feelings of guilt for many years.[646] It may instead involve a significant internal struggle. We saw in Chapter 5 how Peter held a virtual court of law in his own head, weighed up the evidence for and against his guilt, accepted that he was a child and did not choose to be abused, and found himself innocent. Ron Coleman[647] describes a similar process in regard to a fellow voice-hearer, Jenny, with whom he was working:

> She had to find herself innocent of any fault within the abuse... It did not matter that I like many others told Jenny that she was the victim in this situation... what mattered is what Jenny thought... [She] had to put herself on trial and in order to do this had to go through the experience again and again from every conceivable angle until she could say with real conviction I am innocent.

Although we are talking here about the person becoming more compassionate towards themselves, if we accept the argument that voices represent parts of the self, then becoming more compassionate towards the voices themselves may also be of benefit. For example, Eleanor Longden[648] describes the results of being compassionate towards the very hostile and angry voices she heard:

> 'Awful things have happened to you,' I said to them one day, 'and you've carried all the negative emotions and memories. And all I've ever done in return is attack and criticize you. It must have been really hard to be so vilified and misunderstood.' There was a very long pause before a response finally came: 'Yes. Thank you.'

The recently developed avatar therapy,[649] created by Julian Leff, can be seen to employ the ideas of relating therapy and CFT, in addition to ideas from CBT and the HVM. Given this, it is unsurprising that no one is quite sure what precisely it was that resulted in an initial trial of this approach finding beneficial effects for people who hear voices. Avatar therapy involves getting people to engage with their dominant voice and to change their relationship with it. The idea has echoes in the past. In the 1700s, when William Cowper (Chapter 8) was hearing voices, Samuel Johnson sent encouraging suggestions down a speaking tube secreted behind the bed.[650] Although times have changed, we are still faced with the problem of how to engage effectively with invisible entities. Fortunately, technology has advanced beyond the speaking tube. In avatar therapy, the patient is invited to create an avatar of their voice (a visual representation of what they think the face of the voice would look like), which is then displayed on a computer screen in front of them. The therapist then goes into a separate room and speaks to the hearer via headphones, alternatively pretending to be the voice (in which case the avatar moves its lips on the screen and appears to speak, in a distorted version of the therapist's voice) or speaking as themselves to offer coaching on how to respond to the voice or how to challenge what it just said. You can see the process in action on YouTube.[651] During six half-hour sessions the avatar, as voiced by the therapist, comes to stop abusing the hearer, to start offering them support, and to be more under the hearer's control. The initial results were positive, with some people's voices even vanishing altogether, which no one expected. A larger randomized controlled trial of avatar therapy is now underway. Bringing voices into the light appears to be the best way out of the darkness.

The cognitive model of voice-hearing also suggests that because distress is, in part, dependent on what you believe about voice-hearing, then the same words spoken by a voice may cause distress and disability in one culture but not in another. We have already seen (Chapter 8) how Western and non-Western views of the self can influence the way voice-hearing is experienced. Yet even in cultures where occasional voice-hearing experiences are seen as normal, some voice-hearing experiences will be viewed as sliding into an illness state. For example, while some experiences of voice-hearing in the Māori culture are viewed as resulting from *matakite*, a spiritual gift in which an individual is considered to be able to see beyond the physical realm, others which are more intrusive and negative are viewed as problematic.[652] In cultures where spirits are understood to cause voices there are prescribed theological and social ways to control them, to give the experience meaning and to offer the hearer control and hope. For example, in the Inuit culture the ability to hear voices is called 'thinness' and is a characteristic of the valued Shaman.[653] If the hearer is able to take up such a role they are kept within society's embrace rather than abandoned at its borders. This raises the question as to whether meaning can be as therapeutic as medication.

CHAPTER 44

The Voice-Hearer's Stone

One of the founders of the Hearing Voices Movement (HVM), Marius Romme, once had a conversation with the psychologist Richard Bentall. 'The trouble is,' said Romme to Bentall, 'you want to cure hallucinations, whereas I want to liberate them. I think they [voice-hearers] are like homosexuals in the 1950s – in need of liberation, not cure.'[654] The analogy is not perfect, but it is powerful. It offers someone hearing voices the opportunity of accepting their experiences, recognizing them as a natural human variation, and not feeling ashamed. Of course, this is unlikely to be something someone can do alone. As Audre Lorde put it, without community, there is no liberation. This is why there is a Hearing Voices *Movement*, rather than merely a Hearing Voices Approach. Indeed, Romme's goal was explicitly 'to offer the hearers of voices an organization through which they can emancipate themselves'.[655] Chapter 43 focused on psychological therapies for distressing voice-hearing, and we may now ask what the HVM's views on 'treatment' are.

The HVM has views on how to help voice-hearers because it does not romanticize the experience and recognizes it can be highly problematic. Indeed, the analogy between the LGBTQI social movement and the HVM breaks down precisely because it is recognized in the HVM that voice-hearing may often be a sign of a problem (trauma) and can be viewed as an illness state. For example, Romme describes how:

> Voice hearers become ill, in the sense of becoming dysfunctional, as a result of not being able to cope with their voices and the problems that lie at their roots... To recover, voice hearers learn to cope with the social and emotional consequences of their original problems... Gradually they discover that voices are expressing emotions, and these emotions are those the voice hearer experienced as the result of the traumatic situation... The recovery process is one of the turning points in the relationship with the voices, with the person becoming more powerful and independent... Voices are the stories of threatening emotions, hopelessness, feelings of guilt, aggression and anxiety.[656]

What, then, is to be done? The HVM approach shares many similarities with psychological therapies, in part because such therapies have absorbed many of the lessons of the HVM: normalizing voice-hearing, trying to understand it in the context of the person's life, and attempting to change the person's relationship with their voices. Yet there is a notable difference. The Maastricht approach, developed by some in the HVM, attempts to help voice-hearers to recover by exploring the meaning of their voices. At its heart is the idea that voice-hearing is a personal reaction to life stresses, whose meaning and purpose can be deciphered, with the voice often taking the form of a metaphor. The approach stresses how voice-hearers who come to psychiatric services have become stuck in destructive communication patterns with their voices. The Maastricht approach looks for a way for people to change their relations with their voices, make sense of them and cope better. A key tool to do this is the Maastricht hearing voices interview.[657] This aims to create structured information about the voice-hearer and their voices. It is completed in conjunction with the voice-hearer (often being administered by another person with experience of hearing voices) and helps them to explore their own experiences, achieve distance from the voices and plan treatment. The interview includes sections on the characteristics of the voices, personal history of voice-hearing (e.g., 'What were the personal and social circumstances when the voices appeared for the first time?'), what the voices say, triggers, the impact of the voices on life, one's balance of relationship with one's voices, coping strategies, and experiences in childhood. The authors suggest that the interview itself can have a therapeutic effect because voice-hearers became 'aware of the meaning of their voices, the relationship with their emotions and important issues in their lives, and felt stimulated to try other coping strategies'. For some, this may be the voice-hearer's stone, capable of transforming base experiences into valuable ones.

As part of the interview, two key questions are to be answered: 'Who do the voices represent?' and 'What problems do the voices represent?' An active collaboration between the voice-hearer and interviewer 'breaks the code' of the voices and results in what is termed the 'construct'. This then forms the basis for treatment, which has three goals: 1) to identify the most hindering aspects of the voices, choose a strategy to deal with this, and practise it; 2) to improve the voice-hearer's relationship with difficult emotions and provide alternative coping mechanisms for dealing with those emotions; 3) to deal with historical events that have been difficult to accept, and work through any associated anxiety and guilt. As should be clear, at the heart of this approach is working with the voice-hearer's emotions. Indeed, Romme has argued that voices may be emotions, echoing a young Sigmund Freud (Chapter 18). For example, if it is identified that someone has not been allowed to express anger or sadness, and this is related to their voices, then working on these emotions may cause the voices to disappear or place their relationship with the person on a more positive footing.

Another technique that has evolved out of the Hearing Voices Movement is voice dialogue. This goes directly to the voice for information. In it, the therapist asks permission from the hearer to directly speak with their voice(s), and then proceeds to respectfully 'interview' the voice(s) as one might a new acquaintance. The timing and reasons for the voice coming into being, its relation to the person and what it 'wants' are all explored. Take Karen's experience.[658] Although she had heard voices since her childhood, she had a steady job and coped well until, aged 20, she joined a religious sect. The sect told her that her voices were 'instruments of the devil' and that she should get rid of them. The four male voices she heard then became more negative and disturbing, commenting on her behaviour and her thinking and telling her to kill herself. After receiving a range of diagnoses, including schizophrenia and borderline personality disorder, and spending four years living in a psychiatric hospital where antipsychotic medication helped her anxiety but not her voices, she sought an HVM-style intervention. The first session started with the therapist asking Karen for her permission to talk to her voices. She agreed, and the therapist interviewed each voice in turn. Each voice reported that they entered into Karen's life when she was aged four, a time when she was feeling quite lonely and had been sexually abused. The voices said their job was to help Karen feel less lonely and overcome difficult moments. Before the sect had made her reject the voices, Karen had accepted the voices and they felt acknowledged, but when she began to reject her voices, they also rejected her by becoming very negative and telling her to kill herself. The voices told the therapist that they wanted Karen to accept them again, as she used to do. Karen, who was able to 'overhear' the therapist talking with the voices, agreed and began setting aside time in the evening to engage with the voices. By the next session, two of the voices had disappeared, and those that remained were easy to ignore. The voices became more positive, no longer criticizing Karen or telling her to kill herself. Therapy ended a few sessions later. When Karen contacted the therapist four years later, she reported that she was happy and living with her two young children in a new city. She had not been psychiatrically hospitalized but still took a very low dose of antipsychotic medication. She only heard only one voice, but it was positive and supportive and she liked talking to it.

This vignette suggests that the HVM may be able to achieve the goal, for those who wish it, of reducing the negative content of voices. Take the further following example.[659] Nelson, a 47-year-old ex-army sergeant diagnosed with schizophrenia, attended a four-day HVM 'Working with Voices' training session to try and make sense of his voices. Previously he had begun to taper down his medication after he encountered the HVM, reporting that antipsychotics dulled his emotions and had no impact on his voices. During the training course it emerged that severe childhood abuse and neglect were related to the onset of his voices, which first appeared when he was aged seven. The loss of his best friend in military action ten years previously had triggered his psychosis. Until that time he always had been able to deal with his voices, but feelings of grief and guilt about his deceased friend, combined with being the victim of a serious sexual assault, hindered his ability to cope with voices that became increasingly aggressive (like Ken Steele's voices in Chapter 1). Trauma had never been addressed in his previous psychiatric treatment, and this was the first time he had ever been asked about the context or content of his voice-hearing. Trainers talked with one of his voices using voice dialogue. This voice identified itself as 'Judas', a military-type figure that encouraged Nelson to be assertive. Judas revealed that he was 'the protector of Christ' and not 'the traitor of Christ'. Symbolic meanings are proposed by the HVM to often be hidden in voices, and Nelson acknowledged that when Judas first appeared in his childhood, it was as a protector who helped him cope emotionally with the abuse. In recent years, Judas had become aggressive and challenging whenever the second voice (a seven-year-old boy called 'John') became emotionally overwhelmed. Judas said that John couldn't cope with the memories of trauma. This often happened in response to the third voice, 'Mother', who embodied Nelson's abusive parent. During the session the relationship between Judas and John was restored through mutual understanding, and Judas pledged to support John and Nelson more positively, both in response to 'Mother' and to external challenges and responsibilities. Judas also collaborated with Nelson and the trainers to develop a recovery plan. When Nelson woke up the next day, the first thing that Judas said was 'good morning'. Nelson reported that this was the first time in recent memory that Judas had uttered anything pleasant or companionate.

In summary, the HVM has much in common with psychological therapies, which have now adopted many of its tenets and techniques, although differences remain. The HVM has a more explicit focus on understanding any emotional problems that may underlie the voices and in emancipating and empowering voice-hearers. This latter facet involves helping hearers to develop as experts in their own experiences, enabling their development into people who themselves can go on to train mental health professionals, leaping up the power hierarchy. Another key difference is the evidence base for each, and what each views as evidence. The effectiveness of CBT has been deemed best tested by expensive RCTs, for which funding has been supplied. At the time of writing, there has only been one very small pilot RCT of a therapeutic approach directly based on the HVM approach.[660] The findings of this were promising, but much more research of this type is needed before reliable conclusions can be reached. There has been much debate within the HVM regarding the need to evidence-base its approach through RCTs. This debate has not only challenged the traditional hierarchy as to what counts as evidence, but has raised the larger question as to whether evidence is what leads to change anyway.

CHAPTER 45

The Master's Tools

The dethroning of man, begun in 1543 by Copernicus, was completed in Ann Arbor, Michigan, in 1977. Two psychologists, Richard Nisbett and Timothy Wilson, published a paper entitled 'Telling more than we can know: verbal reports on mental processes'.[661] Our conscious experience, it showed, is not at our centre, but merely orbited at some distance around the burning neural powerhouse that drives us. Nisbett and Wilson provided empirical evidence that people often do not know why they believe what they believe, why they feel what they feel or why they do what they do. It won blind assent (especially among anagram fans) and established psychology as a necessary science to get such answers. In stark contrast to the HVM's approach, it was now possible for psychology to not only claim that voice-hearers did not know what caused their voices, but also that they *could not* know. People's claims that child abuse was the cause of their voice-hearing, or that a given therapy helped them, could now be discounted, or at least their truth claims suspended, pending an expensive technical investigation by a professional class.

It was in the 1960s, notes Joanna Moncrieff, that there became an increasing acceptance that medical treatments should be scientifically evaluated through organized, controlled trials.[662] There is a long history of quack interventions that take people's money but give no discernible benefit beyond a placebo effect. The scientific method was supposed to empower people by protecting them from charlatans. Yet this erected towering entry barriers to the hallowed hall of truth. Unless you had substantial research training and, more to the point, substantial research funding, your truth ticket could not be punched. In the new hierarchy of evidence, people's own experiences came dead last. The person on the street's claims to know truth were dismissed by privileged academics, the new Masters of Truth, as 'anecdata', and derided with smug quips ('the plural of anecdote is not data'). Dr Peter Venkman summed it up best: 'Back off man, I'm a scientist.'[663]

This led to an understandable backlash. Torture survivors, for example, have protested the overlooking of the expertise of the person with lived experience. One survivor writes that, 'like guinea pigs and laboratory mice, we are providers of data, objects of someone else's curiosity, nothing more. I think to myself...I am an expert on torture and its effects, but do scientists seek input from me or other survivors?' 'We look forward to the day,' says another torture survivor, 'when we will be regarded more as their colleagues than as research objects.'[664] The HVM has gone further by arguing not only that individuals with lived experience have expertise, but also that such individuals can identify causation from their own personal experience. This means that someone saying 'this therapy helped me' would be taken as a valid insight into causality, and hence as evidence of the effectiveness of this therapy. For example, writing on the effectiveness of hearing voices groups, Jacqui Dillon and Gail Hornstein[665] argue that '[we] reject the idea that randomized research designs or statistically significant findings constitute the only bases for making evaluations. Whether a hearing voices peer support group is effective or not for a given person can only be determined by him or her.'

The key phrase here is 'for a given person'. Dillon and Hornstein have identified a genuine Achilles heel of the scientific method, which they are effectively able to poke at. Scientific studies of the effectiveness of a treatment, such as a drug, basically work as follows. People are randomly assigned to either a group which is given the drug or a group which is given a placebo. At the end of treatment, if the average level of symptoms in the drug group is significantly lower than the average level of symptoms in the placebo group, then the drug is deemed to be effective. The problem is that this tells us about groups, not individuals. A clinical trial could find that the drug group did not improve more than the placebo group, and conclude that the drug was ineffective. Yet for at least some individual people the drug may have genuinely been effective, but this signal could have been lost in the noise. We are hence left in a position where science yells at individuals, saying they cannot know what helps them, and individuals shout back at science that it cannot know what helps them either. One way out of this impasse comes from newer statistical techniques that can pull out different trajectories that distinct groups of people follow in response to treatment. Indeed, as we have seen in earlier chapters, the question being asked of many therapies now is not so much do they work, but who do they work for and why?

Even if the HVM was to participate in the formal scientific endeavour, it remains unclear as to whether this would actually do the movement any good. Ron Coleman, a voice-hearer and influential figure in the HVM, has argued that:

> We have been told over and over again that we need to create an evidence base. People like Romme and Escher...and many others have done this only to see the evidence ignored... [W]e need to realize it is not about evidence, it is about us taking back power and running things outside of the system as communities of recovery where decisions are not made by the evidence or professionals but by the local communities of recovery based on the real needs of our communities as decided by those communities.[666]

We begin to be confronted by an uneasy feeling that 'evidence', which many of us have been raised to revere, may be one of the master's tools which, as Audre Lorde observed, is unlikely to dismantle the master's house.

Direct evidence for this comes from the Soteria study which, according to its designer, Loren Mosher (1933–2004), committed the four deadly sins of psychiatry: 'demedicalizing madness, de-hospitalizing people, de-psychopharmacologizing and de-professionalizing'. Soteria, from the Greek for deliverance/salvation, was a community-based, experimental residential treatment run in the San Francisco Bay area in the 1970s and 1980s. It drew on the power of human relationships, was not run by doctors and nurses, tried to use antipsychotic medication as infrequently as possible and offered an alternative to hospitalization for patients. The non-professional staff did not wear uniforms, provided a simple home-like atmosphere and were taught that human involvement and understanding were critical to healing interactions. They were not there to observe in experimental fashion, but worked 36–48-hour shifts in order to 'be with' the patients, like an LSD trip guide might be. There were no locks on the doors and no restraints or seclusion rooms. The contextual restraints were that everyone should be treated with dignity and respect, have sanctuary, quiet, safety, support and protection, and that the atmosphere be imbued with hope. The effect of this environment on patients was rigorously studied. People experiencing their first diagnosed episode of schizophrenia were randomly assigned to either Soteria (82 patients) or standard medical treatment (97 patients). After six weeks both groups showed comparable improvements. Two years later, it was found that patients in the Soteria group had significantly better outcomes.[667]

Mosher had played the evidence game, but it did him little good. His study was largely ignored by the mainstream therapeutic community, and what little reaction there was has been hostile. For example, Carpenter and Buchanan attacked the study by arguing that its approach was 'based on an anti-medication model and anti-disease model ideology'.[668] The relevance of this criticism to the *results* of the study is unclear. When America put a man on the moon, the Russians didn't argue that because this endeavour had been based on an anti-communism ideology that there was therefore no Apollo 11, no Neil Armstrong, and no footprints on the moon. Furthermore, given evidence that antipsychotics, in addition to their potent side effects, reduce brain volumes,[669] an approach that tries to use medications only when essential seems a good model of work. In relation to this, Carpenter and Buchanan pointed to an earlier study which reported that continuous maintenance of antipsychotic treatment was more effective than targeted drug treatment for relapse prevention. However, a study by Lehtinen and colleagues has since found evidence that points in the other direction.[670] This study had an experimental group in which antipsychotics were used minimally. In the first three weeks after these patients' admission, antipsychotics were, whenever possible, not started. If the patient's condition had clearly improved during this initial phase, drug use was postponed even further or avoided totally. This group was then compared with another condition where antipsychotics were used as per normal practice, which in most cases meant immediately. Both groups also received treatment by the psychotherapeutic and family-centred principles of a Finnish treatment model. At the two-year follow-up, the two groups were comparable on all outcome measures except that the minimal drug-use group actually had significantly fewer hospitalizations. There is hence some evidence for the effectiveness of a Soteria-style intervention, yet this has not advanced the widespread trialling or clinical adoption of this approach, and it only continues on the margins. Salvation remains hard to find.

What can we make of all this? It is clear that people's claims to know the causes of their experiences are problematic, but it is also clear that lived experience is likely to be a very important source of insight. Such claims are perhaps best taken as a key starting point for investigation, but not the end of it. This entails researchers and those with lived experience respectfully partnering in investigations, using appropriate statistical methods to try and get to the truth. There is a clear reason for the HVM to go down the accepted route of evidence-basing their approach because, as Christopher Hitchens puts it, 'that which can be asserted without evidence, can be dismissed without evidence'. Unfortunately, it is clear that evidence without influence is like a car without petrol. The question for the HVM and for Soteria-style interventions hence becomes where the power and influence to translate research findings into widespread practice will come from. A more cautious assessment would be to say that people's claims from their lived experience that the techniques of the HVM helped them, and the results of the Soteria-style studies, are highly suggestive but still require more evidence to convince us of their effectiveness. The problem is where funding will come from for sufficiently large trials to evaluate these claims rigorously. As Vaughan Bell notes,[671] 'Who gets the power to have their hypotheses recognized and tested? Rarely the people who have the experiences.'

In the meantime, and to caution against an overly pessimistic assessment, we may ask to what extent the insights of the HVM are already feeding through to mental health services. Psychological services seem to be listening, as we have seen in the uptake of the HVM's ideas by psychological therapies, but the response from psychiatry appears to be slower.

CHAPTER 46

I Came a Stranger, I Depart a Stranger[672]

If I tell you that I saw an upsetting documentary last night, and you try to establish why I was upset by asking about the cathode ray tube in my television, I'm going to find someone else to talk to. Similarly, many people have gone to hearing voices groups because mental health professionals were primarily interested in their hardware. We saw in earlier chapters some of the factors that have contributed to us being in this situation. Yet, in an environment free of stigma and judgement, people who are hearing voices typically want to talk about their voices and what they say. Despite this, in mental health services, particularly psychiatry, asking the question 'What do the voices say?' may be done merely to categorize (i.e., diagnose) and assess risk ('Do the voices tell you to hurt anyone?'), if it is done at all. In this chapter we will look at how psychiatrists engage with people's voices.

In psychiatric training, listening can be taught as a means to categorization, which is often a poor cousin of understanding. For example, imagine an individual hears distressing voices, which have their roots in childhood sexual abuse, and they undergo a psychiatric interview that takes the form of that taught in a contemporary introductory psychiatry textbook.[673] First of all this book states that:

> If the patient indicates that he or she has been hearing voices, the differential diagnosis includes a variety of disorders that produce this type of psychotic symptom, such as schizophrenia, schizophreniform disorder, psychotic mania, substance misuse involving hallucinogens, or alcoholic hallucinosis.

This is not a promising start. It omits two of the psychiatric conditions where voices most commonly occur (PTSD and borderline personality disorder; see Chapters 8 and 10), and suggests that magic mushrooms are being considered a more likely cause of the person's voice-hearing than rape.

The next instruction is to ask the patient to describe their voices in more detail, including what the voices say and whether they are male or female. One would hope that this is being done as an initial foray into assessing whether there are meaningful links between the voices and the person's life, along the lines of the Maastricht interview. No. We are told it is done because the more detail the patient can give about their voices, the more confident the interviewer can be that they genuinely are hearing voices. The trainee is then told that they may want to focus in on 'some personal topic…such as sexual or interpersonal relationships'. One would again hope this was being done to assess if the root of the person's voices may lie in trauma, or to see how the content of the person's voices mirrors their actual social relations in the world. No. We are told this is to be done to give the interviewer clues about the patient's ability to demonstrate 'emotional responsiveness'. The trainee is next told that novice interviewers are sometimes embarrassed to ask about experiences such as voice-hearing. The reason for this? 'To the interviewer these symptoms seem so "crazy" that the patient might be insulted by being asked about them.' At the end of the interview the trainee is told to compliment the client 'on having told his or her story well' and to '[i]ndicate you now have a much better understanding of his or her problems'. It is hard to see how this statement could possibly be true.

In the example above, it is the presence of voices, not their content, which is seen as informative. When content is asked about, it is only to offer assurances that voices really are present. The interviewer is simultaneously listening and not listening. In case you think this doesn't reflect the real world, consider this observation from a medical director of a psychiatric hospital in the Netherlands:

> As a psychiatrist I was trained to listen. But also not to listen. There is little or no place for psychotic content in textbooks... My own experience is that taking some time to discuss seriously the...messages that voices bring is highly appreciated by patients and, believe it or not, often time saving. It taught me a lot about these psychotic experiences that is found nowhere in psychiatry textbooks.[674]

Seemingly contradicting this claim, one study found that only 15 per cent of psychiatrists said they had received little or no training about dealing with the content of hallucinations/delusions.[675] In order to try and resolve what's happening here, let's peer behind the closed doors of the consulting room.

When we look at actual clinical encounters, we see psychiatrists asking about voice content, but often in a similar way to someone trying to understand Picasso's *Guernica* by asking what paints and brushes were used. A recent study found that only in 23 per cent of exchanges did psychiatrists ask open, broad and non-leading questions to explore the meaning patients attributed to their psychotic experiences. Instead, they most commonly asked questions about the location and frequency of the voices.[676] Consider the following exchange:[677]

Doctor: Where does it come from? Is it within your head or do you hear it from outside?

Patient: It is like the perception or conception of God, but it is not God.

Doctor: But do you hear it through your ears?

Patient: I hear it and feel it at the same time.

Doctor: Yeah, do you hear it through your ears?

Moses never had to put up with this.

In contrast to many psychiatrists' aural fixation, patients tend to focus on the perceived identity, intentions and power of the voice, as well as their relationship to it. Patients talk about people, psychiatrists talk about perceptions. Psychiatrists' failure to talk about the meat of voices, picking over the bones they come on instead, seems to be a common problem. A study by McCabe and colleagues found that patients actively tried to talk about the content and meaning of their voices but that psychiatrists were often reluctant and uncomfortable talking about this.[678] The conflict between the patient wanting to talk about the content of their symptoms, and the psychiatrist not wanting to, unsurprisingly led to notable tension. As Steele notes, this goes against a patient-centred model in which the concerns and interests of the patient, as well as those of the psychiatrist, should be addressed in the consultation.[679]

One reason for the failure of some psychiatrists to engage with the content of voices is that it is seen as having no therapeutic relevance. If medication is the only tool psychiatric training has given them, then it is broadly irrelevant what the voices are saying – the treatment will still be the same. Psychiatrists are not routinely trained in psychological therapies, although they can of course refer patients to such services. Another reason is that, as Romme and Escher argue,[680] many psychiatrists believe that listening to the content of voices 'increases the hearer's undesirable fixation on this "unreal" world'. We can add to this that a lack of time is a hindrance to discussing voice-content in depth. McCabe and colleagues' study, mentioned above, found that a typical 15-minute consultation involved the psychiatrist reviewing the patient's mental state, medication regime and any side effects, their social and occupational activities, living arrangements, finances and contact with other mental health professionals. One psychiatrist commenting on this study suggested that the lack of engagement with the content of voices McCabe and colleagues found was precisely due to the limited time of the session.[681] In response McCabe and colleagues[682] asked 'when the right occasion is and to whom patients should talk about their psychotic symptoms if not their psychiatrist?' While this was clearly meant as a rhetorical question, it is nevertheless still in search of an answer.

Despite a lack of routine, detailed engagement by psychiatry with the content of people's voices, there are some signs that things are beginning to change. The recently developed avatar therapy, discussed in Chapter 43, actively engages with the content of patients' voices. It can be seen to strongly draw on the HVM technique of voice dialogue.[683] Avatar therapy was developed by a psychiatrist, Julian Leff, and has generated interest in psychiatry departments across the world. This change has come too slowly for many though, who have instead taken matters into their own hands. It is part of the reason why members of the HVM, such as Peter who we met in Chapter 5, have themselves set up centres where people hearing voices can be referred to do the Maastricht interview, often administrated by fellow voice-hearers trained in the interview. In time, clinical psychology will adopt a version of this interview too. As psychology and psychiatry colonize the therapeutic wing of the HVM, what then will become of what Jung called 'the wounded healer'? It is likely this will force the HVM to become even more of a political movement, focusing on continuing to empower voice-hearers and on rectifying the upstream causes of voices. This raises the question as to what the upstream causes of voices are.

CHAPTER 47

What Causes the Causes?

So far we have examined how trauma, brains, genes and their interaction may sit at the potter's wheel of our brain and shape it into one that hears voices. But who shapes the shapers? In a famous scene in the movie *Ghost*, Patrick Swayze sits behind Demi Moore at the pottery wheel. He shapes what she shapes. Moore may be seen as the proximal, immediate cause of the pot, but Swayze sits behind her as a more distal, further removed cause. Unfortunately, distal causes don't often attract attention by being tanned and shirtless. They tend to be more hidden.

Sometimes though, they stare us in the face, but we just don't see them. Mark Steel makes this point beautifully in relation to Freud:

> There can be no doubt that Freud was a genius. Here is a man who looked around the world at the start of the twentieth century, saw brutal empires, millions sucked into soulless factories, impending world war, and said I know what causes the problems: we want to have sex with our mothers.[684]

Having established that child abuse, particularly child sexual abuse (CSA), can cause some people's voice-hearing, we can climb up the rungs of the ladder of voice-hearing causation by asking what causes people to perpetrate such crimes. As men are responsible for over 95 per cent of CSA,[685] we are primarily asking why men sexually abuse children. There are many potential answers to this question. 'Is child sex offending about violence, sex, power, mental illness, personality disorders or deviance?' ask Plummer and Cossins.[686] What we know is that risk factors for a man perpetrating CSA include having difficulties with intimate relationships, social skills deficits, having experienced harsh discipline as a child, loneliness and having a sexual interest in children.[687] There is also another factor. Compared with men who have not suffered CSA, men who have suffered CSA are more likely to go on to perpetrate sexual abuse themselves.

Around one in four adult men who commit CSA have themselves suffered CSA, leading to a cycle of abuse.[688] This happens cross-culturally. Consider this example from Australia:

> HG was born in a remote Barkly community in 1960. In 1972, he was twice anally raped by an older Aboriginal man. He didn't report it because of shame and embarrassment. He never told anyone about it until 2006 when he was seeking release from prison where he had been confined for many years as a dangerous sex offender. In 1980 and 1990, he had attempted to have sex with young girls. In 1993, he anally raped a 10-year-old girl and, in 1997, an eight-year-old boy (ZH). In 2004, ZH anally raped a five-year-old boy in the same community.[689]

To be clear, it is a minority of male CSA victims who go on to be perpetrators themselves. A 45-year follow-up study of 2759 cases of CSA[690] found that 5 per cent of male CSA victims were themselves convicted of a sex offence later in life. This rate rose to 9.2 per cent if the CSA had been suffered when they were aged 12 or older. These rates were both significantly higher than the rate of sexual offence convictions in men who had not suffered CSA, which was 0.6 per cent. Another study followed up 224 male victims of CSA and found that 12 per cent went on to perpetrate sexual abuse themselves (predominantly of children). The men who did this were more likely than those who didn't to have been abused by a woman, to have been neglected as children and to have witnessed serious violence within their family.[691]

Other studies have concluded that male CSA victims are more likely to become perpetrators themselves if they have been abused by someone with whom they have a relationship of dependency, such as a father figure, and then have interpreted such findings through the lens of power/powerlessness theory.[692] Cossins argues that men's experiences of power/powerlessness are shaped by their social relationships with other men, and that the more experiences of powerlessness a boy experiences, and the more these inform his sexuality, the more likely he will seek out sex with people low in power, such as children. This can make powerlessness and sexuality central and defining features of his masculinity and self-worth.[693] Speculatively, this may be why rates of CSA in China have been found to be lower than in the West.[694] David Finkelhor and colleagues note that Chinese masculinity has two strains, a 'wu' masculinity emphasizing more conventional Western macho virtues, but also a, possibly more influential, 'wen' masculinity that stresses virtues like culture, spirituality and self-control.[695] Of course, other explanations are possible.

What about more distal causes of child abuse? Having just focused on the potential role of power, we should be unsurprised to hear that patriarchal structures have been implicated. In a study of father–daughter incest, Judith Herman describes how in many families it was considered a male prerogative to supervise and restrict the activities of women.[696] Herman found fathers isolating their family from the outside world and making their wives financially dependent on them. This encouraged mothers to side with their husbands over their daughters. More generally, child abuse has been argued, in part, to result from what author and feminist bell hooks[697] has described as patriarchal thinking: the embrace of 'an ethics of domination which says the powerful have the right to rule over the powerless and can use any means to subordinate them', with both men and women abusing children, either physically or emotionally.

Other factors influencing rates of child abuse are socio-economic ones. As unemployment lines lengthen and poverty deepens, the abuse and maltreatment of children increases.[698] Poverty is particularly pernicious, as it not only makes you more likely to be exposed to trauma, but also reduces the probability you will be able to cope with it. Childhood impoverishment increases your risk of developing PTSD in response to traumas that you suffer decades later.[699] It is, of course, important to stress that there is no necessary connection between poverty/unemployment and child abuse, and that child abuse is perpetrated by people across of all classes. Indeed, part of the relation between poverty and child abuse may be due to wealthier families having greater resources to conceal abuse.

Both absolute and relative poverty may be distal causes of voice-hearing. Relative poverty refers to the extent of the differential between rich and poor in society and is often referred to as 'income inequality'. This imbalance, claimed Plutarch, is the oldest and most fatal ailment of all republics. He may have been right.[700] As greater levels of income inequality are associated with greater levels of child maltreatment,[701] it is unsurprising that it is associated with voice-hearing too.[702] Absolute poverty may also play a role. Consider a study of children in Mauritius.[703] One group of three- to five-year-olds went to a traditional school with a standard curriculum, a teacher–pupil ratio of 1:30 and had no specific lunch, milk or structured exercise provided (lunch was typically bread and/or rice). Another group of three- to five-year-olds were given an enriched environment. This involved specially constructed nursery schools with a teacher–pupil ratio of 1:6, a physical exercise programme, a structured nutrition programme (milk, fruit juice, a hot meal and a salad each day) and enhanced educational activities. The children were followed up 14–20 years later, and it was found that those who had been placed in the enriched environment had lower levels of hallucination- and delusion-like experiences. The recognition of the link between poverty and mental health has now led to trials of simply giving money to people diagnosed with schizophrenia, to see if this helps.[704] Reducing poverty and income inequality would not only reduce rates of distressing voice-hearing (and much more besides) but also facilitate recovery. Hallucinations of first-episode psychosis patients from the upper and middle classes improve faster than those of people from lower social classes.[705]

Once we introduce poverty as a cause of voice-hearing then, due to the unequal distribution of poverty by race, we also open up racism as an intersecting cause. In 2014 the US Census Bureau reported that 26.2 per cent of Black Americans were living in poverty, compared with 12.7 per cent of White Americans.[706] This offered some explanation for why a 2012 study found that 14 in every 1000 black children suffered reported maltreatment, compared with eight white children in 1000.[707] We have already seen that people of Caribbean origin living in the UK are twice as likely as the white population to hear voices,[708] and it emerges that being in an ethnic minority increases the risk of people having psychotic experiences in general. As Bentall and Fernyhough describe:

> The risk of being diagnosed as psychotic is increased by × 4–8 in ethnic minorities living in the United Kingdom... Incidence rates are greatest in those immigrants who are living in neighborhoods in which they form a clear minority, suggesting that discrimination, experiences of social defeat and powerlessness and/or lack of social support may be important in conferring risk of illness.[709]

All this is consistent with the surprisingly unsurprising idea that knowledge, money, power and prestige can both protect against distressing voice-hearing and facilitate recovery from it.

Ascending up the next rung of the causal ladder leads us to ask: what causes poverty? This is somewhat beyond the reach of this book; nevertheless, when we look around we see Adam Smith's invisible hand leaving visible bruises. Unless we want to spend our entire lives fishing each other out of rivers, we need to go upstream and deal with the hand that is pushing people in. In the medical world, this concept is referred to as 'upstream doctoring'.[710]

One way to start making the invisible visible is through reducing the isolation of people, which has led them to think that their problems are limited to them. As Barbara Susan put it, writing about women's consciousness-raising groups:

> Consciousness raising is a way of forming a political analysis on information we can trust is true. That information is our experience… Unless we talk to each other about our so called personal problems and see how many of our problems are shared by other people we won't be able to see how these problems are rooted in politics.[711]

In other words, the personal is political. Such realizations occur in hearing voices groups, when individual experiences of abuse and oppression come to be seen as what they are: not just personal problems but political ones. Judith Herman notes that a new generation of trauma researchers has arisen whose interest stems not primarily from engagement with traumatized people, but from an abstract scientific curiosity, which lacks the passionate social commitment of many earlier researchers. Voice-hearing research faces the same problem, and hence has the same need to rediscover what Herman terms the interconnection between biological, psychological, social and political dimensions.[712] We need to go into the brain and out to the world to join levels of explanation, and more importantly, people, together.

Conclusions

Once associated with lofty prophetic communications, the experience of hearing voices has fallen low. It has been delegitimized by religion, decontextualized by psychiatry and demonized by society. As a result, it is unsurprising that many of the 2.5 per cent of contemporary Westerners who have more-than-mere-fleeting voice-hearing experiences will be distressed and impaired by this. Yet the twenty-first century has seen voice-hearing rehabilitated and raised up again, albeit with the recognition that it tells us more about this world than the next. It emerges that many people are not impaired or distressed by voice-hearing, and we are learning much from this that can help those who are troubled by voices. The failure of standard psychiatric treatment to be helpful for everyone has been met not with apathy but activism, spurring voice-hearers, psychiatrists, psychologists and others to find new ways to facilitate recovery. Those unhelped by medications who wish to turn towards their voices now have opportunities to reinterpret, reclaim and re-engage with the experience, be this through psychological therapies, psychiatric innovations such as avatar therapy or the Hearing Voices Movement. Of course, the provision of these services needs to be improved and particular attention paid to ensure all are able to access these, irrespective of factors such as socio-economic status or race. Those who prefer to turn away from their voices have options such as neurostimulation and neurofeedback on the horizon. As a result of these efforts by the diverse voice-hearing village (which like any society still comprises distinct tribes, interests and power disparities that need to be addressed), the field has now opened up to allow a wide range of causes and meanings of voice-hearing to be considered.

Causation

Hamlet knew there was something rotten in the world, because a phantom appeared and told him so. Unseen voices have been bringing us similar messages, but we have failed to hear them. For too long, voices have been bruises hidden by the long sleeves of schizophrenia. It is now clear that one contributor to voice-hearing is the fire of trauma, often childhood trauma. This is a fire stoked by poverty, patriarchy and prejudice. Those who hear what should not be heard have often led lives that saw what should not be seen.

What remains less clear is exactly *how* trauma leads to voice-hearing, and why it only does so in certain people. It would not be surprising if specific neurobiological variations present in someone before a trauma, such as a short paracingulate sulcus or idiosyncrasies in the structure or function of language-processing regions of the brain, make it more likely for that person to hear voices after a trauma. If the trauma is processed in a dissociated manner, with the person being overwhelmed by its sensory qualities and unable to anchor it in context, this may cause memories of it to float unmoored, apart from other securely harboured memories, bobbing up as voices. Unresolved traumas, involving a sense of ongoing threat, which are more likely to be experienced by people with fewer social, emotional or financial resources to aid coping, may also promote voice-hearing. Indeed, perceiving an ongoing threat seems to actively encourage visitation. This threat could be to one's body, one's social worth, or both. Yet we have also noted that not all threats appear equally potent causes of voice-hearing. Social threats, signalled through the emotions of shame and guilt, seem particularly hallucinogenic. The association between shame and voice-hearing can be understood in many ways. At a biological level, shame can be linked to voice-hearing through its potential effects on increasing dopamine levels in the striatum. At a psychological level, shame may seed voice-hearing through hypervigilance for social threats or conversely through suppression of thoughts about the trauma. Another intriguing though highly speculative possibility is that shame and voice-hearing are linked because self-consciousness exists in our species, at least in part, precisely because it facilitates the experiences of shame and guilt.

At least part of our experience of making a conscious decision to act is an illusion. Your brain has decided so long ago what you are about to do, at least in the case of simple actions, that it almost has time to inform your conscious self by post. A recent fMRI study was able to predict which finger people would use to press a button based on brain activity occurring up to ten seconds before they consciously decided which finger to use.[713] Despite this, we not only feel strongly that we caused ourselves to act, but we also perceive that we could have acted differently. The potential purpose of this, Frith and Metzinger argue, is that it allows us to experience emotions such as shame and guilt, which we couldn't experience unless we felt we could have done otherwise.[714] Experiencing shame can be useful, particularly when it discourages evolutionarily, costly, interpersonal violence by non-dominant members of a group. It can also allow group preferences to manifest in the individual, potentially increasing the stability of a society and the likelihood of individuals thriving in it. If self-consciousness were, to some extent, to exist because it facilitates shame, then should we be surprised that powerful experiences of shame are associated with compelling contents of consciousness – that is, voices? While this theory may only apply to a subset of people's voice-hearing experiences, I would like to put forward the idea that shame is potentially hallucinogenic.

Our understanding of the immediate neurological causes of voice-hearing is progressing, albeit slowly. Changes to the structure of the paracingulate sulcus, to the myelination of fronto-temporal white matter tracts such as the arcuate fasciculus and to the activity of the supplemental motor area, culminating in altered functioning in a potentially already structurally different superior temporal gyrus, have been suggested to lead to altered source-monitoring abilities. This in turn is thought to contribute to our brain's own output being experienced as others' voices. We have seen a neural orchestra, consisting of the left hemisphere language network, right hemisphere speech production regions and areas involved in memory, striking up when voices speak. Yet we still have much to learn: how do interactions between these neural regions summon voices, what is the role of dopamine in voice-hearing, and how is the mind-wandering network involved?

Particularly encouragingly, we have seen how biological, psychological and trauma-based understandings of voice-hearing may be combined into an integrated model. The predictive coding framework is able to combine psychological, software causes (heightened expectations of communications, particularly relating to threat, often stemming from traumas) with biological, hardware causes (neural changes that prevent prediction error signals from flowing). While such hardware changes could result from the neural impact of traumatic life events, they could also be related to other non-trauma-related neurodevelopmental factors, including genetic variations that impact on language processing in the brain, myelination or dopamine/glutamate metabolism.

This offers a way to overcome the dichotomy between trauma-dominated models of the 1960s and biology-dominated models of the 1980s. More generally, this can be done by stressing the biological effects of trauma, as well as how the impact of trauma may be moderated by the pre-existing biology of the brain of the exposed person. Yet this should not be done in a manner that simply equates trauma with a biological toxin, subsumes it into a biological model and treats it with a pill. The impact and consequences of trauma stem in a large part from the meaning that is made of the experience, which therefore forms a key therapeutic target. It may be correct to state that a traumatized person has a hyperactive amygdala, but this does not imply that this is the most appropriate level at which to understand or treat. Instead, the amygdala's activity may be better understood at the psychological level – the person feels unsafe in the world – and this problem is most effectively intervened with by simply helping the person to feel safe. Of course, in cases where neural changes are not caused or maintained by events happening in the world, then a different approach is needed. If a hyperactive superior temporal gyrus is causing voices to be spat out, and this activity doesn't directly relate to any event in the world, then trying to dampen this activity down with drugs, neurostimulation or neurofeedback may be the most appropriate way to help. Voice-hearing can be understood and addressed at multiple levels of explanation. Those working in a therapeutic capacity have the difficult task of determining, in conjunction with the person who is hearing voices, the appropriate level to explain a given person's voice-hearing, which will then strongly suggest what may be the best way to help with the voices. As indicated earlier, this may involve neither biology nor trauma, but other factors such as spirituality. At present we really don't know what proportion of voice-hearing is best understood as stemming from a problem in the world, what proportion stems from a problem with its origin more purely in the genes and brain and what proportion involves the confluence of both these factors.

By allowing these multiple routes to voices, we have not shut the door to a classical neurodevelopmental route to voice-hearing that does not require the presence of traumatic life events. We have seen how the possession of specific genetic variants, such as those associated with metachromatic leukodystrophy (which involves altered myelination in the frontal and temporal lobes), is strongly associated with the development of voice-hearing. Furthermore, we have seen how a neurodevelopmental trajectory towards voice-hearing may be set up by genetic variations, a loss of oxygen at birth (hypoxia) or maternal infection during pregnancy. Voices could subsequently manifest, not due to a trauma occurring, but due to the natural process of synaptic pruning (or an exaggerated form of this) occurring in late adolescence. Not all voices will be born from trauma. Similarly, we have seen suggestions (Chapter 21) that not all voices with their origins in trauma need to be midwifed by a brain genetically pre-wired for voice-hearing, and that trauma may be sufficient for voice-hearing to occur.

If we did want to play a classical neurodevelopmental route off in a dichotomous manner against a trauma-based route, then it appears that the latter may be more common. We saw in Chapter 39 that your odds of being diagnosed with schizophrenia are increased twofold by early insults (e.g., early infection, pregnancy difficulties). Suffering a single childhood trauma (sexual, physical, emotional abuse or neglect) is associated with a comparable two- to threefold increase in your odds of being later diagnosed with psychosis.[715] However, if that single trauma is being raped as a child, this increases your odds of hearing voices as an adult by roughly sixfold.[716] Furthermore, if you suffer three or more childhood traumas you have a more than tenfold increase in your odds of being diagnosed with psychosis[717] or hearing voices. This suggests a particularly prominent role for childhood abuse in voice-hearing, which would be consistent with the relatively low heritability of voice-hearing and its prominent presence across a range of diagnoses associated with the presence of traumatic life events (e.g., schizophrenia, PTSD, borderline personality disorder). As we have seen though, it is still likely to often be more fruitful to think about how trauma and non-trauma-based neurodevelopmental factors may combine together to contribute to the development of voice-hearing.

Meaning

Hamlet turned to Horatio to deal with his phantom: 'Thou art a scholar; speak to it, Horatio.' This was because Horatio spoke Latin, deemed the most appropriate language to deal with spirits. Who do we turn to today to tell us about voice-hearing, and what is the most appropriate language to talk about it in? Whose voices get heard, and whose do not? It is something of an understatement to say that the meaning of voice-hearing is contested. Voice-hearing is the Kashmir of the mental world. The battle for voice-hearing has always begun on the field of meaning, where competing guilds have raised their banners. We have seen how the most prominent contemporary dispute is between traditional biomedical psychiatry and the Hearing Voices Movement (HVM). It appears that both parties have valid arguments for at least some voice-hearers, but that psychiatry's voice is still privileged. More broadly, we exist in a system where there are 'deep divides across social, economic and political interest groups of patients, doctors, advocacy groups, governmental agencies, insurance companies and pharmaceutical corporations'.[718] Is it possible to bring multiple perspectives on voice-hearing together, without one drowning out the others? Can we find ways to overcome what is a persistent underlying problem – namely how, in an economic system that concentrates wealth, can one expect to have a mental health system that distributes power?

One radical move the HVM has made is to stress that voice-hearing may be a potentially adaptive response to traumatic events, rather than a symptom of a disorder caused by a trauma. We have seen that voice-hearing does not need to be understood as surviving through the millennia because it is a cost worth paying for language, for effective threat detection, for self-consciousness, or for genes that would have been helpful in the absence of trauma. It could still be with us because it is beneficial in its own right. In some examples, this case is easy to make. Think back to the protective voice that Mrs A first heard after her trauma (Chapter 13), or the helpful and motivating voices heard by Joe Simpson and Oliver Sacks while descending mountains in distress (Chapter 29). Voices may be able to persuade and comfort us when our own words and voice are simply not enough. The idea that hostile, critical or derogatory voices are helpful messengers in disguise remains a harder sell. We saw from the story of Peter (Chapter 5) how apparently negative voices can be understood as helpful, albeit challenging, messengers. Eleanor Longden has also made a convincing case that the negative voices she heard were actually helpful messengers. For Eleanor, voices warning her not to leave the house were communicating to her that she still didn't feel safe in the world. Voices that berated her for being timid and weak represented her fear of being victimized again. In her experience, the most negative, aggressive voices she heard represented the parts of her that had been hurt the most, drawing attention to emotional conflicts that she needed to deal with, and being, in some ways, attempts to keep her safe.[719] Viewing her voices in this way meant she could thank the voices for their concern, deal with the issues they raised and have a better relationship with them. In this sense, as Eleanor argues, voices may be part of a solution, flagging the dangers of a post-traumatic world, and not part of the problem. We saw a parallel to this idea in a contemporary psychological theory of PTSD, which suggested that negative voices could be seen as warning signals that the trauma may be about to occur again (Chapter 20). However, this theory represented such experiences as being inappropriate indications of threat, rather than helpful alerting to actual ongoing problems.

This idea from the HVM offers a profoundly different meaning to the voice-hearing experience to the 'symptom of brain disease just like blindness' perspective. Voices are no longer symptoms of a broken brain but reminders of enduring pain. They are not the enemy. A conference presentation I recently attended mentioned a story featuring the Sesame Street character, Grover.[720] The story was called 'The Monster at the End of this Book'. In this, Grover gets more and more worked up at the thought of encountering a monster at the end of the book. He undertakes increasingly frantic and desperate manoeuvres to avoid the monster, tying pages together, nailing pages shut, building walls.[721] They all fail. At the end of the book (spoiler alert!), it emerges that the only monster is 'lovable, furry old Grover'. The use of antipsychotic after antipsychotic at escalating doses, the deployment of short-term psychological avoidance strategies, and desperate trials of neurostimulation may all be ways to try and avoid what is not actually a monstrous non-self being, but the languishing pain of a loveable self. This has important implications for the process of recovery. Compassion and conversation, involving the hearer and their voices, come front and centre. Silence, shame and seclusion are to be replaced by listening, loving and, perhaps most importantly of all, living. This is not to say that medication has no potentially helpful short-term role within this framework. It may be able to bring people to a position where they feel less overwhelmed and hence more able to engage with their voices and their potential messages. There is no need to advocate an either/or approach.

Yet, it may be queried if understanding voices as meaningful messengers is a coping strategy, an act of cognitive jujitsu or reframing that makes the experience easier to live with, rather than a truth about the nature of the voices. For Eleanor, due to the way her voices changed when she took a compassionate stance towards them, it seems very fair to understand these voices as helpful manifestations of unresolved pain. However, for other people this may not be the case. Indeed, automatically reading autobiography into voices has the potential for harm. For example, you could imagine, and I have seen, someone hearing highly critical and abusive voices being put on the spot to answer questions as to why they 'really' hate themselves, even when they protest they don't. Some voices may be full of sound and fury, but signify nothing about the person's past. Here other explanations of voice-hearing, such as it being due to right Broca's area activation creating vitriol, may be appropriate. For me, this question as to the relative proportions of voices that are and are not grounded in ongoing emotional conflicts is one of the most important questions we have to answer. The answer has profound implications for how we conceive of, and offer support for, voice-hearing. It also raises the question as to whether there may be overlapping and non-overlapping magisteria for psychiatry and the HVM.[722] Some people's voices may best be helped by a combination of psychiatrically delivered medication and a search for personal meaning in the voices; others may best be helped solely through medication, or solely through exploring and addressing the meaning of the voices. We have a vast array of expertise, and we need to know how and why to deploy it.

In addition to the question of how much power the HVM needs to decentralize from psychiatry, other questions are how it can do this and how successful it is likely to be. One strand of the HVM's approach will be to continue to build a parallel system that people find helpful and whose appeal spreads through word of mouth. Another strand will attempt to expand the evidence base for the HVM approach from largely first-person experience to formal randomized controlled trials, a process that has already started.[723] Arguments that the approach of the HVM is not amenable to testing through this latter method not do convince me. A greater problem than doing such work will be getting funding to do it.

Whatever approach is taken, shifting this centre of gravity of authority is not likely to be easy. Half a millennium ago, Martin Luther was lamenting that people were taught by doctors what to say about their voices. Today, the meaning and management of voice-hearing remains not just primarily taught by psychiatry, but ruled by it. A public relations firm[724] recently engaged by the American Psychiatric Association (APA) proposed repositioning the APA 'from wise sage to caring ruler'.[725] Defensive reactions will naturally be engendered by any proposed decentralization of power. For example, consider a historian of psychiatry who raised the question as to what it is like to live in a world without psychiatry, and then rhetorically answered this with an example from Ireland in 1817 in which a mad person was put in a five-foot-deep hole with a cover over it and left to die.[726] If a patient today was stood in a five-foot-deep hole, all that would be seen of them would be their head. It is unclear how far removed from this situation we actually are. Defensive reactions are likely to be exacerbated by the perception, promulgated by a former president of the APA, that 'psychiatry has been victimized' and that psychiatry 'doesn't get any respect'.[727] Having met a litany of people in this book who were victimized and disrespected, one could be forgiven for being uncertain about adding psychiatry to this list. In reality, few are calling for the complete abolition of psychiatry, and none for the restoration of hole-based treatments (aside from a few misunderstood psychoanalysts). Instead, most are calling for reform: a decentralization of power, a reconsideration of the meaning of hearing voices and improved psychiatric (and dedicated psychotherapeutic) training for medical students who will specialize in psychiatry and come to work with people who hear voices. We can already see such reform occurring. For example, psychiatry can be seen to be embracing some of the ideas of HVM in the psychiatrist-led development of avatar therapy, in which voice-hearers seek to change their relationship with their voices. Yet there needs to be a more widespread engagement of psychiatry with the ideas of the HVM. I suspect many of the ideas of the HVM will ring true with the clinical experience of psychiatrists, and may actually liberate not only patients, but also psychiatrists, by allowing them to voice ideas that the dominant paradigm they work in has kept suppressed.

If there were to be a psychiatric Götterdämmerung, the subsequent forensic investigation would likely find the sparks that set Valhalla alight came from within: an overemphasis on biology, questionable relations with pharmacological companies and a lack of training and resources.[728] For example, the psychiatrist Julian Leff (developer of avatar therapy) has argued that a key threat to psychiatry is that 'the excitement over biological technology eclipses the importance of human relationships, which are at the heart of good psychiatric practice'.[729] As Theodore Roosevelt once put it, 'No one cares how much you know, until they know how much you care.' Psychiatrists are often maligned as overly focused on the role of medication in recovery, but a former president of the UK's Royal College of Psychiatrists, who should know, has argued that most psychiatrists would prefer to engage in face-to-face, in-depth relationships and, if they are prevented from doing so, it is 'as much the fault of factors beyond their control as any medically dominated attitudes of their own'.[730] To facilitate this, it would seem sensible to follow through with the argument of Julian Leff that it is 'essential for all psychiatrists to have a working ability in psychotherapy' and that medical students should all be given the opportunity to take on patients (under supervision) for psychotherapy.[731] How amenable the current training regime is to this is questionable.

Another former president of the UK's Royal College of Psychiatrists, Dinesh Bhugra, who at the time of writing is president of the World Psychiatric Association, argues that part of the problem with psychiatric training, and its solution, is as follows:

> What we do now is take the brightest students as medics, drill competition in and drill empathy out… If I could change the world, I'd have all the disciplines, medical, nursing, psychology, doing a first year of humanities together, learning anthropology, sociology and literature… We need psychiatrists who can put themselves in their patients' shoes.[732]

In addition to these suggestions for improving the empathy of medical students, I would simply add the injunction for them to put the books down and spend more time with voice-hearers as equals (i.e., not when interviewing them, treating them or telling them what the books say) by going to events such as the Intervoice annual conference. To understand the suffering of others is a profound experience. 'I call him religious who understands the suffering of others,' said Gandhi. Threats to the empathic treatment of people hearing voices may come from a lack of professional training in how to deal with both talking about the content of voices and potential underlying experiences of child abuse.[733] The primarily biological lens through which voice-hearing is still seen may also impact the empathy which patients are dealt with. There is some evidence that if clinicians hold a biological explanation for mental health symptoms their patients are reporting, this results in the clinician having less empathy.[734] Yet a significant part of this is not the psychiatrist's personal fault, but rather a training and cultural issue. Pinpointing factors in psychiatric/medical training that increase the risk of negative patient–physician interactions in relation to voice-hearing, allowing changes to be made and improved care to result, seems the way to go.

It is unclear how the HVM will evolve. Its future relation with biology is particularly intriguing. The HVM argues that voices are to be celebrated, yet the biological changes that result in voices are often denied, and those highlighting such changes can be viewed as contributing to a pathology discourse. This raises the question as to why one can be proud to be a voice-hearer but be ashamed of the brain that permits it. The answer is, of course, because many in the HVM have been disempowered and stigmatized by brain-based discourses. This does not need to be the case though. Conceding that brain changes are associated with voice-hearing does not inevitably mean voice-hearing is a dysfunction, that it must be treated by drugs and that it doesn't have a basis in emotionally overwhelming life events. For example, brain changes are recognized and celebrated as a marker of difference by autism neurodiversity activists. Acknowledging a causal role for neurology does not dictate the meaning of voice-hearing. Those who understand their voices in a spiritual framework need not be overruled by neurology. We have seen how, for people like Thomas Aquinas, arcuates would be seen as facilitating angels, not replacing them. Of course, if a spiritual interpretation leads to voices being wielded as a sword (my voices say X, therefore you should do Y), a challenge to this meaning is to be expected, quite likely with a counterthrust of neural reductionism. This is not colonialism but rather the normal contestation of life.

As voice-hearers are able to explore their voices more freely, it is hopeful that more people will find their own meaning in their voices, rather than that meaning being dictated by others. For example, as Amanda Waegeli says of her own voice-hearing:

> Psychiatry, professionals and academics...will all put their own interpretations on my experience and explain it in whatever way they like to, but the bottom line is it doesn't matter to me anymore now what they think. I accept my voice-hearing experiences as being normal for me. I once wanted to know what they thought, and needed to know what they thought or diagnosed it as, because I thought they were the experts and I had something wrong with me and needed their knowledge to help me with my problem. Now knowing I have this innate God given gift and ability to heal, help myself with God's love, support and guidance I am empowered on my recovery, there is nothing wrong with me, and it is more about what has happened to me.[735]

Going forward

The changing meanings of voice-hearing have led the HVM to promote a shift away from the implicit question 'What is wrong with you?' towards the more open inquiry 'What happened to you?'[736] This has occurred in the wider context of child maltreatment now being recognized as one of the major preventable causes of mental (and physical) health problems.[737] It has been estimated that eliminating five specific types of child abuse (sexual, physical and emotional abuse, plus neglect and bullying) would reduce the number of cases of psychosis by a third.[738] So, in good part, *we know what to do*. Men, who constitute the overwhelming majority of perpetrators of sexual violence, need to stop raping people.[739] We need to give greater support to parents, particularly to poor, young, frightened, ill or domestically abused mothers. We need to improve childhoods by creating a secure emotional base for children to explore the world from, allowing them to grow into healthy and resilient adults. We need to better fund child protection and children's health services. My heuristic for judging a city or a country at a glance is to look at the quality of its children's hospitals and maternity wards. Both should be palaces.

We need to rethink not only what we spend our limited research funds on, but also on how research is done. In 2014 the US National Institute of Health (NIH), whose goal is to uncover new knowledge that will lead to better health for everyone, funded more research into food allergies ($35 million) than into child abuse and neglect ($30 million).[740] Funders are enthusiastically supporting new and exciting genetic research that promises answers, while listlessly acting on the solid but less glamorous answers already provided by psychosocial research. The NIH has pumped more than $1000 million into schizophrenia research over the past four years, with little to show for it in terms of improved ways to help. You don't spend a billion dollars without someone benefiting though, so, *cui bono*? Bricks, machines and scientists have advanced, forests have receded and patients have remained more or less where they were, warmed only in their increasing isolation by the burning sincerity of promises.

This ties into a problem highlighted by Nev Jones, drawing on ideas from Arne Naess, namely that much current research could be characterized as 'shallow'. This refers to research done by professional university-based researchers, in which people with lived experience are mere adjunct 'advisers'. Its goals are to improve selected outcomes of patients, get further research grants and to elevate the researcher to a tenured position. It is symptom-driven, detached from real-world concerns, and the researchers are not responsible for the implementation of their findings. An alternative research paradigm, as Nev Jones argues, is 'deep research'. This is done by a diverse team embedded in the community, which, in this context, gives positions of power to people with direct experiences of voice-hearing (voice-hearers, family members, front-line clinicians) and a stake in this area. It emerges from a real-world context, works with multiple practical constraints and has change and a better life for voice-hearers as its goal. To enable this, researchers need to increase their humility and decrease their power in research teams, in order to empower people with lived experience and other direct stakeholders, and in order to create genuine change. It is naive to think that this will happen widely without systemic change that alters the way incentives are structured for researchers. Rewarding researchers for what change they drove and for how they were able to open up discourses to previously unheard voices, rather than what journal they published in, what size grant they delivered to their university and to what extent they were able to dominate the discourse, is one clear direction to move in. Going beyond funding research, we also need to resource voice-hearers themselves more. What the Hearing Voices Movement has achieved on a shoestring budget is remarkable, and much more public money should be made available to support the work, research and activism of such grassroots movements.

Returning to the immediate present, more personalized help should be developed. We have seen that antipsychotics help some people's voices (in the short term at least), but not everyone's. There is an urgent need to find out what predicts whether someone's voices will respond to antipsychotics, in order to save people who wish to go down this route unnecessarily risking dangerous side effects. Given that there may be traumatic life events in some people's route to voice-hearing, but not others, it may be that one of these types of voice-hearing may be preferentially helped by antipsychotics. For example, a recent study found preliminary evidence that people diagnosed with schizophrenia who had suffered child sexual abuse were less likely to be helped by antipsychotics.[741] It also needs to be established why only some people benefit from neurostimulation techniques (e.g., TMS, tDCS). Early answers have focused on those with specific patterns of neural connectivity ('connectomes') preferentially benefiting from these techniques, and there are hints that genes may also help us predict response to these treatments.[742] Similarly, there is a need to understand who benefits from psychological interventions and what the key components of therapy are, whether it be the therapeutic alliance between the distressed hearer and their helper-guide,[743] or specific techniques. Overall, the problem we face is not a lack of new ideas, but a lack of provision of services based on these ideas.

Another issue to address is the probability of recovery. We have met a large number of people who recovered from, or came to live with, their voices and who are able to speak eloquently about this. This neglects a lot of people who have not recovered and who cannot communicate clearly about their voices. The promotion of the idea that voices are something one can recover from is a noble sentiment, but to do this without acknowledging that many people have not recovered is problematic.[744] Furthermore, as we noted at the outset, voices do not occur in a vacuum (quite literally), and even if people can come to cope with their voices, other problems may remain, such as disordered thoughts, delusions or negative symptoms (e.g., a lack of pleasure, motivation, etc.). It is unclear how to balance hope with current clinical realities. The best way, of course, is to improve the current clinical reality.

Finally, given the potential benefits of voice-hearing, we may ask if they can be summoned in a controlled manner and listened to for any insights they might have. The lure of being able to freely access otherwise inaccessible information lurking below the surface of our consciousness is great. Neurostimulation techniques, which have shown some promise in reducing voice-hearing in patients, could, in theory, be thrown into reverse to create voice-hearing in anyone who wanted it. Whether we will soon see people, from the business professional to the poet, seeking insights and information in this way remains to be seen. Yet, we may want to be careful what we wish for, as we may not like what the voices have to say.

End/beginning

The light we have shone is the darkness from which future generations must emerge. Our elementary understandings of the neurology and genetics of voice-hearing will progress, as will our understanding of how trauma and pain transmute into voices. Causation will yield to time, but meaning may not. In particular, one struggle whose outcome is not yet certain is whether shame will be overcome, shame that should not be: shame associated with hearing voices, shame associated with being abused, and a wider shame we can all relate to, the shame of being different somehow. Ancient problems are still current concerns. R.R. Wilson observed that '[w]ithout support from the society, or at least from a group within it, prophets can find no permanent place within the social order and are likely to be regarded simply as sick individuals who must be cured or expelled'.[745] If shame is both a route into voice-hearing and a consequence of it, then belonging and connection may be a road out. We need to ensure that people who hear voices realize that they belong to this wonderfully diverse world we all inhabit and not just in voice-hearing cantons. More generally, we need to guarantee that all children grow up with a sense of belonging and connection to community to make them resilient to the problems life will pose. Perhaps most importantly, we need to listen. To listen to the stories of voice-hearers and to listen to pain, whatever form it may take, without turning away. We may disagree with Hemingway that the world is a fine place, but we can agree it's worth fighting for. This is a task for all of us. For good or for ill, voices have now spoken to you too.

ENDNOTES

1 *Joe Simpson*: Simpson, J. (1988). *Touching the Void*. London: Cape. *Virginia Woolf*: See Woolf's last letter to her sister: 'I feel that I have gone too far this time to come back again. I am certain now that I am going mad again. It is just as it was the first time, I am always hearing voices, and I know I shan't get over it now… I have fought against it, but I can't any longer.' In Nicolson, N. *et al.* (eds) (1978) *The Letters of Virginia Woolf, Volume VI: 1936–1941*. New York, NY: Harcourt Publishers Ltd. *Francoise Chatelin*: Malone, D. (Producer and Director) (2006, 18 June). *Voices in my Head* [television broadcast]. London: Channel 4. *Brian Wilson*: A powerful interview at http://abilitymagazine.com/past/brianW/brianw.html.

2 *The Broken Brain* (Nancy Andreasen) and *The Unbalanced Mind* (Julian Leff) have already been written. *Biology Gone Wild* is merely biding its time.

3 Wahass, S. *et al.* (1997) 'A cross-cultural study of the attitudes of mental health professionals towards auditory hallucinations.' *International Journal of Social Psychiatry*, 43(3), 184–92.

4 Rowling, J.K. (1998) *Harry Potter and the Chamber of Secrets*. London: Bloomsbury.

5 Andreasen, N. (1985) *The Broken Brain: The Biological Revolution in Psychiatry*. New York, NY: William Morrow.

6 See Andreasen (1985), as cited above.

7 Stephane, M. *et al.* (2001) 'Auditory verbal hallucinations and dysfunctions of the neural substrates of speech.' *Schizophrenia Research*, 50, 61–78.

8 See https://thepsychologist.bps.org.uk/volume-28/january-2015/are-understandings-mental-illness-mired-past.

9 Shorter, E. (1998) *A History of Psychiatry: From the Era of the Asylum to the Age of Prozac*. New York, NY: Wiley.

10 Cook, C. *et al.* (eds) (2009) *Spirituality and Psychiatry*. London: RCPsych Publications; Jackson, M. *et al.* (1997) 'Spiritual experience and psychopathology.' *Philosophy, Psychiatry, & Psychology*, 4, 41–65; McCarthy-Jones, S. *et al.* (2013) 'Spirituality and hearing voices: considering the relation.' *Psychosis*, 5(3), 247–58; Watkins, J. (2010) *Unshrinking Psychosis: Understanding and Healing the Wounded Soul*. Melbourne: Michelle Anderson.

11 Williams, L.C. (2014) 'Virginia Woolf's history of sexual victimization: a case study in light of current research.' *Psychology*, 5(10), 1151–64; DeSalvo, L. (1989) *Virginia Woolf: The Impact of Childhood Sexual Abuse on Her Life and Work*. New York, NY: Ballantine Books.

12 Dunn, J. (1991) *A Very Close Conspiracy: Vanessa Bell and Virginia Woolf.* Boston, MA: Little, Brown.

13 Wilson, B. (1996) *Wouldn't It Be Nice: My Own Story*. London: Bloomsbury.

14 Kjelby, E. *et al.* (2015) 'Suicidality in schizophrenia spectrum disorders: the relationship to hallucinations and persecutory delusions.' *European Psychiatry*, 30(7), 830–36.

15 For an example of a study on the differential relation of commanding voices to harming self or other, see Haddock, G. *et al.* (2013) 'Psychotic symptoms, self-harm and violence in individuals with schizophrenia and substance misuse problems.' *Schizophrenia Research*, 151(1), 215–20.

16 Jones, N. *et al.* (2014) 'Beyond easy answers: facing the entanglements of violence and psychosis.' *Issues in Mental Health Nursing*, 35(10), 809–11.

17 Quotes from Ken Steele are taken from his autobiography, Steele, K. (2002) *The Day the Voices Stopped*. New York, NY: Basic Books, and reproduced with permission.

18 Jääskeläinen, E. *et al.* (2012) 'A systematic review and meta-analysis of recovery in schizophrenia.' *Schizophrenia Bulletin*, 39(6), 1296–306. This study examined studies over the period 1921–2011, and defined recovery as both social and clinical recovery lasting for more than two years.

19 Peters, E. *et al.* (2012) 'It's not what you hear, it's the way you think about it: appraisals as determinants of affect and behaviour in voice hearers.' *Psychological Medicine*, 42(7), 1507–14.

20 Moncrieff, J. (2013) *The Bitterest Pills: The Troubling Story of Antipsychotic Drugs*. Basingstoke: Palgrave Macmillan.

21 Ho, B.C. *et al.* (2011) 'Long-term antipsychotic treatment and brain volumes: a longitudinal study of first-episode schizophrenia.' *Archives of General Psychiatry*, 68(2), 128–37. This result was more recently confirmed via meta-analysis; see Fusar-Poli, P. *et al.* (2013) 'Progressive brain changes in schizophrenia related to antipsychotic treatment? A meta-analysis of longitudinal MRI studies.' *Neuroscience & Biobehavioral Reviews*, 37(8), 1680–91. Nevertheless, this picture has been complicated recently, with both increases and decreases in brain volumes being linked to antipsychotics; for example, see Ansell, B.R.E. *et al.* (2015) 'Divergent effects of first-generation and second-generation antipsychotics on cortical thickness in first-episode psychosis.' *Psychological Medicine*, 45, 515–27. The impact of antipsychotics on the brain is still poorly understood.

22 Shorter (1998), as cited above.

23 Jensen, D. (2006) *Endgame, Volume 1: The Problem of Civilization*. New York, NY: Seven Stories Press.

24 Jenkins, J.H. (2015) *Extraordinary Conditions: Culture and Experience in Mental Illness*. Oakland, CA: University of California Press.

25 Mann, S. (1999) 'First person account: talking through medication issues: one family's experience.' *Schizophrenia Bulletin*, 25(2), 407–09.

26 Woods, S.W. *et al.* (2010) 'Incidence of tardive dyskinesia with atypical and conventional antipsychotic medications: prospective cohort study.' *Journal of Clinical Psychiatry*, 71(4), 463–74; Morgenstern, H. *et al.* (1993) 'Identifying risk factors for tardive dyskinesia among long-term outpatients maintained with neuroleptic medications: results of the Yale Tardive Dyskinesia Study.' *Archives of General Psychiatry*, 50(9), 723–33.

27 Appelbaum, P.S. (1989) *Paul Appelbaum on Law & Psychiatry: Collected Articles from Hospital and Community Psychiatry.* Washington, DC: American Psychiatric Association.

28 Quotes from Mel come from her own writings, access to which was kindly provided to me by her parents, Bruce and Faye Roberts, and which are reproduced here with their permission.

29 'La chair est triste, hélas! et j'ai lu tous les livres' [The flesh is sad, alas! and I've read all the books], lines from the 1865 poem 'Brise Marine' [Sea Breeze] by Stéphane Mallarmé.

30 Read, J. *et al.* (2010) 'The effectiveness of electroconvulsive therapy: a literature review.' *Epidemiologia e Psichiatria Sociale*, 19(4), 333–47.

31 The importance of this question is stressed by, among others, Eleanor Longden. See Longden, E. (2013a) *Learning from the Voices in My Head.* TED Books.

32 Kapur, S. *et al.* (2005) 'From dopamine to salience to psychosis – linking biology, pharmacology and phenomenology of psychosis.' *Schizophrenia Research*, 79(1), 59–68.

33 Casson, J.W. (2004) *Drama, Psychotherapy and Psychosis: Dramatherapy and Psychodrama with People Who Hear Voices.* London: Brunner-Routledge.

34 Elkes, J. *et al.* (1954) 'Effects of chlorpromazine on the behaviour of chronically overactive psychotic patients.' *British Medical Journal*, 2, 560–76.

35 Mizrahi, R. *et al.* (2005) 'How antipsychotics work: the patients' perspective.' *Progress in Neuropsychopharmacology and Biological Psychiatry*, 29(5), 859–64.

36 Jones (1969), taken from Obermeier, A. and Kennison, R. (1997) 'The privileging of visio over vox in the mystical experiences of Hildegard of Bingen and Joan of Arc.' *Mystics Quarterly*, 23, 137–63. Apologies for the gendered language in the quote.

37 Cook, L.S. (2011) *On the Question of the 'Cessation of Prophecy' in Ancient Judaism.* Tübingen: Mohr Siebeck. This is also the source of my information on Malachi.

38 Greenspahn, F.E. (1989) 'Why prophecy ceased.' *Journal of Biblical Literature*, 108(1), 37–49.

39 See http://forward.com/culture/13776/daughter-of-a-voice-02187.

40 Rothkoff, A. (2007) 'Bat Kol.' In M. Berenbaum *et al.* (eds) *Encyclopaedia Judaica.* 2nd ed. Vol. 3. Detroit: Macmillan Reference. Gale Virtual Reference Library. For more on *bat kol* see www.jewishencyclopedia.com/articles/2651-bat-kol.

41 Blumenfeld-Kosinski, R. (2006) *Poets, Saints, and Visionaries of the Great Schism.* University Park, PA: Pennsylvania State University Press.

42 Gerson, J. (1998) *Jean Gerson: Early Works* (trans. B.P. McGuire). New York, NY: Paulist Press.

43 Heyd, M. (1995) *Be Sober and Reasonable: The Critique of Enthusiasm in the Seventeenth and Early Eighteenth Centuries.* New York, NY: Brill.

44 Midelfort, H.C.E. (1999) *A History of Madness in Sixteenth-century Germany.* Stanford, CA: Stanford University Press.

45 It is possible, just possible, that correlation may not imply causation here.

46 See Heyd, as cited above.

47 See Heyd, as cited above.

48 MacDonald, M. (1983) *Mystical Bedlam: Madness, Anxiety and Healing in Seventeenth-century England.* Cambridge, UK: Cambridge University Press.

49 Peterson, D.E. (1982) *A Mad People's History of Madness.* Pittsburgh, PA: University of Pittsburgh.

50 On humoral theory see: Simon, B. (2008) 'Mind and madness in classical antiquity.' *History of Psychiatry and Medical Psychology*, 1, 175–97.

51 Scull, A. (1981) *Madhouses, Mad-doctors and Madmen.* Pennsylvania, PA: University of Pennsylvania Press.

52 Marneros, A. (2008) 'Psychiatry's 200th birthday.' *British Journal of Psychiatry*, 193, 1–3.

53 Smith, L. (2007) *Lunatic Hospitals in Georgian England, 1750–1830.* London: Routledge.

54 Scull, A. (1979) *Museums of Madness: The Social Organization of Insanity in Nineteenth-century England.* New York, NY: St Martin's Press.

55 Scull (1981), as cited above.

56 Scull, A. (2006) *The Insanity of Place/The Place of Insanity: Essays on the History of Psychiatry.* London: Routledge.

57 Goldstein, J.E. (2001) *The French Psychiatric Profession in the Nineteenth Century.* Chicago, IL: University of Chicago Press.

58 Shorter (1998), as cited above.

59 Scull (1979), as cited above.

60 Lieberman, J.A. *et al.* (eds) (2006) *The American Psychiatric Publishing Textbook of Schizophrenia.* Washington, DC: American Psychiatric Publishing.

61 Source: Healthcare Finance News (2009) www.healthcarefinancenews.com/press-release/pipeline-antipsychotic-drugs-drive-next-market-evolution, via Read, J. *et al.* (eds) (2013) *Models of Madness*, 2nd edition. New York, NY: ISPS.

62 Neill, J. (1990) 'Whatever became of the schizophrenogenic mother?' *American Journal of Psychotherapy*, 44(4), 499–505.

63 Harris, G. (2009) 'Drug makers are advocacy group's biggest donors.' *New York Times*, 21 October.

64 Andreasen, N. (2004) *Brave New Brain: Conquering Mental Illness in the Era of the Genome.* Oxford: Oxford University Press.

65 Read, J. *et al.* (2003) 'Sexual and physical abuse during childhood and adulthood as predictors of hallucinations, delusions and thought disorder.' *Psychology and Psychotherapy: Theory, Research and Practice*, 76, 1–22; Ellenson, G.S. (1986) 'Disturbances of perception in adult female incest survivors.' *Social Casework: Journal of Contemporary Social Work*, 67, 149–59.
66 Schiffman, J. *et al.* (2002) 'Perception of parent–child relationships in high-risk families, and adult schizophrenia outcome of offspring.' *Journal of Psychiatric Research*, 36(1), 41–47.
67 Ahrens, C.E. (2006) 'Being silenced: the impact of negative social reactions on the disclosure of rape.' *American Journal of Community Psychology*, 38, 263–74.
68 Romme, M. *et al.* (2009) *Living With Voices: 50 Stories of Recovery*. Ross: PCCS Books.
69 With the obvious, honourable exception of post-traumatic stress disorder.
70 To be clear, I'm not claiming these disorders are only or always caused by sexual abuse, only that they can be.
71 Ho *et al.* (2011), as cited above.
72 Technically there is a seven-second delay, but what's a few seconds between friends?
73 Warner, R. (2013) *Recovery from Schizophrenia: Psychiatry and Political Economy*. London: Routledge.
74 Wolff, R.D. (2012) *Democracy at Work: A Cure for Capitalism*. Chicago, IL: Haymarket Books.
75 Mitchell, J. *et al.* (1989) 'Delusions and hallucinations as a reflection of the subcultural milieu among psychotic patients of the 1930s and 1980s.' *Journal of Psychology*, 123(3), 269–74.
76 Peter's story is retold in this chapter with his permission.
77 I have changed this name.
78 Again, I have changed this name.
79 Of course, the reality is more complicated and ruins my analogy: www.stuffyoushouldknow.com/podcasts/is-there-a-dark-side-of-the-moon.
80 Kate's story is retold in this chapter with her permission.
81 Kinzie, J.D. *et al.* (1989) 'Post-traumatic psychosis among Cambodian refugees.' *Journal of Traumatic Stress*, 2(2), 185–98.
82 Benjamin, L.S. (1989) 'Is chronicity a function of the relationship between the person and the auditory hallucination?' *Schizophrenia Bulletin*, 15, 291–310.
83 Romme, M.A. *et al.* (1989) 'Hearing voices.' *Schizophrenia Bulletin*, 15(2), 209.
84 Baker, P. (1990) 'I hear voices and I am glad to!' *Critical Public Health*, 1(4), 21–27.
85 Woods, A. (2014) 'The voice-hearer.' *Journal of Mental Health*, 22(3), 263–70.

86 Corstens, D. *et al.* (2014) 'Emerging perspectives from the Hearing Voices Movement: implications for research and practice.' *Schizophrenia Bulletin*, 40, S285–94.
87 www.jacquidillon.org.
88 www.workingtorecovery.co.uk/home.aspx.
89 Longden (2013a), as cited above.
90 Taken from Cortsens *et al.* (2014), as cited above.
91 Watkins, J. (1998) *Hearing Voices: A Common Human Experience*. Melbourne: Hill of Content.
92 Sidgwick, H. *et al.* (1894) 'Report on the census of hallucinations.' *Proceedings of the Society for Psychical Research*, 10, 24–422.
93 Posey, T.B. *et al.* (1983) 'Auditory hallucinations of hearing voices in 375 normal subjects.' *Imagination, Cognition and Personality*, 2, 99–113.
94 Cochrane, R. (1994) 'Accepting voices.' *British Medical Journal*, 308(6944), 1649.
95 For example, see www.huffingtonpost.com/allen-frances/psychiatry-and-hearing-vo_b_4003317.html.
96 Woods (2014), as cited above.
97 The following draws on: McCarthy-Jones, S. *et al.* (2014) 'Listening to voices: the use of phenomenology to differentiate malingered from genuine auditory verbal hallucinations.' *International Journal of Psychiatry and the Law*, 37(2), 183–89.
98 Seriously, why are you reading this endnote? Were you really hoping for me to tell you more about goats? If you want to pursue your knowledge of goats then I'd suggest applying to the American Goat Society for a $500 educational scholarship. Experience with goats is advantageous, but don't worry if you're a newbie; 20 per cent of the marks for your application are for 'experiences not goat related'. The most recent awardee of such a scholarship was Mr Boring of California. Seriously. For more details see *The Voice of the AGS*, Volume 55, Issue 3, Fall 2014, www.americangoatsociety.com/voice_of_ags.php. For the love of God don't click on this link.
99 McCarthy-Jones, S. *et al.* (2014) 'A new phenomenological survey of auditory hallucinations: evidence for subtypes and implications for theory and practice.' *Schizophrenia Bulletin*, 40(1), 231–35.
100 Perlin, M. (1990) 'Unpacking the myths: mythology of insanity defense jurisprudence.' *Case Western Reserve Law Review*, 40, 599.
101 People v. Schmidt (1915) Court of Appeals of New York, 216 N.Y. 324.
102 Jaffe, M.E. and Sharma, K.K. (1998) 'Malingering uncommon psychiatric symptoms among defendants charged under California's "Three Strikes and You're Out" law.' *Journal of Forensic Psychiatry*, 43, 549–55.
103 Schmidt, R. (2009) *Psychiatry Board Review: Pearls of Wisdom*. New York, NY: McGraw-Hill.
104 McCarthy-Jones, S. and Resnick, P.J. (2014) 'Listening to voices: the use of phenomenology to differentiate malingered from genuine auditory verbal hallucinations.' *International Journal of Law and Psychiatry*, 37(2), 183–89.

105 McCarthy-Jones and Resnick (2014), as cited above.

106 MacDonald (1983), as cited above.

107 Esquirol, E. (1845) *Mental Maladies: A Treatise on Insanity* (trans. E.K. Hunt). Philadelphia, PA: Lea and Blanchard.

108 Siris, S.G. *et al.* (2012) 'Qualitative content of auditory hallucinations and suicidal behavior in schizophrenia.' *Schizophrenia Research*, 134(2), 298–99.

109 McCarthy-Jones *et al.* (2014), as cited in endnote 99.

110 St Teresa of Avila (2008) *The Life of St Teresa of Avila*. New York, NY: Cosimo.

111 Peterson (1982), as cited above.

112 de Jager, A. *et al.* (2015) 'Investigating the lived experience of recovery in people who hear voices.' *Qualitative Health Research* 26(10), 1409–23.

113 McCarthy-Jones *et al.* (2014), as cited in endnote 99.

114 Genesis 22.2. God says to Abraham: 'Take now thy son, thine only son Isaac, whom thou lovest, and get thee into the land of Moriah; and offer him there for a burnt offering upon one of the mountains.' I prefer Bob Dylan's *Highway 61 Revisited* version to the King James – at least Abraham puts up something of a fight there.

115 Chadwick, P. *et al.* (1994) 'The omnipotence of voices: a cognitive approach to auditory hallucinations.' *British Journal of Psychiatry*, 164(2), 190–201.

116 Jenner, J.A. *et al.* (2008) 'Positive and useful auditory vocal hallucinations: prevalence, characteristics, attributions, and implications for treatment.' *Acta Psychiatrica Scandinavica*, 118, 238–45.

117 Anketell, C. *et al.* (2010) 'A preliminary qualitative investigation of voice hearing and its association with dissociation in chronic PTSD.' *Journal of Trauma and Dissociation*, 12(1), 88–101. Although this person had a diagnosis of PTSD, similar phenomena are seen in schizophrenia.

118 Jenner *et al.* (2008), as cited above; Hartigan, N. *et al.* (2014) 'Hear today, not gone tomorrow? An exploratory longitudinal study of auditory verbal hallucinations ("hearing voices").' *Behavioural and Cognitive Psychotherapy*, 42(1), 117–23.

119 For example, see the first four minutes of Jonny Benjamin's story here: www.youtube.com/watch?v=KIfw-ljOQGg.

120 Favrod, J. *et al.* (2004) 'Benevolent voices are not so kind: the functional significance of auditory hallucinations.' *Psychopathology*, 37, 304–08; MacKinnon, A. *et al.* (2004) 'Factors associated with compliance and resistance to command hallucinations.' *Journal of Nervous and Mental Disease*, 192(5), 357–62.

121 Suhail, K. *et al.* (2002) 'Effect of culture on environment on the phenomenology of delusions and hallucinations.' *International Journal of Social Psychiatry*, 48, 126–38.

122 Luhrmann, T. *et al.* (2015) 'Differences in voice-hearing experiences of people with psychosis in the U.S.A., India and Ghana: interview-based study.' *British Journal of Psychiatry*, 206(1), 41–44.

123 https://simonmccarthyjones.wordpress.com/2016/12/25/silence-of-the-ancients.
124 Livy's *History of Rome*, book 5:32; Cicero, *On Divination*, book 1.45:101.
125 For a fuller discussion of this, see my previous book, McCarthy-Jones (2012), McCarthy-Jones, S. (2012). Hearing Voices: The Histories, Causes and Meanings of Auditory Verbal Hallucinations. Cambridge: Cambridge University Press., or Leudar, I. and Thomas, P. (2000) *Voices of Reason, Voices of Insanity: Studies of Verbal Hallucinations.* London: Routledge.
126 Dodds, E.R. (1951) *The Greeks and the Irrational.* California, CA: University of California Press.
127 Woods, A. *et al.* (2015) 'Experiences of hearing voices: analysis of a novel phenomenological survey.' *The Lancet Psychiatry*, 2(4), 323–31.
128 Bell, V. (2013) 'A community of one: social cognition and auditory verbal hallucinations.' *PLoS Biology*, 11(12), e1001723.
129 Benjamin (1989), as cited above.
130 Wible, C.G. (2012) 'Schizophrenia as a disorder of social communication.' *Schizophrenia Research and Treatment.* Article ID 920485.
131 Schneider, K. (1959) *Clinical Psychopathology.* New York, NY: Grune & Stratton.
132 Cf. Rosenhan, D.L. (1973) 'On being sane in insane places.' *Science*, 179(4070), 250–58.
133 Adapted from Benjamin (1989), as cited above. The patient's name is not given by Benjamin; Jane is a pseudonym.
134 Kinderman, P. (2014) *A Prescription for Psychiatry: Why We Need a Whole New Approach to Mental Health and Wellbeing.* London: Palgrave Macmillan.
135 French, P. *et al.* (eds) (2010) *Promoting Recovery in Early Psychosis: A Practice Manual.* London: Wiley Blackwell.
136 Kaufman, J. *et al.* (1997) 'Case study: trauma-related hallucinations.' *Journal of the American Academy of Child & Adolescent Psychiatry*, 36(11), 1602–05.
137 Kessler, R.C. *et al.* (1995) 'Posttraumatic stress disorder in the national comorbidity survey.' *Archives of General Psychiatry*, 52, 1048–60.
138 See the Centers for Disease Control and Prevention's (CDC) report, *The National Intimate Partner and Sexual Violence Survey: 2010 Summary Report*, available in full online.
139 This estimate starts from a paper by Bentall, R.P. *et al.* (2012; 'Do specific early-life adversities lead to specific symptoms of psychosis? A study from the 2007 Adult Psychiatric Morbidity Survey.' *Schizophrenia Bulletin*, 38(4), 734–40). This study looked at rates of voice-hearing in people in the general population who reported being raped as children (2 per cent of the sample reported suffering childhood rape). Let's assume: 1) that based on the figures from Kessler *et al.* (cited above), half of these people developed PTSD; 2) that only those who developed PTSD heard voices; 3) that all voice-hearing in people who had been raped was due to the childhood rape (note that all these assumptions are questionable). Bentall and colleagues found that 8 per cent of all people raped as children reported voice-hearing, allowing us to estimate that 16 per cent of people with child rape-related PTSD

heard voices. To understand this calculation, imagine that 100 people have been raped, and of these 8 heard voices. Kessler *et al.* suggest that around 50 of the 100 would go on to develop PTSD, and 50 wouldn't. Assume all the eight voice-hearers were in the PTSD group. Although the rate of voice-hearing in the 100 raped people would be 8 per cent, the rate would be 8/50 = 16 per cent in the group with PTSD. Bentall and colleagues also found that 1 per cent of non-raped people went on to hear voices, bringing down the percentage of voice-hearing in people with child rape-related PTSD attributable to the child rape to 15 per cent. A comparable study by Mark Shevlin and colleagues found 21 per cent of people raped as children heard voices. Following the same reasoning and assumptions as above (and taking into account the 8 per cent rate of people not raped as children who Shevlin and colleagues found to hear voices), this suggests that 34 per cent of people with child rape-related PTSD heard voices attributable to their rape (Shevlin, M. *et al.* (2007) 'Childhood traumas and hallucinations: an analysis of the National Comorbidity Survey.' *Journal of Psychiatric Research*, 41, 222–28).

140 Ahrens (2006), as cited above.

141 Herman J.L. (2003), *Father-Daughter Incest*. Cambridge, MA: Harvard University Press.

142 Jonzon, E. *et al.* (2004) 'Disclosure, reactions, and social support: findings from a sample of adult victims of child sexual abuse.' *Child Maltreatment*, 9(2), 190–200.

143 MacKinnon, C. (1993) *Only Words*. Cambridge, MA: Harvard University Press.

144 McCarthy-Jones, S. *et al.* (2013) 'What is psychosis? A meta-synthesis of inductive qualitative studies exploring the experience of psychosis.' *Psychosis: Psychological, Social and Integrative Approaches*, 5, 1–16.

145 Fowler, D. *et al.* (2006) 'The Catastrophic Interaction Hypothesis: How do Stress, Trauma, Emotion and Information Processing Abnormalities Lead to Psychosis?' In A. Morrison *et al.* (eds) *Trauma and Psychosis*. London: John Wiley and Sons.

146 Lampshire, D. (2012) 'Living the dream.' *Psychosis*, 4(2), 172–78.

147 Jones, E. and Wessely, S. (2005) *Shell Shock to PTSD: Military Psychiatry from 1900 to the Gulf War*. London: Psychology Press.

148 Obermeyer, Z. *et al.* (2008) 'Fifty years of violent war deaths from Vietnam to Bosnia: analysis of data from the world health survey programme.' *British Medical Journal*, 336(7659), 1482–86.

149 Van Der Kolk, B. (2014) *The Body Keeps the Score: Brain, Mind, and Body in the Healing of Trauma*. New York, NY: Penguin.

150 Herman, J.L. (2001) *Trauma and Recovery*. London: Pandora.

151 Yehuda, R. (2002) 'Post-traumatic stress disorder.' *New England Journal of Medicine*, 346(2), 108–14, states that 6.4 per cent of men will experience combat, and that 39 per cent will experience PTSD as a result, meaning around *2.5 per cent* (39 per cent × 6.4 per cent) of the male population will have PTSD as a result of combat. Yehuda then states that 0.7 per cent of

men will experience rape (with 65 per cent going on to develop PTSD) and 2.8 per cent will experience molestation (of which 12.2 per cent will go on to develop PTSD). This gives us *0.8 per cent* of men having PTSD due to sexual assault ((65 per cent × 0.7 per cent) + (12.2 per cent × 2.8 per cent)). For women, Yehuda cites 9.2 per cent experiencing rape (of whom 46 per cent go on to experience PTSD) and 12.3 per cent experiencing molestation (of whom, 27 per cent go on to experience PTSD). This means *7.5 per cent* of women will experience PTSD as a result of sexual assault ((9.2 per cent × 46 per cent) + (12.3 per cent × 27 per cent)).

152 Bleich, A. *et al.* (2000) 'Post traumatic stress disorder with psychotic features.' *Croatian Medical Journal*, 41, 442–45.

153 Holmes, D.S. *et al.* (1995) 'The problem of auditory hallucinations in combat PTSD.' *Traumatology*, 1, 1; Brewin, C.R. *et al.* (2010) 'Auditory pseudohallucinations in United Kingdom war veterans and civilians with posttraumatic stress disorder.' *Journal of Clinical Psychiatry*, 71, 419–25; Anketell, C. *et al.* (2010) 'An exploratory analysis of voice hearing in chronic PTSD: potential associated mechanisms.' *Journal of Trauma and Dissociation*, 11, 93–107.

154 David, D. *et al.* (1999) 'Psychotic symptoms in combat-related posttraumatic stress disorder.' *Journal of Clinical Psychiatry*, 60, 29–32.

155 David *et al.* (1999), as cited above. Also see Mueser, K. *et al.* (1987) 'Auditory hallucinations in combat-related chronic posttraumatic stress disorder.' *American Journal of Psychiatry*, 44, 299–302.

156 Mueser *et al.* (1987), as cited above.

157 Bosson, J.V. (2011) 'The comorbidity of psychotic symptoms and posttraumatic stress disorder: evidence for a specifier in DSM-5.' *Clinical Schizophrenia & Related Psychoses*, 5(3), 147–54.

158 Gerrity, E. *et al.* (eds) (2001) *The Mental Health Consequences of Torture.* New York, NY: Plenum Publishers.

159 Larkin, W. *et al.* (2006) 'Relationships Between Trauma and Psychosis: From Theory to Therapy.' In A. Morrison *et al.* (eds) *Trauma and Psychosis.* London: John Wiley and Sons.

160 Scott, J.G. *et al.* (2007) 'Hallucinations in adolescents with post-traumatic stress disorder and psychotic disorder.' *Australasian Psychiatry*, 15(1), 44–48.

161 McCarthy-Jones, S. and Longden, E. (2015) 'Auditory verbal hallucinations in schizophrenia and post-traumatic stress disorder: common phenomenology, common cause, common interventions?' *Frontiers in Psychology*, 6, 1071.

162 McCarthy-Jones and Longden (2015), as cited above.

163 Scott *et al.* (2007), as cited above.

164 Butler, R.W. *et al.* (1996) 'Positive symptoms of psychosis in posttraumatic stress disorder.' *Biological Psychiatry*, 39(10), 839–44.

165 McCarthy-Jones and Longden (2015), as cited above.

166 McCarthy-Jones and Longden (2015), as cited above.

167 Bleuler, E. (1950) *Dementia Praecox or the Group of Schizophrenias* (trans. J. Zinkin). New York, NY: International Universities Press.

168 Kathy's story is taken from the Colin A. Ross Institute for Psychological Trauma: www.rossinst.com/case_studies.html.

169 Dorahy, M. *et al.* (2009) 'Auditory hallucinations in dissociative identity disorder and schizophrenia with and without a childhood trauma history: similarities and differences.' *Journal of Nervous and Mental Disease*, 197(12), 892–98.

170 Honig, A. *et al.* (1998) 'Auditory hallucinations: a comparison between patients and non-patients.' *Journal of Nervous and Mental Disease*, 186, 646–51.

171 Paris, J. (2009) *Treatment of Borderline Personality Disorder: A Guide to Evidence-based Practice.* London: Guilford Press.

172 See McCarthy-Jones (2012), as cited above.

173 Slotema, C.W. *et al.* (2012) 'Auditory verbal hallucinations in patients with borderline personality disorder are similar to those in schizophrenia.' *Psychological Medicine*, 16, 1–6; Kingdon, D.G. *et al.* (2010) 'Schizophrenia and borderline personality disorder: similarities and differences in the experience of auditory hallucinations, paranoia, and childhood trauma.' *Journal of Nervous and Mental Disease*, 198, 399–403.

174 Kingdon *et al.* (2010), as cited above.

175 Polivy, J. *et al.* (2002) 'Causes of eating disorders.' *Annual Review of Psychology*, 53(1), 187–213; Rayworth, B.B. *et al.* (2004) 'Childhood abuse and risk of eating disorders in women.' *Epidemiology*, 15(3), 271–78.

176 Rome, E.S. (2004) 'Eating disorders: uncovering a history of childhood abuse?' *Epidemiology*, 15(3), 262–63.

177 Pugh, M. (2015) 'The internal "anorexic voice": a feature or fallacy of eating disorders?' *Advances in Eating Disorders*, 1–9.

178 Noordenbos, G. *et al.* (2014) 'The relationship among critical inner voices, low self-esteem, and self-criticism in eating disorders.' *Eating Disorders: The Journal of Treatment and Prevention*, 22, 337–51.

179 Tierney, S. *et al.* (2010) 'Living with the "anorexic voice": a thematic analysis.' *Psychology and Psychotherapy: Theory, Research and Practice*, 83, 243–54; Tierney, S. *et al.* (2011) 'Trapped in a toxic relationship: comparing the views of women living with anorexia nervosa to those experiencing domestic violence.' *Journal of Gender Studies*, 20, 31–41.

180 Noordenbos *et al.* (2014), as cited above.

181 Dorahy *et al.* (2009), as cited above.

182 Moebius, 1893, as cited in Lewis, 1971, p.191: Lewis, A. (1971) '"Endogenous" and "exogenous": a useful dichotomy?' *Psychological Medicine*, 1, 191–96.

183 Beer, M.D. (1995) 'The importance of the social and intellectual contexts in a discussion of the history of the concept of psychosis.' *Psychological Medicine*, 25, 317–21.

184 Lifton, R.J. (2000) *The Nazi Doctors: Medical Killing and the Psychology of Genocide.* New York, NY: Basic Books.

185 Baker, M.G. *et al.* (2002) 'The wall between neurology and psychiatry: advances in neuroscience indicate it's time to tear it down.' *British Medical Journal*, 324(7352), 1468.
186 Crossley, N.A. *et al.* (2015) 'Neuroimaging distinction between neurological and psychiatric disorders.' *British Journal of Psychiatry*, 207, 429–34.
187 Braun, C.M. *et al.* (2003) 'Brain modules of hallucination: an analysis of multiple patients with brain lesions.' *Journal of Psychiatry and Neuroscience*, 28, 432–49.
188 Currie, S. *et al.* (1971) 'Clinical course and prognosis of temporal lobe epilepsy: a survey of 666 patients.' *Brain*, 94, 173–90.
189 Kasper, B.S. *et al.* (2010) 'Phenomenology of hallucinations, illusions, and delusions as part of seizure semiology.' *Epilepsy & Behavior*, 18(1–2), 13–23.
190 Korsnes, M.S. *et al.* (2010) 'An fMRI study of auditory hallucinations in patients with epilepsy.' *Epilepsia*, 51, 610–17.
191 Serino, A. *et al.* (2014) 'Auditory verbal hallucinations of epileptic origin.' *Epilepsy & Behavior*, 31, 181–86.
192 Sasaki, T. *et al.* (2013) 'Experiential auditory hallucinations due to chronic epileptic discharges after radiotherapy for oligoastrocytoma.' *Epileptic Disorders*, 15(2), 188–92.
193 Dold, M. *et al.* (2012) 'Benzodiazepines for schizophrenia.' Cochrane Database of Systematic Reviews, 14, 11:CD006391. Indeed, a 2010 Danish study found the use of benzodiazepines (a class of drugs which clonazepam is a member of) was associated with greater rates of death in people diagnosed with schizophrenia who also used antipsychotics (Baandruo, L. *et al.* (2010) 'Antipsychotic polypharmacy and risk of death from natural causes in patients with schizophrenia: a population-based nested case-control study.' *Journal of Clinical Psychiatry*, 71(2), 103–08).
194 Serino *et al.* (2014), as cited above.
195 Chang, Y.T. *et al.* (2011) 'Bidirectional relation between schizophrenia and epilepsy: a population-based retrospective cohort study.' *Epilepsia*, 52(11), 2036–42.
196 James, W. (1960/1902) *The Varieties of Religious Experience*. London: Collins.
197 D'Orsi, G. *et al.* (2006) '"I heard voices…": from semiology, a historical review, and a new hypothesis on the presumed epilepsy of Joan of Arc.' *Epilepsy & Behavior*, 9, 152–57.
198 Storm, D. (2012) *Older People and Hearing Voices.* A Cumbrian NHS service which has responded to voice-hearers both with and without dementia. Presentation given at the 2012 Intervoice conference, Cardiff, Wales, 21 September.
199 In 1988 Waser and Streichenberg actually put forward the 'provocative proposal' to use small doses of sarin to treat Alzheimer's disease. What became of this, I don't know. See Waser, P.G. and Streichenberg, C. (1988) 'Use of Longacting Organophosphates in Alzheimer's Disease.' In E. Giacobini and R. Becker (eds) *Current Research in Alzheimer Therapy.* New York: Taylor & Francis. For a useful review, see Singh, M. *et al.* (2013)

'Acetylcholinesterase inhibitors as Alzheimer therapy: from nerve toxins to neuroprotection.' *European Journal of Medicinal Chemistry*, 70, 165–88.

200 Patel, S.S. *et al.* (2010) 'Acetylcholinesterase inhibitors (AChEI's) for the treatment of visual hallucinations in schizophrenia: a case report.' *BMC Psychiatry*, 10, 68.

201 Inzelberg, R. *et al.* (1998) 'Auditory hallucinations in Parkinson's disease.' *Journal of Neurology, Neurosurgery & Psychiatry*, 64, 533–35; Fénelon, G. *et al.* (2000) 'Hallucinations in Parkinson's disease.' *Brain*, 123(4), 733–45; Graham, J.M. *et al.* (1997) 'Hallucinosis in idiopathic Parkinson's disease.' *Journal of Neurology, Neurosurgery & Psychiatry*, 63, 434–40.

202 Fénelon *et al.* (2000), as cited above.

203 Fénelon *et al.* (2000), as cited above.

204 Inzelberg *et al.* (1998), as cited above.

205 Fénelon *et al.* (2000), as cited above.

206 Honig *et al.* (1998), as cited above.

207 Beavan, V. *et al.* (2011) 'The prevalence of voice-hearers in the general population: a literature review.' *Journal of Mental Health*, 20(3), 281–92.

208 Rees, W.D. (1971) 'The hallucinations of widowhood.' *British Medical Journal*, 210, 37–41.

209 Eliot, T.S. (1943) *Four Quartets*. New York, NY: Harcourt.

210 Grimby, A. (1993) 'Bereavement among elderly people: grief reactions, post-bereavement hallucinations and quality of life.' *Acta Psychiatrica Scandinavica*, 87, 72–80.

211 Carlsson, M.E. *et al.* (2007) 'Bereaved spouses' adjustment after the patients' death in palliative care.' *Palliative & Supportive Care*, 5(4), 397–404.

212 Baethge, C. (2002) 'Grief hallucinations: true or pseudo? Serious or not?' *Psychopathology*, 35(5), 296–302.

213 Julie and Aggie's accounts are taken from Hayes, J. and Leudar, I. (2016) 'Experiences of continued presence: on the practical consequences of "hallucinations" in bereavement.' *Psychology and Psychotherapy: Theory, Research and Practice*, 89, 194–210.

214 Davies, M.F. *et al.* (2001) 'Affective reactions to auditory hallucinations in psychotic, evangelical and control groups.' *British Journal of Clinical Psychology*, 40, 361–70.

215 Luhrmann, T.M. (2005) 'The art of hearing God: absorption, dissociation and contemporary American spirituality.' *Spiritus: A Journal of Christian Spirituality*, 5, 133–57.

216 Act III, Scene I.

217 Dein, S. *et al.* (2015) 'God put a thought into my mind: the charismatic Christian experience of receiving communications from God.' *Mental Health, Religion & Culture*, 18(2), 97–113.

218 Dein, S. *et al.* (2007) 'The voice of God.' *Anthropology and Medicine*, 14, 213–28.

219 Gide, A. (1973) *The Counterfeiters: With Journal of 'The Counterfeiters'* (trans. D. Bussy and J. O'Brien). New York, NY: Vintage, p.444.

220 http://writersinnervoices.com.

221 Descriptions of this process were given in an interview by Peter to Anna Sexton, and are more fully described at: https://mentalhealthrecovery.omeka.net/exhibits/show/peter-bullimore/hearing-voices/a-village-called-pumpkin. These extracts are reproduced with kind permission from Peter and Anna.

222 Johns, L.C. *et al.* (2002) 'Occurrence of hallucinatory experiences in a community sample and ethnic variations.' *British Journal of Psychiatry*, 180, 174–78.

223 Posey, T.B. *et al.* (1983) 'Auditory hallucinations of hearing voices in 375 normal subjects.' *Imagination, Cognition and Personality*, 2, 99–113.

224 Johns, L.C. *et al.* (2004) 'Prevalence and correlates of self-reported psychotic symptoms in the British population.' *British Journal of Psychiatry*, 185(4), 298–305.

225 Daalman, K. *et al.* (2010) 'Same or different? Auditory verbal hallucinations in healthy and psychotic individuals.' *Schizophrenia Research*, 117, 188–89.

226 Escher, S. *et al.* (2010) *Children Hearing Voices: What You Need to Know and What You Can Do.* Ross-on-Wye, UK: PCCS Books.

227 Hanssen, M. *et al.* (2005) 'The incidence and outcome of subclinical psychotic experiences in the general population.' *British Journal of Clinical Psychology*, 44, 181–91.

228 Poulton, R. *et al.* (2000) 'Children's self-reported psychotic symptoms and adult schizophreniform disorder: a 15-year longitudinal study.' *Archives of General Psychiatry*, 57(11), 1053–58.

229 Hanssen *et al.* (2005), as cited above.

230 van Os, J. *et al.* (2009) 'A systematic review and meta-analysis of the psychosis continuum: evidence for a psychosis proneness–persistence–impairment model of psychotic disorder.' *Psychological Medicine*, 39(2), 179–95.

231 Mackie, C.J. *et al.* (2011) 'Developmental trajectories of psychotic-like experiences across adolescence: impact of victimization and substance use.' *Psychological Medicine*, 41(1), 47–58; Wigman, J.T.W. *et al.* (2011) 'Evidence for a persistent, environment-dependent and deteriorating subtype of subclinical psychotic experiences: a 6-year longitudinal general population study.' *Psychological Medicine*, 41(11), 2317–2329; see also van Os *et al.* (2009), as cited above.

232 Daalman, K. *et al.* (2012) 'Childhood trauma and auditory verbal hallucinations.' *Psychological Medicine*, 42(12), 2475–84.

233 Andrew, E.M. *et al.* (2008) 'The relationship between trauma and beliefs about hearing voices: a study of psychiatric and non-psychiatric voice hearers.' *Psychological Medicine*, 38(10), 1409–17.

234 Longden (2013a), as cited above.

235 Powers III, A.R. *et al.* (2016) 'Varieties of voice-hearing: psychics and the psychosis continuum.' *Schizophrenia Bulletin.* First published online 7 October 2016; doi:10.1093/schbul/sbw133.

236 Henrich, J. *et al.* (2010) 'The weirdest people in the world.' *Behavioral and Brain Sciences*, 33, 61–135.

237 Murphy, H.B.M. *et al.* (1963) 'A cross-cultural survey of schizophrenia symptomatology.' *International Journal of Social Psychiatry*, 10, 237–49. For other references to all these people's voice-hearing see McCarthy-Jones (2012), as cited above.

238 Johns *et al.* (2002), as cited above.

239 Mueser *et al.* (1987), as cited above.

240 Annual prevalence of schizophrenia taken from McGrath, J. *et al.* (2008) 'Schizophrenia: a concise overview of incidence, prevalence, and mortality.' *Epidemiologic Reviews*, 30, 67–76. Annual prevalence of bipolar I disorder taken from Merikangas, K.R. *et al.* (2011) 'Prevalence and correlates of bipolar spectrum disorder in the world mental health survey initiative.' *Archives of General Psychiatry*, 68(3), 241–51. Annual prevalence of PTSD is hard to judge. In the USA it has been estimated as 3.7 per cent (Kessler, R.C. *et al.* (2012) 'Twelve-month and lifetime prevalence and lifetime morbid risk of anxiety and mood disorders in the United States.' *International Journal of Methods in Psychiatric Research*, 21, 169–84), but most other countries have rates less than 1 per cent (Kessler, R. *et al.* (2008) *The WHO World Mental Health Surveys: Global Perspectives on the Epidemiology of Mental Disorders.* New York, NY: Cambridge University Press). It is hard to know what figure to opt for. We will go for 1 per cent. Annual prevalence of borderline personality disorder population prevalence – estimates of this are again much higher in the USA than in Europe. In Europe the prevalence of BPD has been found to be 0.7 per cent in studies from Norway (which appeared to be a five-year prevalence; Torgersen, S. *et al.* (2001) 'The prevalence of personality disorders in a community sample.' *Archives of General Psychiatry*, 58, 590–96) and the UK (which appeared to be a point prevalence; Coid, J. *et al.* (2006) 'Prevalence and correlates of personality disorder in Great Britain.' *British Journal of Psychiatry*, 188(5), 423–31). We will go with this more conservative 0.7 per cent figure. Annual prevalence of non-clinical voice-hearing is estimated based on the average figure found by Johns *et al.* (2002) and Johns *et al.* (2004), as discussed in Chapter 13. Rate of voice-hearing in schizophrenia estimated from Thomas, P. *et al.* (2007) 'Correlates of hallucinations in schizophrenia: a cross-cultural evaluation.' *Schizophrenia Research*, 92(1), 41–49. Rate of voice-hearing in bipolar I disorder taken from Shinn, A.K. *et al.* (2012) 'Auditory hallucinations in a cross-diagnostic sample of psychotic disorder patients: a descriptive, cross-sectional study.' *Comprehensive Psychiatry*, 53(6), 718–26. Rate of voice-hearing in borderline personality disorder taken from Yee, L. *et al.* (2005) 'Persistent hallucinosis in borderline personality disorder.' *Comprehensive Psychiatry*, 46, 147–54. Rate of voice-hearing in PTSD is estimated based on the discussion in Chapter 10.

241 Lifetime prevalence of schizophrenia being the median lifetime morbid risk reported by McGrath *et al.* (2008), as cited above. Lifetime prevalence of bipolar I disorder taken from Merikangas *et al.* (2011), as cited above. Lifetime prevalence of PTSD is again hard to judge. Estimated as 10.1 per cent in the USA (Kessler *et al.* (2012), as cited above); in many other countries it is estimated as 2 per cent (Kessler *et al.* (2008), as cited above). We will go with this more conservative 2 per cent estimate. Lifetime prevalence of borderline personality disorder: although estimated as high as 5.9 per cent in the USA (Grant, B.F. *et al.* (2008) 'Prevalence, correlates, disability, and comorbidity of DSM-IV borderline personality disorder: results from the Wave 2 National Epidemiologic Survey on Alcohol and Related Conditions.' *Journal of Clinical Psychiatry*, 69, 533), this seems very high. We will simply double our estimate of the annual prevalence of this disorder, giving a lifetime rate of 1.4 per cent. Lifetime prevalence of non-clinical voice-hearing: no study has asked the Johns *et al.* question about voices which speak a few words or sentences in the context of lifetime prevalence. Again, we will simply double the annual prevalence, as an approximation of this figure.

242 Szasz, T. (1988) *Schizophrenia: The Sacred Symbol of Psychiatry.* Syracuse, NY: Syracuse University Press.

243 Rosenthal, D. *et al.* (1977) 'Quadruplet hallucinations: phenotypic variations of a schizophrenic genotype.' *Archives of General Psychiatry*, 34, 817–27.

244 Mirsky, A.F. *et al.* (2000) 'A 39-year followup of the Genain quadruplets.' *Schizophrenia Bulletin*, 26(3), 699–708.

245 Davila, G.W. *et al.* (2003) 'Bladder dysfunction in sexual abuse survivors.' *The Journal of Urology*, 170(2), 476–79.

246 Kook, S.D. *et al.* (2010) 'Psychotic features as the first manifestation of 22q11.2 deletion syndrome.' *Psychiatry Investigation*, 7(1), 72–74.

247 The paper that forms the source for this chapter is Cooper-Rompato, C. (2013) 'The talking breast pump.' *Western Folklore*, 72(2), 181–209.

248 Fairbrother, N. and Woody, S.R. (2008) 'New mothers' thoughts of harm related to the newborn.' *Archives of Women's Mental Health*, 11(3), 221–29.

249 Smailes, D. *et al.* (2015) 'Tailoring cognitive behavioural therapy to subtypes of voice-hearing.' *Frontiers in Psychology*, 6, 1933.

250 Dodgson, G. *et al.* (2009) 'Avoiding false negatives: are some auditory hallucinations an evolved design flaw?' *Behavioural and Cognitive Psychotherapy*, 37, 325–34.

251 For example, Dodgson *et al.* (2009), as cited above.

252 Warren, R.M. *et al.* (1970) 'Auditory illusions and confusions.' *Scientific American*, 22, 30–36.

253 Levine, R. *et al.* (1942) 'The relation of a need to the amount of perceptual distortion: a preliminary report.' *The Journal of Psychology*, 13, 283–93.

254 Dudley, R. *et al.* (2014) 'The effect of arousal on auditory threat detection and the relationship to auditory hallucinations.' *Journal of Behavior Therapy and Experimental Psychiatry*, 45(3), 311–18.

255 Garwood, L. *et al.* (2015) 'A preliminary investigation into the existence of a hypervigilance subtype of auditory hallucination in people with psychosis.' *Behavioural and Cognitive Psychotherapy*, 43(1), 52–62.
256 Adler, A.B. *et al.* (2009) 'Battlemind debriefing and battlemind training as early interventions with soldiers returning from Iraq: randomization by platoon.' *Journal of Consulting and Clinical Psychology*, 77(5), 928–40.
257 Whitson, J.A. *et al.* (2008) 'Lacking control increases illusory pattern perception.' *Science*, 322(5898), 115–17.
258 Smailes *et al.* (2015), as cited above.
259 Read, J. *et al.* (2008) 'Child maltreatment and psychosis: a return to a genuinely integrated bio-psycho-social model.' *Clinical Schizophrenia & Related Psychoses*, 7, 235–54.
260 Darves-Bornoz, J.M. *et al.* (1995) 'Sexual victimization in women with schizophrenia and bipolar disorder.' *Social Psychiatry and Psychiatric Epidemiology*, 30, 78–84.
261 Fisher, H.L. *et al.* (2011) 'Reliability and comparability of psychosis patients' retrospective reports of childhood abuse.' *Schizophrenia Bulletin*, 37, 546–53.
262 Read, J. (1997) 'Child abuse and psychosis: a literature review and implications for professional practice.' *Professional Psychology: Research and Practice*, 28, 448–56.
263 Torrey, E.F. *et al.* (2000) 'Familial and genetic mechanisms in schizophrenia.' *Brain Research Reviews*, 31(2), 113–17. Italics added.
264 Flensmark, J. (2004) 'Is there an association between the use of heeled footwear and schizophrenia?' *Medical Hypotheses*, 63(4), 740–47.
265 For example, Cerruto, M.A. *et al.* (2008) 'Stilettos, schizophrenia and sexuality.' *Journal of Andrological Sciences*, 15, 130–34.
266 For a more general discussion, not limited to voice-hearing, see McNally, R.J. (2003) *Remembering Trauma*. London: Belknap Press.
267 Rhodes, J. (2015) *Instrumental*. London: Canongate Books.
268 Longden (2013a), as cited above.
269 John Irving argues that Freud was 'a novelist with a scientific background. He just didn't know he was a novelist'. See www.theparisreview.org/interviews/2757/the-art-of-fiction-no-93-john-irving.
270 Letter of Freud to W. Fliess, 1 January 1896, in Masson, J.M. (1985) *The Complete Letters of Sigmund Freud to Wilhelm Fliess 1887–1904*. Cambridge, MA: Harvard University Press.
271 Letter of Freud to W. Fliess, 22 December 1897, in Masson (1985), as cited above.
272 Letter of Freud to W. Fliess, 21 September 1897, in Masson (1985), as cited above.
273 Masson, J.M. (2003) *The Assault on Truth: Freud's Suppression of the Seduction Theory*. New York, NY: Ballantine Books.
274 Esterson, A. (1998) 'Jeffrey Masson and Freud's seduction theory: a new fable based on old myths.' *History of the Human Sciences*, 11(1), 1–21.

275 Williams, L.M. (1994) 'Recall of childhood trauma: A prospective study of women's memories of child sexual abuse.' *Journal of Consulting & Clinical Psychology*, 62, 1167–76.
276 McNally (2003), as cited above; McNally, R.J. (2005) 'Debunking myths about trauma and memory.' *Canadian Journal of Psychiatry*, 50(13), 817–22.
277 Ferenczi, S. (1949) 'Confusion of the tongues between the adults and the child.' *International Journal of Psychoanalysis*, 30, 225–30.
278 Masson, J.M. (1988) *Against Therapy: Emotional Tyranny and the Myth of Psychological Healing.* New York, NY: Atheneum; Masson (2003), as cited above.
279 Webster, R. (1996) *Why Freud Was Wrong: Sin, Science and Psychoanalysis.* New York, NY: Basic Books.
280 Simon, B. (1992) '"Incest – see under Oedipus complex": the history of an error in psychoanalysis.' *Journal of the American Psychoanalytic Association*, 40(4), 955–88.
281 Herman (2001), as cited above.
282 For example, Sariola, H. *et al.* (1996) 'The prevalence and context of incest abuse in Finland.' *Child Abuse & Neglect*, 20(9), 843–50.
283 Romme *et al.* (2009), as cited above.
284 Laing, R. D., and Esterson, A. (1964). Sanity, Madness and the Family. London: Tavistock Publications.
285 McCarthy-Jones and Longden (2015), as cited above.
286 King, M. L., Jr. (1967, April 4th). Beyond Vietnam: a time to break silence. Riverside Church, New York, NY. https://www.youtube.com/watch?v=3Qf6x9_MLD0
287 Jung, C.G. (1960) *The Psychogenesis of Mental Disease* (trans. R.F.C. Hull). London: Routledge and Kegan Paul.
288 Teicher, M.H. *et al.* (2009) 'Length of time between onset of childhood sexual abuse and emergence of depression in a young adult sample: a retrospective clinical report.' *The Journal of Clinical Psychiatry*, 70(5), 684–91.
289 Torrey, E.F. (2001) *Surviving Schizophrenia: A Manual for Families, Consumers, and Providers.* 4th edition. New York, NY: HarperCollins. Quote on page 167, italics added.
290 Daalman *et al.* (2012), as cited above.
291 Surgeon General's Advisory Committee on Smoking and Health (1964) *Smoking and Health: Report of the Advisory Committee to the Surgeon General of the Public Health Service.* US Public Health Service. This was later elaborated on by Hill, A.B. (1965) 'The environment and disease: association or causation?' *Proceedings of the Royal Society of Medicine*, 58, 295–300. Spoiler alert: smoking causes health problems.
292 Cf. Kelleher, I. *et al.* (2013) 'Childhood trauma and psychosis in a prospective cohort study: cause, effect, and directionality.' *Childhood*, 170(7), 734–41.

293 Bentall, R.P. *et al.* (2012) 'Do specific early-life adversities lead to specific symptoms of psychosis? A study from the 2007 Adult Psychiatric Morbidity Survey.' *Schizophrenia Bulletin*, 38(4), 734–40.
294 Honig, A. *et al.* (1998) 'Auditory hallucinations: a comparison between patients and non-patients.' *Journal of Nervous and Mental Disease*, 186, 646–51.
295 Read, J. *et al.* (2003) 'Sexual and physical abuse during childhood and adulthood as predictors of hallucinations, delusions and thought disorder.' *Psychology & Psychotherapy: Theory, Research and Practice*, 76(1), 1–22.
296 Read, J. *et al.* (1999) 'Hallucinations, delusions, and thought disorder among adult psychiatric inpatients with a history of child abuse.' *Psychiatric Services*, 50, 1467–72.
297 See Bentall *et al.* (2012), as cited above.
298 van Nierop, M. *et al.* (2014) 'Psychopathological mechanisms linking childhood traumatic experiences to risk of psychotic symptoms: analysis of a large, representative population-based sample.' *Schizophrenia Bulletin*, 40(Suppl 2), S123–S130; Longden, E. *et al.* (2015) 'Childhood adversity and psychosis: generalised or specific effects?' *Epidemiology and Psychiatric Sciences*, 25(4), 349–59.
299 Kelleher *et al.* (2013), as cited above.
300 Janssen, I. *et al.* (2004) 'Childhood abuse as a risk factor for psychotic experiences.' *Acta Psychiatrica Scandinavica*, 109, 38–45.
301 Sideli, L. *et al.* (2012) 'Do child abuse and maltreatment increase risk of schizophrenia?' *Psychiatry Investigation*, 9, 87–99.
302 Walker, E. *et al.* (1994) 'Neuromotor precursors of schizophrenia.' *Schizophrenia Bulletin*, 20(3), 441–51.
303 Fleming, J. *et al.* (1997) 'A study of potential risk factors for sexual abuse in childhood.' *Child Abuse & Neglect*, 21(1), 49–58.
304 https://en.wikipedia.org/wiki/Rind_et_al._controversy.
305 Rind, B. *et al.* (1998) 'A meta-analytic examination of assumed properties of child sexual abuse using college samples.' *Psychological Bulletin*, 124(1), 22–53.
306 Kendler, K.S. *et al.* (2000) 'Childhood sexual abuse and adult psychiatric and substance use disorders in women: an epidemiological and cotwin control analysis.' *Archives of General Psychiatry*, 57(10), 953–59.
307 Beckett, S. (1979) *The Beckett Trilogy: Molloy, Malone Dies and The Unnamable.* London: Picador.
308 Corstens, D. *et al.* (2013) 'The origins of voices: links between life history and voice hearing in a survey of 100 cases.' *Psychosis*, 5(3), 270–85.
309 Raune, D. *et al.* (2006) 'Event attributes and the content of psychotic experiences in first-episode psychosis.' *Psychological Medicine*, 36(2), 221–30.
310 Thompson, A. *et al.* (2010) 'Psychotic symptoms with sexual content in the "ultra high risk" for psychosis population: frequency and association with sexual trauma.' *Psychiatric Research*, 177, 84–91.

311 Reiff, M. *et al.* (2012) 'Childhood abuse and the content of adult psychotic symptoms.' *Psychological Trauma: Theory, Research, Practice, and Policy*, 4(4), 356–69.
312 Hardy, A. *et al.* (2005) 'Trauma and hallucinatory experiences in psychosis.' *Journal of Nervous and Mental Disease*, 193, 501–07.
313 Anketell *et al.* (2010), as cited above.
314 Jessop, M. *et al.* (2008) 'Hallucinations in adolescent inpatients with post-traumatic stress disorder and schizophrenia: similarities and differences.' *Australasian Psychiatry*, 16(4), 268–72.
315 Hardy *et al.* (2005), as cited above.
316 Hoffman, R.E. (1986) 'Verbal hallucinations and language production processes in schizophrenia.' *Behavioral and Brain Sciences*, 9(3), 503–17.
317 Eyerman, R. *et al.* (2004) *Cultural Trauma and Collective Identity.* Berkeley: University of California Press.
318 Ehlers, A. *et al.* (2000) 'A cognitive model of posttraumatic stress disorder.' *Behaviour Research & Therapy*, 38(4), 319–45.
319 Brewin, C. (2001) 'A cognitive neuroscience account of posttraumatic stress disorder and its treatment.' *Behaviour Research & Therapy*, 39(4), 373–93.
320 Ehlers, A. *et al.* (2002) 'The nature of intrusive memories after trauma: the warning signal hypothesis.' *Behaviour Research & Therapy*, 40(9), 995–1002.
321 Brewin, C.R. *et al.* (1996) 'A dual representation theory of post traumatic stress disorder.' *Psychological Review*, 103, 670–86.
322 Fernyhough, C. (2012) *Pieces of Light: The New Science of Memory.* Profile Books. Kindle Edition.
323 Thompson, H.S. (2010) *Fear and Loathing in Las Vegas: A Savage Journey to the Heart of the American Dream.* New York, NY: Vintage.
324 Waters, F. *et al.* (2012) 'Self-recognition deficits in schizophrenia patients with auditory hallucinations: a meta-analysis of the literature.' *Schizophrenia Bulletin*, 38(4), 741–50.
325 McNally, R. *et al.* (2005) 'Reality monitoring in adults reporting repressed, recovered, or continuous memories of childhood sexual abuse.' *Journal of Abnormal Psychology*, 114(1), 147–52.
326 Stein, M.B. *et al.* (1997) 'Full and partial posttraumatic stress disorder: findings from a community survey.' *American Journal of Psychiatry*, 154(8), 1114–19.
327 Stein *et al.* (1997), as cited above; Kessler *et al.* (1995), as cited above.
328 Dvir, Y. *et al.* (2014) 'Childhood maltreatment, emotional dysregulation, and psychiatric comorbidities.' *Harvard Review of Psychiatry*, 22(3), 149.
329 Watters, E. (2010) *Crazy Like Us: The Globalization of the American Psyche.* New York, NY: Free Press.
330 This may sound like a phrase from Philip Pullman, but is actually from George Eliot (*Middlemarch*).
331 Corstens *et al.* (2013), as cited above.
332 Leff, J. *et al.* (2014) 'Avatar therapy for persecutory auditory hallucinations: what is it and how does it work?' *Psychosis*, 6(2), 166–76.

333 Andrews, B. *et al.* (2000) 'Predicting PTSD symptoms in victims of violent crime: the role of shame, anger, and childhood abuse.' *Journal of Abnormal Psychology*, 109, 69–73.

334 Feiring, C. *et al.* (2002) 'Trying to understand why horrible things happen: attribution, shame, and symptom development following sexual abuse.' *Child Maltreatment*, 7, 25–39.

335 Canton-Cortes, D. *et al.* (2011) 'A model of the effects of child sexual abuse on post-traumatic stress: the mediating role of attributions of blame and avoidance coping.' *Psicothema*, 23, 66–73.

336 Gilbert, P. (1989) *Human Nature and Suffering*. Hove, Sussex: Erlbaum.

337 As cited in Gilbert, P. (1997) 'The evolution of social attractiveness and its role in shame, humiliation, guilt and therapy.' *British Journal of Medical Psychology*, 70(2), 113–47.

338 Gilbert (1997), as cited above.

339 Turner, M.H. *et al.* (2013) 'The contribution of shame to post-psychotic trauma.' *British Journal of Clinical Psychology*, 52(2), 162–82.

340 Matos, M. *et al.* (2013) 'The effect of shame and shame memories on paranoid ideation and social anxiety.' *Clinical Psychology & Psychotherapy*, 20(4), 334–49.

341 Anstrom, K.K. *et al.* (2009) 'Increased phasic dopamine signaling in the mesolimbic pathway during social defeat in rats.' *Neuroscience*, 161(1), 3–12.

342 Rows, R.G. (1916) 'Mental conditions following strain and nerve shock.' *British Medical Journal*, 1, 441–43.

343 Esquirol, E. (1845) *Mental Maladies: A Treatise on Insanit* (trans. E.K. Hunt). Philadelphia, PA: Lea and Blanchard.

344 Wegner, D.M. (1989) *White Bears and Other Unwanted Thoughts*. New York, NY: Viking/Penguin.

345 Badcock, J.C. *et al.* (2011) 'The role of emotion regulation in auditory hallucinations.' *Psychiatry Research*, 185(3), 303–08.

346 Brewin, C.R. *et al.* (2000) 'Meta-analysis of risk factors for posttraumatic stress disorder in trauma-exposed adults.' *Journal of Consulting and Clinical Psychology*, 68, 748–66.

347 Hoffman, R.E. (2007) 'A social deafferentation hypothesis for induction of active schizophrenia.' *Schizophrenia Bulletin*, 33, 1066–70.

348 Santhouse, A.M. *et al.* (2000) 'Visual hallucinatory syndromes and the anatomy of the visual brain.' *Brain*, 123(10), 2055–64.

349 Sacks, O.W. *et al.* (2012) 'Musical Hallucinations.' In J.D. Blom and I.E.C. Sommer (eds) *Hallucinations: Research and Practice*. New York, NY: Springer.

350 Classen, C.C. (2005) 'Sexual revictimization: a review of the empirical literature.' *Trauma Violence Abuse*, 6(2), 103–29.

351 Read *et al.* (2003), as cited above.

352 Bebbington, P. *et al.* (2011) 'Childhood sexual abuse and psychosis: data from a cross-sectional national psychiatric survey in England.' *British Journal of Psychiatry*, 199, 29–37.

353 Bowlby, J. (1973) *Separation: Anxiety and Anger*. London: Hogarth Press.

354 Hazan, C. *et al.* (1987) 'Romantic love conceptualized as an attachment process.' *Journal of Personality and Social Psychology*, 52, 511–24; Bartholomew, K. *et al.* (1991) 'Attachment styles among young adults: a test of a four-category model.' *Journal of Personality and Social Psychology*, 61, 226–44.

355 Sitko, K. *et al.* (2014) 'Associations between specific psychotic symptoms and specific childhood adversities are mediated by attachment styles: an analysis of the National Comorbidity Survey.' *Psychiatric Research*, 217, 202–09.

356 Arseneault, L. *et al.* (2011) 'Childhood trauma and children's emerging psychotic symptoms: a genetically sensitive longitudinal cohort study.' *American Journal of Psychiatry*, 168(1), 65–72.

357 Read, J., et al. (2016). 'The relationship between child abuse and psychosis.' In A. Morrison et al. (eds) Trauma and Psychosis. London: John Wiley and Sons.

358 Raichle, M.E. *et al.* (2002) 'Appraising the brain's energy budget.' *Proceedings of the National Academy of Sciences*, 99(16), 10237–39.

359 Bernstein, H.G. *et al.* (2015) 'Glial cells as key players in schizophrenia pathology: recent insights and concepts of therapy.' *Schizophrenia Research*, 161(1), 4–18.

360 Goldstein, G. *et al.* (eds) (1998) *Neuropsychology.* New York, NY: Plenum Press.

361 Sorry, physics joke (comma optional). Beitia, A.O. *et al.* (2002) 'Spontaneous discharge of a firearm in an MR imaging environment.' *American Journal of Roentgenology*, 178(5), 1092–94.

362 Bennett, C.M. *et al.* (2009) *Neural correlates of interspecies perspective taking in the post-mortem atlantic salmon: an argument for proper multiple comparisons correction.* 15th Annual Meeting of the Organization for Human Brain Mapping. San Francisco, CA. For a good summary of this, see http://blogs.scientificamerican.com/scicurious-brain/ignobel-prize-in-neuroscience-the-dead-salmon-study.

363 Weinberger, D.R. *et al.* (2015) 'Finding the elusive psychiatric "lesion" with 21st-century neuroanatomy: a note of caution.' *American Journal of Psychiatry*, 173(1), 27–33.

364 Modinos, G. *et al.* (2013) 'Neuroanatomy of auditory verbal hallucinations in schizophrenia: a quantitative meta-analysis of voxel-based morphometry studies.' *Cortex*, 49(4), 1046–55; Palaniyappan, L. *et al.* (2012) 'Structural correlates of auditory hallucinations in schizophrenia: a meta-analysis.' *Schizophrenia Research*, 137(1), 169–73.

365 Chen, X. *et al.* (2015) 'Reduced cortical thickness in right Heschl's gyrus associated with auditory verbal hallucinations severity in first-episode schizophrenia.' *BMC Psychiatry*, 15(1), 152.

366 Chen *et al.* (2015), as cited above; Mϕrch-Johnsen, L. *et al.* (2015) 'Auditory cortex characteristics and association with auditory hallucinations in schizophrenia patients.' *European Psychiatry*, 30, 298.

367 Lenroot, R.K. *et al.* (2009) 'Differences in genetic and environmental influences on the human cerebral cortex associated with development during childhood and adolescence.' *Human Brain Mapping*, 30(1), 163–74.

368 van Tol, M.J. *et al.* (2014) 'Voxel-based gray and white matter morphometry correlates of hallucinations in schizophrenia: the superior temporal gyrus does not stand alone.' *NeuroImage: Clinical*, 4, 249–57.

369 Simons, J.S. *et al.* (2008) 'Separable forms of reality monitoring supported by anterior prefrontal cortex.' *Journal of Cognitive Neuroscience*, 20(3), 447–57.

370 Palaniyappan *et al.* (2012), as cited above.

371 Buda, M. *et al.* (2011) 'A specific brain structural basis for individual differences in reality monitoring.' *The Journal of Neuroscience*, 31(40), 14308–13.

372 Garrison, J. *et al.* (2015) 'Paracingulate sulcus morphology predicts hallucinations in schizophrenia.' *Nature Communications*, 17(6), 8956.

373 The BBC: www.bbc.com/news/science-environment-34832284; and George Takei: https://twitter.com/georgetakei/status/667560774143864834.

374 Lewis, J. (1983) *Something Hidden: A Biography of Wilder Penfield.* Toronto: Doubleday Canada Ltd.

375 The brain itself feels no pain when poked, so it can be operated on while you're awake, after a local anaesthetic to your scalp.

376 Penfield, W. and Perot, P. (1963). The brain's record of auditory and visual experience. Brain, 86, 595–694.

377 Hunter, M.D. *et al.* (2006) 'Neural activity in speech-sensitive auditory cortex during silence.' *Proceedings of the National Academy of Sciences of the United States of America*, 103, 189–94.

378 Nazimek, J.M. *et al.* (2012) 'Auditory hallucinations: expectation–perception model.' *Medical Hypotheses*, 78(6), 802–10.

379 Hoffman, R.E. *et al.* (2013) 'Transcranial magnetic stimulation of Wernicke's and right homologous sites to curtail "voices": a randomized trial.' *Biological Psychiatry*, 73(10), 1008–14.

380 David, A.S. (1994) 'The Neuropsychological Origin of Auditory Hallucinations.' In A.S. David *et al.* (eds) *The Neuropsychology of Schizophrenia.* London: Psychology Press.

381 Jardri, R. *et al.* (2011) 'Cortical activations during auditory verbal hallucinations in schizophrenia: a coordinate-based meta-analysis.' *American Journal of Psychiatry*, 168(1), 73–81.

382 This figure is taken from a later 2013 symptom-capture study by Jardri and colleagues: Jardri, R. *et al.* (2013) 'The neurodynamic organization of modality-dependent hallucinations.' *Cerebral Cortex*, 23(5), 1108–17.

383 Diederen, K.M.J. *et al.* (2012) 'Auditory hallucinations elicit similar brain activation in psychotic and nonpsychotic individuals.' *Schizophrenia Bulletin*, 38(5), 1074–82.

384 Diederen, K.M.J. *et al.* (2010) 'Deactivation of the parahippocampal gyrus preceding auditory hallucinations in schizophrenia.' *American Journal of Psychiatry*, 167, 427–35; Shergill, S.S. *et al.* (2004) 'Temporal course of auditory hallucinations.' *British Journal of Psychiatry*, 185, 516–17.

385 Dierks, T. (1999) 'Activation of Heschl's gyrus during auditory hallucinations.' *Neuron*, 22(3), 615–21.

386 Raij, T.T. *et al.* (2009) 'Reality of auditory verbal hallucinations.' *Brain*, 132, 2994–3001.

387 Della Sala, S. *et al.* (1994) 'The Anarchic Hand: Fronto-mesial Sign.' In F. Boller *et al.* (eds) *Handbook of Neuropsychology*, Vol. 9 (pp.233–55). Amsterdam: Elsevier.

388 www.youtube.com/watch?v=A9ihKq34Ozc.

389 Linden, D. *et al.* (2010) 'The brain's voices: comparing nonclinical auditory hallucinations and imagery.' *Cerebral Cortex*, 21(2), 330–37.

390 McGuire, P.K. *et al.* (1993) 'Increased blood flow in Broca's area during auditory hallucinations in schizophrenia.' *The Lancet*, 342(8873), 703–06.

391 Hurlburt, R.T. *et al.* (2016) 'Exploring the ecological validity of thinking on demand: neural correlates of elicited vs. spontaneously occurring inner speech.' *PloS ONE*, 11(2), e0147932.

392 Kühn, S. *et al.* (2012) 'Quantitative meta-analysis on state and trait aspects of auditory verbal hallucinations in schizophrenia.' *Schizophrenia Bulletin*, 38(4), 779–86.

393 Marner, L. *et al.* (2003) 'Marked loss of myelinated nerve fibers in the human brain with age.' *Journal of Comparative Neurology*, 462(2), 144–52.

394 Gieselmann, V. *et al.* (1994) 'Molecular genetics of metachromatic leukodystrophy.' *Human Mutation*, 4(4), 233–42.

395 Walterfang, M. (2005) 'Diseases of white matter and schizophrenia-like psychosis.' *Australian and New Zealand Journal of Psychiatry*, 39(9), 746–56.

396 Koubeissi, M.Z. *et al.* (2016) 'A white matter tract mediating awareness of speech.' *Neurology*, 86(2), 177–79.

397 Geoffroy, P.A. *et al.* (2014) 'The arcuate fasciculus in auditory-verbal hallucinations: a meta-analysis of diffusion-tensor-imaging studies.' *Schizophrenia Research*, 159(1), 234–37.

398 McCarthy-Jones, S. *et al.* (2015) 'Reduced integrity of the left arcuate fasciculus is specifically associated with auditory verbal hallucinations in schizophrenia.' *Schizophrenia Research*, 162(1–3), 1–6.

399 Song, S.K. *et al.* (2003) 'Diffusion tensor imaging detects and differentiates axon and myelin degeneration in mouse optic nerve after retinal ischemia.' *Neuroimage*, 20(3), 1714–22; Song, S.K. *et al.* (2005) 'Demyelination increases radial diffusivity in corpus callosum of mouse brain.' *Neuroimage*, 26(1), 132–40.

400 Choi, J. *et al.* (2009) 'Preliminary evidence for white matter tract abnormalities in young adults exposed to parental verbal abuse.' *Biological Psychiatry*, 65, 227–34.

401 Poletti, S. *et al.* (2015) 'Adverse childhood experiences influence white matter microstructure in patients with schizophrenia.' *Psychiatry Research: Neuroimaging*, 234(1), 35–43.

402 Mandl, R.C. *et al.* (2013) 'Altered white matter connectivity in never-medicated patients with schizophrenia.' *Human Brain Mapping*, 34(9), 2353–65.

403 de Weijer, A.D. *et al.* (2013) 'Aberrations in the arcuate fasciculus are associated with auditory verbal hallucinations in psychotic and in non-psychotic individuals.' *Human Brain Mapping*, 34(3), 626–34.

404 Ćurčić-Blake, B. *et al.* (2013) 'When Broca goes uninformed: reduced information flow to Broca's area in schizophrenia patients with auditory hallucinations.' *Schizophrenia Bulletin*, 39(5), 1087–95.

405 Oestreich, L.K.L. *et al.* (2016) 'Decreased integrity of the fronto-temporal fibers of the left inferior occipito-frontal fasciculus (IOFF) associated with auditory verbal hallucinations in schizophrenia.' *Brain Imaging and Behavior*, 10(2), 445–54.

406 Poletti *et al.* (2015), as cited above.

407 Brunelin, J. *et al.* (2012) 'Examining transcranial direct-current stimulation (tDCS) as a treatment for hallucinations in schizophrenia.' *American Journal of Psychiatry*, 169(7), 719–24.

408 Mondino, M. *et al.* (2015) 'Effects of fronto-temporal transcranial direct current stimulation on auditory verbal hallucinations and resting-state functional connectivity of the left temporo-parietal junction in patients with schizophrenia.' *Schizophrenia Bulletin*, 42(2), 318–26.

409 Khan, O.H. *et al.* (2014) 'The role of left inferior fronto-occipital fascicle in verbal perseveration: a brain electrostimulation mapping study.' *Brain Topography*, 27(3), 403–11.

410 Crapse, T.B. *et al.* (2008) 'Corollary discharge across the animal kingdom.' *Nature Reviews Neuroscience*, 9(8), 587–600.

411 Morin, A. (2009) 'Self-awareness deficits following loss of inner speech: Dr. Jill Bolte Taylor's case study.' *Consciousness and Cognition*, 18(2), 524–29.

412 Whitford, T.J. *et al.* (2012) 'Schizophrenia, myelination, and delayed corollary discharges: a hypothesis.' *Schizophrenia Bulletin*, 38(3), 486–94.

413 Whitford, T.J. *et al.* (2011) 'Electrophysiological and diffusion tensor imaging evidence of delayed corollary discharges in patients with schizophrenia.' *Psychological Medicine*, 41(5), 959–69.

414 Langdon, R. *et al.* (2009) 'The phenomenology of inner speech: comparison of schizophrenia patients with auditory verbal hallucinations and healthy controls.' *Psychological Medicine*, 39(4), 655–63.

415 This chapter's title comes from Keat's poem, *Ode to a Nightingale.*

416 St John of the Cross (1943) *The Complete Works of Saint John of the Cross.* Vol. I (trans. E.A. Peers). London: Burns Oates.

417 Rapin, L. *et al.* (2013) 'An EMG study of the lip muscles during covert auditory verbal hallucinations in schizophrenia.' *Journal of Speech, Language and Hearing Research*, 56(6), S1882–93.

418 Green, P. *et al.* (1981) 'Reinforcement of vocal correlates of auditory hallucinations by auditory feedback: a case study.' *British Journal of Psychiatry*, 139, 204–08.

419 See www.nasa.gov/home/hqnews/2004/mar/HQ_04093_subvocal_speech.html and www.forbes.com/free_forbes/2006/0410/084.html.

420 Bick, P.A. *et al.* (1987) 'Auditory hallucinations and subvocal speech in schizophrenic patients.' *American Journal of Psychiatry*, 144, 222–25.

421 Green, M.F. *et al.* (1990) 'Subvocal activity and auditory hallucinations: clues for behavioural treatments.' *Schizophrenia Bulletin*, 16, 617–25.
422 Schönfeldt-Lecuona, C. *et al.* (2004) 'Stereotaxic rTMS for the treatment of auditory hallucinations in schizophrenia.' *Neuroreport*, 15(10), 1669–73.
423 Brinthaupt, T.M. *et al.* (2012) 'Differences in self-talk frequency as a function of age, only-child, and imaginary childhood companion status.' *Journal of Research in Personality*, 46(3), 326–33.
424 Bell (2013), as cited above.
425 Fernyhough, C. (2004) 'Alien voices and inner dialogue: towards a developmental account of auditory verbal hallucinations.' *New Ideas in Psychology*, 22, 49–68.
426 Plato (1987) *Theaetetus* (trans. R.H. Waterford). London: Penguin.
427 Feynman as cited in Szasz, T.S. (1996) *The Meaning of Mind: Language, Morality and Neuroscience.* Westport, CT: Praeger.
428 Puchalska-Wasyl, M.M. (2015) 'Self-talk: conversation with oneself? On the types of internal interlocutors.' *Journal of Psychology*, 149(5), 443–60.
429 Vygotsky, L.S. (1934/1987) *Thinking and Speech: The Collected Works of L.S. Vygotsky*, Vol. 1. New York, NY: Plenum.
430 As described in Stephens, G.L. *et al.* (2000) *When Self-consciousness Breaks: Alien Voices and Inserted Thoughts.* Boston, MA: MIT Press.
431 Simpson (1988), as cited above.
432 Sommer, I.E.C. *et al.* (2008) 'Auditory verbal hallucinations predominantly activate the right inferior frontal area.' *Brain*, 131, 3169–77.
433 Listen, for example, to this: www.youtube.com/watch?v=Oehry1JC9Rk.
434 Aziz-Zadeh, L. *et al.* (2005) 'Covert speech arrests inducted by rTMS over both motor and nonmotor left hemisphere frontal sites.' *Journal of Cognitive Neuroscience*, 17, 928–38.
435 For references and discussion see Sommer *et al.* (2008), as cited above; Sommer, I. *et al.* (2009) 'Language production in the non-dominant hemisphere as a potential source of auditory verbal hallucinations.' *Brain*, 132, 1–2.
436 Sommer *et al.* (2009), as cited above.
437 Aron, A.R. *et al.* (2003) 'Stop-signal inhibition disrupted by damage to right inferior frontal gyrus in humans.' *Nature Neuroscience*, 6(2), 115–16.
438 Gazzaniga, M.S. *et al.* (1978) *The Integrated Mind.* New York, NY: Plenum Press.
439 Gallagher, S. (2004) 'Neurocognitive models of schizophrenia: a neurophenomenological critique.' *Psychopathology*, 37, 8–19.
440 Corbetta, M. *et al.* (2002) 'Control of goal-directed and stimulus-driven attention in the brain.' *Nature Reviews Neuroscience*, 3(3), 201–15.
441 Aristotle (1984) 'On dreams.' *The Complete Works of Aristotle: The Revised Oxford Translation* (trans. J.I. Beare). Princeton, NJ: Princeton University Press.
442 Goldstein (2001), as cited above.
443 Diederen *et al.* (2010), as cited above.

444 Waters, F.A.V. *et al.* (2006) 'Auditory hallucinations in schizophrenia: intrusive thoughts and forgotten memories.' *Cognitive Neuropsychiatry*, 11, 65–83.

445 Waters, F.A.V. *et al.* (2003) 'Inhibition in schizophrenia: association with auditory hallucinations.' *Schizophrenia Research*, 62, 275–80.

446 Waters, F.A.V. *et al.* (2006) 'The "who" and "when" of context memory: different patterns of association with auditory hallucinations.' *Schizophrenia Research*, 82, 271–73.

447 Waters, F.A.V. *et al.* (2006) 'Auditory hallucinations in schizophrenia: intrusive thoughts and forgotten memories.' *Cognitive Neuropsychiatry*, 11, 65–83.

448 Attademo, L. (2015) 'History and conceptual problems of the relationship between obsessions and hallucinations.' *Harvard Review of Psychiatry*, 23(1), 19–27.

449 Byrne, S. *et al.* (2006) *A Casebook of Cognitive Behaviour Therapy for Command Hallucinations: A Social Rank Theory Approach.* London: Routledge.

450 Peng, Z. *et al.* (2012) 'Brain structural abnormalities in obsessive–compulsive disorder: converging evidence from white matter and grey matter.' *Asian Journal of Psychiatry*, 5(4), 290–96.

451 Poyurovsky, M. (2013) *Schizo-obsessive Disorder.* Cambridge, UK: Cambridge University Press.

452 Stephane, M. *et al.* (2000) 'A subtype of auditory verbal hallucinations responds to fluvoxamine.' *Journal of Neuropsychiatry and Clinical Neurosciences*, 13(3), 425–27.

453 Fuller Torrey, E. *et al.* (2011) 'Adjunct treatments for schizophrenia and bipolar disorder: what to try when you are out of ideas.' *Clinical Schizophrenia & Related Psychoses*, 5(4), 208–16.

454 Deamer, F. *et al.* (2015) 'The speaker behind the voice: therapeutic practice from the perspective of pragmatic theory.' *Frontiers in Psychology*, 6, 817.

455 Arzy, S. *et al.* (2006) 'Induction of an illusory shadow person.' *Nature*, 443, 287.

456 Wible (2012), as cited above.

457 Slotema, C.W. *et al.* (2012) 'Meta-analysis of repetitive transcranial magnetic stimulation in the treatment of auditory verbal hallucinations: update and effects after one month.' *Schizophrenia Research*, 142(1–3), 40–45.

458 Homan, P. *et al.* (2012) 'Cerebral blood flow identifies responders to transcranial magnetic stimulation in auditory verbal hallucinations.' *Translational Psychiatry*, 2, e189.

459 Hoffman, R.E. *et al.* (2007) 'Probing the pathophysiology of auditory/verbal hallucinations by combining functional magnetic resonance imaging and transcranial magnetic stimulation.' *Cerebral Cortex*, 17, 2733–43.

460 Kindler, J. *et al.* (2013) 'Reduced neuronal activity in language-related regions after transcranial magnetic stimulation therapy for auditory verbal hallucinations.' *Biological Psychiatry*, 73(6), 518–24.

461 Moseley, P. *et al.* (2014) 'The role of the superior temporal lobe in auditory false perceptions: a transcranial direct current stimulation study.' *Neuropsychologia*, 62, 202–08.

462 Brunelin, J. *et al.* (2006) 'Low frequency repetitive transcranial magnetic stimulation improves source monitoring deficit in hallucinating patients with schizophrenia.' *Schizophrenia Research*, 81, 41–45.

463 Andrews-Hanna, J.R. (2014) 'The default network and self-generated thought: component processes, dynamic control, and clinical relevance.' *Annals of the New York Academy of Sciences*, 1316, 29–52.

464 Jardri, R. *et al.* (2013) 'The neurodynamic organization of modality-dependent hallucinations.' *Cerebral Cortex*, 23(5), 1108–17.

465 Bonnelle, V. *et al.* (2012) 'Salience network integrity predicts default mode network function after traumatic brain injury.' *Proceedings of the National Academy of Sciences*, 109(12), 4690–95.

466 Sridharan, D. *et al.* (2008) 'A critical role for the right fronto-insular cortex in switching between central-executive and default-mode networks.' *Proceedings of the National Academy of Sciences*, 105(34), 12569–74.

467 Palaniyappan, L. and Liddle, P.F. (2012) 'Does the salience network play a cardinal role in psychosis? An emerging hypothesis of insular dysfunction.' *Journal of Psychiatry & Neuroscience*, 37(1), 17–27.

468 Ghaemi, S.N. (2015) 'A new nomenclature for psychotropic drugs.' *Journal of Clinical Psychopharmacology*, 35(4), 428–33.

469 Moncrieff (2013), as cited above.

470 Elkes *et al.* (1954), as cited above.

471 Lomas, J. (1955) 'Uses of chlorpromazine in mental hospital patients.' *British Medical Journal*, 1(4918), 879–82.

472 Schneider, S.D. *et al.* (2011) 'What happened to the voices? A fine-grained analysis of how hallucinations and delusions change under psychiatric treatment.' *Psychiatry Research*, 188(1), 13–17.

473 López-Muñoz, F. (2005) 'History of the discovery and clinical introduction of chlorpromazine.' *Annals of Clinical Psychiatry*, 17(3), 113–35.

474 Cited in Read *et al.* (2010), as cited above.

475 Cole, J.O. *et al.* (1964) 'Phenothiazine treatment in acute schizophrenia.' *Archives of General Psychiatry*, 10, 246–61.

476 Dr Peter Venkman uses thorazine, aka chlorpromazine, to sedate the possessed Dana Barrett. Why does he inject her with 300ccs worth, an amount equivalent to a can of coke? A good question. Given the evening started out as a date, why does he have a coke can's worth of chlorpromazine on him? Another good question. Let's go with the answer: IT'S A MOVIE.

477 http://psychodiagnosticator.blogspot.ie/2015/05/shrinks-to-fit.html. In fact doctors who don't wear white coats tend to be psychiatrists (or paediatricians), as these groups think the white coat might have a negative effect on their rapport with patients (see Farraj, R. and Baron, J.H. (1991) 'Why do hospital doctors wear white coats?' *Journal of the Royal Society of Medicine*, 84(1), 43).

478 Fuller Torrey, E. and Yolken, R.H. (2010) 'Psychiatric genocide: Nazi attempts to eradicate schizophrenia.' *Schizophrenia Bulletin*, 36, 26–32.

479 Moncrieff, J. (2007) *The Myth of the Chemical Cure: A Critique of Psychiatric Drug Treatment.* London: Palgrave Macmillan; Moncrieff (2013), as cited above.

480 Shorter (1998), as cited above.

481 Sommer, I.E. *et al.* (2012) 'The treatment of hallucinations in schizophrenia spectrum disorders.' *Schizophrenia Bulletin*, 38(4), 704–14.

482 Marques, T.R. *et al.* (2011) 'The different trajectories of antipsychotic response: antipsychotics versus placebo.' *Psychological Medicine*, 41(7), 1481–88.

483 Nordon, C. *et al.* (2014) 'Trajectories of antipsychotic response in drug-naive schizophrenia patients: results from the 6-month ESPASS follow-up study.' *Acta Psychiatrica Scandinavica*, 129(2), 116–25.

484 Cole *et al.* (1964), as cited above; Goldberg, S.C. *et al.* (1965) 'Changes in schizophrenic psychopathology and ward behaviour as a function of phenothiazine treatment.' *British Journal of Psychiatry*, 111, 120–23.

485 Adams, C.E. *et al.* (2007) 'Chlorpromazine versus placebo for schizophrenia.' *Cochrane Database of Systematic Reviews*, 2, CD000284.

486 McEvoy, J.P. *et al.* (2007) 'Efficacy and tolerability of olanzapine, quetiapine, and risperidone in the treatment of early psychosis: a randomized, double-blind 52-week comparison.' *American Journal of Psychiatry*, 164, 1050–60.

487 Kahn, R.S. *et al.* (2008) 'Effectiveness of antipsychotic drugs in first-episode schizophrenia and schizophreniform disorder: an open randomised clinical trial.' *The Lancet*, 371(9618), 1085–97.

488 www.theguardian.com/society/2015/jun/02/dont-use-john-nash-schizophrenia-a-beautiful-mind-promote-anti-psychotics.

489 Crump, C. *et al.* (2013) 'Comorbidities and mortality in persons with schizophrenia: a Swedish national cohort study.' *American Journal of Psychiatry*, 170(3), 324–33; Laursen, T.M. *et al.* (2012) 'Life expectancy and cardiovascular mortality in persons with schizophrenia.' *Current Opinion in Psychiatry*, 25(2), 83–88; Tiihonen, J. *et al.* (2009) '11-year follow-up of mortality in patients with schizophrenia: a population-based cohort study (FIN11 study).' *The Lancet*, 374(9690), 620–27.

490 Parks, J. *et al.* 'Morbidity and mortality in people with serious mental illness.' National Association of State Mental Health Program Directors (NASMHPD) Medical Directors Council – cited in Tiihonen *et al.* (2009), as cited above.

491 It is important to note that other factors in addition to antipsychotics may be responsible for increased cardiac disease in schizophrenia. A recent study found a number of genetic variations linked to increased risk for cardiac disease were associated with schizophrenia: Schizophrenia Working Group of the Psychiatric Genomics Consortium (2014) 'Biological insights from 108 schizophrenia-associated genetic loci.' *Nature*, 511(7510), 421–27.

492 Rattehalli, R.D. *et al.* (2010) 'Risperidone versus placebo for schizophrenia.' *Cochrane Database of Systematic Reviews*, 20, CD006918.

493 Lecrubier, Y. *et al.* (2007) 'Physician observations and perceptions of positive and negative symptoms of schizophrenia: a multinational, cross-sectional survey.' *European Psychiatry*, 22(6), 371–79.

494 Shooter, M. (2005) 'Dancing with the devil.' *Psychiatric Bulletin*, 29, 81–83.

495 Spurling, G.K. *et al.* (2010) 'Information from pharmaceutical companies and the quality, quantity, and cost of physicians' prescribing: a systematic review.' *PLoS Medicine*, 7(10), 1292.

496 Reduced superior longitudinal fasciculus integrity was found to be associated with worse treatment response by Luck *et al.* (2011) but not by Marques *et al.* (2014). See Luck, D. *et al.* (2011) 'Fronto-temporal disconnectivity and clinical short-term outcome in first episode psychosis: a DTI-tractography study.' *Journal of Psychiatric Research*, 45(3), 369–77; Marques, T.R. *et al.* (2014) 'White matter integrity as a predictor of response to treatment in first episode psychosis.' *Brain*, 137(1), 172–82.

497 Hassan, A.N. *et al.* (2015) 'The effect of lifetime adversities on resistance to antipsychotic treatment in schizophrenia patients.' *Schizophrenia Research*, 161(2), 496–500.

498 Emsley, R. *et al.* (2007) 'Remission in early psychosis: rates, predictors, and clinical and functional outcome correlates.' *Schizophrenia Research*, 89(1), 129–39.

499 Lencz, T. *et al.* (2006) 'DRD2 promoter region variation predicts sustained response to antipsychotic medication in first episode schizophrenia.' *American Journal of Psychiatry*, 163, 529–31.

500 Seeman, P. *et al.* (1976) 'Antipsychotic drug doses and neuroleptic/dopamine receptors.' *Nature*, 261, 717–19.

501 Howes, O. and Kapur, S. (2009) 'The dopamine hypothesis of schizophrenia: version III – the final common pathway.' *Schizophrenia Bulletin*, 35(3), 549–62.

502 van Tol *et al.* (2014), as cited above.

503 Hoffman, R.E. *et al.* (2011) 'Elevated functional connectivity along a corticostriatal loop and the mechanism of auditory/verbal hallucinations in patients with schizophrenia.' *Biological Psychiatry*, 69(5), 407–14.

504 For example, Howes, O. *et al.* (2009) 'Mechanisms underlying psychosis and antipsychotic treatment response in schizophrenia: insights from PET and SPECT imaging.' *Current Pharamaceutical Design*, 15(22), 2550–59.

505 Howes and Kapur (2009), as cited above.

506 Laruelle, M. *et al.* (1996) 'Single photon emission computerized tomography imaging of amphetamine-induced dopamine release in drug-free schizophrenic subjects.' *Proceedings of the National Academy of Sciences*, 93(17), 9235–40.

507 Again, details taken from Howes and colleagues, as cited above.

508 Lodge, D.J. *et al.* (2007) 'Aberrant hippocampal activity underlies the dopamine dysregulation in an animal model of schizophrenia.' *Journal of Neuroscience*, 27(42), 11424–30.

509 Kapur, S. (2003) 'Psychosis as a state of aberrant salience: a framework linking biology, phenomenology, and pharmacology in schizophrenia.' *American Journal of Psychiatry*, 160(1), 13–23.

510 Howes, O.D. *et al.* (2014) 'Schizophrenia: an integrated sociodevelopmental-cognitive model.' *The Lancet*, 383(9929), 1677–87.

511 Lush, I.E. (1975) 'A comparison of the effect of mescaline on activity and emotional defaecation in seven strains of mice.' *British Journal of Pharmacology*, 55, 133–39.

512 Kyzar, E.J. *et al.* (2012) 'Effects of hallucinogenic agents mescaline and phencyclidine on zebrafish behavior and physiology.' *Progress in Neuro-Psychopharmacology and Biological Psychiatry*, 37(1), 194–202.

513 Machiyama, Y. (1992) 'Chronic methamphetamine intoxication model of schizophrenia in animals.' *Schizophrenia Bulletin*, 18, 107–13.

514 Nielsen, E.B. *et al.* (1983) 'Apparent hallucinations in monkeys during around-the-clock amphetamine for seven to fourteen days: possible relevance to amphetamine psychosis.' *Journal of Nervous and Mental Disease*, 171(4), 222–33.

515 Turner, T.H. *et al.* (1984) 'Psychotic reactions during treatment of pituitary tumours with dopamine agonists.' *British Medical Journal*, 289(6452), 1101–03.

516 Depatie, L. *et al.* (2001) 'Apomorphine and the dopamine hypothesis of schizophrenia: a dilemma?' *Journal of Psychiatry & Neuroscience*, 26, 203–20.

517 Buchanan, F.H. *et al.* (1975) 'Double blind trial of L-dopa in chronic schizophrenia.' *Australian and New Zealand Journal of Psychiatry*, 9(4), 269–71.

518 Demjaha, A. *et al.* (2014) 'Antipsychotic treatment resistance in schizophrenia associated with elevated glutamate levels but normal dopamine function.' *Biological Psychiatry*, 75, e11–e13.

519 For references, see Pollak, T.A. *et al.* (2014) 'Prevalence of anti-N-methyl-D-aspartate (NMDA) receptor antibodies in patients with schizophrenia and related psychoses: a systematic review and meta-analysis.' *Psychological Medicine*, 44(12), 2475–87.

520 See Pollak *et al.* (2014), as cited above.

521 Powers III, A.R. *et al.* (2015) 'Ketamine-induced hallucinations.' *Psychopathology*, 48(6), 376–85.

522 McCarthy-Jones, S. *et al.* (2017) 'Occurrence and co-occurrence of hallucinations by modality in schizophrenia-spectrum disorders.' Manuscript submitted for publication.

523 Hugdahl, K. *et al.* (2015) 'Glutamate as a mediating transmitter for auditory hallucinations in schizophrenia: a 1 H MRS study.' *Schizophrenia Research*, 161(2), 252–60.

524 Stone, J.M. *et al.* (2012) 'Ketamine effects on brain GABA and glutamate levels with 1H-MRS: relationship to ketamine-induced psychopathology.' *Molecular Psychiatry*, 17(7), 664–68.

525 Vine, T. (2010) *The Biggest Ever Tim Vine Joke Book.* London: Random House.

526 Howes, O.D. *et al.* (2013) 'Dopaminergic function in the psychosis spectrum: an [18F]-DOPA imaging study in healthy individuals with auditory hallucinations.' *Schizophrenia Bulletin*, 39(4), 807–14.

527 Kühn, T. (1962) *The Structure of Scientific Revolutions.* Chicago, IL: University of Chicago Press.

528 Palaniyappan *et al.* (2012), as cited above.

529 Stanghellini, G. *et al.* (2012) 'Quality of hallucinatory experiences: differences between a clinical and a non-clinical sample.' *World Psychiatry*, 11(2), 110–13.

530 www.psychiatrictimes.com/blogs/couch-crisis/psychiatry-new-brain-mind-and-legend-chemical-imbalance.

531 http://psychcentral.com/blog/archives/2011/08/04/doctor-is-my-mood-disorder-due-to-a-chemical-imbalance.

532 Read, J. *et al.* (2001) 'The role of biological and genetic causal beliefs in the stigmatization of "mental patients".' *Journal of Mental Health*, 10(2), 223–35.

533 Whitaker, R. *et al.* (2015) *Psychiatry Under the Influence: Institutional Corruption, Social Injury, and Prescriptions for Reform.* New York, NY: Palgrave Macmillan.

534 Whitaker *et al.* (2015), as cited above.

535 Katz, J. (1996) *Human Sacrifice and Human Experimentation: Reflections at Nuremberg.* Occasional Papers. Paper 5. http://digitalcommons.law.yale.edu/ylsop_papers/5.

536 https://en.wikipedia.org/wiki/Noble_lie.

537 http://guides.library.jhu.edu/c.php?g=202502&p=1335759.

538 Fulford, K.W.M. *et al.* (eds) (2013) *The Oxford Handbook of Philosophy and Psychiatry.* Oxford: Oxford University Press.

539 Shooter (2005), as cited above.

540 For good reviews of this area see Clark, A. (2013) 'Whatever next? Predictive brains, situated agents, and the future of cognitive science.' *Behavioral and Brain Sciences*, 36(3), 181–204; and Hohwy, J. (2013) *The Predictive Mind.* Oxford: Oxford University Press.

541 Dawkins, R. (2009) *The God Delusion.* London: Transworld.

542 Egner, T. *et al.* (2010) 'Expectation and surprise determine neural population responses in the ventral visual stream.' *Journal of Neuroscience*, 30(49), 16601–08.

543 Jardri, R. and Denève, S. (2013) 'Circular inferences in schizophrenia.' *Brain*, 136(11), 3227–41; Jardri, R. and Denève, S. (2013) 'Computational Models of Hallucinations.' In R. Jardri *et al.* (eds) (2014) *The Neuroscience of Hallucinations.* New York, NY: Springer.

544 Friston, K.J. (2005) 'Hallucinations and perceptual inference.' *Behavioral and Brain Sciences*, 28(6), 764–66.

545 Vercammen, A. *et al.* (2008) 'Hearing a voice in the noise: auditory hallucinations and speech perception.' *Psychological Medicine*, 38, 1177–84.

546 Horga, G. *et al.* (2014) 'Deficits in predictive coding underlie hallucinations in schizophrenia.' *Journal of Neuroscience*, 34(24), 8072–82.

547 Wilkinson, S. (2014) 'Accounting for the phenomenology and varieties of auditory verbal hallucination within a predictive processing framework.' *Consciousness and Cognition*, 30, 142–55.

548 Sam Wilkinson, personal communication.

549 Bartels-Velthuis, A.A. *et al.* (2010) 'Prevalence and correlates of auditory vocal hallucinations in middle childhood.' *British Journal of Psychiatry*, 196(1), 41–46.

550 Dalman, C. *et al.* (1999) 'Obstetric complications and the risk of schizophrenia: a longitudinal study of a national birth cohort.' *Archives of General Psychiatry*, 56(3), 234–40.

551 Cannon, M. *et al.* (2002) 'Obstetric complications and schizophrenia: historical and meta-analytic review.' *American Journal of Psychiatry*, 159(7), 1080–92.

552 Schmidt-Kastner, R. *et al.* (2006) 'Gene regulation by hypoxia and the neurodevelopmental origin of schizophrenia.' *Schizophrenia Research*, 84(2), 253–71.

553 Arias, I. *et al.* (2012) 'Infectious agents associated with schizophrenia: a meta-analysis.' *Schizophrenia Research*, 136(1), 128–36.

554 Mortensen, P.B. *et al.* (2007) 'Toxoplasma gondii as a risk factor for early-onset schizophrenia: analysis of filter paper blood samples obtained at birth.' *Biological Psychiatry*, 61(5), 688–93.

555 Bartels-Velthuis *et al.* (2010), as cited above.

556 Huttenlocher, P.R. (1979) 'Synaptic density in human frontal cortex: developmental changes and effect of aging.' *Brain Research*, 163, 195–205.

557 Hoffman, R.E. and McGlashan, T.H. (1997) 'Synaptic elimination, neurodevelopment, and the mechanism of hallucinated "voices" in schizophrenia.' *American Journal of Psychiatry*, 154(12), 1683–89.

558 Boksa, P. (2012) 'Abnormal synaptic pruning in schizophrenia: urban myth or reality?' *Journal of Psychiatry & Neuroscience: JPN*, 37(2), 75.

559 Read, J. *et al.* (2014) 'The traumagenic neurodevelopmental model of psychosis revisited.' *Neuropsychiatry*, 4(1), 65–79.

560 De Bellis, M.D. *et al.* (2002) 'Superior temporal gyrus volumes in maltreated children and adolescents with PTSD.' *Biological Psychiatry*, 51(7), 544–52.

561 Tomoda, A. *et al.* (2011) 'Exposure to parental verbal abuse is associated with increased gray matter volume in superior temporal gyrus.' *Neuroimage*, 54, S280–S286.

562 Huang, H. *et al.* (2012) 'White matter disruptions in adolescents exposed to childhood maltreatment and vulnerability to psychopathology.' *Neuropsychopharmacology*, 37(12), 2693–701; Choi, J. *et al.* (2009) 'Preliminary evidence for white matter tract abnormalities in young adults exposed to parental verbal abuse.' *Biological Psychiatry*, 65(3), 227–34.

563 Philip, N.S. *et al.* (2013) 'Regional homogeneity and resting state functional connectivity: associations with exposure to early life stress.' *Psychiatry Research: Neuroimaging*, 214(3), 247–53.

564 Bluhm, R.L. *et al.* (2009) 'Alterations in default network connectivity in posttraumatic stress disorder related to early-life trauma.' *Journal of Psychiatry & Neuroscience*, 34(3), 187.

565 Elton, A. *et al.* (2014) 'Effects of childhood maltreatment on the neural correlates of stress- and drug cue-induced cocaine craving.' *Addiction Biology*, 2(4), 820–31.

566 Pruessner, J.C. *et al.* (2004) 'Dopamine release in response to a psychological stress in humans and its relationship to early life maternal care: a positron emission tomography study using [11C] raclopride.' *Journal of Neuroscience*, 24(11), 2825–31.

567 For example, Huang, H. *et al.* (2012) 'White matter disruptions in adolescents exposed to childhood maltreatment and vulnerability to psychopathology.' *Neuropsychopharmacology*, 37(12), 2693–701; Teicher, M.H. and Samson, J.A. (2013) 'Childhood maltreatment and psychopathology: a case for ecophenotypic variants as clinically and neurobiologically distinct subtypes.' *American Journal of Psychiatry*, 170(10), 1114–33.

568 Rossell, S.L. *et al.* (2001) 'Corpus callosum area and functioning in schizophrenic patients with auditory–verbal hallucinations.' *Schizophrenia Research*, 50(1), 9–17; Knöchel, C. *et al.* (2012) 'Interhemispheric hypoconnectivity in schizophrenia: fiber integrity and volume differences of the corpus callosum in patients and unaffected relatives.' *Neuroimage*, 59(2), 926–34.

569 Briere, J. (1992) 'Methodological issues in the study of sexual abuse effects.' *Journal of Consulting and Clinical Psychology*, 60(2), 196–203.

570 Lampshire, D. (2009) 'Lies and lessons: ramblings of an alleged mad woman.' *Psychosis*, 1(2), 178–84.

571 Baumeister, D. *et al.* (2016) 'Childhood trauma and adulthood inflammation: a meta-analysis of peripheral C-reactive protein, interleukin-6 and tumour necrosis factor-α.' *Molecular Psychiatry*, 21(5), 642–49; Slopen, N. *et al.* (2013) 'Childhood adversity and inflammatory processes in youth: a prospective study.' *Psychoneuroendocrinology*, 38, 188–200.

572 Dennison, U. *et al.* (2012) 'Schizophrenia patients with a history of childhood trauma have a pro-inflammatory phenotype.' *Psychological Medicine*, 42(9), 1865–71.

573 For example, Galton, F. (1906) 'Cutting a round cake on scientific principles.' *Nature*, 75, 173.

574 Kendler, K.S. *et al.* (1985) 'Psychiatric illness in first-degree relatives of schizophrenic and surgical control patients: a family study using DSM-III criteria.' *Archives of General Psychiatry*, 42(8), 770–79. This 7 per cent figure is low but still much higher than the less than 1 per cent of average people who have a first-degree relative with a psychotic disorder.

575 Bentall, R. (2009) *Doctoring the Mind: Is Our Current Treatment of Mental Illness Really Any Good?* New York, NY: NYU Press.

576 Dick, D.M. (2011) 'Gene–environment interaction in psychological traits and disorders.' *Annual Review of Clinical Psychology*, 7, 383.

577 For example, Hur, Y.M. *et al.* (2012) 'Heritability of hallucinations in adolescent twins.' *Psychiatry Research*, 199(2), 98–101.

578 Zavos, H.M. *et al.* (2014) 'Consistent etiology of severe, frequent psychotic experiences and milder, less frequent manifestations: a twin study of specific psychotic experiences in adolescence.' *JAMA Psychiatry*, 71(9), 1049–57.

579 True, W.R. *et al.* (1993) 'A twin study of genetic and environmental contributions to liability for posttraumatic stress symptoms.' *Archives of General Psychiatry*, 50(4), 257–64.

580 DNA is two strands joined together, and we are referring here to the 'sense' strand of the DNA. RNA polymerase reads off the other side, the antisense strand, and creates a sequence the same as the sense strand.

581 Hernaus, D. *et al.* (2013) 'COMT Val158Met genotype selectively alters prefrontal [18F]Fallypride displacement and subjective feelings of stress in response to a psychosocial stress challenge.' *PLoS ONE*, 8(6), e65662.

582 Severi, G. *et al.* (2007) 'The common variant rs1447295 on chromosome 8q24 and prostate cancer risk: results from an Australian population-based case-control study.' *Cancer Epidemiology Biomarkers & Prevention*, 16(3), 610–12.

583 Cheah, S.Y. *et al.* (2015) 'Dysbindin (DTNBP1) variants are associated with hallucinations in schizophrenia.' *European Psychiatry*, 30(4), 486–91.

584 Wei, J. *et al.* (1999) 'The CCK-A receptor gene possibly associated with auditory hallucinations in schizophrenia.' *European Psychiatry*, 14(2), 67–70; Sanjuan, J. *et al.* (2004) 'A possible association between the CCK-AR gene and persistent auditory hallucinations in schizophrenia.' *European Psychiatry*, 19(6), 349–53; Toirac, I. *et al.* (2007) 'Association between CCK-AR gene and schizophrenia with auditory hallucinations.' *Psychiatric Genetics*, 17(2), 47–53.

585 See Fisher, S.E. *et al.* (2009) 'FOXP2 as a molecular window into speech and language.' *Trends in Genetics*, 25, 166–77.

586 Watkins, E.R. *et al.* (2002) 'MRI analysis of an inherited speech and language disorder: structural brain abnormalities.' *Brain*, 125, 465–78.

587 Liégeois, F. *et al.* (2003) 'Language fMRI abnormalities associated with FOXP2 gene mutation.' *Nature Reviews Neuroscience*, 6, 1230–37.

588 Tolosa, A. *et al.* (2010) 'FOXP2 gene and language impairment in schizophrenia: association and epigenetic studies.' *BMC Medical Genetics*, 11, 114.

589 McCarthy-Jones, S. *et al.* (2014) 'Preliminary evidence of an interaction between the FOXP2 gene and childhood emotional abuse predicting likelihood of auditory verbal hallucinations in schizophrenia.' *Journal of Psychiatric Research*, 50, 66–72.

590 Zou, M. *et al.* (2012) 'Association between two single nucleotide polymorphisms at corresponding microRNA and schizophrenia in a Chinese population.' *Molecular Biology Reports*, 39(4), 3385–91.

591 Beveridge, N.J. *et al.* (2010) 'Schizophrenia is associated with an increase in cortical microRNA biogenesis.' *Molecular Psychiatry*, 15(12), 1176–89.
592 Dugas, J.C. *et al.* (2010) 'Dicer1 and miR-219 are required for normal oligodendrocyte differentiation and myelination.' *Neuron*, 65(5), 597–611.
593 Beveridge *et al.* (2010), as cited above.
594 Schizophrenia Working Group of the Psychiatric Genomics Consortium (2014) 'Biological insights from 108 schizophrenia-associated genetic loci.' *Nature*, 511(7510), 421–27.
595 Takahashi, N. *et al.* (2011) 'Linking oligodendrocyte and myelin dysfunction to neurocircuitry abnormalities in schizophrenia.' *Progress in Neurobiology*, 93(1), 13–24.
596 Fanous, A.H. *et al.* (2012) 'Genome-wide association study of clinical dimensions of schizophrenia: polygenic effect on disorganized symptoms.' *American Journal of Psychiatry*, 169(12), 1309–17.
597 Murphy, K.C. *et al.* (1999) 'High rates of schizophrenia in adults with velo-cardio-facial syndrome.' *Archives of General Psychiatry*, 56(10), 940–45.
598 Horowitz, A. *et al.* (2005) 'A survey of the 22q11 microdeletion in a large cohort of schizophrenia patients.' *Schizophrenia Research*, 73(2), 263–67.
599 Debbané, M. *et al.* (2006) 'Psychotic symptoms in children and adolescents with 22q11.2 deletion syndrome: neuropsychological and behavioral implications.' *Schizophrenia Research*, 84(2), 187–93.
600 Barnea-Goraly, N. *et al.* (2003) 'Investigation of white matter structure in velocardiofacial syndrome: a diffusion tensor imaging study.' *American Journal of Psychiatry*, 160(10), 1863–69.
601 Rihs, T.A. *et al.* (2013) 'Altered auditory processing in frontal and left temporal cortex in 22q11.2 deletion syndrome: a group at high genetic risk for schizophrenia.' *Psychiatry Research: Neuroimaging*, 212(2), 141–49.
602 Chun, S. *et al.* (2014) 'Specific disruption of thalamic inputs to the auditory cortex in schizophrenia models.' *Science*, 344(6188), 1178–82.
603 This effect may be specific to people of Asian heritage. See Wall, T.L. *et al.* (2000) 'Hangover symptoms in Asian Americans with variations in the aldehyde dehydrogenase (ALDH2) gene.' *Journal of Studies on Alcohol*, 61(1), 13–17.
604 Caspi, A. *et al.* (2003) 'Influence of life stress on depression: moderation by a polymorphism in the 5-HTT gene.' *Science*, 301(5631), 386–89. A later meta-analysis supported this result: Karg, K. *et al.* (2011) 'The serotonin transporter promoter variant (5-HTTLPR), stress, and depression meta-analysis revisited: evidence of genetic moderation.' *Archives of General Psychiatry*, 68, 444–54. For a review of this still-debated area see Duncan, L. *et al.* (2011) 'A critical review of the first 10 years of candidate gene-by-environment interaction research in psychiatry.' *American Journal of Psychiatry*, 168, 1041–49.
605 Pitman, R.K. *et al.* (2006) 'Clarifying the origin of biological abnormalities in PTSD through the study of identical twins discordant for combat exposure.' *Annals of the New York Academy of Sciences*, 1071(1), 242–54.

606 Alemany, S. *et al.* (2011) 'Childhood abuse, the BDNF-Val66Met polymorphism and adult psychotic-like experiences.' *British Journal of Psychiatry*, 199(1), 38–42.

607 Duncan *et al.* (2011), as cited above.

608 van IJzendoorn, M.H. *et al.* (2015) 'Genetic differential susceptibility on trial: meta-analytic support from randomized controlled experiments.' *Development and Psychopathology*, 27(1), 151–62.

609 Hygen, B.W. *et al.* (2015) 'Child exposure to serious life events, COMT, and aggression: testing differential susceptibility theory.' *Developmental Psychology*, 51(8), 1098.

610 This phrasing assumes that there is nothing beneficial about hearing voices in itself, and so we should reiterate the argument from many in the HVM that voice-hearing may be understood as a helpful response to trauma (see Conclusions chapter).

611 Dias, B.G. *et al.* (2014) 'Parental olfactory experience influences behavior and neural structure in subsequent generations.' *Nature Neuroscience*, 17(1), 89–96.

612 Franklin, T.B. *et al.* (2010) 'Epigenetic transmission of the impact of early stress across generations.' *Biological Psychiatry*, 68(5), 408–15.

613 Liu, J. *et al.* (2014) 'Methylation patterns in whole blood correlate with symptoms in schizophrenia patients.' *Schizophrenia Bulletin*, 40(4), 769–76.

614 Radford, E.J. *et al.* (2014) 'In utero undernourishment perturbs the adult sperm methylome and intergenerational metabolism.' *Science*, 345(6198), 1255903.

615 Meaney, M.J. *et al.* (2005) 'Environmental programming of stress responses through DNA methylation: life at the interface between a dynamic environment and a fixed genome.' *Dialogues in Clinical Neuroscience*, 7(2), 103–23.

616 Szyf, M. (2011) 'DNA methylation, the early-life social environment and behavioral disorders.' *Journal of Neurodevelopmental Disorders*, 3(3), 238–49; Suderman, M. (2014) 'Childhood abuse is associated with methylation of multiple loci in adult DNA.' *BMC Medical Genomics*, 7, 13.

617 Liu *et al.* (2014), as cited above.

618 de Jager, A. *et al.* (2016) 'Investigating the lived experience of recovery in people who hear voices.' *Qualitative Health Research*, 26(10), 1409–23.

619 McGlashan, T.H. *et al.* (1975) 'Integration and sealing over: clinically distinct recovery styles from schizophrenia.' *Archives of General Psychiatry*, 32, 1269–72.

620 Frank, A.W. (1995) *The Wounded Storyteller – Body, Illness and Ethics.* Chicago, IL: University of Chicago Press.

621 Laan, W. *et al.* (2010) 'Adjuvant aspirin therapy reduces symptoms of schizophrenia spectrum disorders: results from a randomized, double-blind, placebo-controlled trial.' *Journal of Clinical Psychiatry*, 71(5), 520.

622 Kulkarni, J. *et al.* (2014) 'Estradiol for treatment-resistant schizophrenia: a large-scale randomized-controlled trial in women of child-bearing age.' *Molecular Psychiatry*, 20, 695–702.

623 Amminger, G.P. *et al.* (2010) 'Long-chain ω-3 fatty acids for indicated prevention of psychotic disorders: a randomized, placebo-controlled trial.' *Archives of General Psychiatry*, 67(2), 146–54.

624 www.medscape.com/viewarticle/843261; www.mssociety.org.uk/node/690821.

625 deCharms, R.C. *et al.* (2005) 'Control over brain activation and pain learned by using real-time functional MRI.' *Proceedings of the National Academy of Sciences of the United States of America*, 102(51), 18626–31.

626 McCarthy-Jones, S. (2012) 'Taking back the brain: could neurofeedback training be effective for relieving distressing auditory verbal hallucinations?' *Schizophrenia Bulletin*, 38, 678–82.

627 Jackson, L.J. *et al.* (2010) 'Developing positive relationships with voices: a preliminary grounded theory.' *International Journal of Social Psychiatry*, 57, 487–95.

628 Lampshire (2009), as cited above.

629 NiaNia, W. *et al.* (2013, 20 November) *New Zealand Māori traditional healing approaches to voice-hearing.* Paper presented at the World Hearing Voices Congress, Melbourne, Australia.

630 A point made by Neil Thomas: Thomas, N. (2015) 'What's really wrong with cognitive behavioral therapy for psychosis?' *Frontiers in Psychology*, 6, 323.

631 Just to be clear, Müller had, of course, brought this statue with him.

632 De Young, M. (2015) *Encyclopedia of Asylum Therapeutics, 1750–1950s.* London: McFarland.

633 Birchwood, M. *et al.* (2004) 'Interpersonal and role-related schema influence the relationship with the dominant "voice" in schizophrenia: a comparison of three models.' *Psychological Medicine*, 34(8), 1571–80.

634 Example from Mankiewicz, P.D. *et al.* (2014) 'Cognitive restructuring and graded behavioural exposure for delusional appraisals of auditory hallucinations and comorbid anxiety in paranoid schizophrenia.' *Case Reports in Psychiatry*, 2014.

635 Perlis, R.H. *et al.* (2014) 'Industry sponsorship and financial conflict of interest in the reporting of clinical trials in psychiatry.' *American Journal of Psychiatry*, 162(10), 1957–60.

636 For a meta-analysis whose results question the evidence base for the effectiveness of CBT for hallucinations, see Jauhar, S. *et al.* (2014) 'Cognitive-behavioural therapy for the symptoms of schizophrenia: systematic review and meta-analysis with examination of potential bias.' *British Journal of Psychiatry*, 204(1), 20–29. For a meta-analysis whose results claim support for the effectiveness of CBT for voice-hearing, see van der Gaag, M. *et al.* (2014) 'The effects of individually tailored formulation-based cognitive behavioural therapy in auditory hallucinations and delusions: a meta-analysis.' *Schizophrenia Research*, 156(1), 30–37.

637 Goldsmith, L.P. *et al.* (2015) 'Psychological treatments for early psychosis can be beneficial or harmful, depending on the therapeutic alliance: an instrumental variable analysis.' *Psychological Medicine*, 45(11), 2365–73.

638 Ehlers, A. *et al.* (2014) 'A randomized controlled trial of 7-day intensive and standard weekly cognitive therapy for PTSD and emotion-focused supportive therapy.' *American Journal of Psychiatry*, 171, 294–304.

639 Birchwood, M. *et al.* (2014) 'Cognitive behaviour therapy to prevent harmful compliance with command hallucinations (COMMAND): a randomised controlled trial.' *The Lancet Psychiatry*, 1(1), 23–33.

640 Chin, J.T. *et al.* (2009) '"Relating" to voices: exploring the relevance of this concept to people who hear voices.' *Psychology and Psychotherapy: Theory, Research and Practice*, 82, 1–17.

641 Hayward, M. *et al.* (2009) 'Relating therapy for people who hear voices: a case series.' *Clinical Psychology & Psychotherapy*, 16(3), 216–27.

642 Jenner, J.A. *et al.* (2006) '"Hitting" voices of schizophrenia patients may lastingly reduce persistent auditory hallucinations and their burden: 18-month outcome of a randomized controlled trial.' *Canadian Journal of Psychiatry*, 51, 169–77.

643 www.bit.ly/1QsUC4o.

644 Connor, C. *et al.* (2013) 'Through the looking glass: self-reassuring meta-cognitive capacity and its relationship with the thematic content of voices.' *Frontiers in Human Neuroscience*, 7.

645 Mayhew, S. *et al.* (2008) 'Compassionate mind training with people who hear malevolent voices: a case series report.' *Clinical Psychology and Psychotherapy*, 15, 113–38.

646 www.youtube.com/watch?v=ZQht2yOX9Js. Sometimes you can find ways to show people they are innocent of what they feel guilt for; see this clip for a movie depiction of this: www.youtube.com/watch?v=RUBaRqY_NqA. If you don't want the clip to be spoilt, don't read the spoiler the YouTube poster gives, just make the clip full screen. The backstory to the clip, from the film *Fearless*, is that Rosie Perez's child, Bubble, has died when he slipped out of Rosie's arms during a plane crash. She could not have held onto him, due to the force of the impact, but she still feels it was her fault. Jeff Bridges' character, who was a fellow passenger, tries to talk her out of this belief, which doesn't go too well, so he comes up with an alternative plan...

647 Coleman, R. (2000) *Recovery: An Alien Concept?* Gloucester, UK: Handsell.

648 Longden (2013a), as cited above.

649 Leff, J. *et al.* (2013) 'Computer-assisted therapy for medication-resistant auditory hallucinations: proof-of-concept study.' *British Journal of Psychiatry*, 202(6), 428–33.

650 www.poetryfoundation.org/bio/william-cowper.

651 http://bit.ly/1UBj8ik.

652 Bush, A. *et al.* (2012) 'Voice hearing and pseudoseizures in a Māori teenager: an example of mate Māori and Māori traditional healing.' *Australasian Psychiatry*, 20(4), 348–51.

653 Murphy, J.M. (1976) 'Psychiatric labelling in cross-cultural perspective.' *Science*, 191, 1019–28.

654 Bentall, R.P. (2003) *Madness Explained.* London: Penguin.

655 Baker, P. (1989) *Hearing Voices.* Manchester, UK: Hearing Voices Network.

656 Romme *et al.* (2009), as cited above.

657 Escher, S. *et al.* (2000) 'Maastricht Interview with a Voice Hearer.' In M. Romme and S. Escher (eds) *Understanding Voices: Coping with Auditory Hallucinations and Confusing Realities.* Gloucester, UK: Handsell; Corstens, D. *et al.* (2008) 'Accepting and Working with Voices: The Maastricht Approach.' In A. Moskowitz *et al.* (eds) *Psychosis, Trauma and Dissociation: Emerging Perspectives on Severe Psychopathology.* Chichester, UK: Wiley-Blackwell.

658 www.dirkcorstens.com/talking-to-the-voices.

659 Corstens, D. *et al.* (2014) 'Emerging perspectives from the Hearing Voices Movement: implications for research and practice.' *Schizophrenia Bulletin*, 40, S285–94.

660 Schnackenberg, J. *et al.* (2017) 'A randomised controlled pilot study of Experience Focused Counselling with voice hearers.' *Psychosis*, 9(1), 12–14.

661 Nisbett, R.E. *et al.* (1977) 'Telling more than we can know: verbal reports on mental processes.' *Psychological Review*, 84(3), 231–59.

662 Moncrieff (2013), as cited above.

663 www.youtube.com/watch?v=sEbSABWJiJc.

664 Gerrity *et al.* (2001), as cited above.

665 Dillon, J. *et al.* (2013) 'Hearing voices peer support groups: a powerful alternative for people in distress.' *Psychosis*, 5(3), 286–95.

666 Coleman (2000), as cited above.

667 Mosher, L.R. *et al.* (1978) 'Community residential treatment for schizophrenia: two-year followup data.' *Hospital & Community Psychiatry*, 29, 715–23; Mosher, L.R. *et al.* (1995) 'The treatment of acute psychosis without neuroleptics: six-week psychopathology outcome data from the Soteria project.' *International Journal of Social Psychiatry*, 41, 157–73; Mosher, L.R. *et al.* (2004) *Soteria: Through Madness to Deliverance.* San Francisco, CA: XLibris.

668 Carpenter, W.T. *et al.* (2002) 'Commentary on the Soteria project: misguided therapeutics.' *Schizophrenia Bulletin*, 28, 577–81.

669 Ho *et al.* (2011), as cited above.

670 Lehtinen, V. *et al.* (2000) 'Two-year outcome in first-episode psychosis treated according to an integrated model: is immediate neuroleptisation always needed?' *European Psychiatry*, 15, 312–20.

671 Personal communication.

672 Credit for the title comes from the liberetto of Franz Schubert's *Winterreise* (Op. 89, D 911), 'Fremd bin ich eingezogen, Fremd zieh' ich wieder aus'. You can hear it sung here: www.youtube.com/watch?v=iJETtWr47PY. It is also worth listening to Quasthoff and Barenboim's awesome end to the cycle: www.youtube.com/watch?v=pze4NxCOjg0.

673 Black, D.W. *et al.* (2014) *Introductory Textbook of Psychiatry.* Washington DC: American Psychiatric Publishing.

674 Van Meer, R. (2003) 'To listen or not to listen.' *British Medical Journal*, 326, 549.

675 Aschebrock, Y. *et al.* (2003) 'Is the content of delusions and hallucinations important?' *Australasian Psychiatry*, 11, 306–11.

676 Steele, A. *et al.* (in press) 'Let's talk about psychosis.' *Clinical Schizophrenia & Related Psychoses.*

677 Steele, A. (2014) 'Let's talk about psychosis' (unpublished doctoral thesis). Institute of Psychiatry, King's College London, UK.

678 McCabe, R. *et al.* (2002) 'Engagement of patients with psychosis in the consultation: conversation analytic study.' *British Medical Journal*, 325, 1148–51.

679 Steele *et al.* (2016), as cited above.

680 Romme, M. *et al.* (2000) *Making Sense of Voices: A Guide for Professionals Who Work with Voice Hearers.* London: MIND.

681 Rajesh, G.S. (2003) 'Design of study has several problems [Letter to editor].' *British Medical Journal*, 326, 549.

682 McCabe, R. *et al.* (2003) 'Author's reply [Letter to editor].' *British Medical Journal*, 326, 550.

683 Corstens, D. *et al.* (2012) 'Talking with voices: exploring what is expressed by the voices people hear.' *Psychosis*, 4(2), 95–104.

684 Steel, M. (2003) *The Mark Steel Lectures: Sigmund Freud.* Accessed at http://marksteelinfo.com/videos.

685 Dubé, R. *et al.* (1988) 'Sexual abuse of children under 12 years of age: a review of 511 cases.' *Child Abuse & Neglect*, 12(3), 321–30.

686 Plummer, M. and Cossins, A. (in press) 'The cycle of abuse: when victims become offenders.' *Trauma, Violence, & Abuse.*

687 Whitaker, D.J. *et al.* (2008) 'Risk factors for the perpetration of child sexual abuse: a review and meta-analysis.' *Child Abuse & Neglect*, 32(5), 529–48.

688 Hanson, R. *et al.* (1988) 'Sexual victimization in the history of child sexual abusers: a review.' *Annals of Sex Research*, 1, 485–99. See also Ryan, G. *et al.* (1996) 'Trends in a national sample of sexually abusive youths.' *Journal of the American Academy of Child & Adolescent Psychiatry*, 35(1), 17–25; Ogloff, J.R.P. *et al.* (2012) 'Child sexual abuse and subsequent offending and victimisation: a 45 year follow-up study' (Trends & Issues in Crime & Criminal Justice No. 440). Canberra: Australian Institute of Criminology.

689 Anderson, P. *et al.* (2007) *Ampe akelyernemane meke mekarle: 'little children are sacred'. Report of the Northern Territory Board of Inquiry into the Protection of Aboriginal Children from Sexual Abuse.* Darwin, Australia: Northern Territory Government.

690 Ogloff *et al.* (2012), as cited above.

691 Salter, D. *et al.* (2003) 'Development of sexually abusive behaviour in sexually victimised males: a longitudinal study.' *The Lancet*, 361(9356), 471–76.

692 Plummer and Cossins (2016), as cited above.

693 Cossins, A. (2000) *Masculinities, Sexualities, and Child Sexual Abuse.* The Hague: Kluwer Law International; Plummer and Cossins (2016), as cited above.

694 Ji, K. *et al.* (2013) 'Child sexual abuse in China: a meta-analysis of 27 studies.' *Child Abuse & Neglect*, 37(9), 613–22.

695 Finkelhor, D. *et al.* (2013) 'Explaining lower rates of sexual abuse in China.' *Child Abuse & Neglect*, 37(10), 852–60.

696 Herman, J.L. (2000) *Father–Daughter Incest.* Cambridge, MA: Harvard University Press.

697 hooks, b. (1984) *Feminist Theory: From Margin to Center.* Boston, MA: South End Press.

698 Drake, B. *et al.* (1996) 'Understanding the relationship between neighbourhood poverty and specific types of child maltreatment.' *Child Abuse & Neglect*, 20, 1003–18; Gillham, B. *et al.* (1998) 'Unemployment rates, single parent density, and indices of child poverty: their relationship to different categories of child abuse and neglect.' *Child Abuse & Neglect*, 22, 79–90.

699 Koenen, K.C. *et al.* (2007) 'Early childhood factors associated with the development of post-traumatic stress disorder: results from a longitudinal birth cohort.' *Psychological Medicine*, 37(2), 181–92.

700 Wilkinson, R. and Pickett, K. (2009) *The Spirit Level: Why Equality is Better for Everyone.* Harmondsworth: Penguin. See also: www.ted.com/talks/richard_wilkinson?language=en.

701 Eckenrode, J. *et al.* (2014) 'Income inequality and child maltreatment in the United States.' *Pediatrics*, 133(3), 454–61.

702 Johnson, S.L. *et al.* (in press) 'Economic inequality is related to cross-national prevalence of psychotic symptoms.' *Social Psychiatry and Psychiatric Epidemiology.*

703 Raine, A. *et al.* (2003) 'Effects of environmental enrichment at ages 3–5 years on schizotypal personality and antisocial behavior at ages 17 and 23 years.' *American Journal of Psychiatry*, 160, 1627–35.

704 Ljungqvist, I. *et al.* (2015) 'Money and mental illness: a study of the relationship between poverty and serious psychological problems.' *Community Mental Health Journal.* doi:10.1007/s10597-015-9950-9.

705 Brown, A.S. *et al.* (2000) 'Social class of origin and cardinal symptoms of schizophrenic disorders over the early illness course.' *Social Psychiatry and Psychiatric Epidemiology*, 35(2), 53–60.

706 DeNavas-Walt, C. *et al.* (2014) 'Income and poverty in the United States: 2013, current population reports.' US Department of Commerce, Economics and Statistics Administration, US Census Bureau.

707 US Department of Health and Human Services (2013) *Child Maltreatment 2012.*

708 Johns *et al.* (2002), as cited above.

709 Bentall, R.P. *et al.* (2008) 'Social predictors of psychotic experiences: specificity and psychological mechanisms.' *Schizophrenia Bulletin*, 34(6), 1012–20.

710 Manchanda, R. (2013) *The Upstream Doctors: Medical Innovators Track Sickness to Its Source.* TED Books.

711 As cited in Rhodes, J. (2005) *Radical Feminism, Writing, and Critical Agency: From Manifesto to Modem.* New York, NY: State University of New York Press.

712 Herman (2001), as cited above.

713 Soon, C.S. *et al.* (2008) 'Unconscious determinants of free decisions in the human brain.' *Nature Neuroscience*, 11(5), 543–45.

714 Frith, C.D. *et al.* (2016) 'What's the Use of Consciousness? How the Stab of Conscience Made Us Really Conscious.' In A.K. Engel *et al.* (eds) *Where's the Action? The Pragmatic Turn in Cognitive Science.* Boston, MA: MIT Press; Frith, C.D. (2015, July) *What's the use of consciousness?* Paper presented at the meeting of the Association for the Scientific Study of Consciousness, Paris, France.

715 Varese, F. *et al.* (2012) 'Childhood adversities increase the risk of psychosis: a meta-analysis of patient-control, prospective- and cross-sectional cohort studies.' *Schizophrenia Bulletin*, 38(4), 661–71.

716 Varese *et al.* (2012), as cited above.

717 This is a harder number to estimate. See Table 4 in Shevlin, M. *et al.* (2008) 'Cumulative traumas and psychosis: an analysis of the national comorbidity survey and the British Psychiatric Morbidity Survey.' *Schizophrenia Bulletin*, 34(1), 193–99.

718 Jenkins (2015), as cited above.

719 Longden (2013a), as cited above; Longden, E. (2013b) 'Listening to voices.' *Scientific American Mind*, 24(4), 34–39.

720 Britz, B. (2016, September) *Practicing presence: moving towards healing and wholeness.* Paper presented at the International Consortium on Hallucinations and Related Symptoms (ICHR) 2016 Satellite conference, Chicago, IL.

721 See http://smollin.com/michael/tmonstr/mon001.html.

722 The 'magisteria' concept is taken from work by Stephen J. Gould.

723 Schnackenberg *et al.* (2016), as cited above.

724 http://psychnews.psychiatryonline.org/doi/full/10.1176%2Fappi.pn.2014.5a21.

725 http://creative.porternovelli.com/portfolio/american psychiatric-association-rebranding-to-move-the-field-forward.

726 Shorter (1998), as cited above.

727 www.youtube.com/watch?v=pYIcmz2c9Xs.

728 Whitaker *et al.* (2015), as cited above.

729 Fannon, D. (2004) 'E-interview: Julian Leff.' *British Journal of Psychiatry Bulletin*, 28(3).

730 Shooter (2005), as cited above.

731 Fannon (2004), as cited above.

732 Bland, J. (2014) 'Profile: stigma and the psychiatrist – Julia Bland talks to Dinesh Bhugra.' *Psychiatric Bulletin*, 38(4), 180–82.

733 Read, J. *et al.* (2007) 'Why, when and how to ask about childhood abuse.' *Advances in Psychiatric Treatment*, 13(2), 101–10.

734 Lebowitz, M.S. *et al.* (2014) 'Effects of biological explanations for mental disorders on clinicians' empathy.' *Proceedings of the National Academy of Sciences*, 111(50), 17786–90.

735 McCarthy-Jones *et al.* (2013), as cited above.

736 A position convincingly and eloquently argued by Longden (2013a), as cited above, in particular.

737 See the publications stemming from the landmark Adverse Childhood Experience (ACE) study: www.cdc.gov/violenceprevention/acestudy/index.html.

738 Varese *et al.* (2012), as cited above.

739 Helpful rape prevention advice is given here: https://canyourelate.org/2011/05/24/rape-prevention-tips.

740 http://report.nih.gov/categorical_spending.aspx.

741 Hassan, A.N. *et al.* (2015) 'The effect of lifetime adversities on resistance to antipsychotic treatment in schizophrenia patients.' *Schizophrenia Research*, 161(2), 496–500.

742 Shivakumar, V. *et al.* (2015) 'Effect of tDCS on auditory hallucinations in schizophrenia: influence of catechol-O-methyltransferase (COMT) Val158Met polymorphism.' *Asian Journal of Psychiatry*, 16, 75–77.

743 Goldsmith *et al.* (2015), as cited above.

744 My line of thinking here came from the always insightful Nev Jones. See Jones, N. *et al.* (2015) 'Inconvenient Complications: On the Heterogeneities of Madness and their Relationship to Disability.' In H. Spandler *et al.* (eds) *Madness, Distress and the Politics of Engagement.* Bristol: Policy Press.

745 Wilson, R.R. (1978) 'Early Israelite Prophecy.' In J.L. Mays *et al.* (eds) *Interpreting the Prophets.* Philadelphia, PA: Fortress Press.

INDEX